'Blinker' Hall: Spymaster

'The Machiavelli in him was cruel … But the school-boy was always round the corner, and the love of the dangerous game he, and all of us, were playing would bubble out, and the fun and hazard of it all would fill him with infectious delight. "Adventures are for the adventurous" he would chant, rubbing his hands and grinning like a crafty little French Abbé.

He was a gambler. One of his favourite sayings was "Mistakes may be forgiven, but even God himself cannot forgive the hanger-back." We all followed with a blind devotion the risks he took, because we were sure he was going to win.'

Ruth Skrine, 'Blinker' Hall's secretary.

'BLINKER' HALL: SPYMASTER

THE MAN WHO BROUGHT AMERICA INTO WORLD WAR I

David Ramsay

SPELLMOUNT

British Library Cataloguing in Publication Data:
A catalogue record for this book is available
from the British Library

Copyright © David Ramsay, 2008, 2009

ISBN 978-0-7524-5398-9

First published in the UK in 2008 by
Spellmount, an imprint of the History Press
The Mill, Brimscombe Port
Stroud, Gloucestershire. GL5 2QG
www.thehistorypress.co.uk

This revised paperback edition 2009
Reprinted 2010

1 2 5 7 9 8 6 4 2

The right of David Ramsay to be identified
as the author of this work has been asserted by him
in accordance with the Copyright, Designs
and Patents Act 1988

All rights reserved. No part of this publication may be
reproduced, stored in a retrieval system or transmitted in
any form or by any means, electronic, mechanical,
photocopying, recording or otherwise,
without prior permission in writing from
Spellmount Limited, Publishers.

Printed in Great Britain

Front cover: Blinker Hall as a Rear-Admiral by Sir Gerald Kelly PRA.
Reproduced by kind permission of his great-grandson, Toby Stubbs.

Contents

Preface		7
Acknowledgements		11
List of Abbreviations		15
I	1870–1914	17
II	'The Miraculous Draught of Fishes' – The Endowment of Room 40 (1914)	23
III	Director of Naval Intelligence (1914–1915)	39
IV	The Eyes and Ears of The Fleet (1914–15)	55
V	Eastern Adventures (1915–16)	75
VI	Unrestricted Submarine Warfare: the Sinking of *Lusitania* (1915)	89
VII	The Ides of May (May 1915)	107
VIII	The Great Game I (Operations and intelligence in the US, Ireland and Spain (1915–17)	123
IX	Jutland – An Intelligence Failure (1916)	145
X	Hall takes charge of Room 40 (1916–1917)	161
XI	Arthur Zimmermann Sends a Telegram (January–February 1917)	177
XII	War Comes to America: 'Alone I did it' (February–April 1917)	195

XIII	All Change at the Admiralty (May–December 1917)	225
XIV	The Great Game II (1917–18)	247
XV	The Road to Victory (1918–19)	265
XVI	1919–43	293
XVII	The Hall Legacy (World War II and after)	301
Index		317

Preface

Whilst the fleet commanders of World War I, Jellicoe and Beatty, Keyes and Tyrwhitt, became household names, Admiral Sir Reginald 'Blinker' Hall, the Director of Naval Intelligence (DNI) for almost the entire war, is much less well known. Arthur Marder, doyen of naval historians, described Hall as one of the five outstanding naval leaders of the war – 'a genius in his own sphere and brilliantly successful'. Indeed he was one of the pivotal figures of that conflict. In 1935 Keyes wrote of his friend: 'Reggie Hall was a great ally … I hope some day a true record of his great services and his contribution to victory will be written.' Fortunately for the allied cause, the post of DNI had become vacant when Hall had to give up command of the battlecruiser HMS *Queen Mary* for health reasons and his appointment proved providential.

The ability of the Admiralty's famous Room 40 to read the German naval and political decrypts from November 1914 onwards gave Hall a focal authority in the British intelligence community, including direct access to Cabinet Ministers, far greater than any previous or later DNI ever enjoyed. Hall was given a free hand in political and non-naval matters and worked closely and usefully with the Foreign Office. He acted as the effective co-ordinator of Intelligence, a position filled in World War II by the full-time Chairman of the Joint Intelligence Committee.

Naval intelligence, through its ability to analyse German naval and diplomatic signals, made a very significant contribution towards the allied victory. Hall's initiative, taken with the full knowledge of his superiors, to bribe Turkey out of the war early in 1915 came close to success. Had this endeavour come off, the course of the war would have been altered to the considerable advantage of the allies. The revelation of the Zimmermann telegram, astutely handled by Hall and the greatest of his wartime achievements, was the catalyst that brought America into the war in April 1917 at a time when the German unrestricted submarine warfare campaign was coming dangerously close to cutting Britain's supply routes. American entry into the war gave the allied cause a huge boost and had catastrophic consequences for Germany.

The effective interface between intelligence and operations, instituted by Hall and the anti-submarine chief, Admiral Duff, together with the institution of convoy and other successful anti-submarine measures at sea, resulted in the eventual defeat of the U-boats. Hall had a remarkable talent for disseminating misinformation and he was an effective interrogator. His dynamic leadership and force of personality were essential to these successes. He was often called Machiavellian. A more realistic verdict might be that he was endowed with the ruthlessness necessary in wartime which enabled him to combat and keep one step ahead of a formidable and determined enemy and his widespread espionage and subversion operation.

He had a remarkable capacity for foresight. As early as 1918 he had anticipated the threat from Soviet communism and also warned the Government of Japanese expansionism. Ever distrustful of the 'huns', he repeatedly informed Whitehall of the potential menace of Nazi Germany.

After he retired from the Navy at the end of World War I, he remained active in public life, serving as a Conservative MP for nearly ten years and maintaining many contacts within the intelligence community. His greater legacy was to shape the nature of British naval intelligence in and beyond World War II and well into the Cold War era. He placed his experience at the disposal of Rear-Admiral John Godfrey, the DNI in the early years of that War, who readily admitted his debt to Hall. The Admiralty's Operational Intelligence Centre, which played a vital part in winning the Battle of the Atlantic, was developed from the model Hall had helped set up in World War I. The staff at Bletchley Park who used the ENIGMA machines to decode ULTRA (German signal traffic) included several Room 40 veterans. The OSS, the predecessor of the CIA, was formed with the assistance of Admiral Godfrey and adopted many of the principles of British naval intelligence as originally developed by Hall.

The co-author of Hall's autobiography unfortunately lost Hall's correspondence with his 'old chief' and close friend Beatty. Hall did not leave many papers and he took many of his secrets to the grave with him. In 1933 the Admiralty had vetoed the publication of his autobiography on grounds of security. The only previous life of Hall, *The Eyes of the Navy* by Admiral Sir William James, was published as long ago as 1955. James had served under Hall both at sea and as Head of Room 40 and, like Keyes and so many of his friends and colleagues, he believed that his great services to the country should be recorded for future generations.

The Admiralty sought to ban James's book, on the same grounds that it had objected to Hall's autobiography, that it revealed that coded wireless signals could be intercepted and deciphered. Their attitude, almost forty years after the end of World War I, when the technology of decoding these signals had long ceased to be a secret, is astonishing. As a result of the Admiralty's back-seat driving, James was forced to play down certain aspects of the work of the NID and of Room 40. Although James vividly described Hall's personality and his remarkable leadership qualities, much had to be left untold or cut out.

Ninety years after the allied victory in 1918, to which he had made such a remarkable contribution (principally in the disclosure of the Zimmermann telegram) the time is now ripe for a new assessment of Hall, as one of the significant figures of that war and one of the most successful intelligence chiefs in modern history. As Alan Judd, the recent biographer of his contemporary Mansfield Cumming, head of the Special Intelligence Service, noted, echoing what Keyes wrote in 1935: 'Hall deserves further and more contemporary attention.' This book describes in detail Hall's remarkable and unique achievements in both naval and political intelligence, which won him an outstanding reputation and widespread admiration among so many of his contemporaries.

Acknowledgements

I am pleased to express my gratitude to the Hall family for their constant support and encouragement while I was researching the book and particularly to Timothy Stubbs, who lent me his collection of 164 letters written by Blinker Hall to his sister, May Templar, between 1939 and 1943, which had not been seen by any previous author. These letters are now part of the Hall Papers at the Churchill Archives Centre. He has kindly given me permission to quote from his grandfather's papers. I would also like to thank the late Mrs Margaret Hall and her daughter, Mrs Claire Wheway, for information about Admiral Hall's forebears, and the late James Stubbs, one of only two sources whom I interviewed who knew Hall as a young man and who related many memories of his meetings with him in the late 1930s.

I was saddened to learn of the recent death of Peter Freeman, the author of 'The Zimmermann Telegram Revisited: A Reconciliation of the Primary Sources', published in the April 2006 issue of *Cryptologia*. He kindly gave me access to his extensive research into the background of the telegram, the most important single event in Hall's tenure as Director of Naval Intelligence. His detailed examination of the circumstances in which the telegram was sent from Berlin to Washington has enabled me to avoid a number of errors made by previous authors. He could not have been more helpful and I am considerably in his debt.

I am once again indebted to Captain David Garstin RN, naval engineer by profession and enthusiastic naval historian, who has read the naval chapters of the book in draft, correcting my errors and making a number of valuable suggestions, almost all of which I have incorporated. At my request he prepared an account of the connection between the Paymaster branch of the RN and naval intelligence, which appears in Chapter 10. He recently and generously gave me his collection of the books of Arthur Marder, doyen of naval historians, whose *From Dreadnought To Scapa Flow* (Oxford), the definitive study of the RN in the First World War, was one of my prime sources.

Allen Packwood, the Director of the Churchill Archives Centre, Churchill College, Cambridge, where Hall's papers are lodged along with those of many other admirals (including the author's father), has been a staunch supporter. He kindly gave me access to Hall's letters to his American friend, Percy Madeira, written between 1928 and 1942, which were rescued by a collector, Dr David Shneidman, who presented them to the Archives Centre. I would also like to thank his helpful staff, notably Sandra Marsh and Caroline Herbert.

I should like to express my gratitude to Philip Atkins, formerly Archivist of the National Railway Museum, York, for providing me with details of the career of Sir Eric Geddes, First Lord of the Admiralty from 1917 to 1918 and a major figure in this story; and to Captain Christopher Page RN and Commander Malcolm Llewellyn-Jones of the Naval Historic Branch, Portsmouth and the staff of The National Archives, Kew (formerly the PRO); the National Archives and Records Administration, College Park, Maryland and to the National Maritime Museum, Greenwich, all of whom gave me full measure of assistance. Judy Collingwood carried out additional research for me in the Admiralty and Intelligence files at TNA. I would especially like to thank Andrew Lambert, Laughton Professor of Naval History, Department of War Studies, King's College, London for giving me access to a PhD thesis, 'Sharpening the Trident', written by his former pupil, Richard Mullins, on the formation of the Naval Intelligence Division in the 1880s. Hall's father, Captain W. H. Hall, was its first Director.

Robin Denniston and Lord Herschell, whose fathers had served in Room 40, the latter as one of Hall's PAs, and Anthony de Grey, whose grandfather Nigel was the lead cryptographer on deciphering the Zimmermann telegram, gave me much valuable information about their forebears' time in the NID, as did Ned Serocold, whose great-uncle Claud was Hall's other PA and Tom Winnifrith, whose great-uncle George Young was the first head of Room 40's political section.

My thanks are also due to many others who helped me in my research, particularly Lt Col. John Abbatielo, USAF, Stuart Ball, Gill Bennett, Correlli Barnett, Dr John Brooks, David K. Brown, Warwick Brown, Elizabeth Burke, Jack Darrah and Peter Wescombe (Bletchley Park), Dr Thomas Boghardt (International Spy Museum, Washington DC), Bernard Cazenove (Cazenove & Co.), George Newkey-Burden (*Daily Telegraph*), Tam Dalyell, James Denning, John Ehrman, (who also knew Hall when he was a young man), Adam Fergusson, Barry Gough, Sir Michael Howard, John Hughes-Wilson, Lawrence James, Penny Jenison (Associate Professor of History-College of the Desert, Palm Desert, California), Alan Judd, Dr Peter Martland, Ian Nelson (Edinburgh Central Library), David Stafford and Steve Torrington (Library Editor, Associated Newspapers).

ACKNOWLEDGEMENTS

I acknowledge the authors and publishers of the following works from which I have quoted:

Patrick Beesly, *Very Special Admiral. Room 40* and *British Naval Intelligence 1914–1918* (Hamish Hamilton)
Francis Birch and W.F. Clarke, 'Contribution to the History of German Naval Warfare 1914–1918' (unpublished)
W. S. Chalmers, *The Life and Letters of David Earl Beatty* and *Full Cycle: The Biography of Admiral Sir Bertram Home Ramsay* (Hodder & Stoughton)
Winston S. Churchill, *The World Crisis* (Thornton Butterworth)
Percy Cradock *Know Your Enemy: How the Joint Intelligence Community Saw the World* (John Murray)
Robin Denniston, *Thirty Secret Years: A.G. Denniston's Work in Signals Intelligence 1914–1918* (Polperro Heritage Press)
Blanche Dugdale, *Arthur James Balfour 1906–1930* (Putnam)
A. W. Ewing, *The Man of Room 40* (Hutchinson)
Penelope Fitzgerald, *The Knox Brothers* (Macmillan)
Lionel Fraser, *All to the Good* (Heinemann)
William F. Friedman and Charles J. Mendelsohn, *The Zimmermann Telegram of January 16 1917 and its Cryptographic Background* (Aegean Park Press)
Guy Gaunt, *The Yield of the Years* (Hutchinson)
James W. Gerard, *My Four Years in Germany* (Hodder & Stoughton)
Martin Gilbert, *Winston S. Churchill*, Vol. 3 (Heinemann)
Andrew Gordon, *The Rules of the Game* (John Murray)
Roger Lancelyn Green, *A.E.W. Mason: The Adventures of a Story-Teller* (Max Parrish)
Keith Grieves, *Eric Geddes* (Manchester University Press)
Paul Halpern, *A Naval History of World War One* (Naval Institute Press)
Burton J. Hendrick, *The Life and Letters of Walter H. Page* (Doubleday, Page)
Arthur Hezlet, *Electronics and Sea Power* (Stein & Day)
Christopher Hitchens, *Blood, Class & Nostalgia* (Farrar, Strauss & Giroux)
Richard Hough, *The Great War at Sea 1914–18* (Oxford)
William James, *The Sky Was Always Blue* and *The Eyes of the Navy* (Methuen)
Roy Jenkins, *Churchill* (Macmillan)
Geoffrey Jones, *The State and the Emergence of the British Oil Industry* (Macmillan)
Alan Judd, *The Quest for C: Mansfield Cumming and the Founding of the Secret Service* (Harper Collins)

David Kahn, *Seizing the Enigma The Race to Break the German U-boat Codes 1939–1943* (Barnes & Noble)
John Keegan, *Intelligence in War* (Hutchinson)
Roger Keyes, *The Naval Memoirs of Admiral of the Fleet Sir Roger Keyes: Scapa Flow to the Dover Straits 1916–1918* (Thornton Butterworth)
David Kynaston, *Cazenove & Co. A History* (Batsford)
David Lloyd George, *The War Memoirs of David Lloyd George* (Little Brown)
Elizabeth Longford, *Wellington The Years of the Sword* (Weidenfeld & Nicolson)
Ruddock Mackay, *Fisher of Kilverstone* (Oxford)
Donald McLachlan, *Room 39 Naval Intelligence in Action 1939–1945* (Weidenfeld & Nicolson)
Robert Massie, *Castles of Steel* (Random House)
Nathan Miller, *Theodore Roosevelt A Life* (Quill William Morrow)
David Paull Nickles, *Under the Wire: How the Telegraph Changed Diplomacy* (Harvard University Press)
Joseph E. Persico, *Roosevelt's Secret War* (Random House)
Diana Preston, *Wilful Murder The Sinking of the Lusitania* (Doubleday)
Reinhard Scheer, *Germany's High Sea Fleet* (Peter Smith)
Stephen Roskill, *Hankey: Man of Secrets* 1877-1918 and *Earl Beatty: The Last Naval Hero* (Collins)
Joseph P. Sims (ed), *Three Wars With Germany* (Putnam)
Michael Smith, *The Spying Game* (Politeos)
David Stafford, *Churchill and Secret Service* (John Murray)
Barbara Tuchman, *The Zimmermann Telegram* (Macmillan)
Nigel West, *GCHQ: The Secret Wireless War 1900-86* (Weidenfeld & Nicolson)
John Winton, *Jellicoe* (Michael Joseph)
Jules Witcover, *Sabotage at Black Tom: Imperial Germany's Secret War in America 1914-1917* (Algonquin).

David Ramsay
Indian Wells, California

List Of Abbreviations

ACNS	Assistant Chief of the Naval Staff
Admiralstab	German Naval Staff
ASW	Anti-Submarine Warfare
ASWD	Anti-Submarine Warfare Division
BCF	Battlecruiser Force, later Battlecruiser Fleet
CID	Committee of Imperial Defence
DCNS	Deputy Chief of the Naval Staff
DF	Direction Finding
DID	Director of the Intelligence Division of the Naval Staff, renamed DNI, Director of Naval Intelligence Division 1918
DNI	See above
DSO	Distinguished Service Order
FdU	Führer der U-booten. Senior Officer Submarines, Kriegsmarine
FSL	First Sea Lord
GC & CS	Government Code & Cipher School. The inter-Service cryptological Organisation which took over Room 40 in 1922
GMT	Greenwich Mean Time
HMAS	His Majesty's Australian Ship
HSF	*Hochseeflotte* The High Seas Fleet
HVB	*Handelsverkehrsbuch* (Kriegsmarine/German Merchant Navy Code)
ID	Intelligence Division of the Naval Staff
ID 25	Official designation of Room 40 from May 1917 as Section 25 of the ID
JIC	Joint Intelligence Centre
JIS	Joint Intelligence Staff
MI5	British Secret Service department responsible for counter-espionage inside the UK
MI6	British Secret Service department responsible for intelligence and espionage outside the UK. See also SIS
NID	Naval Intelligence Division. See also ID

OIC	Operational Intelligence Centre, a Division of the Admiralty in World War II
ONI	Office of Naval Intelligence (USN)
OSS	Office of Strategic Services (USA)
RAN	Royal Australian Navy
RNR	Royal Naval Reserve, formed from officers and men of the Merchant Navy
RNVR	Royal Naval Volunteer Reserve
SIS	Special Intelligence Service. See also MI6
SKM	*Signalbuch der Kaiserlichen Marine;* the principal German Naval Code
SOO	Staff Officer Operations
USN	United States Navy
VA	Vice-Admiral
VB	*Verkehrsbuch*: The Kriegsmarine code used for communicating with Naval Attachés, warships stationed overseas, consuls and Flag Officers
W/T	Wireless Telegraphy
Y Stations	Wireless stations which intercepted and recorded enemy WT traffic

CHAPTER I
1870-1914

William Reginald Hall, Reggie or 'Blinker' in the service and Rex to his family, was born on June 28 1870, the second of the four children of William Henry, Lieutenant, later Captain, RN and Caroline Hall, daughter of the Rev. Henry Armfield, Canon of Salisbury Cathedral. W. H. Hall became the first Director of Naval Intelligence, the position his son was to hold with such distinction in World War I. The family naval connection stretched back to the end of the 18th century when Hall's great-grandfather, John, became a naval chaplain. He served as both secretary and chaplain to Vice-Admiral Sir James Wallace, C-in-C North American Station and Governor of Newfoundland and later as chaplain at the Naval Hospital at Haslar.

William Henry was the predominant influence in his son's early life, encouraging him to make the Navy his career. In January 1883 Hall joined HMS *Britannia*, the hulk moored in the River Dart, the training establishment for future officers. In 1885 he went to sea for the first time in the armoured cruiser HMS *Northampton*, the flagship of the North American and West Indies Squadron. He quickly established himself as a keen and highly competent officer: his commendations describing him as 'zealous, promising, smart and intelligent'.

In 1889 he was promoted Sub-Lieutenant, passing his examination for Lieutenant with First-Class certificates in five subjects, including Gunnery and Torpedoes. His record coupled with the considerable reputation his father had earned as Director of Intelligence helped to secure Hall prime appointments. In January 1890, he was promoted Lieutenant, returning to sea in the armoured cruiser HMS *Imperieuse*, the flagship of the China station. On her Captain's recommendation, he was accepted for the Gunnery course.

He graduated second in his term, serving for a year on the junior staff at HMS *Excellent*, the Navy's gunnery school at Whale Island, near Portsmouth. As a qualified gunnery officer, he was now a fully-fledged member of what was then and for many years afterwards the elite of the Navy.

Physically, Hall was slim and slightly below medium height but with a considerable presence. As a young man he had the bright red hair and the piercing blue eyes indicative of a quick temper. He normally had this trait well under control but there were occasions when it could explode into bursts of startling anger. He owed his nickname 'Blinker', prosaically enough, to his constant blinking. The most likely explanation for this condition, suggested to the author by an eye specialist, is that Hall suffered severely from sarcoidosis or dry-eye and his blinking was a subconscious attempt to keep his eyes lubricated.[1]

When he was 24, Hall married Ethel Abney, always known as Essie, whose father, Sir William, an eminent scientist, had been closely involved in the development of photography. They had three children, two sons, John and Richard, who both became naval officers, and a daughter, Faith, who married a naval officer, Peter Stubbs.

A successful term as Gunnery Officer on the armoured cruiser HMS *Australia* secured him the sought-after appointment as Senior Staff Officer at *Excellent* in June 1898. The officers and men who passed through the School remembered his electrifying presence and his blazing blue eyes which missed little of what was going on around him. In January 1901 he was promoted Commander. Hall spent three and a half years at sea as Commander (Executive Officer) of the battleships HMS *Magnificent* and HMS *Cornwallis*, forging a reputation as a strict disciplinarian. His earlier biographer, Admiral Sir William James, wrote:

> ... Hall's method of command was unusual. He had no mercy on men who broke the disciplinary bonds or who avoided hard work but he could not do enough for the loyal, hard-working men and their fear of him soon turned to devotion when they realised that, although he demanded a very high standard, he had their interests at heart, and would do all that he could to help them with their private or domestic troubles.[2]

Hall was promoted Captain on December 31 1905 at the age of 35, indicating that his career was on a fast track. John 'Jacky' Fisher, his father's old friend, now First Sea Lord, selected Hall for the newly created post of Inspector-Captain of the Mechanical Training Establishments, one of his measures to improve the service's technical skills. He successfully built the network from scratch, receiving a glowing Admiralty appreciation.

In December 1907 Hall became Captain of the armoured cruiser HMS *Cornwall*, where he had his first successful experience of intelligence work. By 1908 a warship construction race was in progress between Britain and Germany. (As Sir Michael Howard points out in his book *Empires, Nations and Wars*, 'The security of the British Isles depended on the maritime subordination of everyone else.') The Naval Intelligence Division particularly wanted to discover how many shipyard slips the

Germans had earmarked for building warships. As *Cornwall* was due to visit Kiel and other German ports that summer, Hall was asked to investigate their naval shipbuilding capacity. He found that Kiel's dockyards and the forts were well guarded. He ingeniously got round this difficulty by enlisting the support of Bendor, the Duke of Westminster, who was visiting Kiel in his yacht. He borrowed Bendor's fast motor boat and with two of his officers, Lieutenant Brandon and Captain Trench, Royal Marines, he sped round the harbour, staging a 'convenient' breakdown opposite the dockyard. While 'running repairs' were in progress, Brandon and Trench surreptitiously photographed the building slips under the noses of the unsuspecting harbour police. The Intelligence Division was well satisfied with Hall's investigation.

Hall's next appointment was as Captain of the large armoured cruiser HMS *Natal*, the champion gunnery ship of the service in each of her three types of guns. Under his command, *Natal* surpassed her earlier gunnery records. Her gunnery officer, William 'Bubbles' James, was to be closely associated with Hall: as his Commander on *Queen Mary*, as Head of Room 40 in 1917–18, as his effective deputy as Director of Naval Intelligence, and his first biographer in the 1950s.

After two years as Assistant to the Third Sea Lord or Controller of the Navy, responsible for warship design and construction, Hall took command of the new second generation battlecruiser HMS *Queen Mary* (26,260 tons, 8 13.5-in and 16 4-in guns) which was commissioned in October 1913, and joined the elite battlecruiser squadron, commanded by Hall's old friend, David Beatty.

On August 28 the battlecruisers, now based at Scapa Flow, saw action for the first time. Commodore Roger Keyes, commanding the Navy's submarine force, which had been patrolling off the German North Sea coast, had discovered that German destroyers, unescorted by light cruisers, were regularly patrolling northwest of the island of Heligoland searching for British submarines and minelayers. Keyes and Commodore Reginald Tyrwhitt, commanding the Harwich Force, proposed an audacious plan to attack these warships with Keyes's submarines and Tyrwhitt's two cruisers and thirty-one destroyers. As the operation would be conducted close to the German coast, it was inevitably risky. Jellicoe, commanding the Grand Fleet, concerned that Tyrwhitt's task force was not strong enough to deal with forceful German opposition, persuaded the Admiralty to send the battlecruisers to support the operation. Beatty's squadron, with six modern light cruisers, sailed from Scapa at 5 am on August 27.

At 11.35 am on the following day Beatty decided that he must intervene to support Tyrwhitt's Force, which was in some trouble in an action against three German light cruisers, with five more being sent to reinforce them. Beatty increased his squadron's speed to 26 and then to 28 knots and by 12.37 pm he was within range of the action. His intervention proved decisive. Three German cruisers and a destroyer were sunk and their losses would have been higher if the action had been fought in better visibility. Correctly reasoning that the German battlecruisers had been ordered to sea to engage him and with his task completed, he turned for home. Despite the damage to Tyrwhitt's force, no British warships had been sunk in the war's first naval engagement.

Hall was well pleased with *Queen Mary*'s performance in her first action. Beatty wrote to his wife: 'I gave the Germans a very good shock right at their front door and got all our ships out safely which was an intense relief as at one time I thought we would never do it but by hard steaming the *Lion* family flew at 28 knots. Even Captain Hall admits it.'[3] The battle of the Heligoland Bight was the only occasion on which Hall saw action in his thirty-five years in the service, as illness was soon to strike him down.

Anxiety about Hall's health (he suffered from a weak chest and lungs) had surfaced as early as November 1910. Following his inspection of Hall's then command, HMS *Natal*, Rear Admiral Lowry reported: 'Hall's health is not very good at present and he would be better for a spell of shore employment.'[4] The sub-arctic conditions at Scapa did him no good. On September 10, Beatty told his wife: 'We have bad news here. I hear Captain Hall is far from well and I must have a good talk with him ... He looks so terribly grey and tired ... [and two days later] Hall is still alive and going strong in his diet ... I have not seen him but will do so tomorrow.'[5] On October 12 Beatty wrote: 'Hall has been appointed to be the Director of Intelligence at the War Staff. I am sorry to lose him but it will save his life. He could not last if he continued as he gets no better, in fact worse and looks an awful colour. I am getting him out as soon as I can as I think he has reached the limit of human endurance.'[6] Two days later, Hall gave up command of *Queen Mary*. His Executive Officer, William James, believed (like Beatty) that his new appointment had literally saved his life. He described the reaction of the ship's company: 'The ship was plunged into gloom when they heard that he was leaving. They had begun by fearing him: now they loved him.'[7]

If Hall had remained in command of *Queen* Mary, he would probably have been killed when she was blown up with the loss of all but eighteen of her crew at Jutland.

Fortuitously, the post of Director of Naval Intelligence had just become vacant. The outgoing Director, Rear Admiral Henry Oliver, now Naval Secretary to the First Lord and responsible for the appointments of senior officers, noted that the understandably distraught Essie Hall successfully lobbied him to secure the vacancy for her husband.[8] Beatty wrote to his wife: 'I am glad now that Hall is at the Admiralty – he might be of some use to me there – he is not afraid of speaking his mind – he knows my views.'⁹ Hall's appointment as DNI was certainly inspired and in the four years in which he held the post he came face to face with his destiny.

Notes

1. Communication to the author from Dr. Bart Ketover May 2005
2. Admiral Sir William James, *The Eyes of the Navy* p.6
3. Beatty to Lady Beatty, August 30 1914 Beatty papers NMM BTY 17/28
4. Hall Service Record, TNA
5. Beatty to Lady Beatty, September 10 and 12 1914 NMM BTY 17/29
6. Ibid, October 12 1914 NMM BTY 17/30
7. James, *The Sky was Always Blue* p.85
8. Henry Oliver, *Recollections* Vol. II p.164 NMM OLV/12
9. Beatty to Lady Beatty, October 20 1914 NMM BTY 17/30

CHAPTER II

'The Miraculous Draught of Fishes' – The Endowment of Room 40

Cryptography can be traced back at least as far as the time of Julius Caesar. Before the invention of the telegraph cable and later of wireless telegraphy, the Navy had made use of a simple form of signals intelligence: SIGINT in the jargon of the intelligence world. In pursuing the French fleet carrying Napoleon and his army to Egypt in 1798, Nelson was at a disadvantage as he had no frigates under his command to act as scouts and provide him with valuable intelligence. As he later ruefully remarked 'The lack of frigates will be emblazoned on my heart.' As C-in-C of the Mediterranean Fleet, he was able to use the experience he had gained in that campaign to achieve an even greater success.

In the run-up to the battle of Trafalgar, Nelson purposefully deployed his frigates to keep a close watch on the French and Spanish fleets, while his battleships remained out of sight below the horizon. His frigates, his eyes and his ears as he memorably called them, formed a chain with one end in sight of the port and the other in signalling range of his battle fleet, all of them remaining in visual contact with each other. In a process known as line-of-sight intelligence, the scouting frigates were able to relay any enemy fleet movements more or less in real time to the C-in-C. The system had been made possible by the Home Popham signal book, named after the Admiral who had introduced it two years earlier. Every ship in Nelson's fleet had a copy of the codebook. The system was simple and effective, using coloured flags or pennants to denote numbers and letters. These were hoisted to the yardarm where the signals could be read by the intended recipient ship. The signal book included standard phrases, such as number 370, which read 'Enemy ships are coming out of port'. Nelson placed considerable reliance on his senior frigate Captain, the resourceful Henry Blackwood of HMS *Euralyus*. On October 4 1805 he wrote to him: I am confident that you will not let these gentry slip through your fingers.' Five days later, he wrote again: 'As *Weazle* [a sloop under Blackwood's command] sails faster you can send her to me with accounts, when you can't communicate by signals. I should never wish to be more than 48 hours without hearing from you. In short watch all points and winds and weathers for I shall have to depend on you.'[1] Blackwood did not let him down, nor did his other captains. On October 14, Nelson wrote to Captain George Hope of HMS *Defence*:

> You will with the *Agamemnon* take a station west from Cadiz from 7 to 10 leagues, by which means, if the enemy should move, I hope to have instant information, as 2 or 3 ships will be kept, as at present between the fleet and your 2 ships, and it seems thought by Capt. Blackwood that a ship or 2 may attempt to drive the frigates off and if that should be the case you will be at hand to assist.

He left little to chance. On the day before the battle he signalled:

> Capt. Blackwood to keep with 2 frigates in sight of the enemy in the night, 2 other frigates to be placed between him and *Defence*. [And that night] If the enemy are standing to the southward, or towards the Straits [of Gibraltar] burn 2 blue lights together, every hour and make a greater blaze if the enemy are standing to the westward.[2]

Nelson's insistence on this detailed intelligence paid off. In his famous letter from HMS *Victory* on October 19 1805 to Emma Lady Hamilton, now in the possession of the British Library, he wrote: 'The signal has been made that the Enemy's Combined Fleet are coming out of port.' Interestingly, the letter which was found open on his desk and later brought to Emma Hamilton by Captain Hardy, noted that *Victory*'s position at noon that day was 16 leagues (48 miles) east south east of Cadiz. On the same day, Blackwood wrote to his wife: '… though our fleet was at sixteen leagues off, I have let Lord N. know of their coming-out … At this moment we are within four miles of the enemy, and talking to Lord Nelson by means of Sir H Popham's signals, though so distant, but repeated along by the rest of the frigates of this Squadron.' Nelson wrote in his private diary on October 20: 'In the afternoon Captain Blackwood telegraphed the enemy seemed determined to go to the westward. At 5 I telegraphed Capt. Blackwood that I relied on his keeping sight of the enemy. At six o'clock [the frigate] *Naiad* made signal for 31 sail of the enemy … the frigates and look-out ships kept sight of the enemy most admirably all night, and told me by signals what tack they were on.'[3]
Nelson, ever a forward-looking fleet commander, had used this early form of SIGINT to great effect and the resultant knowledge of enemy movements had made a splendid contribution towards one of the most decisive victories in the history of warfare.

Throughout the 19th century the Navy actively developed communications, instituting a chain of interconnecting semaphore stations during the Napoleonic wars which linked the Admiralty in London with the main naval bases at Portsmouth, Plymouth and Chatham. By contemporary standards this system was remarkably fast. By 1806 a message could be transmitted to and be acknowledged by Plymouth in only three minutes.[4] The system had a drawback: it could only work in daylight and in reasonably clear weather. The Prussian Army instituted a similar system, connecting Berlin with the main garrison towns. The arrival of the telegraphic cable and the electrically operated Morse code made the semaphore redundant.

In its Victorian heyday, the British Government was quick to grasp the potential of the submarine cable as a tool to maintain control over its widespread Empire. In 1858 the first transatlantic cable had connected Britain and Canada. By 1870 a British-owned cable system, routed through traditional allies like Portugal and colonies such as Gibraltar, Malta and Aden and Egypt, the latter effectively under British control from 1882, linked Whitehall with India, that jewel in the Imperial crown. The link was later extended to Australia, New Zealand and Britain's other Pacific possessions. By the turn of the century the British dominated the world's cable systems, ensuring that wherever possible the cables were laid at sea, effectively preventing any foreign interference with their operations. In time of war the Government could and did demand priority for its own signal traffic. In November 1900 the French Government noted: 'England owes her influence in the world perhaps more to her cable communications than to her navy. She controls the news and makes it serve her policy and commerce in a marvellous manner.'[4]

From a naval point of view, the advantages of communicating by telegraphic cable were nugatory. Although the Admiralty could now keep in touch with shore bases in real time, it could not relay intelligence to fleets or squadrons at sea. In the 1890s fleet commanders were thus effectively as dependent on line-of-sight intelligence as Nelson had been nearly a century before.

Between 1897 and 1900 Guglielmo Marconi had developed his discovery of wireless telegraphy to a state where it was of serious interest to every leading naval power. The anglophile Marconi enjoyed a close relationship with the British Admiralty and particularly with its leading expert in and enthusiast for wireless telegraphy, Captain (later Admiral of the Fleet Sir) Henry Jackson. Its huge potential at sea and its ability to revolutionise communications both between ships afloat and from ship to shore was quickly realised. In 1900 the Admiralty decided to adopt the Marconi system, ordering 50 of his sets for installation both afloat and ashore. An entrepreneur and a prolific inventor, Marconi continued throughout his active life to produce dramatic improvements in the range and capability of his system and its derivatives. In December 1901 he successfully transmitted the first transatlantic wireless signal from his station at Poldhu in Cornwall to Cape Cod in Massachusetts. A month later the Cunarder *Philadelphia* in mid-Atlantic received a signal from the same station at a range of 1,500 miles. Well before 1914, every leading navy had equipped all its important warships with wireless and had set up a series of shore stations to relay the traffic to its destinations.

The technology developed by the Marconi company and its bitter German rival Telefunken transformed naval command and control systems and radically influenced the evolution of signals intelligence. The story of the most famous early example is worthy of repetition.

In 1910 Dr Crippen murdered his wife and fled to Belgium with his girlfriend, Ethel Le Neve, dressed as a boy, intending to take a ship to Canada, boarding the Canadian Pacific liner *Montrose* in Antwerp. Their plan came unstuck when the liner's astute Captain, Henry Kendall, suspected that Crippen and Le Neve were on board. On July 22, the third day of the voyage, and while he was 130 miles west of the Marconi station at Poldhu and thus within the ship's transmitting range (150 miles) he asked his radio operator to send this signal to the Canadian Pacific Head Office in Liverpool: 'Have strong suspicions that Crippen London cellar murderer and accomplice are among Saloon passengers. Moustache taken off growing beard. Accomplice dressed as boy. Voice manner and build undoubtedly a girl.'

It took five hours to transmit this vital intelligence from Poldhu to Scotland Yard. Detective Inspector Walter Dew, in charge of the investigation, rushed to Liverpool on the next train. With only minutes to spare, he boarded the White Star liner *Laurentic* bound for Quebec. The newer *Laurentic* had a cruising speed of 17 knots, four knots faster than *Montrose* and steering a more direct course could reach Canadian waters several days earlier. Two days later, an anxious Kendall, able to receive signals at a distance of 600 miles, received a signal relayed from a London newspaper to its reporter on board *Laurentic*: 'What is Inspector Dew doing? Are passengers excited over chase? Rush reply.' The relieved Captain now knew that his intelligence had successfully reached its destination. Relaying signals via other ships, Kendall kept Scotland Yard fully informed about the suspects and prevented them knowing of the pursuit now in hand. With superb irony, the unsuspecting Crippen, enjoying the sun in a deckchair and watching the aerial above him crackling with electricity from incoming signals, observed to Kendall: 'What a marvellous invention wireless is.'

On July 27 *Laurentic* overtook *Montrose* and Dew arrested Crippen and Le Neve, when the liner called in at Rimouski Point, her first port of call on the St. Laurence River. Crippen was extradited to Britain, tried for murder at the Old Bailey and hanged. This incident, which attracted a media furore at the time, dramatically demonstrated the potential of Marconi's invention as a source of signals intelligence.

Germany was acutely aware that Britain dominated the world's cable systems and could cut their access to these routes in time of war. To overcome this disadvantage, she commissioned a number of long-range shore based wireless transmitters, a quantum leap which put them well ahead of Britain, whose Imperial Wireless Chain, commissioned from Marconi in 1912, did not finally come on stream until 1916. By 1914 Telefunken had improved the range of the main transmitter at Nauen, a Berlin suburb, to 3,300 miles, capable of reaching Kamina in the African colony of Togoland. The radio station at Kamina relayed Nauen's signals to other African colonies. The German colonies in the Pacific and Tsingtao, the base of the East Asia Squadron, were also in range of Nauen either directly or through relay. Another radio link connected Nauen with two radio stations in the United States, at Sayville on Long Island and Tuckerton, New Jersey. (Curiously, these two stations had been partly financed by French capital.)

In 1912 the Committee for Imperial Defence, the high-level coordinating body set up as part of the review of defence policy after the Boer War, decided that all German-owned transatlantic cables were to be cut immediately following any declaration of war. Britain had twenty-eight cable ships, twice as many as those of any other cable-owning country and its own cable network was thus relatively secure from an enemy cable-cutting effort. Early on the morning of August 5 1914, the cable ship *Telconia* cut each of the five German cable systems connecting the port of Emden with Spain, Africa and North and South America. In her book on the Zimmermann telegram, Barbara Tuchman vividly described this remarkable operation:

> ... before the sun rose the next morning [August 5] a ship moved slowly through the mist over the North Sea until she reached a point some miles off Emden, where the Dutch Coast joins the German. In the half-darkness she began to fish in a manner that was strangely clumsy yet purposeful .... Heavy grappling irons were plunged into the water, dragged along the bottom, and hauled up, bringing with them an eel-shaped catch dripping mud and slime, that clanged against the ship's side with a metallic sound. Several times, the maneuver was repeated and each time the eel-like shapes were cut and cast back into the sea.[5]

Later that day a Royal Navy cruiser dragged up two German-owned cables near the Azores. Only one German cable system, a joint venture with an American company operating between Monrovia in Liberia and Pernambuco in Brazil, survived this determined and successful onslaught. Over the objections of the Foreign Office, a British cable company persuaded the American partner to cut the system early in 1915. Twice during the war a German cable ship managed to cut the cable between

Britain and Norway but as the Royal Navy effectively had command of the North Sea, the system was quickly repaired.

The Committee of Imperial Defence's decision paid Britain a dividend far greater than could ever been envisioned and its results were to shape the course and eventual outcome of the conflict. With the loss of its cable systems at the very outset of the war, Germany was forced to communicate by wireless with its embassies and overseas stations, particularly those in Spain and the Americas.

Cable traffic was relatively secure and at risk only to cutting. In 1914 wireless telegraphy was a much newer technology and its vulnerability to interception seriously underrated. The 1914 Naval Annual asserted that there was no threat of any interception of radio traffic, a view accepted at that time even by Churchill. He told Vice-Admiral Lewis Bayly that: '...our wireless orders will be in cypher, and we ought not to assume that they can be instantly intercepted and decoded'.[6]

Such complacency was soon to be shattered. From the first day of the war a huge volume of coded German signals was received by the naval radio stations and those of the Post Office and the Marconi Company and passed on to the Admiralty. During the course of the war Marconi estimated that it received no less than 80 million words transmitted by Nauen.

Hall's predecessor as DNI, Rear-Admiral Henry Oliver, was faced with the problem of how to read this traffic. Early in August 1914 he had lunch at the United Services Club in Pall Mall, the Senior to generations of naval and army officers, with Sir Alfred Ewing, the Director of Naval Education and one of Britain's most distinguished engineers. The two men were old friends and both were protégés of Jacky Fisher. Ewing, 59 in August 1914, was a dapper Scotsman, renowned for his sartorial elegance, with a liking for grey suits, striped waistcoats and blue polka dot bow ties. The son of a Church of Scotland minister and a graduate of Edinburgh University, his talent had been recognised as early as 1878 when he had been chosen as Professor of Engineering in the newly formed Imperial University of Tokyo, a mere ten years after the Meiji Revolution which had opened Japan up to Western technology. In 1890, when he was 35, he was appointed to the prestigious position of Professor of Mechanism and Applied Mechanics at Cambridge.

In 1903, as part of the so-called Fisher-Selborne reforms, Fisher had brought Ewing from academia into the Admiralty in the new post of Director of Naval Education. His remit was to upgrade the technical skills of all ranks in the Navy to enable the service to take full advantage of the ongoing developments in engineering, gunnery and other sciences, an area of considerable importance in an increasingly technological profession. The post of Inspecting Captain of Mechanical Establishments, which Hall had held between 1905 and 1908, was created as a part of the same initiative. Fisher had made an inspired choice. Ewing had a working knowledge of maritime engineering as he had been closely involved in the development of the marine turbine by his contemporary, Sir Charles Parsons. His success in this new appointment had been recognised by the knighthood he had received in the 1911 Coronation Honours List.

Oliver wrote: 'Before 1914 the Intelligence Department had been trying without success to decode wireless cyphers. I wanted to put a big man on it ... as we walked together to the club it occurred to me that he was my man. He had studied at a German University and spoke the language fluently. I asked him to take charge of a department and he agreed as the War had closed his schools and he was rather at a loose end.'[7]

Oliver had made an astute choice in asking Ewing to organise a decoding operation. Not only did he have time on his hands, he had a deep interest in both wireless telegraphy and cryptology. The two men returned to the Admiralty and put the proposal to Churchill. With his fascination for intelligence, the First Lord had little hesitation in confirming Ewing's appointment.

The cryptanalysts were originally based in Ewing's already cramped office and the small box-like room occupied by Mountstephen, Sir Alfred's secretary. They had to compete for space with the staff of the Education Division. Ewing made his greatest contributions towards Room 40's success in its earliest days. Through his interest in the technology he had got to know Russell Clarke, a barrister and a prominent amateur enthusiast for wireless telegraphy. He told Ewing of the considerable volume of German wireless traffic which was being transmitted on a lower frequency than the signals emanating from the Kriegsmarine's main station at Norddeich in Schleswig-Holstein. With Ewing's support, Clarke and his fellow wireless devotee, Colonel Hippisley, a Somerset landowner, set up a facility in the coastguard station at Hunstanton in Norfolk, which successfully intercepted this traffic. The Hunstanton group grew to include seven other stations.

Ewing had to start from scratch in recruiting cryptologists: at that time no such profession existed. Initially he picked men with two qualifications, knowledge of German and a reputation for discretion. One of his first choices was Alastair Denniston, a fellow-Scot and former hockey international, who had been the Professor of German at the Naval College at Osborne. Denniston, the future head of the Government Code and Cipher School, was to become one of the stalwarts of British cryptology over the next thirty years. His papers give a real insight into the operations and development of Room 40. He was joined by R. D. Norton, a former company promoter, by Lord Herschell, another fluent German speaker and one of Hall's future PAs, by two Naval instructors, Parrish and Curtis, who were already on Ewing's staff, and Professor Henderson, a mathematician from the Naval College at Greenwich – when they could be spared from other duties. The first weeks of the operation were almost entirely given over to research, much of the work, according to Denniston, proving fruitless.

In the autumn of 1914, through a succession of fortuitous circumstances, British Naval Intelligence enjoyed a stroke – or more precisely three strokes – of monumental good fortune. On August 11 the German steamship *Hobart* was captured off Melbourne by a boarding party from the Royal Australian Navy under the command of Captain J.A.T. Richardson. *Hobart*'s Captain, unaware that war had been declared, was taken by surprise by the arrival of the boarders who were wearing civilian clothes and who alleged that they were customs inspectors. Richardson kept the Captain under close observation and arrested him while he was attempting to remove his confidential records from a secret panel in his cabin with the intention of destroying them. Among the captured documents was a copy of the Handelsverkehrbuch or HVB, the code used by the Admiralstab, the German Admiralty, for communicating not only with merchant ships but also with the Hochseeflotte, the High Seas Fleet. The RAN did not at first realise the importance of their discovery and not until September 9 did they dispatch the captured codebook to the Admiralty, who received it at the end of October.

On August 23 the German Baltic Fleet sent a task force, including the cruisers *Augsburg* and *Magdeburg* and three destroyers, to attack Russian shipping in the Gulf of Finland. *Magdeburg* was the proverbial unlucky ship, plagued by repeated trouble with her turbines; her crew was inexperienced and she was commanded by a relatively junior officer, Korvettenkapitan Richard Habenicht. At around 12.30 am on the morning of August 25, *Magdeburg* ran aground in fog on shallows off the Russian island of Odensholm at the entrance to the Gulf. Every effort Habenicht made to free the luckless ship, including an attempt by one of the escorting destroyers, V-26, to pull her off, failed. By 9 am Habenicht was uneasily aware that the lighthouse keepers had reported the incident to the Russian naval base at Tallinn, some fifty miles to the east, and that Russian naval units had been sent to the island.

He ordered that *Magdeburg* be blown up to avoid her falling into the hands of the Russian Navy and instructed his radio officer, Walther Bender, to destroy all the confidential documents carried aboard the cruiser, including charts of German minefields, her war diary and most importantly the main Kriegsmarine codebook, the SKM, and the cipher key. Bender burnt the codebook and cipher in the steering room. Two further copies of the codebooks and a cipher key from the radio room and bridge were to be retained for communication with rescuers and with higher command. A fourth copy kept under lock and key in the captain's cabin was forgotten.

Habenicht had by then set charges for the destruction of the cruiser and V-26 came alongside to take off the crew. The ill-fortune which had plagued the hapless *Magdeburg* did not relent. The charges were set off prematurely. In the resultant chaos, Bender ordered three of his radiomen, Szillat, Neuhaus and Kiehnert, to recover the codebooks and cipher keys from the radio room and the bridge and bring them to V-26, which was still alongside the cruiser. Before they could reach her, the first officer ordered 'abandon ship'. Before leaping overboard, Szillat threw the bridge's copy of the codebook into the water where it immediately sank. Kiehnert, carrying the cipher key, jumped into the sea where several other sailors jumped on top of him. He was unable to hold onto the valuable document. At that moment the forward charge exploded, blowing large chunks of steel on to the sailors. Neuhaus also lost the radio room's codebook, which he was carrying. The stern charge never exploded.

While V-26 was rescuing survivors, several Russian ships arrived and opened fire. One shot blew several men overboard and another hit her wardroom, killing all its occupants. Her Captain did, however, manage to evade the Russian gunnery and escape. Bender, with his dog Schuhmchen, *Magdeburg*'s mascot, and a number of sailors, among them Neuhaus, swam to the nearby island where they were rounded up by Russian guards. A Russian gunboat, *Lejtenant Burakov*, put a boarding party commanded by her first officer Lieutenant Galibin on board what remained of *Magdeburg*. Habenicht and those officers and men who had remained aboard surrendered.

In *World Crisis* Churchill dramatically described the recovery of this code: 'The body of a drowned German under-officer was picked up by the Russians ... and clasped in his bosom by arms rigid in death, were the cypher and signal books of the German Navy.' The reality was more prosaic than this Churchillian flight of fancy. While Galibin was searching Habernicht's cabin he discovered his copy of the codebook hidden in a locker, and divers quickly located the two other codebooks, which Szillat and Neuhaus had lost in the sea. The cipher book was never found.

In one single, minor sea action, the Russian Navy had struck gold. Keeping the waterlogged copies recovered from the sea for their own use, they recognised that Britain, as the major allied naval power, would derive the greatest advantage from this unexpected discovery. They generously offered the undamaged codebook, serial number 151, which they had discovered in Habenicht's cabin, to the Admiralty in London. Count Constantine Benckendorff, the son of the Russian Ambassador in London and a former cipher officer, was detailed to take the precious codebook to Britain. Once again, there was delay in transferring it to the RN. Travelling in a naval steamship, escorted by the cruiser HMS *Theseus*,

Benckendorff sailed from the Arctic port of Alexandrovsk early in October. On the morning of October 13, two days before Hall was appointed DNI, Benckendorff and the Russian naval attaché, Captain Wolkoff, handed the *Signalbuch der Kaiserlichen Marine* or SKM, to a delighted Winston Churchill. The writer David Kahn eloquently described this gift as 'more precious than a dozen Fabergé eggs ... one of the most significant moments in the long history of secret intelligence'. The SKM was a sophisticated code used for communicating with both warships and naval attachés overseas.[8]

Four days later Captain Cecil Fox, commanding the light cruiser HMS *Undaunted* with the destroyers HMS *Lance*, *Legion*, *Lennox* and *Loyal*, was on a sweep off the Dutch coast. His instructions were to protect the allied forces then defending Antwerp. Steaming north off the Dutch island of Texel, Fox encountered an inferior force of four older German destroyers, S-115, S117, S-118 and S-119, heading south on a mine laying mission. The German force was outgunned and Fox quickly sank all four destroyers. Before his ship went down the senior German officer on S-119 correctly threw all his confidential documents, including his codebooks, overboard in a lead-lined chest. On November 30 a British trawler, fishing off Texel, dragged the case up in its nets. Four days later the case and its valuable contents were in the hands of Room 40. Among the documents discovered in the case was the Verkehrsbuch (VB), another relatively sophisticated code for communicating with both warships and overseas naval attachés. This important find was thereafter humorously referred to by the staff of Room 40 as 'The Miraculous Draught of Fishes'. By December 1914 Room 40 had obtained access to all three of the German Navy's most important codes.

Denniston recalled the excitement when Wolkoff, after seeing Churchill, delivered the SKM to Ewing. 'Some time about the middle of October Sir Alfred's desk was cleared mysteriously ... on the arrival of the Russian attaché ... and the cryptographers were almost rudely discouraged from their visits to Mountstephen's room, now occupied by an unknown naval officer, who came early and stayed late.'[9] This quiet, hardworking naval officer was Fleet Paymaster C.J.E. Rotter, the head of the German section of the Intelligence Division, whom Hall, in one of his first acts since succeeding Oliver as DNI, had transferred to Ewing's staff to help decode the German messages. Rotter spoke fluent German, had spent long periods in that country and could pass for a native. Without the cipher key, which had not been recovered from *Magdeburg* and blocked by the extra level of security it provided, the cryptographers had found that they could only solve a small number of the messages, principally weather forecasts and instructions for auxiliary vessels. The astute Rotter guessed that the cipher key to the HVB code recovered from *Hobart* might use the same system as the key to SKM. Analysing a large volume of enciphered traffic and the serial numbers used, he succeeded in breaking the key. As Denniston acidly noted: 'Their folly was greater than our stupidity.'[10] By mid-November 1914 the Admiralty was able to intercept and read all the principal German Naval codes and as a result was aware in close detail of the High Seas Fleet's movements and plans.

Incredibly, the Kriegsmarine never held any inquiry into the security aspects of the loss of *Magdeburg*. The Admiral commanding the task force merely reported that the encipherment key had not been destroyed with certainty. The Admiralstab complacently concluded that: 'no serious consequences are feared here from the possible loss of the codebook.' Prince Heinrich of Prussia, the Kaiser's younger brother and C-in-C of the Baltic Fleet and often thought to have been promoted beyond his ability, was unsatisfied. His investigation determined that the Russians may well have got hold of the lost cipher key and that: '... finally the possibility must also be considered that the Russians, by diving, got one of the codebooks out of the water'.[11] Heinrich, more perceptive than his detractors believed, recommended that the SVB should be replaced and that mechanical encipherment be introduced. The Admiralstab overruled him. In August 1915 Lieutenant Galibin, who had led the boarding party on *Magdeburg*, was captured. Under interrogation, he revealed that the codebook had fallen into enemy hands. Once again the Admiralstab took no notice.

The decrypting operation had now outgrown its original home. Denniston remembered that 'Sir Alfred's visitors were now refused entrance to the room ... the august Assistant Secretary to the Admiralty [Oswyn Murray] was denied admittance by a temporary civilian ignorant of his identity.' This error might have helped, for very early in November a new room was placed at the disposal of the section. The watchkeepers were now housed in Room 40 after its location in the Old Admiralty building, or OB 40 as it was known. The operation quickly outgrew Room 40 and expanded into a number of adjoining Rooms, although Room 40 remained its generic title.

Ewing's staff was increased to cope with the volume of signal traffic that could now be read. He then performed his second conspicuous service to Room 40. With a real understanding of the requirements of cryptology, he widened his net to recruit academics, particularly mathematicians, whose analytic skills made them extremely useful as cryptanalysts. Availing himself of his contacts in the academic world, he descended on King's College, Cambridge where he had been a fellow, recruiting several dons, most notably Alfred Dillwyn Knox, who, like Denniston, became a stalwart of British cryptology. Knox was the son of the then Bishop of Manchester and one of four remarkably talented brothers. He was the very epitome of the unworldly professor, so absent-minded that according to his niece Penelope Fitzgerald in her acclaimed book *The Knox Brothers*, he forgot to invite his brothers to his wedding. Although he was a classicist, he had a passionate interest in mathematics and was once reputed to have cracked a German code while taking a bath. He relished correcting inaccurately translated ancient manuscripts by a process of analysis, similar to cryptology, and was a first rate if unconventional bridge player. He proved to be a natural cryptologist, spending the rest of his life, until his premature death from cancer during World War II, in that vocation.

Unlike practically every other contemporary British politician, Winston Churchill had been a soldier and had seen active service in three wars, on the North-West Frontier of India, in the Sudan, and South Africa. In 1895 he had been an observer in the Cuban rebellion against Spain, where he had gained his first intelligence experience. Before leaving for Cuba he had been briefed and given maps by the Director of Military Intelligence, Colonel Edward Chapman. He was specifically instructed to collect information and statistics, notably on the effect and striking power of the new bullet. During the Battle of Diamond Hill in the Boer War, he had carried out a spectacular piece of 'line-of-sight-intelligence'. Climbing the reverse side of a hill, out of sight of the Boers, he had detected a weakness in their position which could be advantageously exploited by the British cavalry. Using a handkerchief tied to a stick, he successfully signalled the intelligence to the Divisional Commander, Ian Hamilton, who grasped the opportunity and inflicted a decisive defeat on the Boers. The British victory at Diamond Hill was a turning point in the war, leading to the capture of Pretoria and Johannesburg. Hamilton, recognising what he owed to Churchill's act of cool courage, recommended him for a medal. Roberts and Kitchener, then C-in-C and Chief of Staff in South Africa, shared a prejudice against Churchill and overruled him. Fourteen years later, Kitchener would be Churchill's opposite number at the War Office.

Throughout his long career as a Defence Minister, Churchill was habitually and deeply involved in operational matters to a far greater degree than any of his predecessors or successors. With his intelligence background, he took a close interest in Room 40 from the outset, rigorously examining its output. David Stafford, the historian of his involvement in intelligence, wrote: 'Churchill stood head and shoulders above his political contemporaries in grasping the importance of intelligence. Secret service with all its romance and melodrama, trickery, deception, plot and counter-plot, certainly appealed to the schoolboy within him.'[12] Churchill instinctively realised that the Navy had acquired the vital codes, not because of any skill in cryptology but because the Kriegsmarine, encouraged by their extensive network of high-power transmitters on shore and the high quality of the wireless sets afloat, had made too free a use of wireless telegraphy. It has been observed by some historians that their captains and radio officers tended to be garrulous. Confident that their codes and ciphers were unbreakable, the Kriegsmarine paid little or no heed to any security risk for most of the war.

Churchill cited the case of *Magdeburg*, which had not been a flagship, and yet had carried no less than four copies of the SVB. He was determined that the Navy would not make a similar mistake and he insisted on maintaining a high degree of secrecy. It is not easy to hold a balance between using intelligence received from decrypts and running the risk of compromising its source; and in practice the balance, especially in World War I, generally came down on the side of discretion.

Churchill insisted that the decrypts should be controlled by a small group of senior naval officers inside the Admiralty. Only the two most important fleet commanders, Jellicoe and Beatty, and Jellicoe's Chief of Staff, Charles Madden, were even aware of Room 40's existence and its daily interception of the decrypts. Jellicoe was acutely aware of the importance of receiving SIGINT without delay. On December 19 he signalled Fisher, now once again First Sea Lord: 'Time saved by receiving and deciphering on board instead of awaiting news from the Admiralty would be of incalculable value – it is of vital importance that delay caused by deciphering at Admiralty and transmission should be avoided. There are always strong probabilities of messages not reaching me in time for complete action.'[13] Churchill overruled him and vetoed an agreement between Jellicoe and Ewing to send Herschell, who was to be commissioned as a Lieutenant-Commander in the Royal Navy Volunteer Reserve, to join Jellicoe's staff on HMS *Iron Duke* to take charge of cryptography. Under this plan, Jellicoe would have received copies of all important decrypts, especially those detailing Kriegsmarine fleet movements.

Churchill's decision was justified. The quantity of signal traffic being intercepted and the size of the staff necessary for effective decoding and interpretation and dealing with changes to the codes and keys were both far larger then Jellicoe realised. The Admiralty was the most suitable location for a decrypting operation, which could not easily be accommodated even on a flagship. Jellicoe's intuition that the Admiralty might not provide him promptly with all the relevant intelligence in their possession was nevertheless well founded and indeed was to be demonstrated at Jutland.

On November 29 Churchill issued a Most Secret order directing that only one copy of each decrypt received should be issued 'direct and exclusively' to Oliver, as Chief of Staff, who would pass it on to a small number of recipients inside the Admiralty: the First Lord, the First and Second Sea Lords, Sir Arthur Wilson – Old 'Ard Art' to the lower deck – the former First Sea Lord, who had been brought back from retirement following the declaration of war, the Naval Secretary, Hall as DNI, the Director of Operations and his Assistant and the Duty

Captains in the War Staff. The Cabinet and the War Council, a group of senior ministers set up to co-ordinate strategy at top level, did not receive the decrypts and the Prime Minster, Asquith, only saw them at Churchill's discretion. In effect, he did not allow anyone to see the signals without his permission.

Churchill had adopted a highly centralised and inflexible system, from which Jellicoe and Beatty were effectively excluded. The fleet commanders only received decrypts at Oliver's discretion even when they were in action. Beesly, the historian of naval intelligence, adroitly summed up its defects: 'Centralised Intelligence is both necessary and desirable, but only if it ensures that all information does always reach those who are in a position to act on it fully and without delay.'[14] The system prevented the development of an efficient interface between intelligence and operations. These flaws had dangerous consequences which will be examined in later chapters.

By the end of 1914, Ewing was able to report that Room 40's teething troubles, mainly faulty procedures and the inexperience of the cryptanalysts, had largely been overcome. As a result the decrypts were now gaining credibility with the War Staff, although Room 40's request to install a chart of the North Sea was inexplicably forbidden. In January 1915 the Kriegsmarine changed its encryption key. Rotter and his team solved the change in less than twelve hours. Later in the war new keys could be broken in six.

Early in 1915, Room 40's efficiency was further improved by the development of a network of direction finding stations. DF had originally been developed by Marconi from 1911 onwards and by 1912 the company had installed two direction finders aboard the Cunarder *Mauretania*. In August 1914, Captain H. J. Round, one of Marconi's senior engineers with 117 patents to his name and who was described as one of the electronic industry's most prolific inventors, was seconded to the War Office. By mid-December, two Marconi DF receivers were operational on the Western Front. During January 1915, the first weekly maps based on DF information were being produced for Military Intelligence, originally detailing German wireless positions and later indicating movements, not only of troops but of Zeppelins and aircraft.

Through his contacts with Military Intelligence, Hall soon learnt of the success DF had achieved in France and quickly recognised that its naval applications could be even more significant. He reasoned that giving the existing wireless stations DF capability would enable them to track the course of German warships and thus greatly enhance the value of the SIGINT that Room 40 was already providing.

Hall instructed Marconi to set up a DF station, originally at their factory in Chelmsford, which was later moved to the coast at Lowestoft. This was the first unit in the chain of six stations coverering the entire

North Sea that reported directly to Hall. The most northerly was at Lerwick in the Shetland Islands. Some of the stations had a double function, also intercepting German decrypts. As early as May 1915, Room 40 had successfully followed the track of a U-boat across the North Sea from the time it had sailed from its base at Emden. An additional section was set up to handle the information received from the DF stations, plotting rings and determining fixes. Later in the war and to counter the U-boat campaign, an additional five stations were established in Ireland, controlled by the Vice-Admiral Queenstown. The Marconi DF system, designed and continuously improved by the talented Round, proved technically superior to the rival systems used by the Germans and proved its worth to Room 40, particularly at Jutland. Hall's initiative had produced substantial dividends.

Although Room 40 was not then fully operational, SIGINT derived from its decrypts was first used to direct fleet movements in the action known as the Scarborough Raid in December 1914, when Admiral Warrender took a fleet to intercept the German raiding force commanded by Admiral Franz von Hipper. Ironically, the German force narrowly escaped being encircled by Warrender and Jellicoe's Grand Fleet through faulty British signalling and decision-making. By January 1915 Room 40 could accurately forecast German fleet movements. The effectiveness of its SIGINT would be clearly demonstrated in the Battle of the Dogger Bank later that month. Its performance in these actions is described in Chapter 4.

Notes

[1] Nicolas *The Dispatches and Letters of Vice-Admiral Lord Nelson* Vol. 8 p.77 & 96
[2] Ibid Vol. 8 p.122
[3] Ibid Vol. 8 p.137
[4] Keegan *Intelligence in War* p.99
[5] Tuchman The Zimmermann Telegram pp.9-10
[6] Churchill to Bayly 19 April 1913. Quoted in Stafford Churchill and Secret Service p.60
[7] Oliver *Recollections* Vol II p.102 NMM/OLV/12
[8] Kahn *Stealing the Enigma* pp.15-22
[9] CAC DENN 1/2
[10] Ibid
[11] Kahn p.27
[12] Stafford p.363
[13] Beesly *Room 40 British Naval Intelligence 1914-18* p.42
[14] Ibid p.43

CHAPTER III
Director of Naval Intelligence

At the time of his appointment as DNI, Hall was 44, one of a remarkable galaxy of talented naval officers born in the early 1870s, including Beatty, Tyrwhitt, Keyes, Chatfield, Richmond and Horace Hood, who was lost when HMS *Invincible* was blown up at Jutland. An article in the *Liverpool Post* written in 1911 offered a vivid pen picture of him at that stage of his life:

> A dapper, alert figure, clean shaven with perfectly domed head (compensation for premature baldness), large hooked nose, the strong cleft chin of character, eyes of hypnotic force, dark, penetrating, index of an indomitable soul ... something of the appearance of Captain W.R. Hall RN.[1]

What exactly were the characteristics which made Hall such a phenomenally successful DNI? He had total self-confidence allied to astonishing resilience and the ability to deal with a high degree of stress. Despite the life-threatening condition which had struck him down on HMS *Queen Mary*, he did not go on sick leave between the two appointments and according to Oliver he took no leave at all between 1914 and 1917. The naval historian Arthur Marder, who had called him one of the seven outstanding Captains in the Grand Fleet at the outbreak of war, summed up his attributes vividly: 'Full of charm, he was at the same time a man of dynamic energy, force of character and imagination who exuded vitality and confidence. As DNI it was one that gave full play to his gifts and in which he won world wide fame.'[2]

Patrick Beesly, the historian of British naval intelligence in both World Wars, vividly described the unforgettable impression which Hall, then in his mid-sixties, made on him when he met him at a dinner-party he gave:

> He did not conform to my rather stereotyped ideas of a retired British admiral. Small, like Nelson, it is true, the top of his imposing head was bald ... But it was his face and eyes that caught one's attention. A majestic

nose over a rather tight-lipped mouth and a firm, cleft chin made one feel instinctively that this was not a man with whom one could take liberties. He looked rather like a peregrine falcon, an impression which was reinforced by his penetrating eyes, darting round the assembled company. He had a short incisive way of talking.[3]

Hall had a remarkably quick and agile brain, which enabled him to grasp rapidly the reality of a situation. Twenty-five years later when he was approaching seventy, Admiral John Godfrey, the DNI in the early years of World War II, wrote 'I was impressed by the liveliness and ability of his mind ... and his ingenuity.'[4] The historian John Ehrman, whose father was a friend and neighbour of Hall's and who remembers meeting him shortly before World War II, noted, as Marder had, his capacity for imagination. His exceptional talent for lateral thinking enabled him time and again to read the minds and anticipate the intentions of his German adversaries. Admiral William Sims, the C-in-C of the United States Navy in Europe in 1917–18, who became a staunch ally, compared him to Sherlock Holmes, endowed by his creator Arthur Conan Doyle with a similar gift for lateral thinking.

He had an intinctive distrust of the Germans, whom he habitually referred to as the huns. Like Churchill, he was endowed with the ruthlessness necessary in wartime, which enabled him to keep one step ahead of a formidable and determined enemy and his widespread espionage and subversion operation. Although he was called Machiavellian and was sometimes accused of a love of intrigue, his perception was clear: an intelligence war against Germany could not always be conducted according to Queensberry rules.

Ed Bell, the Second Secretary in the American Embassy in London and their point man on intelligence, who had worked closely with Hall and NID, said of him: 'No man could fill his place, a perfectly marvellous person but the coldest blooded proposition that ever was – he'd cut out a man's heart and hand it back to him.'[5] Hall's instinctive judgment of other men's characters and his capacity for guile, which had served him so well in sea-going command, were to prove matchless assets. James called him.

> ... a genius and his genius was given full play because he had a quite remarkable gift for drawing everything that was best from his fellow men. This gift ... was even more conspicuous when he found himself in a world which was quite strange to a man who had so far spent all his life at sea.[6]

Godfrey wondered if Hall had fully realised his great gifts until he became DNI, noting that he had then lost no time in exploiting them.

Hall had the personality, the showmanship, the panache, that touch of eccentricity common to many successful naval officers, which together inspired great professional loyalty. How many Admirals rode around Whitehall on a motor scooter as he did? Lord Northcliffe, the proprietor of the *Daily Mail* once called on Hall in his office at the Admiralty and, without bothering to take his hat off, started to tell him how ineffective and incompetent the intelligence division was. Hall listened to this diatribe in silence for several minutes. He then rang for his messenger and asked him to bring in his cap which he then put on. Now that he was on equal terms with the behatted press baron, he retorted to Northcliffe's impertinent question: 'How many agents do you have in Zeebrugge?' with the elegant riposte: 'If I had any I certainly wouldn't tell you!'

He had a bubbling, almost rambunctious, sense of humour, which never ceased to stimulate those who worked for him, coupled with an almost schoolboyish pleasure whenever he foiled a German plot or staged a successful intelligence coup. His humour could sometimes be cruel and he delighted in pulling the legs of unsuspecting or gullible American visitors. When Franklin D. Roosevelt, then Assistant Secretary for the Navy, came to see Hall during his visit to London in June 1918, Hall introduced him to an officer. Hall invited Roosevelt to question him as to his whereabouts twenty-four hours earlier. 'In Kiel, Sir', he told the astonished Roosevelt. Hall loftily added that his agents were crossing the border between Germany and Denmark almost every night. Roosevelt did not realise that 'The young agent's tale of derring do was a charade concocted by Hall precisely to impress him.'[7] Twenty-three years later Godfrey met Roosevelt during a visit to Washington. Their conversation turned to Hall, for whom the President expressed a considerable admiration. Godfrey was taken aback to discover that Roosevelt still implicitly believed the yarn Hall had invented.

In 1904 Colonel David Henderson, who had been Director of Military Intelligence in South Africa during the Boer War, gave a pen-picture of his ideal intelligence officer:

> He must be cool, courageous and adroit, patient and imperturbable, discreet and trustworthy. He must have resolution to continue unceasingly his search for information, even in the most disheartening circumstances and after repeated failures. He must have endurance to submit silently to criticism, much of which will be based on ignorance or jealousy. And he must be able to deal with men, to approach his source of information with tact and skill, whether the source be a patriotic gentleman or an abandoned traitor.[8]

He could have been describing Hall. Intelligence was in his blood. He had personal intelligence experience from his time in command of

Cornwall, when he had scouted out and sent the Admiralty useful information on dockyard construction and operations at Kiel and other German ports. His father had been the first DNI, successfully creating the Department from scratch. He wrote: 'I had a family interest in the matter and it had always been my ambition to sit in his seat.' Hall's appointment was providential. If he had not been forced by ill-health to give up command of HMS *Queen Mary*, a lesser man, lacking Hall's remarkable talents, would almost inevitably have been appointed DNI. (The senior captains serving in the Grand Fleet, whom Marder rated highly, would have moved heaven and earth to avoid coming ashore at that period of the war when they could reasonably have expected to take part in a victory to rival Trafalgar.) Few of his contemporaries would have been able to exploit the opportunities or run rings round his German opposite numbers as skilfully and effectively as he did. In his book *Greenmantle*, a story of counter-espionage set in the Middle East in World War I, John Buchan, well-versed in the world of intelligence, wrote of Hall's operation: 'If I had a big proposition to handle and I had my pick of helpers, I'd plump for the Intelligence Division of the Admiralty.'[9]

W. H. Hall is not nearly as well known as his son, largely owing to his premature death from peritonitis at the age of 52 before he could reach flag rank. Father and son were similar in temperament and belief, sharing an admiration for St. Vincent and his forward offensive strategy combining blockade and offensive operations against the French and Spanish navies during the French Revolutionary and Napoleonic Wars. In his letters to his sister in World War II, the younger Hall used to quote St. Vincent's maxim that 'only officers of approved firmness should be employed'. In a report to the Board of the Admiralty in 1884, W.H Hall stressed that 'a *defensive* policy ... is utterly at variance with the traditions of the Royal Navy, whose role has always been that of *attack* and not *defence*'. In February 1941, the younger Hall described Andrew Cunningham as ' ... a real thruster [who] does not stand for any slackness or lack of initiative; he just sends them [officers] home when satisfied that they belong to the safety home school.'[10]

Father and son had both been gunnery officers. In the late 1860s the elder Hall had served for some three years as an instructor at HMS *Excellent* together with several influential figures including Jacky Fisher and two other future First Sea Lords, and the naval historian John Knox Laughton, whose teachings inspired the development of strategy throughout the service.

Admiral Sir Geoffrey Phipps Hornby, C-in-C of the Mediterranean Fleet in 1877–78, at a time when war with Russia was narrowly averted, had complained bitterly about the lack of intelligence. In 1882 a Committee on Colonial Defence advocated the formation of a specialist naval intelligence department inside the Admiralty. That December, Vice-Admiral Sir George Tryon, then Secretary of the Admiralty and a noted reformer, established the Foreign Intelligence Committee (FIC). The FIC's terms of reference included reporting on the naval policies and resources of foreign nations, notably the size and armaments of their fleets, naval personnel and construction and maintenance programmes.

Tryon selected W. H. Hall to head the new committee. He was initially supported by a skeleton staff, which by one account consisted of one Royal Marine officer, two clerks and a copyist and one naval attaché based overseas. Hall habitually worked an extremely long day, as one of his staff recalled: 'The work was strenuous ... about nine hours a day for six days in the week and often we took work home with us. W. H. Hall worked from 5 to 8 before breakfast, came to the Admiralty at 10 am. He worked there till 7 and again for 1 ½ hours at home after dinner.'[11]

In 1885 a boundary dispute in Afghanistan known as the Pendjeh crisis once again brought Britain and Russia close to war. Senior officers in the Admiralty expressed concern about the Navy's readiness to conduct operations against the Russian Navy. Prominent among them was Captain Lord Charles Beresford – Charley B to the service – who in the following year was appointed Junior Naval Lord with a seat on the Admiralty Board. Throughout his career Charley B played by his own rules. If W. H. represented the inside face of the service, the flamboyant Beresford embodied its public persona. A born intriguer, he had few scruples, believing that the end always justified the means and he was a habitual leaker to the press. Although he is largely remembered today for his cantankerous opposition to Jacky Fisher's innovations when he was First Sea Lord, he had a genuine claim to have been an ardent naval reformer as a younger man.

In October 1886 Beresford wrote a memorandum for his colleagues arguing that the FIC should be developed into a fully fledged department responsible not only for intelligence but for devising plans for mobilisation. Typically, he leaked his memorandum to the influential *Pall Mall Gazette*. Beresford's calculated manoeuvre infuriated the First Lord, Lord George Hamilton, and the Senior Naval Lord, Admiral Sir Arthur Hood, who commissioned Hall to write a report on the future of naval intelligence. Hall effectively endorsed Beresford's recommendations, adding that the development of strategy be added to the remit. His report was accepted and he was appointed to head an enlarged Naval Intelligence Division, reporting directly to the Senior Naval Lord. Its terms of reference were:

1. To collect, sift, record and lay before the board all the information relating to maritime matters likely to be of use in war.

2. To prepare and keep correct to date, a complete plan for mobilising the Naval forces of the Empire with the utmost possible rapidity, and with the least strain on the Admiralty.
3. When directed, to prepare plans of Naval Campaign for the consideration of the Board.
4. To bring to the notice of the Board all points effecting 'Preparation for War' but it is to be distinctly understood that the Intelligence Department is not to indicate to the Board any policy in connection with shipbuilding, armaments etc, unless called upon to do so.[12]

The new Division started work in February 1887. Hall was supported by a staff headed by two assistant directors, Captains Reginald Custance and S.W. Eardley-Wilmot, responsible respectively for mobilisation and intelligence. Six months later, and not for the first or last time, the Treasury intervened in the affairs of the Admiralty and demanded a cut in the salaries of Hall and his officers in the NID below that of their contemporaries in other departments. Hamilton and Hood meekly agreed. The outspoken Charley B promptly resigned in protest, arguing:' ... the efficiency of the whole service was ... bound up with the efficiency of the Intelligence Department because that department was created for the express purpose of estimating and reporting what was required to fulfil its duties'.[13]

His departure allowed him to join forces with several retired Admirals, including Phipps Hornby, in lobbying to improve the service's strength. Their allies inside the Admiralty, notably Hall and Fisher, then Director of Naval Ordnance, provided detailed data demonstrating that the Navy had too few ships to operate effectively a forward offensive strategy against a Franco-Russian naval alliance. This campaign led to the historic Naval Defence Act of 1889, which mandated a shipbuilding programme costing £21.5m over five years, unprecedented in time of peace, and incorporated the strategic principles developed by Hall and his colleagues of the NID. The Act instituted the two power standard, namely that the strength of the Royal Navy should be at least equal to that of the next two largest European navies.

In January 1889, after six years in the post, W. H. Hall left the NID to return to sea. His achievements were widely recognised in the service. Phipps Hornby, who had been one of his staunchest supporters, said of him: 'No one values more than I do Captain Hall and the remarkable work he has done.' His two immediate successors, Captains Cyprian Bridge and Lewis Beaumont, paid him eloquent tributes illustrating how invaluable his services to the division had been: '... the service and the country are in your debt to an amount which scarcely anyone realises' [Bridge]. 'I ... congratulate you ... on having done six years of most valuable work under circumstances of great difficulty and discouragement .... it will be more and more known throughout the service that but for you, the Department, which is admitted by all to be essential, would have languished and died in the early years' [(Beaumont).[14]

A recent commentator, Robert Mullins, wrote: 'By the time Captain W. H. Hall departed from the Admiralty ... the first D.N.I. had established an intellectual tradition that would be sustained by other strategic thinkers appointed to the position including ... Bridge, Beaumont, Custance, Prince Louis of Battenberg and even his own son Reginald 'Blinker' Hall.'[15]

In 1909 responsibility for mobilisation was transferred to a separate division and in 1912 the NID became part of the new Naval War Staff. One of Hall's first priorities when he took over as DNI was the expansion of the Division to enable it to meet the far greater commitments resulting from the war, not least the collection, analysis and transmission of SIGINT. When Oliver was appointed DNI in September 1913 its establishment was one Commander and one Lieutenant RN, seven Royal Marine officers, two Fleet Paymasters, one Engineer-Commander, one Staff Paymaster, one staff clerk and nine junior clerks, 23 persons in all. Hall described the development of his division from a staff of 29 in December 1914 to an establishment of 360 men and women at the time of the Armistice, paying them this warm tribute:

> The Intelligence Division grew from a minor and purely naval department to a worldwide organization with a multitude of most diverse activities ... I had the most wonderful staff that any man could have hoped to garner. Men and women of every profession and class joined us with little but their own sense to guide them aright. We had few enough precedents to follow and we had to make up our own rules as we went along.[16]

Hall was well aware that he had spent almost all his career either at sea or as a gunnery instructor and that he lacked many of the connections outside the Navy, which would be increasingly necessary for the efficient operation of an intelligence division in the exacting circumstances of a world war. For the first time since the division had been set up, he recruited civilians with appropriate experience and qualifications to fill key positions. Many of these recruits were commissioned in the Royal Naval Volunteer Reserve, known as the Wavy Navy because the patterns of the rings on the sleeves of their officers' uniforms resembled the rise and fall of the sea.

One of his first actions was to appoint two Personal Assistants, Lord Herschell and Claud Serocold, who would provide the connections he sought. Dick Herschell was already working in Room 40, having offered his services to the Admiralty as a German linguist. Hall had employed him to translate the documents which had been captured in the 'Miraculous

Draught of Fishes' along with the VB code. Impressed by his considerable ability, Hall quickly transferred him to his private office.

Herschell's influence lay in his political and royal connections as a son of a former Lord Chancellor in the Gladstone and Rosebery Governments in the 1880s and 1890s, as a former Private Secretary to the Lord Lieutenant of Ireland when the Liberal party returned to power in 1905 and later as a Lord in Waiting to both King Edward VII and George V, a position he continued to hold throughout the War. These connections made him extremely useful to Hall giving him an entrée into worlds with which he was not familiar. Herschell's friendship with King Alfonso XIII of Spain, whose wife was a niece of Edward VII, made him an ideal choice to oversee the NID's operations in Spain and to enable it to out manoeuvre the agents who ran a subversion campaign under the aegis of the German Embassy in Madrid.

Hall's other choice as a Personal Assistant was at first sight less easily explicable. Claud Serocold was then 39, three years older than Herschell. Small in stature but with a strongly outgoing personality, he had had coxed the Eton VIII for three years and the Oxford VIII for four years – a record which still stands. His father, a successful brewer, had given him the sum of £10,000 (equivalent to £600,000 today) to start him in business. In 1903 he became a partner in the stockbrokers Cazenove & Akroyds. David Kynaston, the historian of Cazenove, wrote of Serocold:

> All the signs are that before 1914 he was a relatively minor figure in the city and concentrated more on the fun aspects of life, being considered something of a playboy. His haunts ranged from Cannes to the Empire in Leicester Square; he spoke French well; he appreciated music and art; and in general he seems to have been considered (at least by his somewhat staid family) as slightly raffish ... He was in fact marvellous company: quick, entertaining and generous; he made throughout his life a host of friends. He was also a safe confidant and a born diplomat, capable of cracking the hardest nuts.[17]

It is not quite clear how Hall selected Serocold but it is possible that he may have been introduced to him by Herschell, a gifted pianist, as both men shared an interest in music. Serocold's quick mind and decisiveness appealed to Hall, who, with his own fast mental reactions, consistently valued this talent highly in other people. The two men had a further trait in common – they were outgoing and loved entertaining. Although Serocold's range of contacts reached their zenith in the interwar years, when he became the highly successful senior partner of Cazenove and a major figure in the City, he was responsible for bringing at least one rising city figure, Lionel Fraser, who had been invalided out of the Army, into Room 40.

Whatever reason impelled Hall to select Serocold, his choice proved inspired. Kynaston noted that 'It was a rather different man who returned to Threadneedle Street at the end of the conflict.'[18] Herschell and Serocold both enjoyed considerable success in their new roles at NID and the two men became extremely close to Hall, who trusted them both implicitly and gave them considerable authority. Herschell died in 1929 but Hall and Serocold remained close friends until Hall's death. In 1922 Serocold wrote to Hall:

> I value our friendship and how proud I am of it. From the moment you took me into your confidence in those early days I think I expanded and grew at least two inches round the waist. I had the luck to serve you only a few years and in that comparatively short time you inspired me with the divine feelings which I found among all those who had the same honour and luck as me ...[19]

Serocold's sentiments were echoed by virtually everyone who worked for Hall in naval intelligence or Room 40. To this day Alastair Denniston's family refer to him as The Admiral.

The flood of SIGINT into the Admiralty rapidly created a problem, exacerbated by Churchill's insistence on personally examining the raw decrypts as they were released by the codebreakers without any prior interpretation by the NID. Early in November 1914 he had a major row with Hall on this issue, which was resolved when Churchill implicitly accepted Hall's argument that SIGINT had to be sifted and analysed before it was transmitted to him and to the War Staff. On the following day, he sent this instruction to Oliver and Ewing but not to Hall, which, in a Churchillian touch, he called 'Exclusively Secret' and which was to serve as Room 40's modus operandi:

> An officer of the War Staff, preferably from the ID [Intelligence Division] should be selected to study all the decoded documents, not only current but past, and to compare them continually with what actually took place in order to penetrate the German mind and movements and make reports. All these intercepts are to be written in a locked book with their decodes, and all other copies are to be collected and burnt. All new messages are to be entered in the book, and the book is only to be handled under direction from COS [the Chief of Staff – Oliver]. The officer selected is for the present to do no other work. I shall be obliged if Sir Alfred Ewing will associate himself continually with this work.[20]

Hall complied with Churchill's instruction by making another inspired appointment, selecting Commander Herbert Hope, a highly competent officer who was then serving in the Admiralty's Chart Room, to prepare and issue the daily analyses of decrypts and to provide naval know-how to Ewing's codebreakers, thus assuring their credibility with the War Staff. He was at first given an office in a different part of the Admiralty but within a week, following Fisher's intervention, he was relocated inside Room 40. Hope wrote that Fisher '... told me that I was to visit him twice daily with copies of the messages, a course which I pursued not only with him but with his successors, Sir Henry Jackson and Sir John Jellicoe. This was the beginning of a sphere of work which was probably unique, was absorbingly interesting.'[21] Hope was a quiet, unassuming man. Denniston noted that he self-effacingly admitted:

> ... he knew no German, no cryptography nor why he had come. His official duty was to keep the Operations Division and Intelligence Division informed of the activities of the German Fleet as elucidated by the cryptographic staff. Before very long however, he was able by his constant presence to be the connecting link between the watches and to be the guide and helper of all [who] were in difficulties either with the German language or cryptography.

His task was made harder by the cryptographers' initial ignorance of the subject of their work. 'The watchkeepers knew nothing of the German fleet, very little of the geography of the German coastline, while their ignorance of English and German naval phraseology was profound ... Lord Fisher pointed out that warships did not "run in" and begged the staff to adopt the word "proceed".'[22] Hope's function was to edit the raw translations of the decrypts into accepted naval usage and thus promote their credibility with the understandably sceptical War Staff.

Hope was a man of almost uncannily astute judgment, who earned the unwavering allegiance of his diverse and sometimes undisciplined staff, to whom he became their beloved chief. In effect, he was the real head of Room 40. Hope was ably assisted by another naval officer seconded from the NID, Fleet Paymaster Charles Rotter, who had, as noted in the previous chapter, solved the problem of how to interpret early captured documents. Three Naval officers, Hall, Hope and Rotter, had laid the foundations of Room 40's effectiveness and deserve much of the credit for its achievements.

There was a serious flaw in the status of Room 40, which looks particularly irrational in hindsight. Logically it should have formed part of the NID, whose original terms of reference included the authority 'To collect, sift, record and lay before the board all the information relating to maritime matters likely to be of use in war'. Ignoring this obvious link, Oliver insisted that Ewing should report to him and not to Hall. It was a strange decision by an Admiral who had himself been Director of Naval Intelligence and should have clearly understood its governing tenets. The patient Hope was driven to criticise the Staff's handling of the decrypts, noting the missed opportunities:

> In a very few months we obtained a very good working knowledge of the organisation, operations and internal economy of the German Fleet. Had we been called upon by the Staff to do so, we could have furnished valuable information as to the movements of submarines, minefields, minesweeping etc. But the Staff was obsessed by the idea of secrecy ... they worked on the principle that every effort must be made to keep our knowledge up our sleeves for a really grand occasion such as the German Fleet coming out in all their strength to throw down the gage of battle. In other words the Staff determined to make use of our information defensively and not offensively.[23]

Oliver's decision resulted in a lack of interface between intelligence and operations with unfortunate consequences and until Hall took over full responsibility for Room 40 in May 1917 the War Staff consistently failed to make full use of the decrypts it so tirelessly produced. To make matters worse, Hall and Oliver did not see eye to eye. Although both men were autocrats, their methods were strikingly different. Oliver was an arch centraliser, who was utterly unable to delegate and who insisted on drafting almost every important signal himself. Captain (later Admiral Sir) Herbert Richmond, then Assistant Director of Operations, noted that:

> ... he held all the strings in his hands – indeed too much so. He was so busy allocating craft for convoys of troops across the Channel ... that he has no time for strategical schemes ... It is impossible for work to be done properly in such a way. The principle of decentralising and trusting subordinates has not yet gained ground; so seniors are worked to death and juniors find no use for their brains.[24]

Oliver habitually worked a 105-hour week and was so taciturn that he was known in the service as Dummy. He was by no means an effective communicator. In contrast, Hall was outgoing, exuding confidence and vitality. As he had in sea command, he was ready to assign important responsibilities to able and trusted subordinates, whom – with his intuitive judgment of character – he picked with flair. Writing in 1933, he set out this classic exposition of the advantages of delegation:

> ... a Director of Intelligence who attempts to keep himself informed about every detail of the work being done cannot hope to succeed; but if he so arranges his organisation that he knows at once to which of his colleagues he must go to for the information he requires, then he may expect good results. Such a system ... has the inestimable advantage of bringing out the

best in everyone working under it, for the head will not suggest every move and he will welcome and indeed insist on ideas from his staff. And so it was from first to last in the Intelligence Division.[25]

From the outset, Hall and Ewing were never on close terms and over time their relationship deteriorated. Ewing no doubt suspected, not without reason, that Hall wished to supersede him as Head of Room 40. Although he was a distinguished engineer, he lacked Hall's capacity for imagination and vision of what the decrypting operation, which he had founded and of which he was justly proud, could achieve, as a vital component of an integrated naval intelligence division.

Eventually Ewing complained to Oliver, whom he reminded that Churchill had promised him a free hand when he took on the role. Oliver noted that: 'Hall was always trying to boss Sir. A. Ewing and he would not put up with it, he was not that sort of man. It led eventually to a row and the Ist Lord, Balfour, deputed Sir William Graham Greene, the Secretary to the Admiralty and me to hold an enquiry and we spent a long afternoon restoring peace.'[26] This altercation, inevitably settled by Oliver and Greene in Ewing's favour, must have taken place between May 1915 when Balfour became First Lord and September 1916 when Ewing ceased to have full time control over Room 40. Their decision did nothing to solve the problem, perpetuating the unsatisfactory status quo and preventing the most effective application of Room 40's exceptional talents.

The Admiralty's control over the German naval, and from 1915 the political, decrypts gave Hall a power greater than any previous or later DNI would enjoy in the British intelligence community, including the right of direct access to cabinet ministers (other than the First Lord of the Admiralty) and most importantly to the Foreign Secretary.

During the First World War, there were only four British intelligence agencies, the naval and military intelligence divisions and the Special Intelligence Service (SIS or MI6) and the Security Service (MI5), both of which had only been founded in 1909. In comparison, by the time of the Second World War, their number had grown to include the RAF intelligence division, the Government Code & Cypher School (GC & CS) – the successor to Room 40 and by then under SIS aegis – the Special Operations Executive (SOE) and the Ministry of Economic Warfare. The overall assessment of intelligence produced by this complex network was the task of the Joint Intelligence Committee, originally set up in 1936. Its highly effective Chairman, William Cavendish-Bentinck, a diplomat seconded from the Foreign Office, performed the co-coordinating role between the various ministries in Whitehall which Hall had informally exercised in the previous war. In the process he was to become almost as great a legend in the intelligence world as Hall had been a generation earlier.

This extraordinary degree of authority, one which Hall exploited to the full, was tacitly recognized by the other intelligence chiefs, notably by Mansfield Cumming, the head of SIS, himself a former naval officer. In a letter to Hall in October 1917, congratulating him on his knighthood, Cumming wrote, addressing him as My Dear Chief: 'I have never coveted greater talents as much as since I became one of your "lieutenants" & wished I could have been of greater service to you. I owe you far more than I can ever repay ... such as it is however you have my unswerving loyalty & devotion.'[27] Basil Thomson, the son of a former Archbishop of York, the Director of Special Branch at Scotland Yard and as such Britain's counter-espionage chief, became another staunch Hall ally. The two men kept a close watch for any hint of German-inspired subversion, not least in Ireland. Between them, they were responsible for the arrest and imprisonment of every important German agent based in Britain.

To his credit, Oliver gave Hall a free hand in political and non-naval matters, enabling him to keep the political operations of Room 40 and thus the all-important diplomatic decrypts under his personal control. Hall established excellent relations with the Foreign Office, particularly when Arthur Balfour, to whom he had enjoyed direct access when he was First Lord of the Admiralty, became Foreign Secretary in the Lloyd George Government and Lord Hardinge replaced Sir Arthur Nicolson as Permanent Under-Secretary at the end of 1916. Hall had a low opinion of most politicians, notably of Lloyd George and later Neville Chamberlain, and Balfour was one of the few whom he admired. He greatly preferred the technocrats who were given ministerial rank, especially Eric Geddes in the First World War and Lords Woolton and Leathers in the Second.

Hall was thus able to revive the valuable connections which naval intelligence had traditionally enjoyed in time of war with the diplomatic corps. This was no mean achievement; as Oliver noted: 'Previous to the war, the Foreign Office had hated its consular officers helping Naval Intelligence.'[28] Ernest Maxse, the Consul-General in Rotterdam, became one of his most effective and valued agents. Maxse was following the path set by one of his predecessors in that post, Richard Walters, who had controlled a successful Admiralty intelligence network in Europe during and after the Seven Years War 1756–1763. During the Crimean War

> ... the Royal Navy appealed to British consuls in the Danish and Swedish Baltic ports 'to use the utmost diligence in collecting information that will be useful, and especially such information as regards the munitions of war in the enemy's use. Shortly after the outbreak of the war, the ambassador in Stockholm, Sir Edward Grey, reported that he had asked a Swedish trader called Ekstrom to go to the Aland Islands to find out about the Russian military garrisons there. Ekstrom returned with detailed information.[29]

Hall also renewed the close ties between naval intelligence and the City of London. In 1793 the then Secretary to the Admiralty had enlisted the services of Lloyd's worldwide intelligence network.

Anyone who has examined the State Department records in the National Archives in Washington will grasp the extent of the German intelligence and espionage operations in the United States and indeed throughout the Americas. Hall selected Captain Guy Gaunt, the Naval Attaché in Washington, as the de facto head of British Intelligence in North America. The Australian-born Gaunt was an exceedingly effective operator with a taste for the cloak-and-dagger side of intelligence work. He ran a chain of agents inside the German and Austrian embassies and the New York offices of the German shipping lines, whose managers were deeply involved in espionage. He also had close ties with the Wilson Administration, notably with Col. House, the President's alter ego, and with Robert Lansing, the Secretary of State from June 1915, with whom he lunched regularly. These sources enabled him to supply Hall with excellent and timely information. Gaunt's memoirs unambiguously express his appreciation of Hall:

> Hall stood by me through thick and thin. His loyalty, his trust, his instinctive intuition were a godsend. I could realise what a powerful friend he was when I visited the Admiralty: it opened my eyes when I saw the men who came quietly into his office. I think I saw most of the Cabinet and for that matter, everyone else in England of any note.[30]

Hall worked closely with another powerful figure, Sir Maurice Hankey, the Secretary of the Committee of Imperial Defence (CID), and a former intelligence officer in the Mediterranean Fleet. In January 1915 they conceived a bold scheme to bribe Turkey out of the War, described in chapter 5. A year later, Hankey enlisted Hall's support in a scheme originated by the Governor of the Bank of England to flood Germany with forged banknotes, a proposal that instantly appealed to Hall. During their discussions he learned that Hall had succeeded in breaking the code used by Col. House, then in Berlin as a part of a mission in Europe, to communicate with Wilson. In his diary he wrote: 'This information [that the Germans would plan a major submarine offensive] is of course priceless.'[31]

Whilst Hankey was not apparently troubled by the DNI's spying on a neutral Government, he noted, rather coldly, that he had not shown the decoded telegrams to the First Lord (Balfour). Hall has been criticised for holding back intelligence from Ministers. He would no doubt have defended himself against these charges by expounding two of his cardinal principles: the vital necessity of protecting his sources, the agents (HUMINT) and the decrypts (SIGINT) and of preventing the Germans from realising the scope and extent of his operations. In the case of the

Zimmermann telegram this criticism will be shown to be unjustified. As late as the summer of 1918 Hall declined to reveal certain decrypts of cables between Berlin and the German Washington Embassy for use by Government lawyers in a proposed trial of extremist Irish Nationalist leaders, on the grounds that Germany might learn that Room 40 had been reading its diplomatic signal traffic. Had he revealed that he was reading the American diplomatic codes, Balfour might well have ordered him to desist. Hall would undoubtedly have considered that such an instruction did not serve the national interest in time of war and it can certainly be argued that he used his discretion to good advantage.

He would also have freely expressed his concern about ministerial security leaks which were all too frequent in World War I. Asquith in particular was notorious for poor security, often revealing confidential issues of state in his indiscreet letters to his lady friend Venetia Stanley. On occasions, for all his understanding of intelligence, Churchill treated official documents rather casually. To illustrate Hall's point, the American Ambassador, Walter Hines Page, once dryly noted that his staff's social contacts provided him with the best secret service he could expect.

Notes

[1] James, *The Eyes of the Navy* p.13
[2] Marder, *From Dreadnought to Scapa Flow* Vol. 2 p.16-17
[3] Beesly, Room 40 p.36
[4] CAC MLBE 1/2 J.H. Godfrey, *The Hall Tradition*
[5] CAC HALL 2/2
[6] James p.201
[7] Persico *Roosevelt's Secret War* pp.8-9
[8] Smith, *Spying Game* p.55
[9] CAC MLBE 5/1 Lloyd Hirst papers
[10] CAC HALL 7/ WRH to May Templar February 8 1941
[11] Sir George Aston quoted in 'The Origins of the NID' by Matthew Allen *Mariner's Mirror* February 1993
[12] TNA ADM 231/12 Work of the NID during 1887 to February 1888
[13] Beresford Memoirs p.353
[14] James pp.3-4
[15] Robert E. Mullins 'Sharpening the Trident' PhD Thesis p.62
[16] CAC HALL 3/1
[17] Kynaston, *Cazenove & Co A History* p.100
[18] Ibid
[19] CAC HALL 1/2
[20] Quoted in Stafford, *Churchill and Secret Service* p.64
[21] Beesly, p.19

[22] CAC DENN1/2 Denniston Thirty Secret Years p.33-34
[23] Beesly. p.41
[24] Marder, Vol. 2 p.92
[25] CAC HALL3/1
[26] NMM Oliver, *Recollections* p.164
[27] Judd, *The Quest for C* p.381
[28] NMM Oliver p.93
[29] Smith, p.49
[30] Gaunt, *The Yield of the Years* p.217
[31] Roskill, *Hankey Man of Secrets* Vol. 1 pp.246-247

CHAPTER IV

The Eyes and Ears of The Fleet

At the time Hall took over as Director of Naval Intelligence, the NID had other assets beside SIGINT, which should not be discounted. One of the NID's principal and original responsibilities had been the mobilisation of the fleet in readiness for war, a function transferred to a separate division of the Admiralty in 1909 during Jacky Fisher's first term as FSL. In 1904 Hall's ally Richmond, one of a number of naval officers who were critical of the effectiveness of the NID, had written:

> The NID as it stands is merely a collector of notes on various subjects. It provides badly written and dull blue books ... and publishes the results of naval attaches work and a hundred other things – all of value but generally so dully produced that most people take no trouble to read them.[1]

As C-in-C Mediterranean Fleet, Jacky Fisher, innovative as in so many issues, had set out to develop his own system of obtaining intelligence. He recruited an active and enthusiastic network of agents ranging from the Bishop of Gibraltar to vice-consuls and other diplomats including Gerald Fitzmaurice, the Oriental Counsellor at the British Embassy in Constantinople, a man of unparalleled knowledge of the Middle East who was later to work for Hall, as well as paid informers. His most valuable informants were the managers of the British-owned cable companies, who at the time controlled nearly 80% of the global telegraph traffic outside Europe. These sources provided him with the bulk of diplomatic cipher messages originating in the Mediterranean and again through the helpful British Embassy in Constantinople, keys to these ciphers. Maurice Hankey, who had served on Fisher's staff, wrote: 'I had some inkling of this at the time but it was not until seven years later when I myself became Fleet Intelligence Officer that I learnt the full extent of Fisher's preparations and how he towered above all his predecessors.'[2]

As FSL, Fisher built up a net of NID outstations in addition to the experimental unit already established in Malta to handle the volume of traffic provided by the Mediterranean Fleet's effective organisation. The system succeeded in accurately tracking the Russian fleet sent to the Far East during the Russo-Japanese War.

By 1906 he fully recognised that Germany was the Navy's most likely adversary and he set about improving the Admiralty's knowledge of German naval developments. To this end, he authorised active intelligence including the mission entrusted to Hall at Kiel in 1908. He strengthened the existing and longstanding connections between the Admiralty and Lloyd's, who set up a network of agents inside Germany to monitor HSF movements through the Kiel Canal.

A series of articles headed WORK OF THE SECRET SERVICE written by a former undercover agent which appeared in the *Daily Telegraph* in September 1930 indicated how thoroughly the NID had infiltrated the German and Austro-Hungarian Admiralties from 1905 on. Fisher had scored an initial deception coup:

> Lord Fisher always derived intense amusement from the hoax he practised on the Germans in 1905 in connection with HMS *Invincible*, the first battle-cruiser ever built. She was of course a 'hush hush ship' in every sense of the word, her novel features being a speed of 25 knots and an armament of 12" guns.
>
> As German agents made repeated efforts to penetrate a secret of the *Invincible*, Lord Fisher determined to oblige them. He had prepared a set of plans for the ship which bore every semblance of official origin, but which showed the armament to consist of 9.2" guns. These drawings were put under the nose of a well-known German emissary, who gleefully dispatched them to Berlin, and doubtless received a substantial reward. The Germans appear to have been completely taken in, for a few months later they designed the *Blucher* as a 'reply' to the *Invincible* and gave her an armament of 8.2" guns. While these weapons may have been equal in ballistic properties to the British, they were, of course, hopelessly inferior to our 12" guns, and so it befell that she was outclassed and obsolete even before she was launched.

The intelligence provided by these agents included details of mobilisation, plans and specifications for all Dreadnoughts and battlecruisers, among them the *Konig* class, which was not commissioned until after August 1914, and German ordnance and fire control systems. In particular, the information they passed on showing that the displacement of the second-generation battlecruisers, the *Moltke* class, would be over 25,000 tons and their armament increased to ten 11-in guns as compared to the 19,200 tons and eight 11-in guns of the Kriegsmarine's first battlecruiser *Von Der Tann*. Jellicoe, then Controller of the Navy, was able to improve the specifications of the *Lion* class, then on the Admiralty drawing boards, to match their German rivals. Details of German agents in the UK were also secured, enabling them to be kept under surveillance and arrested when war broke out. As an anonymous writer noted: 'From August 1 1914 onwards, the activities of the British Naval Intelligence Service were transferred from enemy soil, but there still remained in the enemy's country a few courageous men, who, taking their lives in their hands, continued to keep German and Austrian naval affairs under observation.'

The NID's enterprise, which derived from Fisher's insistence in building up networks of active agents, provided Hall with a valuable endowment, which, at least in part, remained available to him throughout the war.

On 30 October 1914, two weeks after Hall had first sat in the chair as DNI, a change took place at the Admiralty that was to have a far-reaching effect. The First Sea Lord, Prince Louis of Battenberg, born in Germany and who had come to England to enter the Navy as a boy of 13 almost fifty years before, was forced to retire, although his integrity and loyalty to his adopted country were unquestionable. An outbreak of xenophobia orchestrated against Battenberg, by that old and unrepentant intriguer, Lord Charles Beresford, once W. H. Hall's ally, was largely to blame; though Churchill and Prime Minister Asquith had both lost confidence in him. Despite a distinguished career, he had not been a complete success as First Sea Lord and he was cynically known in the Admiralty as 'I Concur Battenberg' owing to his frequently adding 'I concur' to the margins of official documents sent to him for his approval.

To succeed Prince Louis, Churchill brought back from retirement the veteran Jacky Fisher, who had driven through so many far-reaching naval reforms during his previous tenure as First Sea Lord from 1904 to 1910. As the creator of HMS *Dreadnought*, which at a stroke had made every battleship in the world obsolete, the flamboyant Jacky Fisher was a true national hero. He was a volcano of a man, with boundless energy and a single-minded determination to achieve his objectives. His motto was: 'Fear God and Dread Nought' and he liked to sign his letters to his close allies: 'Yours until Hell Freezes Over'. This chapter will highlight three naval operations that took place in the three months following Fisher's return to the Admiralty, in each of which the Naval Intelligence Department and Room 40 played a significant role.

The Navy's achievements at the outset of war had been considerable. Exploiting Britain's strategic position abreast of the sea routes connecting Germany with the rest of the world, the German Merchant Marine had been swept from the seas, an effective blockade had been enforced and the British Expeditionary Force had been escorted to France without any loss of life. Despite these successes, the Navy had experienced several setbacks. In the Mediterranean, during the first week of the war, the German battlecruiser *Goeben* and the light cruiser *Breslau* had successfully evaded a much larger British force including three battlecruisers and had sought refuge in Turkish waters. The resultant loss of British prestige was a considerable factor in Turkey's decision to join the war on the German side. On 22 September, the three old cruisers HMS *Aboukir*, *Cressy* and *Hogue*, on blockade patrol off the Dutch coast, were torpedoed by a U-boat with the loss of 1,459 officers and men. Churchill, who had just made an ill-timed speech threatening that 'if the German fleet did not come out and fight they would be dug out like rats in a hole', was strongly criticised for this disaster. In reality he had been alerted to the risks involved in keeping the cruisers in such an exposed position but, against his better judgment, Prince Louis had been persuaded by the War Staff not to implement Churchill's order for their withdrawal, made four days before their sinking. Only a day before Fisher's return the new battleship HMS *Audacious* had struck a mine and her crew were taken off. Three hours later when in tow and without any previous warning, she blew up. Churchill reckoned that Fisher's appointment would restore public confidence in the Navy following this succession of disasters.

Coronel and the Falklands

A worse calamity was to follow. The Kriegsmarine had maintained a powerful and homogeneous East Asiatic Squadron, based at the port of Tsingtao in the German concession in North China, to police their possessions in the Far East. In the summer of 1914, this force included two modern armoured cruisers, *Scharnhorst* and *Gneisenau* (11,400 tons, eight 8.2-in and six 5.9-in guns) and three light cruisers. The Squadron was led by Vice Admiral Maximilian Graf von Spee, a south German aristocrat, who was regarded as one of the Kriegsmarine's most able and effective commanders. At the outbreak of war, the Squadron was in the German Pacific territory of the Caroline Islands as part of a three-month cruise.

Realizing that a return to Tsingtao, which would shortly be besieged by the Japanese, would be impossible, von Spee detached the cruiser *Emden* to act as a commerce raider. Operating in the Indian Ocean, *Emden* sank 16 British merchant ships, a Russian cruiser and a French destroyer between September and November 1914, before she was finally cornered and destroyed by the more powerful cruiser HMAS *Sydney*. With the remainder of his squadron he steamed slowly towards the Pacific coast of South America where he would be able to take on coal and other supplies from islands, whose administrators did not know that war had been declared, or from the efficient Etappenkommando network of colliers which the Admiralstab had set up.

On September 14 von Spee appeared off the port of Apia, the capital of the German colony of Samoa, which had been captured by allied forces at the end of August. Finding the harbour empty, he made out to sea. On September 22, he attacked Papeete, the capital of French Tahiti, sinking a gunboat. Early in October von Spee received a signal from the cruiser *Dresden* which had been transferred from the Atlantic to join his squadron. His reply, instructing her to join him at Easter Island, was intercepted but at that stage of the war it was unlikely that it was decoded. Nevertheless it was now clear that his destination was the west coast of South America.

The Admiralty's response to von Spee was piecemeal and insufficient, ignoring the doctrine of superior force. The main strength in the Pacific was provided by the Australian Navy with the battlecruiser HMAS *Australia* and two modern light cruisers, including *Sydney*, which had sunk *Emden*. The Admiralty decided that this squadron should be deployed in protecting troopship convoys and it was never seriously involved in the hunt for von Spee. To confront his force, they formed two cruiser squadrons, neither of which was strong enough to outgun him. Rear Admiral Sir Christopher Cradock was appointed to command a new South American Squadron with the task of hunting down von Spee. Under his command were an obsolete pre-Dreadnought HMS *Canopus* – which would barely make 15 knots – and two equally obsolete armoured cruisers, HMS *Good Hope* and *Monmouth*, both of whom could be outgunned by *Scharnhorst* and *Gneisenau*. All three ships were manned by inexperienced reservists and none were battle-ready. The rest of this ragtag squadron was the armed merchant cruiser HMS *Otranto*, a converted liner armed with six 4.7-in guns and highly vulnerable to gunfire and the light cruiser HMS *Glasgow*, the only ship under his command with a regular crew who could give a good account of themselves in battle. Rear-Admiral A.C. Stoddard, with three more armoured cruisers including Hall's former command *Cornwall* and one modern light cruiser, remained in the South Atlantic.

The Admiralty had told Cradock that his squadron would be reinforced by the far more modern armoured cruiser HMS *Defence* (14,600 tons, four 9.2-in and 10 7.5-in guns), which had been designed to overmatch the German pair. However, instructions to dispatch her from the Mediterranean to join Cradock were cancelled and were not reinstated until it was too late for her to join his squadron before battle was joined. If she had been present at the Battle of Coronel, the outcome could have been very different.

Cradock sailed from his base at Port Stanley in the Falkland Islands on October 22, bound for the Pacific Coast of Chile. Intelligence was sparse, communications difficult and strategy was faulty. Disaster was almost inevitable. *Glasgow*'s Captain, John Luce, commented:

> It always appeared to me that we fell between two stools. There was not force available at the moment to form two squadrons of sufficient strength

and speed and we should not have advanced into the Pacific until this was forthcoming, but [should] have concentrated on the Straits using the Falklands as a base. The [British] trade was not of vital importance and could have been kept in harbour until von Spee's position was revealed – which was bound to happen if he was to do anything. Cradock (an Admiral in the offensive tradition of St. Vincent and Nelson but known to be impulsive) seems to have thought, however, that the Admiralty was pressing him to attack and his ardent fighting spirit could not brook anything in the nature of defensive strategy.[3]

Von Spee's adroit tactic of allowing only one of his ships, the cruiser *Leipzig*, to break wireless silence led Cradock to believe that he would encounter only one German light cruiser. On November 1 the two squadrons met off the Chilean port of Coronel in the fading light of a South Pacific evening. Although Cradock realised that he was thoroughly outgunned by von Spee, especially in the absence of *Canopus*, which could not keep up with the cruisers, he did not hesitate to engage. The German armoured cruisers' shooting was lethal. *Good Hope* and *Monmouth* went down with the loss of all hands. *Glasgow* and *Otranto* managed to escape. Coronel was the first defeat suffered by the Navy in an action in more than a century – since the War of 1812 – and the first defeat of a squadron since the American War of Independence. The psychological blow was fierce.

By November 4 news of the extent of the disaster had reached the Admiralty. Indomitable as ever, Fisher rose to the challenge in characteristic fashion. With Churchill's support, he ordered two battle cruisers, HMS *Inflexible* and *Invincible*, to be detached from the Grand Fleet and dispatched to the South Atlantic to locate and hunt down von Spee. After Herculean efforts by the dockyard staff, they left Devonport at 4 pm on November 11.

Fisher had arrived at the Admiralty determined to remove the then Chief of the Naval War Staff, Vice Admiral Doveton Sturdee, a supporter of his old adversary, Beresford, whom he cordially detested. Sturdee, an able sea commander, had not been a success as Chief of Staff. He had been largely responsible for the ill-coordinated planning for the action of the Heligoland Bight and had been criticised for initiating the faulty instructions sent to Cradock before the battle of Coronel. Richmond wrote that Sturdee 'more than anyone else is responsible for the loss of Cradock's Squadron'.[4] Churchill, who also had some responsibility for these instructions, had been unwilling to make him a scapegoat for the disaster. Fisher finally achieved his objective of ousting Sturdee by giving him command of the battlecruisers sent to the South Atlantic.

Fisher replaced Sturdee with Henry Oliver, Hall's predecessor as DNI, who had served as Naval Secretary for less than a month. Oliver, promoted Acting Vice Admiral, had been a member of the 'Fishpond', the nickname in the service for those officers who had taken Fisher's side in his feud with Beresford, and had been his Naval Assistant during his earlier term as First Sea Lord. He was a far more able staff officer than his predecessor but unfortunately he was, even by contemporary naval standards, an arch centraliser, totally unwilling or unable to delegate. In his new office Oliver was now Hall's immediate superior. As, sadly, their modi operandi were incompatible, the two men did not get on and were never able to work together effectively.

As the battlecruisers steamed south, Sturdee maintained a rigorous radio silence. Nevertheless, news of his squadron's mission soon leaked out. Their destination had been no secret in Devonport. He advertised his movements when on November 17 his squadron coaled in the port of St. Vincent in the Portuguese colony of the Cape Verde Islands off the West African coast. Several German merchant ships were sheltering in the harbour to avoid the British blockade and news of their arrival was clearly passed on to Berlin. On the same day, Paymaster-Lieutenant Lloyd Hirst, the Intelligence Officer of *Glasgow*, then in dock at Rio de Janeiro while the damage she had suffered at Coronel was being repaired (and who later in the war became the head of the Latin America section of the NID) was taken to lunch in an English club. He was horrified to overhear two Britons at the next table discussing the imminent arrival of the battlecruisers.[5] Although the Admiralstab was well aware that they had been sent to the South Atlantic, this intelligence was, inexplicably, never passed on to von Spee. This failure was all too typical of the ineptitude that German intelligence displayed throughout the war, notably the failure to discover the mutiny in the French Army in 1917.

On November 3 von Spee took *Scharnhorst*, *Gneisenau* and the cruiser *Nurnberg* into the Chilean port of Valparaiso. The laws of neutrality permitted three warships of a belligerent power to visit a neutral port for 24 hours. Von Spee was welcomed by the German Minister and lionized by the influential German community, whose members were delighted by the news of his victory. He then sailed for the Chilean island of Mas Afuera, four hundred miles offshore, which had been his base before Coronel and where, accompanied by colliers, he remained until November 18. During these two weeks he sent his other cruisers, *Dresden* and *Leipzig*, into Valparaiso to allow their crews to go ashore and to collect intelligence.

Some 40% of von Spee's ammunition had been shot off at Coronel and could not be replaced at sea. He had no option but to return to Germany, which accorded with an instruction from the Admiralstab. Despite his successful leadership of his squadron and his victory over Cradock, he now began to exhibit a curious fatalism. Although von Spee must have known that the Admiralty would seek retribution for the disaster, he unaccountably lingered in Chilean waters for a month, while he accumulated the stocks of coal he needed. He did not sail until November 26. For several days he remained in the vicinity of Cape Horn, which he passed on December 1. On December 6, he conferred with his captains. Relying on intelligence that the only warship in Port Stanley was *Canopus*, he proposed an attack on the Falkland Islands to destroy the wireless station and the islands' stocks of coal. Unknown to von Spee, after Coronel, Captain Luce had shepherded the ancient battleship to the Falklands where, to assist their defence, she was beached in a position where her four 12-in guns could cover the entrance to the harbour. Her Marines and lighter guns were landed to reinforce the garrison. Although all his captains bar one, notably Erich Maercker of *Gneisenau*, objected strongly, von Spee overruled them.

Meanwhile Sturdee had reached the Abrolhos Rocks off the Brazilian coast on November 26 where he rendezvoused with Admiral Stoddard and his cruisers, including *Glasgow*, her repairs now complete. Pressed by Luce, he sailed for the Falklands two days later. He did not hurry, only reaching Port Stanley on the afternoon of December 7 and ordering his squadron to coal.

At 7:30 am on December 8, von Spee detached *Gneisenau* and *Nurnberg* to attack Port Stanley. Maercker quickly received two very unpleasant shocks. His gunnery officer reported that he had seen tripod masts in the harbour, indicating the presence of British capital ships. *Canopus* opened fire, straddling *Gneisenau* and forcing Maercker to break off the attack before he could silence the wireless station and make for the open sea to rejoin von Spee, who steamed south-east at top speed in the hope that he could outrun the British squadron.

Sturdee's ships had still been coaling when he heard news of the attack but by 10 am his squadron was at sea and the two battlecruisers, steaming at 25 knots, were inexorably overhauling von Spee. At 12.47 pm Sturdee opened fire. The battle was hard fought on both sides but the result was inevitable. Hit repeatedly, *Scharnhorst* sank at 4.17 pm with the loss of all her crew, including the Admiral. *Gneisenau* fought on valiantly until 6 pm when she finally capsized. Less than 100 of her crew were rescued. Maercker did not survive. Sturdee's cruisers pursued and sank *Leipzig* and *Nurnberg* although *Dresden* managed to escape in the fading light, as *Glasgow* had at Coronel. Sturdee's success had avenged the disaster at Coronel and did much to restore the morale both of the Navy and of the civilian population. He himself was acclaimed as the hero of the day and Fisher's beloved battlecruisers had proved their value in a role for which they had been designed.

The question cries out for an answer. Why did von Spee attack the Falklands? He did not need the coal stocks at Port Stanley as Maercker had been ordered to destroy them. The orders sent to him via Valparaiso had told him to break through to Germany and break off warfare against trade. He could reasonably have interpreted this order as one to avoid any attack on British bases. Had von Spee bypassed the Falklands, he would almost certainly have evaded Sturdee and his battlecruisers and he would have steamed up the east coast of South America with relative impunity. In notes which he prepared for a lecture on Intelligence in Wartime to the Naval Staff College at Greenwich in 1936, Hall wrote: 'Propaganda can be used for various purposes. 1. To deceive the enemy (Falkland Islands) in order to lead him to take a certain course for which you are prepared.'[6]

Hall seldom if ever referred to NID or Room 40 operations in public. He was more forthcoming at the dinner parties he regularly gave in the late 1930s, when he could reasonably depend on the discretion of his friends, old colleagues and close relatives. At one of these dinners, he described how he had successfully instructed a covert agent in Berlin to infiltrate the long-range wireless station at Nauen and send a bogus telegram to Valparaiso to be delivered to von Spee, specifically ordering him to attack Port Stanley. Hall's obituary in the Associated Press, which appeared in several American newspapers, mentioned that he had lured von Spee to the Falklands by misinformation.

Although Hall's account might seem far-fetched and the author can find no corroborating smoking gun, it is feasible and bears the stamp of his skill in the arts of deception. By November 1914 Room 40 was in possession of both the SKM and HVB codes and it is reasonable to believe that such a signal could have been transmitted behind the backs of the authorities. As one of von Spee's cruisers had called at Valparaiso as late as November 18, it is possible that he could have received this signal when the cruiser returned to Mas Afuera. If Hall did, indeed, succeed in luring von Spee to the Falklands, his deception played a significant role in bringing about the German Admiral's downfall and in restoring the Navy's reputation after the disaster at Coronel.

Following her escape after the battle of the Falkland Islands, *Dresden* passed Cape Horn into the South Pacific and spent the next two months evading the Navy, hiding among the hundreds of islands off the Chilean coast. By November 1914 the Australian Navy's lead cryptanalyst, Frederick Wheatley, was successfully reading the HVB code. By his own account, he finally broke the code when he returned to his office after having taken a couple of hours off to watch Australia's premier horse race, the Melbourne Cup. The Navy in South American waters was much more liberal in the use of the codebook than the Admiralty and Captain Luce of *Glasgow*, the senior officer entrusted with *Dresden*'s destruction, was able to read a signal sent by her Captain, Ludecke, to a German collier. The future Vice-Admiral Harold Hickling, then a Sub-Lieutenant on *Glasgow* wrote:

... our luck turned. We intercepted a signal in Telefunken, the German wireless with its distinctive note ... Earlier on, we had captured the German merchant vessel code ... The code book lay on the captain's dining table and every officer spent a few hours a day trying to solve the puzzle. A few days later, Charles Stuart, the Signal Officer, bounced up on the bridge: 'I think I've got it, Sir. ... "Am proceeding Juan Fernandez meet me there 9 March very short of coal".'[7]

Armed with this intelligence, Luce steamed to *Dresden*'s signalled location at Cumberland Bay on the island of Juan Fernandez, arriving on March 14. After a short exchange of gunfire, her Captain ordered her scuttled.

Only one German cruiser, *Konigsberg*, now remained, blockaded in the Rufigi river in German East Africa. Her Captain's signals to Berlin, sent via the Portuguese port of Lourenco Marques, were regularly intercepted by Room 40. After reading these signals, Hall permitted them to be sent on, so that he could continue to monitor the traffic and obtain more intelligence, a practice he would continue later in the war, notably in the case of the Swedish Roundabout (see Chapter 12). SIGINT thus played a considerable part in the sinking of *Konigsberg* by river-going monitors on July 11 1915.

The Scarborough Raid

As already noted, Nelson had used his frigates as intelligence gatherers, keeping a close watch on enemy fleet movements and sending SIGINT by relay to his flagship. By 1914 close-in intelligence on Nelsonian lines was no longer practicable owing to the advent of the submarine. As aerial reconnaissance was not yet available, the War Staff was heavily reliant on the SIGINT received via the decrypts.

The main Grand Fleet base at Scapa Flow was further from the English East Coast than the Kriegsmarine's headquarters at Wilhelmshaven. To counteract this disadvantage, the faster battlecruisers, commanded by Beatty, were relocated to Cromarty and Jellicoe, commanding the Grand Fleet, and Beatty needed constant, timely and accurate intelligence. Unfortunately, the two Admirals received Hope's intelligence digests only at Oliver's discretion. They should have been, but never were fully in the loop, nor was Hall. The situation was further complicated by Oliver's unwillingness to delegate.

On the morning of November 3, Admiral Franz Hipper, commanding the German battlecruisers, bombarded the East Anglian port of Yarmouth while he was covering a mine-laying operation. His squadron was safely back in his base at Wilhelmshaven long before Beatty could have intervened. During the next month, Room 40 was becoming proficient in intercepting and decoding the Kriegsmarine's signal traffic and was thus able, at least in theory, to provide the timely intelligence which Jellicoe and Beatty so desperately needed.

By early December, the German fleet commander, Admiral Friedrich von Ingenohl, had decided to stage another bombardment of coastal towns, this time Scarborough, Whitby and Hartlepool in the north-east of England. His intention was to bring Beatty's battlecruisers to action while HMS *Inflexible* and *Invincible* were in the South Atlantic searching for von Spee. He apparently did not know that a third battle cruiser, HMS *Princess Royal*, had been sent to the Caribbean to forestall von Spee if his squadron had traversed the newly completed Panama Canal. As a result of these moves, Beatty's battlecruiser force was reduced to only four. Hipper's Scouting Group, four battlecruisers and a modern armoured cruiser was thus slightly stronger. Von Ingenohl's Dreadnoughts would cover the battlecruisers with the intention of luring Beatty into a minefield laid immediately west of the Dogger Bank while he remained to the minefield's east, thus obeying an instruction from the Kaiser. The operation was delayed until December 15 to permit the battlecruiser *Von Der Tann* to be released from the dockyard, restoring Hipper's force to its full strength.

This time Room 40 intercepted the German signals relating to the battlecruiser operation. At about 7 pm on December 14 Admiral Wilson, the former First Sea Lord who had volunteered to serve in the Admiralty in an unofficial capacity at the outbreak of the war asked Churchill to convene an immediate meeting with both Fisher and Oliver. In Churchill's book *The World Crisis* he wrote:

> He [Wilson] then explained that his examination of the available evidence indicating the possibility of an impending movement, which would involve the battlecruisers and perhaps – though this was no positive evidence – have an offensive character against our coasts. The German High Sea Fleet, he stated definitely, appeared not to be involved.[8]

Room 40's information was, unfortunately, incomplete, as the decrypts did not mention that the Dreadnoughts had been ordered to sea, nor did they reveal which towns were to be bombarded. The lack of such intelligence adversely affected the orders sent to Jellicoe. Beesly noted how closely Churchill had become engaged in operational decisions and how few officers were involved in taking such an important decision. Hall, the only officer in the Admiralty who had actually seen action during the war, or Ewing and Hope, representing Room 40, were not present to interpret the raw SIGINT. Nor were any staff officers of the Operations Division.

Beesly might also have mentioned Churchill's inconsistency in directing a major fleet action as if the War Staff did not exist, given that he had been sent to the Admiralty with the explicit objective of installing an effective staff system. In effect he was allowing the First Sea Lord to carry on the traditional practice of implementing operational decisions himself together with, on this occasion, Wilson and Oliver, who were to all intents and purposes his deputies. Fisher, dynamic reformer though he was, had never attempted to modernise the Navy's command and control system. In truth, he had never had much more use for a staff than he did the fossil Admirals whom he loved to deride. Now in his mid-seventies, he was not going to change his ways. At 9.30 pm Oliver drafted the following signal for Jellicoe:

> Good information just received shows the German First [Battle] Cruiser Squadron with destroyers will leave the Jade on Tuesday morning early and return on Wednesday night. It is apparent from information that battleships are very unlikely to come out. The enemy force will have time to reach our coast. Send at once, leaving tonight, the Battle Cruiser Squadron and Light Cruiser Squadron supported by a Battle Squadron, preferably the Second. At daylight on Wednesday, they should be at some point, where they can make sure of intercepting the enemy during his return. Tyrwhitt [Commanding the Harwich Force] with his light cruisers and destroyers, will try to get in touch with the enemy off the British coast and shadow him, keeping the Admiral informed. From our information, First [German Battle] Cruiser Squadron consists of four battlecruisers and five light cruisers and there will probably be three flotillas of destroyers.[9]

As on other occasions, Jellicoe's intuitive caution served him well. Using the well-tried principle of using maximum force against the enemy, he queried the Admiralty's instruction to send only one Battle Squadron to support Beatty. He requested permission to send the entire Grand Fleet, three Battle Squadrons in all. He was sharply overruled.

The Second Battle Squadron, with the Royal Navy's most modern battleships then in commission, commanded by Vice-Admiral Sir George Warrender, was the gunnery champion of the Fleet. Warrender had some shortcomings: '… given the complexities of modern naval warfare and the rapidity with which decisions had to be made, Warrender should not have been in command. His mind worked gradually, and his responses were further slowed by a growing deafness.'[10]

Hipper sailed from Wilhelmshaven at 3 am on December 15 with his four battlecruisers, one armoured cruiser, four light cruisers and a destroyer screen. Twelve hours later, von Ingenohl followed with a mighty armada, 14 Dreadnoughts, eight pre-Dreadnoughts, nine cruisers and 54 destroyers – 85 warships in all. Warrender left Scapa at 5:30 am with six battleships and four light cruisers. As a gale was blowing, he left his destroyers behind. Thirty minutes later, Beatty sailed from Cromarty with four battlecruisers, among them Hall's old command, HMS *Queen Mary*, four light cruisers and only seven destroyers. The two squadrons, dangerously weak in destroyers, rendezvoused at 11 am, proceeding south to take up station to the west of the Dogger Bank.

At 6.35 am on December 16, Hipper sent his destroyers and all but one of his cruisers east to join up with the battle fleet. At around 5 am the British and German destroyers had clashed. Although they were outnumbered and suffered some damage, the British ships forced the Germans to retreat. Surprisingly, this destroyer action resulted in von Ingenohl deciding to return to port without informing Hipper.

Between 7 and 8 am, the battlecruisers bombarded the towns of Scarborough, Whitby and Hartlepool, killing 105 civilians and wounding 525. Only at Hartlepool did Hipper face any artillery fire and his ships suffered only minimal damage. Nine sailors were killed or wounded. By 9 am, his task accomplished, he withdrew to the east.

Beatty was almost within range of the cruisers bringing up the rear of the retreating High Seas Fleet when he received a signal from the Admiralty that Scarborough was being shelled. Beatty and Warrender immediately turned west to intercept Hipper. During the morning the visibility worsened and at 11.25 Beatty's light cruisers encountered a German cruiser and eight destroyers, part of the force which Hipper had sent east earlier that morning. Due to communications errors and a vaguely worded signal sent by Beatty's inept Flag Lieutenant, Ralph Seymour, the highly capable Commodore William Goodenough, commanding the cruisers, broke off the action and the German ships vanished into the mists.

This was not the only mistake that morning. A strange incident occurred, which exposed the lack of battle-experience of senior naval officers and their all too frequent failure to act on their own initiative. The B division of Warrender's battleships was commanded by Rear-Admiral Robert Arbuthnott on HMS *Orion*. Her Captain, Frederic Dreyer, one of the navy's top gunnery experts and the inventor of the fire-control system named after him, trained his guns on the German ships and asked Arbuthnott for permission to open fire. Incredibly Arbuthnott refused, telling a frustrated Dreyer that he had to wait until Warrender had given the order. The order from the flagship never came and the German cruisers quickly escaped into the mist. Dreyer later wrote that if *Orion* had opened fire the five other battleships would have followed suit. A few minutes later Warrender sighted the cruisers but he did not react decisively. Rather than opening fire, he ordered his armoured cruisers to pursue the speedier German ships, which were able to get out of range without any damage. The shortcomings of these two Admirals resulted in the opportunity to inflict serious damage on the German cruisers being irretrievably lost.

Nelson's captains would never have squandered such an opportunity but unlike their successors, they were thoroughly battle-hardened by the time of Trafalgar and they were led by an Admiral who required them to use their initiative, as his signal before the battle indicates: 'No Captain will go far wrong if he lays his ship alongside one of the enemy.'

At 12.30 Beatty, wrongly believing that Hipper had slipped past him, turned east. At that moment the German battlecruisers were only 12 miles to his west and had he maintained his course, Beatty would soon have been able to open fire. Despite a number of later changes of course, neither he nor Warrender encountered Hipper. Eventually Hipper reasoned that he was facing two separate opposing forces and turned north to successfully elude them. His battlecruisers had had a lucky escape.

By the morning of December 16, Room 40 was intercepting a constant stream of German signals, including a report of the destroyer action that had caused Ingenohl to retreat. Inevitably, the delay of more than an hour involved in coding and transmitting the intelligence to the commanders at sea reduced its value. It was not until 1.50 pm that the Admiralty received a signal indicating that the battle fleet was at sea, between 70 and 80 miles north-west of Heligoland. They deduced that it was advancing when it was actually making for port. At 3.47 pm Warrender ordered Beatty to break off the action. After a quite unnecessary delay of several hours, the Admiralty ordered Commodore Keyes, commanding the submarines, to attack the returning force. The submarine E-11 fired a torpedo at the battleship *Posen* but owing to the high seas she missed.

The Scarborough Raid had been marked by inept leadership on both sides. The British press was bitterly critical of the Navy for not having prevented the bombardment of the three east-coast towns and then for having allowed Hipper and his battlecruisers to escape unscathed. A furious Fisher demanded that heads should roll, especially Warrender's, whom he castigated as stupid. In the event, no senior Naval officer was sacked and it was not until nearly a year later that Warrender, by then a sick man, was eventually removed. The unfortunate Seymour was chiefly to blame for the lapse in communications which had resulted in Goodenough breaking off his action against the German cruisers. Another Admiral would almost certainly have sacked him for his ineptitude but, strangely, he remained Beatty's Flag Lieutenant throughout the war – although his handling of signals at both the Dogger Bank and Jutland was equally as incompetent. One observer commented: '... he was retained at immeasurable cost to the Navy and to the country.'[11] Only after the war had ended did Beatty turn on Seymour: 'He lost three battles for me.'[12]

Within this dismal catalogue of failure, Room 40 had passed its first test with honours. A thoughtful Churchill, admitting the widespread dissatisfaction, wrote this eloquent tribute to his codebreakers in *World Crisis*:

> ... we could not say a word in explanation. We had to bear in silence the censures of our countrymen. We could never admit, for fear of compromising our secret information, where our squadrons were, or how near the leading German cruisers had been to their destruction. One comfort we had. The indications upon which we acted had been confirmed by events. The sources of information upon which we relied were evidently trustworthy. Next time we might at least have average visibility. Then he pondered: 'but would there be a next time? The German Admiral must have known that he was very near to powerful British ships ... Would it not also be a mystery how they came to be there?[13]

As it turned out, no German Admiral, even the highly capable pair of Scheer and Hipper, ever appears to have questioned why, every time they went to sea to fight a fleet action, they encountered a strong force of British warships so far south of their bases in Scotland.

The German newspapers were jubilant at the success of the bombardment, hypocritically regretting the loss of civilian life. Tirpitz was as enraged by the outcome of the raid as Fisher had been, believing that a golden opportunity to inflict a heavy defeat on the Royal Navy had been thrown away. Magnus von Levetzow, the fire-eating Captain of the battlecruiser *Moltke*, infuriated that Hipper's Scouting Group had been left unsupported, went so far as to accuse Ingenohl of cowardice in retreating when he was confronted by just eleven (in fact only seven) destroyers, which, he wrote, could easily have been eliminated.

To mollify public opinion, which had been badly shaken by the bombardment, four days later the Admiralty moved Beatty's Battlecruiser Force south to the naval base at Rosyth on the Firth of Forth, considerably closer to the German coast, enabling them to more easily counter any further attack on east-coast towns.

The Battle of the Dogger Bank

On January 23 1915, the Admiralstab authorised a reconnaissance operation to the Dogger Bank. That morning Room 40 intercepted their signal:

First and Second Scouting Groups, Senior Officers of Destroyers and two flotillas to be selected by the Senior Officer Scouting Forces [Hipper] are to reconnoitre the Dogger Bank. They are to leave harbour this evening after dark and return tomorrow evening after dark.[14]

Room 40 had been expecting such a message for several days and its intelligence was both timely and accurate. They had reported that one of Hipper's battlecruisers was in dry dock and that the squadron comprising the four most recently completed Dreadnoughts, commanded by Scheer, had been sent to the Baltic for gunnery practice. They reproduced Scheer's instruction detailing the squadrons involved in the operation and the exact time Hipper's ships would be putting to sea. At 2.10 pm that day this signal was sent to Jellicoe, Beatty and Tyrwhitt:

> Four German battlecruisers, six light cruisers and twenty-two destroyers will sail this evening to scout on the Dogger Bank, probably returning tomorrow evening. All available battlecruisers light cruisers and destroyers from Rosyth should proceed to rendezvous in 55.13 N 3.12 E arriving at 7 am tomorrow. Commodore T [Tyrwhitt] is to proceed with all available destroyers and light cruisers to join Vice Admiral *Lion* [Beatty] at above rendezvous. If enemy is sighted by Commodore T while crossing their line of advance, they should be attacked. Wireless telegraphy is not to be used unless absolutely essential.[15]

The last sentence indicates a concern that the development of Direction Finding technology could lead to the detection of the location of ships. At 2.45 pm Jellicoe was instructed to take the entire Grand Fleet to sea, sailing at 6.30 pm. Half an hour earlier Beatty left Rosyth with five battlecruisers and four light cruisers. At dawn he rendezvoused with Tyrwhitt and his destroyers. Hall's old command, *Queen Mary*, was in dock and was absent from the battle: a serious loss as she was the champion gunnery ship of the Battle Cruiser Force. By contrast the newer *Tiger* was notoriously poor at shooting.

In one important aspect, Beatty had a substantial advantage over Hipper. With *Von Der Tann* also in dockyard hands, Hipper had only three battlecruisers, not four as the Room 40 intelligence had indicated. His fourth large ship was the armoured cruiser *Blucher* (15,500 tons, 12 8.2-in guns). As her top speed was only 24 knots, she would have difficulty in keeping up with the battlecruisers.

Confronted by Beatty and Tyrwhitt and fearing that Beatty was being closely followed by the Grand Fleet, Hipper turned south-east at 7:35 am on the morning of January 24 and ran for home at 20 knots with Beatty in hot pursuit. Shortly before 9 am he opened fire at a range of almost 20,000 yards. The rival battlecruisers fought a fierce duel and accurate

German shooting resulted in serious damage to Beatty's ships, with his flagship *Lion* receiving no less than 16 hits.

A series of errors now combined to rob Beatty of what might have been a major victory. As a result of incorrect fire direction by Captain Pelly of *Tiger*, the German battlecruiser *Moltke*, like her sisters an excellent gunnery ship, was left unengaged to fire on *Lion*. As his flagship was eventually forced to drop out of the battle line, Beatty instructed HMS *Indomitable*, the oldest and slowest of his ships, which was bringing up his rear to finish off *Blucher*, already mortally damaged but still putting up a valiant fight. This decision left his three remaining battlecruisers, *Princess Royal*, *Tiger* and *New Zealand*, to fight Hipper's three. His flagship had already been hit eight times by *Lion* and *Tiger*. At 9:47 am a shell from *Lion* struck the battlecruiser *Seydlitz*'s after deck, penetrating the armour of her rear turret. Ammunition being hoisted from the aft magazine set off flash fires, resulting in the destruction of the two aft turrets. Three members of the crew opened the valves, allowing 600 tons of sea water to flood the magazine, almost certainly saving the battlecruiser from a fatal explosion.

At 10.54 am, Beatty saw – or believed he saw – the periscope of a U-boat on *Lion*'s starboard bow. He immediately ordered his entire force to make a 90° change of course to port. During the first three days of their voyage, before they passed out of radio range, the U-boats communicated frequently with their shore command. By the time of the Dogger Bank action, Hope's analyses enabled Room 40 to establish the number of U-boats that were at sea at any one time and plot their positions with reasonable accuracy. Oliver did not pass on this invaluable intelligence, which had accurately plotted the position of the U-boats at 54.9N 5.16 E and 54.17N 5.35E, approximately 40 miles to the south of Beatty's ships, until 1.10 pm, almost two-and-a-half hours later.

Only four minutes after he had ordered his ships to alter course, Beatty realised that this turn had taken him too far from Hipper's rapidly fleeing battlecruisers and made a second signal 'Course North East' combined with a further imprecise signal 'Attack the rear of the enemy'. As *Lion* had lost all electric power, she was forced to make signals by flag and as she was now effectively out of the battle, command of the battlecruisers now devolved on Rear-Admiral Sir Archibald Moore, who had been Controller of the Navy and Hall's former superior. Moore had had little experience of sea command and seems to have been lacking in offensive spirit. He erroneously took the signal to mean that all three battlecruisers should attack the already doomed *Blucher*, which, at the time, was to his north-east. In doing so he abandoned the pursuit of Hipper's battlecruisers. Had the chase been maintained, the heavily damaged *Seydlitz* would almost certainly have been sunk and another battlecruiser, *Derfflinger*, which had also been hit several times, might have suffered the same fate. As a result of this succession of leadership failures

Hipper once again managed to escape and for the second time the Navy was denied a decisive victory.

Fisher's rage was once more a terrible phenomenon to behold, describing the unfortunate Moore as 'despicable' and Captain Pelly of *Tiger*, another Beresford protegé, as a 'poltroon'. Moore was demoted to command a cruiser squadron based near the Canary Islands, far from the German fleet. Pelly survived.

Back in Wilhelmshaven, Hipper wondered why, having sailed in secret and with minimum notice, he had run into both Beatty and Tyrwhitt with his destroyers directly in his path. Scheer went further: 'The unexpected presence of English ships ... leads to the conclusion it was not a matter of chance and our plan in some way or other had become known by the English.'[16] Von Ingenohl, who was sacked nine days after the battle, noted: 'It must be considered a remarkable coincidence that our battlecruisers should encounter the enemy precisely at dawn. It appears as if the enemy had intelligence concerning the operation.' The Admiralstab actually suggested that a British agent had passed information of Hipper's movements through newspaper advertisements. In another example of German ineptitude in handling intelligence and of their scarcely concealed contempt for the British, the Admiralstab did not explain how this could have been achieved in the time frame. Room 40 and its activities remained secure.

Room 40 had performed extremely well in the run-up to the battle. Nevertheless, neither for the first nor the last time, the contrast between the accurate intelligence produced by Hope's traffic analyses and the often inadequate use made of it inside the Admiralty is stark. Fisher had been in bed with a severe cold throughout the battle and the instructions and information sent to Beatty had once again been composed by the triumvirate of Churchill, Oliver and Wilson, without the involvement of Hall or anyone else in the War Staff. The limitations of this over-centralised system and the continued failure to set up an effective interface between operations and intelligence had worked to Beatty's considerable disadvantage. After the battle Fisher told Beatty: '... you are mistaken about the German submarines – we know from themselves [Room 40 intercepts] exactly where they were, hours off you.'[17] He thus tacitly admitted the system's deficiencies. Jellicoe complained, with some justification, that the Admiralty had withheld the intelligence that Hipper was due to proceed to sea for too long. Fisher does not, however, seem to have demanded any improvements to prevent similar mistakes. The results of such inaction would be manifest at Jutland. We can only imagine what Hall thought of this missed opportunity but he must have been highly frustrated and it is small wonder that his relations with Oliver became so difficult.

Notes

1. Richmond to Julian Corbett November 20 1904. quoted by Nicholas Lambert in 'Strategic Command and Control in Warfare', *War & Society* 2004
2. Hankey *Supreme Command* Vol. 1 p.19. Quoted by Lambert, above
3. Massie *Castles of Steel* p.213
4. Marder Vol. 2 p.124
5. Massie p.249
6. CAC HALL 2/1
7. Beesly p. 78
8. Quoted in Beesly p.50
9. Ibid. p.51
10. Massie p.335
11. Hough *Great War at Sea* p.128
12. Marder Vol. 2 p. 140
13. Churchill *World Crisis* p.477-478
14. Beesly pp.58-59
15. Ibid. p.59
16. Scheer *Germany's High Sea Fleet* p.16
17. Chalmers *The Life and Letters of David Earl Beatty* p.147

CHAPTER V

Eastern Adventures

In January 1915, barely three months after his appointment as DNI, Hall instigated a bold endeavour to remove Germany's ally Turkey from the war. Keeping Churchill and Fisher well-informed of the progress of his initiative, he took up a suggestion made to him by Hankey, who as a former Mediterranean Fleet Intelligence Officer, knew the Middle East well. He secured the services of three men who had long experience of dealing with Turkish officials: George Griffin Eady, the local manager of the construction firm of Sir John Jackson & Co., who had been involved in the construction of the Asiatic sections of the Berlin to Baghdad Railway, Edwin Whittall, a merchant banker, and Gerald Fitzmaurice, the former Dragoman or Oriental Counselor in the British Embassy in Constantinople. Fitzmaurice, in particular, knew the political climate of that city intimately. His effectiveness can be judged by an eventually successful campaign to remove him from his post by the German Foreign Office, who saw him as an obstacle to their objective of creating an alliance with Turkey. Fisher, well versed in the Near East from his time as C-in-C in the Mediterranean, had no doubt about Fitzgerald's significance. In a minute to his Naval Assistant, Captain T.E. Crease, he wrote: 'Tell W.R. Hall to find out from the Foreign Office *by 11 am* where Fitzmaurice is – he was last in Sofia and what his orders are. He is now the most important person in the Eastern theatre of war but unfortunately this is not realised.'[1] Hall was soon able to assure Fisher that he had recruited Fitzmaurice, whom he later brought into the Naval Intelligence Division.

Fitzmaurice told Hall that the alliance with Germany, secretly negotiated in August 1914 by Enver Pasha, the Minister for War and leader of the so-called Young Turk Movement which had ruled the country since 1908, was far from popular in Turkey. He believed that the endeavour to break the alliance stood a reasonable chance of success and Eady took a similar view.

Hall instructed the trio to persuade Talaat Pasha, the Minister of the Interior and an influential member of the Turkish government, that they should break off their alliance with Germany and allow the fleet to pass through the Dardanelles unhindered. An additional request was later added. The Admiralty wanted the Turks to hand over the German battlecruiser *Goeben*, which had taken refuge in Turkish waters in August 1914 and which had subsequently been in action against the Russian Black Sea Fleet. To clinch these negotiations, Hall provided his negotiators with his personal guarantee for £3 million and authorised them to offer up to £4 million if necessary. On March 4 Hankey wrote in his diary: 'Saw Captain Hall, Admiralty War Staff, who said that negotiations had been opened to bribe the Turks to oust the Germans, as I had proposed earlier.'[2]

With the assistance of the anglophile Chief Rabbi in Turkey, Hall's agents started negotiations with Talaat, which were inevitably complicated by the fleet's bombardment of the forts at the entrance to the Dardanelles starting in mid-February. The discussions were seriously compromised by growing Turkish awareness that the Foreign Office had offered to hand over Constantinople to the Russians, as well as other Turkish territory in Europe to various Balkan powers. Hall reacted to these delays by threatening to reduce the proposed amount of subsidy. On March 5 he was prepared to offer £500,000 for the surrender of the Dardanelles, providing that all mines had been removed, and a further £500,000 for handing over *Goeben* undamaged. Three days later he reduced the offer for *Goeben* to £100,000. He was still willing to go to £4 million if agreement could be reached at a meeting between his negotiators and Talaat's representatives due to be held in the Bulgarian town of Dedeagatch on March 15.

On March 13 Room 40 intercepted and decoded a VB signal, signed by the Chief of the Kaiser's Naval Cabinet., Admiral Georg von Muller, and transmitted by Nauen to Constantinople:

> Most Secret. For Admiral Usedom [the Inspector-General of Coast Defences and Mines in charge of the Dardanelles]. HM the Kaiser has received the report and telegram relating to the Dardanelles. Everything conceivable is being done to arrange the supply of ammunition. For political reasons it is necessary to maintain a confident tone in Turkey. The Kaiser requests you to use your influence in this direction. The sending of a German or Austrian submarine is being seriously considered.

Hall immediately took this signal to Fisher, whom he found standing in front of the fireplace in Churchill's room at the Admiralty. Both men were excited by this important intelligence, which highlighted the fragile state of the alliance between Germany and Turkey as well as the shortage of ammunition. Fisher, who had been sceptical at the very least concerning the advisability of a naval action in the Dardanelles, surprised Hall by suddenly developing an ardent enthusiasm for the attack. In his eagerness, he shouted: 'By God, I'll go through tomorrow. We shall probably lose six ships but I'm going through.'[3] Churchill observed: 'This means that they have come to the end of their ammunition.' He told Fisher to draft the necessary orders.

Hall had kept both Churchill and Hankey briefed on the negotiations with the Turks. As he was about to leave the First Lord's room, Churchill asked him how they were proceeding. When Hall mentioned the size of the financial guarantee he had personally provided, he provoked a fierce reaction.

> Churchill: 'How much?'
> Hall (telling himself that the figures did look extraordinarily high): 'Three million pounds, with power to go to four million pounds if necessary.'
> Churchill (frowning): 'Who authorised this?'
> Hall: 'I did, First Lord.'
> Churchill: 'But – the Cabinet surely knows nothing about it?'
> Hall: 'No it does not. But if we were to get peace or if we were to get a peaceful passage for that amount, I imagine that they would be glad enough to pay.'
> Churchill, addressing Fisher: 'Do you hear what this man has done? He's told his people that they can go up to four million pounds to buy a peaceful passage! On his own!'
> Fisher: 'Four millions. No, no, I tell you I'm going through tomorrow or as soon as the preparations can be completed.'[4]

Churchill and Fisher instructed Hall to break off the negotiations at once, although his agents were to pursue the offer to buy *Goeben*. As Hall wrote: 'The necessary cables were sent … they not only rendered any future discussions useless but also destroyed the belief in Turkish minds of our good faith.' When his emissaries met the Turks at Dedeagatch two days later, they could only announce that they had received new orders to suspend the discussions. Their continuation was probably moot as Hall was in no position to give the Turks the guarantee they were urgently seeking, namely that they would retain Constantinople after the war. Hall went on to note: 'Ironically enough, when the gallant attempt of March 18 had proved unsuccessful, the Cabinet were asking me to spare no expense to win over the Turks.'[5] Fisher even asked him to increase the offer for *Goeben* to £2 million and for the cruiser *Breslau* to £1 million.

Some commentators have dismissed the chances of this endeavour ever succeeding; and it does read rather like a thriller by John Buchan or Ian Fleming. They have cited it as an example of Hall's alleged penchant for acting independently of his superiors. Their criticism highlights Hall's pursuit of a financial deal with the Turks without the Cabinet's knowledge, as Churchill had suggested to Fisher on the afternoon of March 13. Yet Churchill's statement that afternoon was disingenuous. In October 1916 he cross-examined Hall before the Dardanelles Commission, chaired by Lord Cromer, the highly respected former Agent-General in Egypt, and the minutes reveal Churchill asking Hall: 'Do you remember my authorising you to use the funds on an extraordinary scale?' Hall replied in the affirmative.[6] The critics' suggestion that the attempt was unauthorised does not stand up to examination, as Hankey's confirmation that he had originally proposed the plan to Hall, whom he continued to support, and Fisher's initiative in recommending Fitzmaurice as a member of the negotiating team, amply demonstrate.

In retrospect it is startling that Churchill and Fisher vetoed the scheme apparently without weighing up for a moment the prospects of success against the perils of a naval assault on the Dardanelles. By 1916 Room 40 was reading Turkish signals that confirmed both their shortage of ammunition and their leaders' readiness to accept bribes. In their haste Churchill and Fisher had almost certainly missed an unrepeatable opportunity to reinstate Turkish neutrality, remove the German naval presence off Constantinople, establish a warm water shipping link with Russia (vital to their economy), and significantly improve the allies' strategic position in the Middle East. The huge casualties in the unsuccessful land assault on the Dardanelles would have been averted.

Nor would the £4 million Hall had been prepared to offer (in accountancy terms) have cost the British taxpayer a penny. In August 1914 the Admiralty had commandeered two Turkish battleships then being fitted out in British shipyards with a contract value of approximately £2 million per ship. Acceptance of Hall's offer would effectively have compensated the Turkish Government for this loss. This extract from Hall's evidence to the Dardanelles Commission revealed that his plan had been well conceived and stood a reasonable chance of success.

> Churchill (cross-examining Hall): 'To the end of January you got good information from Constantinople?'
> Hall: 'Yes'.
> Churchill: 'Will you describe as well as you can the state of feeling of affairs in Constantinople, as disclosed by your Intelligence reports and secret sources of information, during the process of the naval attack?'
> Hall: 'The general impression from the information we had from our agents out there, who were in a good position to know, was that the Turkish population in Constantinople were in the habit of going on their housetops and looking for the British Fleet to arrive and relieve them from oppression … '
> Churchill: 'Did the intelligence in your possession favour the idea that the arrival of the British Fleet would have produced a revolution in Constantinople?'

Hall: 'Oh yes, it certainly would. I feel no hesitation in saying that. From very certain information one could say that the entry of Turkey into the war was forced by the guns of the *Goeben*, by the *Goeben* actually arriving there – that the entry of Turkey was by no means a unanimous opinion of the Young Turk party itself: and we had every reason to believe that had the British Fleet got off Constantinople we should have had precisely the same effect on the inhabitants as the *Goeben* had, but in the opposite direction.'
Lord Cromer (Chairman of the Commission): 'You mean, the two German ships, the *Goeben* and the *Breslau*?'
Hall: 'Yes, there is unquestionable evidence that their arrival there forced Turkey into the War.'
Churchill: 'Had you any information to show that there was any anxiety or apprehension or panic in Constantinople as our attack on the forts developed?'
Hall: 'Yes I had. We had direct evidence that the Government was preparing to shift to Asia Minor, and the archives had already started going over there. Undoubtedly as the bombardment went on there was panic in Constantinople and the better families were preparing to pack up and to go over into Asia Minor rather than stay there. We had evidence of that from a number of good sources.'
Churchill: 'During the progress of the bombardment did you attempt to get into communication with the enemy Government and commanders to obtain a passage, if possible?'
Hall: 'Yes.'
Churchill: 'I may say that I have the Prime Minister's permission to refer to this in general terms. Did your negotiations carry you up to high Turkish authorities?'
Hall: 'Yes, the very highest.'
Churchill: 'Did they indicate a readiness on their part to open the passage?'
Hall: 'Yes.'
Cromer: 'At what time?'
Churchill: 'During the bombardment from about the 25th February to the 11th or 12th March.'
Hall: 'We got into very close touch with the highest authorities in Constantinople. Delegates were sent down to meet our agents, and we got on well up to a point, and then it was discovered that it was not so much the passage of the Dardanelles they were prepared to give, but they wanted a separate peace. It was no part of my function to discuss peace terms with the Turks.'
Cromer: 'As I understand it, in following up this thread, you expected to find a traitor who wished to enrich himself, and you found a patriot who wished to make separate peace with England?'

Hall: 'Yes.'
Cromer: 'It was impracticable on general grounds?'
Hall: 'It was impracticable.'[7]

In his evidence Hall confirmed that the alliance with Germany was by no means popular. Ataturk, or Mustafa Kemal, who was then Military Attaché in Sofia, and Djemal Pasha, the Minister of Marine, were among a number of prominent Turks who had opposed the alliance. Kemal had protested strongly to Enver about the risks inherent in pursuing a pro-German policy. Djemal had told Rear-Admiral Arthur Limpus, the head of the British Naval mission in Turkey, that many senior Turkish naval officers shared his reservations about the alliance. Henry Morgenthau, the perceptive American Ambassador in Constantinople, noted that: '... the populace, far from opposing the arrival of the allied fleet, would have welcomed it with joy ... for this would emancipate them from the hated Germans, bring about peace and end their miseries'.[8]

In July 1914 the future Air Marshal Thomas Elmhirst, then a Sub-Lieutenant RN, had been serving on HMS *Indomitable*, the flagship of the Mediterranean Fleet, during a visit which the C-in-C, Admiral Milne, had paid to Constantinople. The German Admiral Souchon had also recently visited the Turkish capital and Elmhirst noted that the Turks had given Milne a far more friendly reception than his Kriegsmarine opposite number.[9]

The German Ambassador in Constantinople, Hans von Wangenheim, had few illusions about the consequences if the British Fleet had arrived off the city. On March 23 1915, five days after the unsuccessful naval assault, he wrote: 'We realise that we would have then had to draw a line under our Turkish policy.' Kapitanleutnant Hermann Baltzer, a Kriegsmarine officer seconded to the Turkish Ministry of Marine, was equally candid, he had '... no doubt whatever that Turkey would have made peace. There would have been a revolution. The appearance of ships before Constantinople would have been sufficient. Constantinople *is* Turkey.'[10] British historian Aspinall-Oglander has pointed out: 'It is important to remember that if Constantinople had been abandoned the Turks would have been unable to continue the war; their only arms and munitions factories were in the capital'[11]

Hankey's biographer, Stephen Roskill, noting that he had experience of naval intelligence work in the Middle East and that he had worked closely with Hall on the plan, came to the same conclusion. He wrote: '... it seems likely that his claim to have originated a proposal, which was by no means as fantastic as it may now appear, was solidly based ... There was considerable opposition to the alliance with Germany and many influential Turks were imbued with feelings of friendship towards Britain. Had these secret negotiations succeeded the whole course of the war would have been altered with the British Fleet steaming up to Constantinople.'[12] As late as August 1915, Hankey seriously considered reopening negotiations with Turkey on the basis which Hall had pursued.

Hall's initiative showed the extent of his creative vision, his audacity and his readiness to use well-positioned agents with a wide range of experience. Roskill paid him a substantial tribute: 'In a conflict from which the Admiralty does not in general emerge well, Hall's work is the outstanding exception.'[13] Admiral Godfrey, the DNI in the early years of World War II, a man of incisive judgment and who was certainly not given to exaggeration, had served on Admiral Wemyss's staff throughout the Dardanelles campaign. He wrote in his memoirs: '… [Hall] would have succeeded if the Foreign Office had not already promised Constantinople to the Russians.'[14]

The Foreign Office's ill-judged and unrealistic proposal to transfer Constantinople to Russia, apparently taken without any regard for the reaction of the local population, who traditionally hated the Russians, constituted a major blunder. The failure of what might have been a successful Admiralty initiative indicated the complete lack of co-ordination of foreign and defence policy and appreciation of intelligence at the highest levels of the Asquith Government. In January 1915 the Foreign Secretary, Sir Edward Grey, had reiterated his assurance about the future of Constantinople to his Russian opposite number, Sergei Sazonov. The Prime Minister and the Foreign Office on the one hand and the Admiralty and the Committee of Imperial Defence on the other were thus pursuing completely contradictory policies towards Turkey.

In his biography of Churchill, Roy Jenkins noted that, after he had been removed from the Admiralty in May 1915, Churchill had criticised 'the creakingly ineffective decision taking capacity of the Dardanelles Committee and still more so that of the Cabinet.' Jenkins added this devastating comment:

> Asquithian though I am and sceptical of how much the direction of the war improved under Lloyd George, I am nonetheless shocked by reading the minutes of the Dardanelles Committee. This, more than its name implies, was the central strategic directing body of the time. Yet it was a forum for the undulating exchange of views rather than for taking any hard decisions.[15]

Against this background of sclerotic leadership, it is easy to understand why Hall and Hankey were driven to instigate policy initiatives. As a result of the debacle, Hall took particular care to establish and maintain close relations with the Foreign Office. He thus minimised the possibility of any of his endeavours being compromised by any Foreign Office actions of which he might have been unaware.

Hall continued to feed another old ally, Commodore Roger Keyes, now Chief of Staff to Vice-Admiral De Robeck, the naval commander at the Dardanelles, with intelligence, particularly on the movement of German U-boats to the Eastern Mediterranean. U-21 with a long distance capability had sailed from Emden on April 25th. Room 40 was well aware of her departure but not her destination. On May 19th she arrived at the Austrian naval base at Cattaro to refuel and take on supplies and the Admiralstab sent her commander a signal listing the location of the British pre-Dreadnought battleships at the Dardanelles, a further indication of unnecessarily lax security, as there was presumably a secure land line connecting the German and Austrian naval bases. Room 40 picked up the signal, which Hall immediately sent to Keyes. Sadly, De Robeck does not seem to have acted on the intelligence as within a little more than a week U-21 had succeeded in sinking HMS *Triumph* and HMS *Majestic*, when both battleships were at anchor.

During World War I there was no Special Operations Executive or Political Warfare Executive propaganda, as in World War II. SIS had only recently been formed and had been unable to build up an effective spy network. Hall provided an ad hoc organisation to cover these deficiencies. The network Hall had built up during the Dardanelles campaign continued to operate through the war and his intelligence of Turkish and German activities in Palestine and Syria proved particularly useful. As Marjorie Napier, one of Hall's most trusted naval intelligence operatives, noted: 'One example of the many pies into which he put his fingers was the Middle East. The intelligence he supplied to Allenby, when he became C-in-C Middle East in 1917, proved highly valuable to him.'

The discovery of the German diplomatic codes

In one paragraph of an affidavit which he swore in December 1926 in connection with the Black Tom case, Hall described his original acquisition of a German Foreign Office diplomatic Code 13040:

> The German cipher book covering this system of ciphering [that used between Berlin and the German Embassy in Washington] is in our possession, it having been captured by the British authorities in the baggage of a German consul named Wassmuss who was stationed at Shiraz while Wassmuss was engaged in an endeavour to cut a British oil pipe line.

The paragraph quoted above does not make total sense and contains two errors. Wilhelm Wassmuss, a known German agent, had only briefly served as a Consul in the Persian Gulf before 1914 and the code (actually two codes) captured on this occasion was not 13040.

The usually accepted account of the acquisition of these codes reads as if it came from the pages of Buchan. Like Lawrence of Arabia, to whom he bore some similarity (down to a shared penchant for wearing Arab robes), Wassmuss considered himself a friend of the local tribes. He knew them well and he advocated enlisting them as Germany's allies in the war against Britain. In February 1915, he was summoned to Constantinople to receive his detailed instructions to commence espionage operations, including the cutting of pipelines owned by the British-controlled Anglo-Persian Oil Co. (APOC), 51% owned by the Admiralty and an important supplier of oil for the Navy; and initiating anti-British propaganda. Having succeeded in cutting the pipeline, he began inciting local rulers against the British.

In traditional fashion, one Khan decided to play both sides off against each other, arresting Wassmuss and then informing the British garrison at Bushire in the hope of obtaining a substantial reward. When a detachment of British troops arrived, the Khan engaged their commander in hustling for his prize money. Alerted to the betrayal, Wassmuss succeeded in escaping on horseback and in his pyjamas, but in his hurry managed to leave all his baggage behind. The British, disappointed at the escape of such a dangerous adversary, consoled themselves by confiscating the baggage and taking it back to Bushire. Legend has it that they found a codebook among other incriminating documents.

The actual chronicle of events is more prosaic. William Friedman, the distinguished American cryptologist of World War II, found it difficult to believe that an agent engaged in an operation to cut a pipeline would have been carrying a code and suggested that the documents in his possession were coded telegrams accompanied by details en clair. The Persian Gulf, with its British-owned oilfields, was strategically important to the British. The India Office, responsible for the region, was infuriated by the cutting of the APOC pipeline and ordered the removal of any German diplomatic presence from the Gulf. C. J. Edmonds, then Acting Vice-Consul in Bushire, wrote an account of the operation, in which he took part, entitled 'The Persian Gulf Prelude to the Zimmermann Telegram' for the *Journal of the Royal Central Asian Society* in 1960. On March 9 1915 British officers detained the German Consul in Bushire, Dr. Helmut Listemann, and removed a quantity of documents, including, as Edmonds remembered, 'two dictionary ciphers'.[16]

When Hall prepared his affidavit in December 1926, which would have been available to the German lawyers involved in the Black Tom case through the process of discovery, he may well have reasoned that his explanation of the acquisition of 13040 better served the ongoing interests of British cryptology. The German Foreign Office would soon have realised that the decrypts that he had provided were genuine. His uncanny insight into the German mindset indicated that they would sooner believe that Naval Intelligence had obtained 13040 by stealing a codebook, often vulnerable to capture by the enemy, rather than by breaking it through persistent Room 40 cryptanalysis. His intuition bore fruit in World War II when the German authorities resolutely refused to believe that British cryptanalysts could ever have decoded their sophisticated ENIGMA system.

Wassmuss's baggage and the documents seized from the Consulate in Bushire were sent to the India Office in London. There, but for Hall, they might have laid unnoticed. That April, he met a young naval officer who had just returned from the Gulf on sick leave and who told him about Wassmuss's activities in espionage, his narrow escapes and the capture of his baggage. Hall's intuition told him that a search of the documents might yield valuable results. A member of his staff, William Cozens Hardy, recovered them from the India Office. Hall found the codebooks among the documents. Denniston is specific on this point: 'April 1915 ... the DID [Hall] procures consular books from Persia.'[17] The available evidence indicates that the two captured codebooks were from the 18470 family and not, as generally believed, the 13040 code widely used by the German Foreign Ministry in communicating with its principal embassies and legations.

Hall's initiative in obtaining these codebooks was vital to the development of Room 40, extending its reach outside the purely naval sphere into the wider worlds of diplomacy and espionage. Denniston noted that by early 1915 Room 40 was intercepting a large volume of signal traffic between the German Foreign Office and the Embassy in Madrid using the Verkehrsbuch. Hall selected George Young, a former diplomat, who, to his family's consternation, had resigned from his post as First Secretary in the Legation at Lisbon, seeking to play a more active role in the war, to head the new section of Room 40, created to decode and analyse the diplomatic cipher traffic. This section, located in Room 45 of the Admiralty, was operational by August 1915. From its outset and with Oliver's agreement it reported directly to Hall, not to Ewing.

Young, an accomplished linguist who had been educated in universities in England, Germany and France, was rumoured to speak over 20 languages, although his niece asserted that his only skill in half of these was how to swear. He had considerable diplomatic experience, having served in Washington, Athens and Constantinople, and was an acknowledged expert on the Near East. Although he had the reputation of being difficult and opinionated, Young proved to be highly effective, a striking example of Hall's remarkable talent for getting those who worked for him to go the extra mile. He was assisted and eventually succeeded by the genial Benjamin Faudel-Phillips, who had been one of Serocold's city contacts. He became one of the most well-liked members of the Room 40 staff, who called him the Lord Mayor as his father and grandfather had both been Lord Mayor of London. Two cryptanalysts, Nigel de Grey and William Montgomery, both talented linguists, were transferred to the diplomatic section. Nigel de Grey had been a publisher in private life and Montgomery was an Ulster minister, a member of the staff of the Westminster Presbyterian College at Cambridge and a well known translator of German theological texts. Known in Room 40 as the Fighting Padre, his talent for lateral thinking made him a highly effective cryptographer. He apparently solved the mystery of a message hidden in a blank postcard sent from Turkey, addressed to Sir Henry Jones, 184 King's Road, Tighnabruaich, Scotland. Sir Henry Jones' son was a POW held by the Turks. Tighnabruaich is a small village on the Firth of Clyde, where the houses were not numbered and there was no King's Road. Using his biblical knowledge Montgomery worked out that the address referred to the Old Testament, the First Book of Kings Chapter 18 Verse 4: 'Obadiah took a hundred prophets, and hid fifty of them in a cave and fed them with bread and water.' He deduced that Sir Henry's son was getting round the censor and was reassuring his father that he was being well treated by his captors.

Before the end of 1915 Room 40 was able to read signals sent in no less than three diplomatic codes, 18470 and the related 2310 and 89734. Contrary to accepted wisdom, Room 40 never acquired a copy of the all-important Code 13040 used for communications between the German Foreign Office, their embassies in Constantinople, Madrid and Washington and their legations throughout Latin America.

In reality, Young and his assistants succeeded in figuring the code out by detailed and effective cryptanalysis. As Friedman noted: '... the structure of Code 13040 is such that a comparatively small amount of decoded material with a number of telegrams in code will enable skilled cryptographers to reconstruct the book.'[18] The acquisition of these codes and the breaking of 13040 was a major coup for the Naval Intelligence Division, potentially as important as their obtaining the three main Kriegsmarine codes, laying the foundation for its greatest success, the interception of the Zimmermann telegram.

With access to these codes and the backlog of previously unreadable diplomatic signals already in Room 40's records, Young and his team were able to track the extent of the more or less worldwide German espionage and subversion operations in which, by 1915, their embassies in Madrid and Washington were deeply involved. With this knowledge, Hall was able to supply sufficient information to the authorities within the Empire to curtail such activities. The espionage operation in the Persian Gulf was quickly shut down. Hall soon became aware of the activities of an American-based network of Indian nationalist agents, run first by one Ram Chandar and then by a Dr Chakravati. He did not take them very seriously and as their cables to Berlin sometimes supplied him with valuable information and as they consumed extensive subventions from the German Embassy, he did not identify the network to the American authorities until after their declaration of war in April 1917.

In August 1914 the German Ambassador in Washington, Johann Heinrich Count von Bernstorff, was in Berlin. He conferred with Rudolf Nadolny, the head of Section 3P of the General Staff responsible for subversion, who authorised him to implement a programme of espionage designed to impede and, if possible, prevent the envisaged shipment of American munitions to Britain and France. When he returned to the US on a Dutch liner, Bernstorff took with him ample funds to finance this programme. He now had a dual role, overtly to keep the United States neutral through diplomacy and covertly to oversee the subversion and espionage programme. He was accompanied by Dr Bernhard Dernburg, a former banker and Minister for the Colonies, who was to take charge of propaganda.

The military and naval attachés in the Washington Embassy, Captains Franz von Papen and Karl Boy-Ed, directly oversaw the ever-escalating espionage operation. Von Papen, an arrogant cavalry officer, who never attempted to conceal his contempt for America and Americans, was one of the more objectionable characters of the period. Fortunately for his adversaries, his love for intrigue and subversion exceeded his ability and he succeeded in leaving a bizarre trail of evidence which pointed straight to him. His masters in Berlin were clearly dissatisfied with him and in the spring of 1915 they insinuated another agent, Franz von Rintelen, a reserve naval officer, the self-styled Dark Invader, into the US. Von Rintelen knew the country well and he was to cross Hall's path on many occasions over the next quarter of a century.

Room 40's acquisition of the diplomatic codes provided valuable intelligence of a potentially more dangerous German threat to Britain than the rather risible espionage operations in India and Persia. From the outset of war the Washington Embassy had been intriguing with the leaders of Clann Na Gael, the radical Irish nationalist movement in New York. Its most important figures, the veteran Fenian, John Devoy, the publisher of the *Gaelic American*, and Judge Daniel Cohalan, both of whom nursed an obsessive hatred for Britain, were far more intransigent than the Parliamentary Nationalist party in Ireland, led by John Redmond. They had close links with Sinn Fein and the Irish National Volunteers, the two main extremist groups in Ireland.

Although Ireland had come close to civil war in 1914, Redmond and the Unionist leader, Sir Edward Carson, had agreed a truce and many thousands of Irishmen, Protestant and Catholic alike, had volunteered for service in the British Army, judging that Britain's fight was also Ireland's.

Devoy had for almost fifty years remained single-mindedly devoted to the cause of Irish independence. Cohalan was a major figure in Tammany Hall and had been indicted for bribery when serving as New York's Commissioner of Public Buildings. Despite this questionable record, he had, in 1913, become a Justice of the New York State Supreme Court.

As an officer in the British Consular Service, Sir Roger Casement had acquired an international reputation for his reports uncovering the vicious ill-treatment of native workers in the Belgian Congo and in the Putumayo basin of the Amazon. He had retired in 1913 on grounds of ill-health and had returned to his native Ireland where he quickly expressed his support for Irish nationalism and joined the armed Irish National Volunteers. At the outbreak of war he was in New York working closely with the leaders of Clann Na Gael to foment trouble in Ireland. As early as August 24 1914 Devoy had met Bernstorff in New York and had briefed him on the prospects for an armed uprising in Ireland and asked for military assistance including the provision of arms. Following in the footsteps of earlier radical nationalists, who had believed that Britain's difficulty was Ireland's opportunity, Devoy, Cohalan and Casement had no compunction in accepting German financial assistance and arms.

One of the earliest cables decoded by the political section of Room 40 had been sent by Bernstorff to the Imperial Chancellor, Bethmann-Hollweg, on September 27 1914:

> We are most likely to find friends if we give freedom to oppressed people, such as the Pole, the Finns and the Irish … I recommend falling in with Irish wishes, provided that there are many Irishmen who are prepared to help us. The formation of an Irish Legion from Irish prisoners of war would be a great idea if it could only be carried out.[19]

By the time Hall had become DNI, the activities of the Irish extremists in New York were well-known in Whitehall and particularly to Basil Thomson, Hall's ally at Scotland Yard. In October 1914, Casement travelled from America to Berlin via Norway. On November 20 the German government assured him of its support for an independent Ireland. With its permission but with an almost total lack of success, he attempted to suborn Irish prisoners of war to join an Irish Legion to fight Britain. His other objective was to arrange for supplies of German arms to be landed from a ship carrying a neutral flag on a remote beach on the west coast of Ireland, where, so he believed, substantial support existed for an armed uprising.

Throughout the war, Hall and Thomson maintained constant surveillance over the activities of the Irish extremists with considerable success owing to Room 40's possession of the diplomatic decrypts. Without this knowledge, the 1916 Easter Rising might have developed into an armed insurrection that would certainly have diverted resources from the Western Front.

Notes

[1] James p.61
[2] Roskill *Hankey* p.159
[3] James p.63
[4] CAC HALL 3/7
[5] Ibid
[6] TNA ADM 116/1437B Dardanelles Commission Proceedings p.282 paras. 4915 & 4916
[7] Ibid. paras 4902-14
[8] Quoted in Massie p.470
[9] TNA AIR 1/2387
[10] Marder *From the Dardanelles to Oran* pp.31-32
[11] Aspinall-Oglander *Military Operations Gallipoli* p.105
[12] Roskill pp.159-160 & 208
[13] Ibid. p.159
[14] Beesly *Very Special Admiral* p.101
[15] Jenkins *Churchill* p.283
[16] Freeman 'The Zimmermann Telegram Revisited: A Reconciliation of the Primary Sources' *Cryptologia* April 2006 p.140-141
[17] CAC DENN 1/2
[18] Friedman & Mendelsohn *The Zimmermann Telegram of January 16 1917* p.28
[19] James pp.43-44

CHAPTER VI

Unrestricted Submarine Warfare: the Sinking of Lusitania

The Kriegsmarine, like the Royal Navy, had originally considered the submarine purely as a defensive weapon. The Navy's increasingly effective blockade of Germany and their ability to bottle up the German surface fleet in the North Sea forced the Admiralstab to reconsider their role. In the early months of the war, their U-boats had achieved considerable success against warships in an offensive capacity, sinking the battleship HMS *Formidable* in the English Channel as well as four cruisers, three in a single morning. Jellicoe, ever cautious, had felt it prudent to move the Grand Fleet to Loch Ewe on the west coast of Scotland until he was satisfied that Scapa Flow was secure against submarine attack.

The Kriegsmarine was fully prepared to use the U-boats aggressively against merchant shipping, as Fisher, with his remarkable ability to foresee events, had forecast. In the early months of the war, they had adhered to the accepted rules of Cruiser Warfare, confirmed by the Hague Conventions of 1899 and 1907, which stipulated that a warship could enforce a stop-and-search order against a merchant ship. If a vessel attempted to escape or resist or if it was escorted by a warship, it lost its immunity to attack and could be sunk by gunfire or torpedo. If it was found to be an enemy vessel or if it was carrying contraband, a merchant ship could only be sunk after adequate steps had been taken to ensure the safety of her passengers and crew. Mere suspicion of contraband did not constitute grounds for attacking a vessel without warning.

The development of the submarine had rendered the existing rules obsolete. The larger the merchant ship, the more effectively it could take aggressive action against a submarine on the surface by, for instance, ramming her before she could submerge: an action which could not be easily taken against a surface warship. Surface raiders could put a prize crew on board their prey and sail it to a friendly port and had the space for the captured passengers and crew. Submarines lacked this capacity.

In October 1914 Churchill issued instructions to British shipping companies requiring their Masters to disregard any instruction to heave to and authorising them to attack or ram U-boats. In the following month, the Admiralty tightened the blockade by designating the North Sea as a military zone, which neutral shipping entered at its peril. These orders were a clear breach, at least in spirit, of cruiser rules and Germany soon followed Britain in abandoning the prevailing practice. Admiral Alfred von Tirpitz, the domineering State Secretary for the Navy, supported by several other Admirals, strongly advocated instituting a policy of unrestricted submarine warfare. Early in 1915 the submarine hawks had succeeded in overcoming the objections of the Foreign Office, understandably worried at the adverse effects on neutral opinion – particularly in the US – and in convincing the Kaiser. On 4 February the Kaiser told his submarine commanders that from 18 February the waters surrounding the British Isles would become a war zone in which any enemy and by implication any neutral vessels could be sunk. In a clear attempt to deter neutral shipping from sailing into the zone, neutral citizens were strongly warned against either travelling on or shipping goods through the zone, 'as torpedoing of neutral shipping cannot always be avoided'. The Kaiser advised his captains: 'if it is possible … to save the crews … do it … if you cannot save them, then it cannot be helped.'

From the outset several U-boat captains including Kapitanleutnant Walther Schwieger, who later sank *Lusitania*, had no compunction in attacking neutral shipping in the war zone. When the Admiralstab initiated unrestricted submarine warfare in February 1915, its U-boats were already operating in the Irish Sea against merchant ships carrying cargoes of war supplies from America.

By February 1915 Hope was using the signal traffic intercepted by Room 40 to prepare a daily analysis of the operational strength, movement and location of the German U-boat fleet. His task was made easier by the frequency of the German radio traffic, transmitted by their high-power station at Norddeich in Schleswig-Holstein (an example of the over-centralisation that wireless tended to encourage). The Führer der Unterbooten (FdU), the senior officer commanding submarines, customarily sent detailed and extremely precise instructions to his U-boat commanders while they were at sea. This traffic continued for the first two or three days of each U-boat's voyage until they passed beyond radio range, during which time the U-boats habitually radioed reports of their position as often as every three hours. This information was of great potential value to the Admiralty as it gave it the power to track each U-boat's path with a reasonable degree of accuracy at least in the early stages of its voyage and to warn local commanders of the threat to warships and merchant shipping where the submarine was likely to penetrate. Once returning U-boats were again in radio range their commanders would report their position, expected time of arrival and details of any sinkings, as Schwieger had after he had sunk *Lusitania*.

Beesly wrote: 'Room 40 knew the total strength of the U-boat fleet, the rate at which it was growing, the number of U-boats at sea or in port, losses, as evidenced by the failure of a U-boat to return, and, in most cases, the size of the threat in any particular area.' He added an important caveat: 'It was information of enormous value, but it did not mean that the position of each and every U-boat on patrol could be pinpointed with any degree of accuracy; the sea was vast, weather and other conditions were unpredictable, and the decisions of individual U-boat commanding officers impossible to guess.'[1]

Hope's daily reports were sent only to Churchill, Fisher, Wilson and Oliver. Hall and the German section of the Naval Intelligence Division were not automatically in the loop. Nor was the Trade Division, responsible for liaising with the shipping lines. According to Beesly, its Director, Captain Richard Webb, may not even have known of Room 40's existence. Neither Hall nor Webb had direct access to its U-boat traffic analysis. As a decrypting centre, Room 40 was not permitted to track the positions either of warships or of merchant shipping. This might not have been a serious defect if an effective tracking operation had been set up elsewhere in the Admiralty. This restricted distribution of the traffic analysis constituted a serious weakness in the system with adverse consequences, which were not be rectified until much later in the war.

In 1915 and indeed until the inception of convoy in April 1917, British merchant shipping was largely left to fend for itself almost on a peacetime basis and Admiralty instructions to their Masters were generally optional rather than compulsory. Nevertheless, confronted with the intelligence that U-boats would be targeting merchant shipping in addition to warships and troopships, Oliver took decisive action to protect some larger merchant ships with important cargoes, ordering them to be held in port or diverted. On January 30th U-21 had sunk three unarmed merchant ships in the Irish Sea, close to the entrance to the port of Liverpool. Although the U-boat had obeyed cruiser rules, Oliver diverted two eastbound Cunarders, *Transylvania* and *Ausonia,* into the Irish port of Queenstown where they arrived on 31 January and 3 February. The two liners were detained there for several days until Oliver was able to provide a destroyer escort for the rest of their voyage to Liverpool.

The death of a liner

The Cunarder *Lusitania*, the first Transatlantic express liner to make the crossing in five days, was one of the most prestigious ships in the British merchant fleet. Since entering service in 1907, the German establishment had regarded her with intense suspicion, almost loathing.

In August 1914, *Lusitania* and her sister ship *Mauretania* had briefly been commandeered as armed merchant cruisers. Before work could start on their conversion the Admiralty decided that the two great Cunarders were too large and vulnerable to be used in this role. That September *Lusitania* was put back onto the Atlantic run while her sister ship was laid up.

At the end of that month, the Secretary to the Admiralty, Sir William Graham Greene, (uncle of the novelist), invoked the terms of the agreement by which the Admiralty had provided financial support for the construction of the two new Cunarders. Greene told the Chairman of Cunard, Alfred Booth, that the cargo space of *Lusitania* and the other Cunarders on the North Atlantic run was to be placed at the Admiralty's disposal to facilitate the rapid transport of vitally needed military supplies, purchased from the US. The Masters of these liners would be subject to Admiralty instructions at sea and Cunard would only be permitted to contact their ships through naval channels. Booth objected to the Admiralty's decision, particularly the proposal to use the liner to run military supplies. He told Greene that he would have preferred to lay her up for the duration. Greene overruled him and under the terms of what now looked like a Faustian deal struck by his predecessor, Booth had little option but to agree to the Admiralty's demands.

On March 3 1915 a signal from the Norddeich transmitter informed U-boats that *Lusitania* was expected to arrive in Liverpool on either of the two following days. At Cunard's request the Trade Division signalled her Master, Captain Dow: 'Owners advise keep well out. Time arrival to cross bar [the Mersey Bar, a sandbank guarding entry to the port of Liverpool] without waiting.' The Admiralty had been given a clear indication of her status as a most important target. Oliver ordered two destroyers, stationed at Milford Haven, to meet her in St. George's Channel and escort her into Liverpool. As the destroyers were not carrying merchant Navy codes and as Dow, reasonably, refused to transmit his position en clair, they failed to make contact until the liner was off North Wales on the last leg of her voyage. A second signal from Norddeich stated that *Lusitania* was due to sail on her next voyage on March 10. Oliver reacted by holding the liner in Liverpool until March 20 by which time the decrypts indicated that no U-boats were operating close to the liner's course.

The first serious breach of cruiser rules had occurred on March 27. U-28, operating in St George's Channel between Wales and Ireland, the sea lane which led directly to Liverpool, sank the cargo liner *Falaba* bound from Liverpool for West Africa, which had ignored her orders to stop. Her Commander eventually forced the liner to heave to and gave her passengers and crew only five minutes to take to the boats. Before this process could be completed, a British trawler appeared and the U-boat promptly torpedoed the liner. She was evidently carrying a cargo of high explosives which blew up and *Falaba* sank immediately with the loss of 104 of the 250 people aboard.

Despite this success the U-boat command was not without its troubles. The defences installed by the Navy in the Straits of Dover were proving effective. As a result, the submarines were forced to take the long voyage round the west coasts of Scotland and Ireland to reach their hunting grounds off the south of Ireland, where the incoming traffic carrying the vitally needed munitions supplies from North America had to pass. The time the predators could spend on patrol was severely limited.

By mid-April the disinformation planted by Hall purporting to indicate an invasion of Schleswig-Holstein had reached the Admiralstab. Several U-boats were retained in German waters to meet this imaginary threat. To increase the pressure on the U-boat command, Hall had circulated false intelligence that a large number of British troop transports were due to sail from southern and western ports. The General Staff demanded that the Kriegsmarine take offensive action. In retrospect, this deception was a double-edged sword.

On 25 April three oceangoing submarines, U-20, U-27 and U-30, were ordered to sea with instructions to attack merchant ships, warships and troop transports. U-20 was to patrol the Irish Sea and Liverpool Bay, U-27 the approaches to the Bristol Channel and U-30 the western end of the English Channel. U-20, commanded by Walter Schwieger, delayed by repairs, did not sail from the submarine base at Emden until 30 April, five days after her sisters, and the day before *Lusitania* left New York. Although these signals were intercepted by Room 40, Oliver did not pass this intelligence to the Trade Division or to the Vice-Admiral, Queenstown, Sir Charles Coke, responsible for Irish coastal waters.

The German agents in New York were well aware that British and French liners, including *Lusitania*, were carrying war supplies, which constituted contraband under international law. On April 21st, George Viereck, an undercover agent and the editor and publisher of a pro-German newspaper *The Fatherland*, subsidised by the Embassy in Washington, convened a meeting of leading members of the city's German-American community. They adopted an aggressive approach, placing newspaper advertisements designed to dissuade American passengers from sailing on British or French ships. These exhortations would be timed to coincide with the departure of the next large liner. Bernstorff endorsed Viereck's project and gave the advertisements greater effect by publishing them in the Embassy's name. On Saturday 1 May, the day *Lusitania* sailed, the advertisement appeared in seven morning papers in New York, two in Philadelphia and one in Boston. It read:

TRAVELERS intending to embark on the Atlantic voyage are reminded that a state of war exists between Germany and her allies and Great Britain and her allies; that the zone of war includes the waters adjacent to the British Isles: that in accordance with formal notice given by the Imperial German Government, vessels flying the flag of Great Britain, or any of her allies, are liable to destruction in those waters and that travelers sailing in the war zone on ships of Great Britain or her allies do so at their own risk.

The timing notwithstanding, it was aimed not merely at *Lusitania* passengers but all travellers intending to make the voyage on allied ships. It immediately created a media sensation, although editorial comment tended to be dismissive. Captain Gaunt did not share this complacent view. Instantly understanding the advertisement's sinister implications, he lost no time in wiring it to Hall, who in turn informed Oliver.

At 12.30 EST that day *Lusitania*, now commanded by Captain Thomas Turner, sailed from New York with 1,265 passengers and a crew of 694 on board. Virtually all the cargo carried on what proved to be her last voyage was contraband within the strict terms of the law.

The ominous concurrence of the advertisement with Room 40's detailed information on U-20's instructions and destination should have set alarm bells ringing in the Admiralty. It is instructive to examine why it did not. On 25 April, Room 40 had intercepted Bauer's instructions to U-30 setting out the patrol areas for her and her two sisters, including U-20, detailed for the Irish Sea. On 1 May, the day after U-20 had left Emden, Hope's traffic analysis recorded 'She was at sea since April 30th: gone NW; under orders for Irish Sea.' Surprisingly in view of U-30's destination, this intelligence was not passed on to Admiral Coke or to the Director of the Trade Division.

Oliver reacted forcefully by sending detailed orders to warships. The battleship HMS *Orion* had been refitting in Devonport and was due to rejoin the Grand Fleet at Scapa Flow. Oliver delayed her departure by two days until he could be reasonably certain that U-30 was no longer in the sea lanes south west of England. He finally instructed her to sail on 4 May, escorted by four destroyers, and with specific orders to steer a course 50 miles west of the Scilly Islands and 100 miles off the Irish Coast. The cruiser HMS *Gloucester*, returning from the Mediterranean Fleet, was ordered to keep 60 miles west of Finisterre, the westernmost point of the French Coast, and to steer a mid-channel course when South of Ireland, whilst zigzagging and maintaining a speed of twenty knots. At 12.51 pm on 7 May, less than two hours before *Lusitania* was torpedoed, Oliver sent a signal to the Admiral at Devonport, instructing the cruiser HMS *Duke of Edinburgh*, due to sail for Scapa, to keep 100 miles off the coast of Ireland and pass 50 miles west of the Scottish island of St Kilda.

The precision of these orders contrasts sharply with the signals sent to the Masters of merchant ships, including Turner aboard *Lusitania*, which in comparison appear vague and obscure. Historian David Stafford has suggested a possible explanation for this disparity:

> ... an Admiralty mindset slow to wake up to the ruthless nature of modern war at sea and still convinced that merchant ships should be treated differently from warships. Although the War Staff had used information derived from the decrypts to warn warship captains of possible submarine attack, they did not consider merchant ships to be at great risk. Nor did they have any system either to monitor or to instruct them to alter their course.[2]

The failure to provide an escort for *Lusitania* has given rise to accusations of conspiracy. The reality is far more prosaic. The Kriegsmarine's unrestricted submarine campaign had not resulted in the expected degree of merchant ship losses. In the final analysis they did not have the number of submarines to achieve their objectives. As Churchill pointedly told the House of Commons after the sinking:

> We do sometimes attempt ... to provide escorts for vessels carrying troops, munitions ... and cargoes vitally needed ... our principle is that the merchant traffic must look after itself ... shocking exceptions like this ought not to divert the attention of the House, or the world ... from the main fact that almost the entire trade of these Islands is being carried on without appreciable loss.[3]

A degree of complacency about the safety of merchant ships had set in. *Lusitania* had survived in March to reach Liverpool without an escort, save on the final approaches to the port. Oliver may have reasoned (if the word 'reason' is applicable to such thinking) that if she had escaped that earlier submarine threat she might do so again. Prevailing belief inside the Admiralty held that speed per se could enable a merchant ship to escape from a submarine. One highly respected contemporary authority did not share the Admiralty's complacency. Three days after the tragedy, J. R. Thursfield, the veteran Naval Correspondent of *The Times*, wrote:

> ... even if the vessel had been proceeding at full speed, providing that she was placed favourably for the discharge of a torpedo from a lurking submarine, this alone would not have been sufficient to save her. As I have pointed out, over and over again, the rate at which a ship is travelling is no certain protection against torpedo attack.[4]

The Admiralty had failed to appreciate that the governing consideration was not the speed of a submerged submarine, less than 10 knots, but that a torpedo fired from a U-boat hidden below the surface could run at 40 knots, almost twice as fast as *Lusitania*'s top speed of 21 knots on her last voyage with only three of her four boiler rooms operational.

A signal from Norddeich, intercepted on March 27, had revealed that the Kriegsmarine had captured the principal British merchant naval code. Until a replacement code could be supplied to every important vessel, a procedure which would necessarily be time-consuming, Oliver quite reasonably refused to send wireless messages to merchant vessels instructing them to change routes, noting that that this would only inform German submarines where to look for prey. It appears that this instruction was not sent to Queenstown.

Schwieger cleared Fastnet, the customary landfall on the south–west coast of Ireland, around 2pm on 5 May and that evening he encountered the schooner *Earl of Lathom* (132 tons) about twelve miles south of the promontory known as the Old Head of Kinsale. He surfaced, ordered the crew to take to the boats and sank the schooner by gunfire. At 8.50 pm when he was off the entrance to Queenstown harbour, he attacked a ship he described as flying Norwegian colours but his torpedo missed. In fact, his intended prey was the British-registered *Cayo Romano*. Her officers notified the attack to the Navy when she arrived at Queenstown later that evening. Before midnight the news of both incidents had been passed on to the Admiralty. The War Staff was thus fully aware that a U-boat was operating less than twenty miles from Queenstown on the main shipping lanes between North America and Britain and directly in the path of *Lusitania*, then still several hundred miles west of Fastnet. Although the danger was clear and present, the alarm bells still did not sound at the Admiralty. The stage had been set for disaster.

Meanwhile Schwieger was continuing his voyage eastwards. On the following day, 6 May, he sank two cargo liners, *Candidate* and *Centurion*, outward bound from Liverpool, south-east of the Coningbeg lightship at the western entrance to St George's Channel. A Naval Auxiliary Patrol Boat rescued 44 members of *Candidate*'s crew and landed them at Milford Haven at 3.00 am on the morning of 7 May. *Centurion*'s crew was picked up by a trawler and landed at Rosslare on the Irish side of St George's Channel early the following morning, by which time both the Admiralty and the Navy at Queenstown were aware of the fate of the two cargo liners. That afternoon the cautious Schwieger, short of fuel and with only three torpedoes left, took stock of his position. He recorded in his war diary:

> Passage to St. George's Channel has already consumed so much fuel oil that a return from Liverpool southward around Ireland would no longer be possible. I shall commence return passage when down to two-fifths fuel,

avoiding the North Channel [between Ireland and Scotland] if at all possible because of the type of patrolling experienced there by U-20 on her previous operation ... Have therefore decided to remain to the south of the entrance to the Bristol Channel and attack steamers until down to two-fifths fuel, especially as there are greater attacking opportunities with *less opposition* [author's emphasis] than in the Irish Sea off Liverpool.

Schwieger had correctly appreciated the low priority and insufficient naval resources allocated by the Admiralty to the waters south of Ireland – an area which was rapidly becoming Britain's maritime Achilles heel. Almost 24 hours after Queenstown had become aware of U-20's presence in such a busy sea lane, Admiral Coke finally took some action, sending a vague and imprecise signal to all British shipping in the area, 'Submarines active off S. Irish coast'. This message was received on board *Lusitania* at 7.52 pm that evening. A second signal, sent 15 minutes later, reminded Captains to avoid headlands, pass harbours at full speed and steer a mid-channel course and those bound for Liverpool were instructed to take on a pilot at the Mersey Bar, a shoal which guarded the entrance to the estuary.

If the alarm bells had been slow to sound in the Admiralty and at Queenstown, the danger signal rang out clearly in Liverpool. By the morning of May 7, the city's shipping community was aware of the loss of *Candidate* and *Centurion*. Alfred Booth arrived at Cunard's offices on the Liverpool waterfront a desperately worried man. Concerned for *Lusitania*'s safety, he called on Admiral Stileman, the SNO at Liverpool, demanding that Turner be specifically warned of the dangers lying directly in his course. The outcome of this meeting is unclear. Booth apparently believed that Stileman had given him to understand that the liner was to be diverted into Queenstown. In fact it was the Admiralty, effectively Oliver, and not Stileman, who had the authority to issue instructions to Turner or, for that matter, any other Master.

At 9 am GMT, Schwieger finally decided to start his return journey to Emden, looking for prey further west. *Lusitania* had made landfall around noon, clearing Fastnet Rock by 18½ miles, a wider margin than on any of her eight previous wartime voyages. Although Turner was criticised heavily by the Admiralty for the course he took after passing Fastnet, his navigation of the liner did conform to the (admittedly vague) Admiralty instructions in his possession. It kept him well clear of the Irish coast and would have brought him into a good position to alter course to the northwards at the appropriate time, entering St Georges's Channel midway between Coningbeg and the Smalls, the rocks on the Welsh side of the channel.

Turner was steaming at 18 knots, three knots slower than the liner's top speed with only three boiler rooms operating. He had chosen this speed as he was faced with the obstacle of the Mersey Bar, the sandbank which guarded the entry to the port of Liverpool. A ship of *Lusitania*'s draft could only cross this barrier in a period of three hours either side of high tide at 6.53 am on 8 May. Knowing the liner's vulnerability to a submarine attack if she had to wait outside the Bar, Turner was anxious to avoid arriving there before 4 am, the earliest time when he could safely cross the sandbank. He had decided not to risk stopping for a pilot as Admiralty Instructions required and to take the liner over the Bar himself in line with a discretion permitted him by Cunard.

Turner's anxiety was increased by the arrival of a further Admiralty signal sent via Queenstown, received at 11.52 am: 'Submarines active in southern part of Irish Channel, last heard of 20 miles south of Coningbeg Light vessel.' The Admiralty had instructed Admiral Coke 'Make certain *Lusitania* gets this.' It is likely that this signal was sent in response to the urgent representations Booth had made to Admiral Stileman earlier that morning. This information put Turner in a quandary as it indicated that a submarine was lurking directly in his path and close to the entrance to St George's Channel. He was not to know that this information, based on the sinkings of *Candidate* and *Centurion,* was out of date.

Turner had no option but to use his own judgment. It was his responsibility to bring his large and valuable ship, with nearly 2,000 people on board, into Liverpool safely and expeditiously. Until he had received this signal and despite the Admiralty's criticism after the event, Turner had steered what could reasonably have been described as a mid-channel course. He had intended to clear both the Old Head and Coningbeg by between 18 and 20 miles. He had several problems to take into account. He had to navigate St George's Channel at night with the likelihood of being delayed by fog and he had to cross the Mersey Bar before 9.30 am on the following morning. In such a situation his first priority, as an experienced and cautious master, would have been to establish his actual position.

He could either come inshore or stand further out to sea. The second option had one major disadvantage. It would have added several hours to the time the vessel had to stay at sea in an area in which the Admiralty had just advised them that submarines (plural) were operating, thus increasing her exposure to attack. While we know that there was only one submarine off the South coast of Ireland, Turner did not.

The information he had just received from the Admiralty indicated that submarines were operating close to the lightship, 75 nautical miles or four hours steaming distance ahead of him. On this basis he would have been justified in believing that he could steer the steady course for the thirty minutes or so required to take the accurate four-point bearing he needed to steer a safe course up St George's Channel at night and ready his vessel for her final approach to Liverpool, without hazarding his vessel. Once the bearing had been completed, he could set course to pass close to Coningbeg and devote his entire attention to coping with the submarine menace.

Bringing *Lusitania* inshore shortened the time she had to remain at sea, retaining the advantage of time in hand to meet the tide at the Mersey Bar. Turner had no margin for error in taking an inshore course at night and as he had pointedly told Lord Mersey during the subsequent Inquiry: 'My Lord, I do not navigate my ship by guesswork.' He probably reasoned that steering an inshore course would put sufficient distance between *Lusitania* and the reported position of the U-boats to avoid them.

Turner's instinct and experience led him to opt for an inshore course. In the light of the inadequate information and the absence of any specific instructions provided by the Admiralty, his decision appears rational and defensible. At 12.40 pm, Turner ordered a change of course of 30° to port. When he turned to starboard one hour later and resumed his original course of S 87 E magnetic, *Lusitania* was approximately 9 nautical miles closer inshore.

Schwieger, then on the surface, had sighted the liner at 1.20 pm and had concluded that he could not intercept her if she maintained her then course of N 63 E. He recorded that he submerged to periscope depth at 1.25 pm: '... and proceeded at high speed on intercepting course toward steamer in the hope that the steamer will alter course to starboard along the Irish Coast. At 1440 CET (1.40 pm GMT) the steamer turns to starboard ... permitting an approach for a shot. Proceed at high speed until 1500 (2.00 pm) in order to gain bearing ...'

U-20's position gave Schwieger the opportunity to get into range for a torpedo attack, provided that Turner maintained a course of S 87 E, whether he was steaming at 10 or 18 miles off the coast. Turner's decision to alter course and come inshore made Schwieger's task more difficult but alas, not difficult enough to save the liner. Ironically, if Turner had taken his peacetime course, passing the Irish headlands at a distance of about one mile, Schwieger would probably have been unable to have intercepted.

At 2.10 pm, U-20 fired one torpedo at *Lusitania*, then 11 miles south-south-west of the Old Head of Kinsale. It hit close to the bulkhead between the two forward boiler rooms, an area where the liner was particularly vulnerable. The resultant asymmetrical flooding caused her to founder only eighteen minutes later with the loss of 1,198 lives – including 125 American citizens.

The Admiralty's reaction was to scapegoat the hapless Captain Turner, relying on a subjective and hastily compiled report prepared by Captain Webb, the Director of the Trade Division, on the grounds that he had disregarded their instructions to steer a mid-channel course, to zigzag and to avoid proximity to harbours. The tone was set by Churchill, who wrote in the report's margin: 'I consider the Admiralty case against the Captain should be pressed before Lord Mersey by a skilful counsel and that Captain Webb should attend as witness, if not employed as an assessor. We should pursue the Captain without check.'[5] Only days earlier he had told the House of Commons that he did not wish to heap any blame on the Captain of *Lusitania* before the loss had been fully investigated.

An examination of the allegations laid against Turner by the Admiralty would indicate that on the charge of failure to zigzag, the Scots Law verdict of 'not proven' might be applicable. Their other charges, the reduction of speed and the decision to steer an inshore course, do not stand up to scrutiny. In his report, Captain Webb was critical of Turner for not steering a course well out of sight of the Irish Coast. This was written with the benefit of hindsight and begs the question why Turner never received any explicit instruction as to the course he should steer. The subsequent Inquiry was headed by a senior Judge, Lord Mersey. Butler Aspinall, a specialist shipping lawyer, representing Cunard and Captain Turner, exposed serious weaknesses in the Admiralty's case. Mersey, supported by his naval and merchant navy assessors, announced his decision on 17 July. He refused to play the Admiralty's gambit that Turner should be found responsible for the disaster, placing the entire blame on Imperial Germany.

Nevertheless, Mersey's verdict got the Admiralty off the hook. Their responsibility for the loss was considerable and their systems had conspicuously failed. One Admiral, Alexander Duff, saw the situation for what it was; later in the war he became the first Director of the Admiralty's Anti-Submarine Division and then Assistant Chief of the Naval Staff responsible for the entire campaign against the U-boats. Duff commented trenchantly in his diary:

> *Lusitania* is sunk off the Irish Coast ... the disaster lies at the hands of the Admiralty. They knew that the ship was marked as an object lesson of German "frightfulness" and yet they allowed her to run at scheduled time and normal course and provided no protection. Indirectly the Dardanelles operation contributed; the T.B.D.s [destroyers] that should be guarding merchant shipping are being used there.[6]

In April 1975, Edward Beach, a retired Captain U.S.N. and a distinguished World War II submariner told Paul Ryan, the co-author of *The Lusitania Disaster*, a book which was highly critical of Turner, that the warnings and cautionary instructions Turner had received were not adequate in the circumstances.

Duff and Ryan, writing 60 years apart, both attributed the loss of *Lusitania* to a serious breakdown in intelligence. In a 1982 interview, naval historian Stephen Roskill was pressed to explain the Admiralty's omissions. He cited: '… bad control of merchant shipping, because we hadn't learnt how to do it … bad use of intelligence as regards merchant ships … inefficiencies and excessive secrecies in all parts of the Admiralty.'[7]

The Admiralty had the necessary raw intelligence, the ominous advertisement, the knowledge through the decrypts of U-20's destination and instructions and finally Schwieger's appearance off the south coast of Ireland sinking three merchant ships directly in the liner's track. The War Staff's reaction was patently ineffectual. Not only were the warnings sent to Turner vague and imprecise, they failed to order him to divert either round the north of Ireland (an option which was viable as late as 6 am on May 7) or into Queenstown as they had ordered the Cunarders in similar circumstances three months earlier. Diversion or more explicit warnings would have averted disaster.

In the final analysis, *Lusitania* was doomed by what might be described as Admiralty overload, resulting from over-centralisation, the lack of operational experience and risk-assessment and an ineffective staff-system – particularly the inadequate interface between intelligence and operations – which was to plague the Navy for the first two years of the war, most notably during the Battle of Jutland.

Conspiracy?

An event as controversial and dramatic as the torpedoing of *Lusitania* inevitably attracted conspiracy theorists. Conspiracy has many godparents, not least the obsessive secrecy of British Government departments. Although the Admiralty was well aware of the circumstances surrounding the liner's loss, it deliberately chose to 'let sleeping dogs lie'. Their reticence only fired the imaginations of the theorists. Two men in particular have asserted that Churchill and the War Staff, including Hall, deliberately abandoned the liner for political ends.

In the UK edition of *Room 40*, published in 1982, Beesly wrote:

> … the idea of a plot by Churchill positively to sink the ship strikes this author as untenable. Putting aside all questions of humanity, it would have left so much to chance. Although Room 40's knowledge of the movements and intentions of German U-boats at this time was much greater than had previously been supposed, it was not precise. Neither U 30 nor U 20 were in fact where the intercepted orders would have led Oliver or Wilson to believe they would be.[8]

Beesly could have mentioned that a conspiracy would have entailed a constant stream of signals traffic from the Admiralty to *Lusitania* routed through Queenstown. The record is clear: only four naval signals were received on board the liner in the 24 hours before the sinking. Many officers in the Admiralty or at Queenstown would have had to be involved – too large a number to keep the plot secret.

Beesly hedged his bets: 'It is ... far less easy to discount entirely the possibility that the *Lusitania* was deliberately put at risk, that she was knowingly permitted to stand into danger, a danger which must have been apparent to Coke at Queenstown and to Oliver at the Admiralty.'[9] Mistakes and omissions are a common factor in *every* significant military disaster. Despite their failings or inaction in the days leading up to the sinking, neither Admiral would purposely have hazarded the liner. At the very least, Beesly's comment is unwarranted.

In the later American and UK editions of *Room 40*, published two years before Beesly's death in 1986, he shifted his stance. Without giving any supporting reasons, he asserted (reluctantly) that there had been a conspiracy deliberately to put the *Lusitania* at risk hoping that even an abortive attack on her would bring the United States into war. He noted that such a conspiracy could only have been effected with Churchill's express approval. (Beesly's account of the sinking is itself inaccurate. He insisted that the torpedo struck in the liner's cargo hold, echoing an opinion voiced by Light and other conspiracy addicts. Survivor evidence and Schwieger's war diary confirm that it hit aft of the bridge.)[10]

In attacking Churchill, the conspiracy theorists conveniently overlook the fact that he had left the Admiralty to travel to Paris on official business at around noon on May 5, several hours before Schwieger had announced his presence off the south coast of Ireland by sinking *Earl of Lathom*. His actions on and immediately after 7 May do not suggest that he was the mastermind behind a conspiracy to engineer *Lusitania*'s destruction. Had he been so involved, he would surely have returned post haste to London on hearing the news of her sinking to actively direct the next stage of the alleged plot, luring the US into the war. Instead he lingered in France for three days.

The second main theorist is the journalist and author Christopher Hitchens, a man who has manifested an animosity to Churchill. In his book *Blood, Class and Nostalgia*, published in 1990, he accepts Beesly's conversion to the conspiracy theory. Hitchens wrote: 'The Admiralty in 1915 possessed a department under the direction of Winston Churchill. It was called Room 40 and its job was ... intelligence and deception.'[11] In reality it was a cryptological bureau and did not form part of the naval intelligence division until May 1917. He asserts: 'In the first half of the century, British intelligence was principally a machine for involving the United States in war on the British side.'[12] He recycles a number of long discredited myths: 'Escort ships were deployed away from the scene of danger. Churchill's Admiralty conveyed no warnings to the ship.'[13]

UNRESTRICTED SUBMARINE WARFARE: THE SINKING OF *LUSITANIA*

He insinuates from Mersey's conclusion that the liner had been sunk by two torpedoes that he had deliberately covered up the fact that she had only been hit by one. During the war the Admiralty were justified in keeping this knowledge a tightly held secret to avoid revealing their interception of the Kriegsmarine signal traffic. It is highly unlikely that either Mersey or his chief naval assessor, Admiral Sir Frederick Inglefield, even knew of this particular decrypt. While his Report was unsatisfactory in some respects, Hitchens's description of the inquiry as a pantomime is unsupportable. Hitchens accuses Hall of forging the notorious *Lusitania* medal. In reality the medal was genuine and had been created by a Munich goldsmith named Karl Goetz to celebrate Schwieger's achievement in sinking the liner. Under an inscription 'No Contraband' the obverse side of the medal shows the liner sinking, guns clearly visible on her deck, over a further inscription: 'The liner Lusitania sunk by a German submarine May 5 1915.' The message on the reverse was even more vicious. Under the legend 'Business above all' passengers were shown lining up to buy tickets at a Cunard booking office manned by a skeleton. They were depicted as ignoring a man reading a newspaper with a banner headline 'U Boat danger' and a top-hatted Bernstorff, shaking a warning finger. The implication was clear: the passengers who had died had only themselves to blame.

A Dutch dealer featured Goetz's *Lusitania* medal in his catalogue, attracting the eagle eye of Hall's most effective agent in Holland, Ernest Maxse, the Consul General in Rotterdam, who quickly informed Naval Intelligence in London. Hall astutely grasped its potential as a propaganda weapon. Goetz's treatment had been heavy-handed and his mistake in bringing forward the date of the sinking by two days enabled Hall to claim that it had been planned in advance. At Hall's request, Gordon Selfridge, the owner of the London department store, reproduced 300,000 copies of Goetze's medal, which were widely distributed in neutral countries to demonstrate German indifference to the loss of life.

Although Goetz's medal had been purely a private venture, allied propaganda directed by Hall successfully portrayed it as an official German project. Speaking in November 1916, Arthur Balfour strongly attacked the Kriegsmarine's war on commerce. Contrasting the high-minded proposals for conducting war at sea that Germany had presented at the 1909 Hague Conference with repeated examples of their wartime frightfulness including the recent sinking of a Norwegian merchant ship, he declared: 'What are we to make of a nation which makes such a speech ... at an assembly ... considering international law and a few years afterwards strikes a medal for sinking the *Lusitania*.'[14]

In the April 2002 issue of the *Atlantic Monthly* Hitchens revisited the subject in an article on Churchill entitled 'The Medals of his Defeats'. Against all the evidence, he repeated the charge that Churchill had deliberately put *Lusitania* at risk to bring the US into the war, repeating almost word for word the allegation Beesly had made almost twenty years earlier.

Later that year another historian, Diana Preston, revived this discredited conspiracy theory in her book *Wilful Murder*, an otherwise objective account of the liner's last voyage. Her accusation was directed, not at Churchill or Fisher, but at Hall. It appears to have been based on an inspection of Hall's papers, as she quotes the well known observation about Hall by Ed Bell, the intelligence point man at the American Embassy (quoted earlier): '... no man could fill his place – a perfectly marvelous person but the coldest blooded proposition there ever was – he'd cut out a man's heart and hand it back to him'. Bell's admiring hyperbole cannot be enough to indict Hall of conspiracy. Preston paints a dramatic picture of Hall sitting in his office at the Admiralty, aware of the threat to the liner and yet not even making a telephone call to any of his colleagues to alert them to the clear and present danger. She produces no supporting evidence and posits the incredible motive that the sinking would reflect badly on Alfred Ewing and Oliver, noting correctly that Hall was not on good terms with either man.

Her assertion reveals a lack of knowledge of the relationship between Room 40 and the intelligence division and of the difference between the interception and analysis of SIGINT. As Room 40's intelligence was both accurate and timely, Ewing had absolutely no responsibility for the loss of *Lusitania*. Hall's papers reveal the bald, definitive statement: 'I had no executive authority.'[15] He had no power to instruct any commanders ashore or afloat, particularly Coke, two ranks his senior. The Admiralty had received no intelligence of U-20's position since the sinkings of *Candidate* and *Centurion* and Hall could take no action as the day proceeded other than reminding Oliver of the threat.

Preston's animosity towards Hall is evident. She suggests, again without supporting evidence, that he advocated torturing captured German agents. Four further assertions – that his action in attempting to bribe Turkey out of her alliance with Germany was unauthorised, that he had withheld the details of the Zimmermann telegram from ministers for several days and that he had improperly released the notorious Casement black diary – are inaccurate and are refuted here. She alleged that Hall had sacrificed an agent who had purloined a German code to prevent the authorities discovering the theft. Although she does not name the agent, she is clearly referring to Alexander Szek, an Austrian national who had lived in England before 1914 and had been employed as a wireless operator at the transmitter in Brussels after the German invasion. Szek appears to have attempted to flee to England via Holland with a copy of the codebook. The most recent writer to mention Szek is Alan Judd, in his biography of Mansfield Cumming, the head of SIS. He quotes a letter from the German military governor at Charleroi to Szek's father, concluding that he was arrested by the Germans on the Belgian-Dutch frontier and subsequently shot. In March 1920, Alistair Denniston, replying to an inquiry about Szek, wrote: 'Nothing was known of this man in 40 OB [the official designation of Room 40].'[16] Preston's attack on Hall is difficult to understand as she properly concludes that: 'Far from being the subject of conspiracy, *Lusitania* ... was the victim of complacency and neglect.'[17]

We should leave the last word to specialist historians. In his 1982 interview, Stephen Roskill, who was by no means uncritical of Churchill, totally rejected the conjecture that he could have acted so ruthlessly as to allow the *Lusitania* to steam into danger. David Stafford dismisses the theory succinctly: 'Churchill was not the mainspring of a conspiracy to sink the *Lusitania* since none existed.'[18]

Notes

[1] Beesly p.91
[2] Stafford p.74
[3] Hansard May 10 1915 Quoted in Ramsay *Lusitania Saga and Myth* p.115
[4] Ramsay p.224
[5] TNA ADM 137/1058
[6] CAC Roskill Papers 3/20
[7] Roskill was interviewed by Sir Ludovic Kennedy. The transcript is in the Imperial War Museum.
[8] Beesly pp.120-121
[9] Ibid. p.121
[10] Beesly Room 40 US Edition 1983. Quoted in Hitchens *Blood, Class & Nostalgia* pp.190-191
[11] Ibid. p.189
[12] Ibid p.320
[13] Ibid. p.190
[14] *Imperial War Museum Review* Vol. 1 1986
[15] CAC HALL 3/1
[16] Judd p.370
[17] Preston *Wilful Murder* p.406
[18] Stafford p.75

CHAPTER VII

The Ides of May

By May 1915 Hall had established his influence throughout Whitehall and was considered to be at the epicentre of the intelligence world. He had gained direct access to Cabinet Ministers, notably to Asquith and to the Home Secretary, Reginald McKenna.

Like many other naval officers both afloat and in the Admiralty, Hall had welcomed Fisher's return as First Sea Lord. In the draft of his autobiography he wrote: 'In those first few weeks at any rate, the new First Sea Lord – in spite of his age – remained the tireless and exacting and magnetic figure we had long known and loved.'[1]

As early as October 1914 the future First Sea Lord, Rosslyn Wemyss, had questioned whether a Churchill–Fisher partnership could endure, perceptively forecasting that 'They will be as thick as thieves at first until they differ on some subject, probably as to who is to be No. 1, when they will begin to intrigue against each other.'[2] The equally prescient Beatty, who had worked with Churchill as his Naval Secretary, told his wife: 'The situation is curious – two very strong and clever men, one old, wily and of vast experience, one young, self-assertive, with a great self-satisfaction but unstable. They cannot work together, they cannot both run the show.'[3]

If the two men had not had very different working habits, they might well have fallen out earlier. Fisher rose early and went straight to the Admiralty and he did not stay late. By contrast Churchill breakfasted in bed, reading the newspapers and attending to correspondence. Walking through the corridors from his grace-and-favour residence at Admiralty House, he reached his desk late in the morning. After an afternoon siesta and a break for dinner he worked long into the night. In a letter to Hall in 1932, Captain T. E. Crease, who had been Fisher's Naval Assistant in 1914–15, described Churchill's nocturnal habits. Returning to the Admiralty after dinner, he would get down to business:

> … starting the nightly strafe of memoranda, full of brilliant ideas that seldom could be taken seriously in the morning. The effect often was that

Lord Fisher, having as he thought settled all outstanding matters with the First Lord before going home ... was confronted only a few hours later, in the early hours of the next morning, with an entirely fresh set of memoranda, minutes, proposals, suggestions etc. In April and May of 1915 these nearly always dealt with various phases of the Dardanelles projects, and it is no doubt that at this time the procedure had become very irksome to him, and got on his nerves, so that he started the day incensed against the First Lord.

Lord Fisher latterly also resented Mr. Churchill's habit of discussing matters, more especially with regard to the Dardanelles, with Sir A. K. Wilson and Sir Henry Jackson, before speaking with him and of thus coming to him with preconceived ideas ... I am sure that these ... matters had ... considerable influence on Lord Fisher's attitude at this time towards Mr. Churchill. Personal trifles often disturb the relations of men more than differences of opinion on grave issues.[4]

In December 1914, Fisher had told Jellicoe:

Winston has so monopolised all initiative in the Admiralty and fires off such a multitude of purely departmental memos (his power of work is absolutely amazing!) that my colleagues are no longer 'superintending Lords' but only 'the First Lord's Registry' ... and the consequence is that the Sea Lords are atrophied and their departments are run really by the Private Office, and I find it a Herculean task to get back to the right procedure and quite possibly I may have to clear out and I've warned Winston of this.[5]

Although Churchill always sounded Fisher out on operational matters, he frequently issued instructions directly to Fleet Commanders and only consulted him after the event. Marder noted:

Long before the May crisis Fisher had reluctantly become convinced ... that he and the First Lord could no longer work together. He did not carry out his many threats to resign, because of his loyalty to and affection for Churchill, his gratitude to the First Lord for having brought him back to the Admiralty, and because of Jellicoe's reiterated advice. The C-in-C pressed him to hold on, as he felt that Fisher could probably check Mr. Churchill's dangerous assumption of executive authority better than anyone else.[6]

The Dardanelles crisis proved to be the catalyst that finally destroyed the relationship. By the beginning of May, Hall and the other Divisional Directors in the Admiralty had become increasingly anxious about the deteriorating relationship between Churchill and Fisher. They feared that they were coming dangerously close to falling out over the Dardanelles campaign, which Churchill had originated and vigorously supported. During the winter of 1914–15 Fisher, who had never made any secret of his dislike for the campaign, had several times threatened to retire in protest. On each occasion he had allowed himself to be talked out of it. The enthusiasm he had displayed for a naval attack when Hall told him that the defenders had almost run out of ammunition quickly faded. After the failure of the assault on March 18, he had reverted to his original opposition to the operation.

Hall noted that Churchill was habitually usurping the First Sea Lord's executive functions. In his earlier tenure as First Sea Lord and in time of peace, Fisher had worked in reasonable harmony with successive First Lords, notably Churchill's immediate predecessor, McKenna, who did not interfere in operations. Fisher, like his predecessors, had always insisted that operational matters were his prerogative. Churchill had no such compunction. Used to getting his own way, Fisher had never had to face such a formidable adversary. Crease believed that the old Admiral was being worn down day by day with the stress of the Dardanelles and by the continual feuding with Churchill, a man of titanic intellect and mental endurance who was at the height of his powers and more than thirty years his junior. Under this stress his powerful ego was gradually retreating into paranoia.

Two incidents early in May 1915 highlight Fisher's declining mental capacity. Martin Gilbert records a bizarre event that occurred during Churchill's absence in Paris, where he was negotiating a convention to co-ordinate the operations of the allied navies in the Mediterranean after Italy joined the war on the allied side later in the month.

> When Churchill left for France on 5th May, the responsibility for the daily conduct of Admiralty affairs had fallen on Fisher … the responsibility agitated him. In an effort to soothe him Clementine Churchill invited him to luncheon at Admiralty House. All went well and the Admiral departed in a cheerful mood … some moments later she found him still lurking in the corridor. 'What is it?' she asked. 'You are a foolish woman' he replied. 'All the time you think Winston's with Sir John French he is in Paris with his mistress.' Clementine Churchill was stunned by such a wounding remark. It was for her a sure sign that Fisher's mind was unbalanced. She reported all this to her husband on his return, fearing that Fisher might break down … she later recalled that the Admiral was as nervous as a kitten.[7]

Churchill's many detractors in his lifetime and the revisionist historians since his death have never accused him of philandering. Fisher seems to have picked up and misunderstood some idle chatter among the civil servants in Churchill's private office, who would jokingly refer to his visits to France as jaunts to see the French mistress.

Fisher's behaviour after the sinking of *Lusitania* was equally irrational. On 13 May, Captain Richard Webb, the Director of the Trade Division, officially submitted his report on the loss of the liner to Oliver, who in turn sent it to the First Sea Lord. Fisher had a vengeful side to his character which had become more pronounced as he grew older. As one obituary noted: 'In later years he tended to treat those who ... found themselves in direct antagonism with a hostility which left bitter feelings behind.'[8] This was usually directed at the not inconsiderable number of Admirals with whom he had fallen out and their associates in the service. For example, after his return to the Admiralty he told Oliver that Rear-Admiral Arthur Leveson, then Director of Operations, was a traitor for no better reason than he had once been Sir William May's Flag-Captain. Willy May was a distinguished Admiral who had fallen out of favour during Fisher's earlier term as First Sea Lord. Fisher's reaction on reading Webb's somewhat subjective report suggested that he was close to losing touch with reality. Webb had blamed the negligence of her Master, the unfortunate Captain Turner, for the loss of the liner. Penning furiously in the margin of the report in his unmistakable handwriting and in the green ink he always used, Fisher minuted:

> The Master appears to have displayed an almost inconceivable negligence and one is forced to conclude that he is either utterly incompetent or he has been got at by the Germans. As Cunard would not have employed an incompetent man, the certainty is absolute that Captain Turner is not a fool but a knave. I feel absolutely certain that Turner is a scoundrel and [has] been bribed. No seaman in his senses would have acted as he did. I hope that Captain Turner will be arrested *immediately* after the inquiry *whatever* the verdict or finding might be.[9]

Hall had got on well with Churchill, who appreciated his energy and enthusiasm, qualities the First Lord fervently believed were in short supply at the Admiralty, commenting that 'He had both courage and vision – a brilliant man if ever there was one. I admired his energy and dash ... his capacity for work was almost frightening. Notes and memoranda of every conceivable subject streamed forth ... at all hours of the day and night.' At the same time, Hall had no illusions about the political head of the Navy:

> But he had the defects of his great qualities; he was essentially a 'one-man show'. It was not in his nature to allow anybody except himself to be the executive authority when any action of importance had to be taken. Even

in matters of the extremest technicality he would insist on elaborate presentation of his own views, and his powers of argument were so extraordinary that again and again tired Admiralty officials were hypnotised – I can think of no better word – into accepting opinions, which differed vastly from those they normally held.

Once, I remember, I was sent for by Mr. Churchill very late at night. He wished to discuss some point or other with me – at once. To be candid, I have not the slightest recollection what it was: I only know that his views were diametrically opposed to mine. We argued at some length. I knew I was right, but Mr. Churchill was determined to bring me round to his point of view, and he continued his argument in the most brilliant fashion. It was long after midnight, and I was dreadfully tired, but nothing seemed to tire the First Lord. He continued to talk, and I distinctly recall the odd feeling that although it would be wholly against my will, I should in a very short space of time be agreeing with everything that he said. But a bit of me rebelled, and recalling the incident of the broken shard in Kipling's Kim, I began to mutter to myself: 'My name is Hall, my name is Hall …'

Suddenly, he broke off to look frowningly at me. 'What's that you're muttering to yourself?' he demanded.

'I'm saying' I told him 'that my name is Hall because if I listen to you much longer I shall be convinced that it's Brown.'

'Then you don't agree with what I've been saying.' He was laughing heartily.

'First Lord' said I, 'I don't agree with one word of it, but I can't argue with you; I've not had the training.'

So the matter was dropped, and I went to bed.[10]

During World War II, Hall told his sister May: 'I worked with the PM in the last war and know what it means to stand up firmly for one's opinions; being at his best about midnight, he starts a hare when everyone else is tired from the day's work. One ought to apply to him the old tag – Never say No to your wife before breakfast or Yes after dinner.'[11] Beesly commented on Hall's nocturnal joust:

> Those who served closely under Churchill …in World War II would immediately recognize the truth of this story. It shows how Churchill could be weeded away from some of his more wild cat ideas by those who had the courage to stand up to him. For a mere captain from a Service whose tradition was 'theirs not to reason why …' it must have taken considerable courage.[12]

Throughout his life Hall, never lacking in moral courage, was consistently outspoken.

The final break between Churchill and Fisher came on the morning of Saturday May 15. The torpedoing of the old battleship HMS *Goliath* by a Turkish destroyer in an unprotected anchorage on the night of May 12 had indicated the fleet was even more vulnerable to attack than an understandably worried Fisher had previously supposed. He reiterated his demand that HMS *Queen Elizabeth*, the Navy's newest and fastest battleship, should immediately be brought home from the Dardanelles. On the afternoon of 14 May Churchill and Fisher met in an attempt to settle their differences and decide the changes to be made to the fleet. After a protracted but relatively harmonious discussion they eventually agreed to the replacement of *Queen Elizabeth* by two old and expendable battleships and to a number of other ship movements. By the time they had finalised these arrangements, it was well into the evening and the old Admiral was exhausted. Churchill said to him kindly: 'Now go home, Fisher, and get a good night's sleep.' Once he had left, Churchill ill-advisedly wrote a note to Fisher suggesting that two newly commissioned submarines be added to the list of the ships earmarked for the Dardanelles. Nothing could have been more guaranteed to ignite the old Admiral's latent paranoia. Churchill's private office and Crease were equally aghast that he should even have suggested altering the agreed plan. The First Lord would not even listen to their protests.

When Fisher reached the Admiralty on the following morning, 15 May, and discovered Churchill's meddling, his reason finally snapped. Without further ado the old Admiral resigned and walked out, leaving the Navy without a professional head in the middle of a war. Hall ran into him outside the Admiralty and thought that he looked extremely distressed. It was not until the following day that he was officially told that the First Sea Lord had resigned. Fisher walked round to the Treasury to break the news to Lloyd George, who vividly described his appearance: 'A combative grimness had taken the place of his usually genial greeting; the lower lip of his set mouth was thrust forward, and the droop at the corner was more marked than usual. His curiously Oriental features were more than ever those of a graven image in an Eastern temple, with a sinister frown.'[13] Lloyd George tried, without success, to persuade him to delay his resignation until the situation could be put before a special meeting of the War Cabinet. After he left the Treasury, Fisher went to ground in a room at the Charing Cross Hotel, refusing a written instruction from Asquith: 'In the name of the King, I order you to return to your post at once.' Unknown either to the Prime Minister or the First Lord, the vengeful Fisher had sent a coded message to the Leader of the Opposition, Andrew Bonar Law, a man who detested Churchill, thus exploding the crisis at the Admiralty into the political arena.

Fisher's resignation sounded the death knell for Asquith's Liberal Government. On the morning of Monday 17 May, Bonar Law called on Lloyd George at the Treasury. Law is a strangely underrated figure in British political history, whom his biographer Robert Blake dubbed the

Forgotten Prime Minister. Despite their very different political views a friendship had grown up between the two men. Law had, for some time, been chafing at the restraints of the political truce he had agreed with Asquith nine months before. In essence, the truce obliged him to support the Government and its policies without enabling him to influence them. Once Lloyd George had confirmed the extent of the disarray at the Admiralty, Law put his cards on the table. He explained that the melancholy succession of losses and setbacks and the revelations of operational and logistical shortcomings at both the Admiralty and the War Office made it impossible for him to continue the truce.

The two men quickly agreed that they could see no alternative to the formation of an all-party Government to provide for more effective direction of the War. Law made it clear that the Conservative party would insist that Churchill had to be replaced at the Admiralty. Lloyd George asked Law to wait while he went to No. 10 Downing St to see the Prime Minister where he recounted his conversation with Law. Asquith had a reputation for being averse to taking hard decisions but as Doctor Johnson once famously remarked: 'There is nothing that concentrates a man's mind so wonderfully as the knowledge that he is to be hanged.' On this occasion he quickly realised that his Government's position was beyond redemption and that Churchill could not remain as First Lord. Bonar Law was called in and told that his terms had been accepted.

Fisher's departure had left a vacuum inside the Admiralty. The remaining Sea Lords had had no responsibility for operations: the Second, Third and Fourth Sea Lords were respectively in charge of personnel and training, ordnance and warship design and construction, and supply. To put it mildly, Fisher had never gone out of his way to consult his colleagues on operational matters. The Sea Lords had been pitchforked into a situation for which they had little recent experience.

On the afternoon of May 17, Room 40 intercepted a decrypt that revealed the Hochseeflotte had put out to sea, heading for the Dogger Bank. The Second Sea Lord, Admiral Sir Frederick Hamilton, who was acting as professional head of the service in Fisher's absence, and Oliver both decided that Churchill should be immediately informed. At that moment Asquith had summoned Churchill to Downing Street to break the unpleasant news that he would have to leave the Admiralty. Hastily alerted by his private office, Churchill hurried back to the Admiralty to take charge of the threatening situation. Meantime Crease went to see Fisher and implored him to return to the Admiralty even if only while the High Seas Fleet remained at sea. He flatly refused, telling Crease that he had full confidence in Oliver's ability to handle the situation, although he knew full well that Oliver – whom he once described as a 'mule' – was grossly overworked. According to his biographer, Admiral Sir Reginald Bacon, he convinced himself that the German Fleet had put out to sea merely 'to test whether we had occult means of reading their cipher signals'[14] – a further example of his mental decline. To everyone's relief the Hochseeflotte had merely been covering a minelaying operation and returned to port long before Jellicoe could bring them to action.

Fisher's decision to resign was badly received by the fleet and particularly by Jellicoe, who implored him to stay on. He wrote to Hamilton: 'Fisher had many enemies, more enemies than friends, in the service, but even his enemies have been saying that his presence at the Admiralty was essential, as he was the only person who could tackle the Ist Lord … Winston Churchill is a public danger to the Empire.'[15] For similar reasons, two other senior fleet commanders, Beatty and Tyrwhitt, were equally opposed to Fisher's departure. The Sea Lords had originally agreed with the fleet commanders that Fisher should return to his post. Disturbed by Fisher's failure to return to the Admiralty when he had been advised that the Hochseeflotte was at sea, they now reversed their position and concluded that he could no longer function effectively as the professional head of the service and that he should be replaced as a matter of urgency.

Marder wrote: 'Fisher's inaction in this crisis made it practically impossible for any Government to keep him in office. Professionally ... he was dead in the wrong, since his place was at the Admiralty until his resignation was accepted.'[16] The King and Asquith were both infuriated by Fisher's desertion of his post. Jellicoe, who had originally believed that the other Sea Lords should have resigned in support of Fisher, now accepted that the old Admiral had to go. He wrote to Hamilton: 'Now that I know all the facts, I feel that you and the other Sea Lords took the right course. Certainly … Lord Fisher was quite wrong in giving up all work without being relieved.'[17]

By the morning of the 18th the news of Fisher's resignation had leaked to the press. With almost total unanimity the editorial columns demanded that he should stay. The *Globe*'s banner headline read: LORD FISHER MUST NOT GO. *The Times* was one of several newspapers who proposed that Fisher should replace Churchill as First Lord with a seat in the Cabinet, noting that the appointment 'would undoubtedly command great popular approval'. The *Army and Navy Gazette* pointed out that in earlier wars Admirals, notably St Vincent and Barham, had successfully held this office. Understandably encouraged by this strong support and believing that the incoming Conservative Ministers, having demanded and secured Churchill's departure, would back him, Fisher was to make a strategically fatal mistake.

On the next morning, May 18, Hamilton came to Hall's office, surprising him by locking the door. He asked him to tell Asquith that he and his fellow Sea Lords did not want Fisher to return to the Admiralty. Hall later described their discussion:

Hamilton: Hall, I want you to do something for me … something I can't order you to do, but something I'd earnestly ask you to do. I want you to take such steps as will make it impossible for Lord Fisher ever to return … I consider him to be a real danger and past his work.
Hall: But surely – this is a matter for the Sea Lords.
Hamilton: No, Hall, we can't act. If we were to make representations we should be suspected not unreasonably of motives of self interest.
Hall: If I agreed to act I could very easily be ruining myself. Yes, I see that you can't act for yourselves but it is a most unpleasant job you've given me.[18]

It could be argued that the Sea Lords should have briefed the Prime Minister themselves on the grounds that they were acting in the best interests of the service, rather than delegate the disagreeable task to Hall. Little seems to be known about Hamilton but Hall described him as a fine sailor and a great gentleman, the kind of man under whom everyone was pleased to serve. It would be fair to say that Fisher's impetuous resignation had put Hamilton in an almost impossible position. It could equally be argued that Hall was better suited to undertake the assignment than the Sea Lords, as by May 1915 he had built up excellent contacts with Asquith and other ministers, with whom he had become persona grata. The close nature of his relationship with the ministers can be illustrated in a chapter heading he prepared for his unwritten autobiography, referring to the political crisis in December 1916: 'Fall of the Asquith Government, breakfast with Carson, lunch with Asquith, tea with Balfour.'[19]

Hall had every reason to be perturbed at what he was being asked to do. It went against the grain as loyalty to the service was a quality in a naval officer valued almost above any other. Fisher and W. H. Hall had been contemporaries, fellow gunnery officers and close friends. Fisher had been extremely supportive of the elder Hall during his tenure as the first Director of Intelligence and in many ways had been Hall's mentor in the service after his father's death. He had helped to advance his career and in particular had appointed him to the challenging post of Inspector-Captain, where he had made a great name for himself. Hall could not overlook the deterioration in Fisher, whom he saw daily, noting that: 'Fisher was a very tired man – the strain of his position made all the more irksome by the divergence between his own views and those of the First Lord. We, in the Admiralty, could not help becoming more aware that the Fisher we had known was no longer with us.'[20]

The more Hall thought of the assignment the less he liked it. Eventually and very reluctantly he agreed to act, telling Hamilton that he had given him a most unpleasant job. The Admiral replied that it had to be done. Hall had his own doubts whether he should contact Asquith directly.

He had developed a considerable admiration for the Prime Minister, who had gone out of his way to be helpful to him. To brief him on detailed intelligence was one issue, to volunteer a controversial suggestion was another. After much thought, he decided to approach a man whom he knew already had Asquith's confidence. He had recently given evidence in the trial of a German agent named Kuepferle before the Court of the Lord Chief Justice, Lord Reading, and had been greatly impressed by his demeanour and his ability as a judge. Before his appointment as Lord Chief Justice, Reading, then Sir Rufus Isaacs, had been Attorney-General in Asquith's Government and, as Hall knew, he had remained close to the Prime Minister. Like his contemporaries, Edward Carson and F. E. Smith, Reading was well-known for his skill in cross-examination, having broken the poisoner Frederick Seddon. Intellectually, he and Hall were well-matched.

> He was obviously the man. I took Dick Herschell into my confidence, he at once agreed, and suggested his own flat as a meeting place. And so it was arranged. That afternoon Reading came round to Herschell's flat and I briefed him on the growing difficulty in the Admiralty of getting organized work done. I mentioned the conditions in which a man like Crease [Fisher's Naval Assistant] was working and the repeated friction between Lord Fisher and Mr. Churchill. I said bluntly that in my opinion Lord Fisher was in no fit state to continue in his post, and exhorted our visitor to represent to the Prime Minister the necessity for accepting the proffered resignation without delay … When I had finished Reading cross-examined me for nearly half an hour, and afterwards Dick Herschell told me that he had never heard anything like it … Question indeed followed question, some purely technical, but others fashioned as to make sure of my motive.
> Reading: Do you yourself object to serving under Lord Fisher?
> Hall: I'd serve under the devil if he were proficient.
> Reading: And would that have been your answer if I had mentioned Mr. Churchill instead?
> Hall: It would.
> Reading (speaking with deliberation, put the crucial question for which Hall had been waiting): Then if either of them is to leave the Admiralty, which would you suggest it be?
> Hall: Regretfully, I have to say both.
> Reading: And why?
> Hall: Because if you wish, as you must, to maintain any confidence between the Fleet and the Admiralty, you mustn't keep a First Lord, who will appear to have driven from office a man like Lord Fisher. The Navy will never forgive him.
> Lord Reading nodded and for a moment there was silence. 'You were quite right' he said at last 'when you said that you were putting your future in

my hands, and if you had answered my questions differently I would have broken you. But I am now satisfied that your view of what is required is correct, and I will see the Prime Minister at once. I shall not mention your name unless he asks for it.' Hall had indeed put his career in Reading's hands and had convinced one of the finest legal minds in the land that the case he had presented was sound.[21]

Meanwhile, in a spectacular act of self-destruction, Fisher proceeded to ensure his own downfall by writing a letter to Asquith setting out in a most overbearing way a list of demands before he would return to the Admiralty. He opened with a broadside:

If the following six conditions are agreed to, I can guarantee the successful termination of the war and the total abolition of the submarine menace. They must be published verbatim so that the Fleet may know my position.

1. That Mr. Winston Churchill is not in the Cabinet, to be always circumventing me, nor will I serve under Mr. Balfour.

2. That Sir A. K. Wilson leaves the Admiralty and the Committee of Imperial Defence and the War Council as my time otherwise will be occupied in resisting the bombardment of Heligoland and other such wild projects ...

3. That there shall be an entire new Board of Admiralty ... *new measures* demand *new men*.

4. That I shall have complete professional charge of the war at sea, together with the absolute sole disposition of the Fleet and the appointment of all officers of all ranks whatsoever, and absolutely untrammelled command of all the sea forces whatsoever.

5. That the First Lord of the Admiralty should be absolutely restricted to policy and parliamentary procedure ...

6. That I should have the sole absolute authority for all new construction, and for all dockyard work of whatever sort whatsoever, and complete control of the whole Civil establishments of the Navy.[22]

Hankey read a draft of the letter and remonstrated with Fisher, bluntly telling him that his terms were impossible. Despite this excellent advice, the old Admiral insisted on sending on May 19 what was in effect an ultimatum to Asquith. His normally loyal biographer, Admiral Sir Reginald Bacon, noted that: 'his age and the strain of the last six months of the Admiralty had begun to warp his calm and clear judgment and had made him more intolerant of opposition'.[23] Between May 17 and 19, he had recklessly thrown away two trump cards, widespread support in the service and the enthusiastic backing of virtually all the leading newspapers. No Prime Minister could ever have agreed to such conditions and Asquith had no hesitation in accepting Fisher's resignation. As Hankey sardonically noted 'Jackie got megalomania and has done for himself.'[24]

The risky and unpleasant assignment given by Hamilton to Hall may well have been moot. Marder believed that Fisher had destroyed himself before Hall's intervention. Strangely, neither of Reading's biographers, Montgomery Hyde and his son Gerald, mentions his meeting with Hall. Nevertheless in taking on this thankless task Hall had demonstrated his characteristic moral courage.

In Hall's entry in the New Oxford Dictionary of National Biography, published in 2004, he is described as having been directly involved in the intrigues surrounding the departure of Fisher in 1915. The use of the word intrigues appears misplaced. Fisher had been in large measure the architect of his own downfall, opinion throughout the service had unanimously concluded that the old Admiral had to go and Hall had only become embroiled in the incident following a direct instruction from Hamilton.

On two occasions in 1917, Hall's and Fisher's paths crossed. In July 1915, the incoming First Sea Lord, Sir Henry Jackson, had appointed Fisher Chairman of the newly formed Board of Invention and Research or the Board of Intrigue and Revenge as it was quickly christened by wits in the service clubs. The Admiralty had set up the Board to secure expert assistance in organising and encouraging scientific effort to meet the Navy's requirements. Fisher presided over a committee that included the inventor of the marine turbine, Sir Charles Parsons, and an advisory panel that boasted Sir J. J. Thomson and Sir Ernest Rutherford amongst its members. Under his leadership the Board did some valuable work including developing new weapon systems for the anti-submarine campaign.

In the summer of 1917 to assist their efforts in this field, the Admiralty arranged that the Board should receive reports of all successful attacks against U-boats. Fisher, wrongly suspecting that the Anti-Submarine Division was not being sufficiently co-operative, demanded that he should see copies of all actions with submarines, whether or not they were successful. Hall was opposed to this suggestion both on security grounds and the likelihood that the ever judgmental Fisher would criticise any unsuccessful actions. He minuted: 'I do not recommend approval of this proposal. The B.I.R. can carry out research on lines suggested to the Admiralty. The extension of circulation of these reports is to be deprecated. It will only lead to irresponsible criticism.'

By some bureaucratic error Hall's minute was sent to the B.I.R. An infuriated Fisher could not resist the opportunity of getting even with Hall, of whose (possibly indirect) involvement in his downfall he must have been well aware. Over-reacting violently, he dashed off an indignant letter to the First Lord, by that time Sir Eric Geddes: 'The remarks of Admiral W. R. Hall are such that it seems to me that unless he is removed it will be necessary for me to resign.'[25]

Geddes, who had been in office for barely a month and was totally unaware of the background, asked Hall what he had done to drive Fisher to threaten resignation. Hall had already summed up Geddes as a forceful character, who could not easily be pushed around. He told Geddes that it did not greatly matter what he had done to Fisher since the latter had ordered his dismissal. The First Lord's reaction was instantaneous. He was not going to take orders from Fisher. Hall replied that Geddes should tell Fisher that he was not going to acquiesce in dismissing any naval officer at his behest. They agreed that all Fisher should receive in return for his ill-considered letter was a message from Hall: 'I regret that the B.I.R. have read the word "irresponsible" in my minute in the wrong sense. The meaning that I intended to convey was that I deprecated the circulation of reports to those who are not responsible for the operations.'[26]

Honour appears to have been satisfied. Within two months of attempting to get Hall dismissed, Fisher, not content with his role at the Board, actually tried to involve Hall in a scheme to get him reinstated as First Sea Lord. Earlier in the year he had even suggested to Jellicoe that he be appointed Third Sea Lord and Controller, a post he had held over twenty years before. Jellicoe had not pursued the offer.

On the morning of October 5, Thomas Marlowe, the Editor of the *Daily Mail* and Hall's close confederate in circulating deception to the Germans, asked to meet him urgently. Citing pressure of work, Hall sent Serocold to see him. He returned with an almost unbelievable story. A Mr. H. W. Wilson, a member of Marlowe's staff, had been in contact with Fisher, who had asked his editor to get in touch with Hall. The objective of the scheme was to arrange Fisher's return to the Admiralty on the grounds that he was the only man who could save Britain from the submarine menace. Marlowe, well informed about Fisher's true physical and mental condition, had no wish to get involved and only passed on the message to Hall at the old Admiral's express request. Hall sent Serocold back to tell Marlowe that he agreed with his assessment, adding that Fisher's judgment was erratic and that he was too old and tired to withstand the stress of high office. Despite his self-confidence, which never flagged, his return could not be seriously considered. To use a Fleet Street term, Marlowe responded by spiking Fisher's plan. In January 1918, Geddes and Wemyss, by then First Sea Lord, abolished the Board and appointed a Director of Experiments and Research inside the Admiralty, responsible to the Third Sea Lord as Controller of the Navy. They thus ended Fisher's active association with the Navy after nearly 64 years service.

Hall's involvement in Fisher's downfall inevitably became known in naval circles, In July 1933 Ralph Straus, the co-author of Hall's projected autobiography, wrote to inform him that the Admiralty had raised objections to the draft chapter, 'Lord Fisher and Mr. Churchill', which included the story of Fisher's late machinations. Straus's source appears to have been Sir Archibald Sinclair, who had been Churchill's Second-in-Command when he commanded a battalion of the Royal Scots Fusiliers on the Western Front in the winter of 1915–16 and who had remained close to him. Sinclair was a former Liberal Cabinet Minister who was to serve as Secretary of State for Air in Churchill's wartime Government.

The Admiralty's reaction, nearly twenty years later, indicates a continuing degree of sensitivity to this incident; although they based their decision, reached two weeks later, to ban the autobiography, on its revelations about the decrypts. Strangely enough when James published his biography of Hall in 1955, he wrote that an unnamed Sea Lord had asked Hall to brief Asquith and he did not mention Hamilton by name.

Notes

[1] CAC HALL3/7
[2] Massie, p.299
[3] Ibid, p. 291
[4] Crease to WRH November 7 1932. Quoted in Marder, *From Dreadnought to Scapa Flow* Vol. 2 pp.267-268
[5] Fisher to Jellicoe December 20 1932. *Marder* Vol. 2 pp.269-270
[6] Marder, *From Dreadnought to Scapa Flow* Vol. 2 p.272
[7] Gilbert, *Winston S. Churchill* Vol. 3 p.419
[8] Fisher Obituary *Dictionary of National Biography 1911-1920*
[9] Fisher's comments can be found in the margin of the Webb Report (TNA ADM137/1058.)
[10] CAC HALL 3/7
[11] CAC HALL 7/4/124 WRH to May Templar June 27 1942

[12] Beesly, p.135
[13] Lloyd George *War Memoirs* Vol.1 p.225-226
[14] Marder, Vol. 2 p.283
[15] Ibid, p.281
[16] Ibid, p.283
[17] Jellicoe to Hamilton May 27 1915, Marder Vol. 2 p.283n
[18] CAC HALL 3/7
[19] CAC HALL 1/4
[20] CAC HALL 3/7
[21] Beesly pp.136-137
[22] Mackay, *Fisher of Kilverstone* p.502
[23] Quoted in Marder, Vol 2 p.285
[24] Mackay, p.512
[25] James, p.87
[26] Ibid

CHAPTER VIII

The Great Game I

Since the Trojan Horse, deception has been a legitimate tool of war. It reached its zenith with Operation Fortitude in the run-up to the Normandy invasion in World War II. The misinformation leaked by double agents about the totally fictional First United States Army Group, complete with papier-mâché tanks and artillery, persuaded the German army that the invasion would take place in the Pas De Calais and the huge Allied armada crossed the Channel bound for Normandy unnoticed and without opposition. Hall had placed considerable importance on the use of deception as a weapon to outwit the enemy and used it to great effect throughout World War I. The hugely successful Operation Fortitude was directly derived from the game book Hall had developed in the Great War.

Working in close collaboration with Col. R.J. Drake of MI5, Hall became a master of deception through the use of faked photographs, forged documents and misinformation. Photographs of the battlecruiser HMS *Lion*, damaged at the Battle of the Dogger Bank, falsely indicating that her refit was by no means complete, persuaded the Kriegsmarine to withdraw the U-boats which they had stationed waiting outside the Tyne estuary in the hope of torpedoing her. *Lion* was thus able to rejoin the fleet safely. Hall and Drake successfully initiated the practice of using captured agents to transmit disinformation, including fictional invasions of the Belgian coast and Schleswig-Holstein and false troop movements.

Interrogation

Using his remarkable talent for guile, which had served him so well in dealing with defaulters in sea-going command, Hall became an exceedingly skilled interrogator. He had an almost uncanny ability to see through impostors, and he would habitually lure suspects into a sense of false security. On one occasion a prisoner under interrogation was stoutly denying that he was a German and insisting that he was an

American who had survived the torpedoing of a merchant ship off the English coast. His cover story did not really add up and Hall's suspicions deepened as the interrogation proceeded. Playing the soft cop routine, he took a sympathetic line with the suspect, congratulating him on his escape. Having ensnared the suspect, who subconsciously dropped his guard, Hall walked behind him and reverting to a hard cop routine, suddenly barked a command in German to stand to attention. The prisoner instantly complied, even clicking his heels in Prussian fashion. He was no longer able to deny his nationality or his identity.

Hall successfully unmasked the notorious trickster, Trebitsch Lincoln, a Hungarian who had moved to England where he pursued a remarkable career. At various times he had been a clergyman, a journalist and Liberal MP for Darlington. He had been forced out of Parliament as a bankrupt and at the beginning of the war applied to join naval intelligence, although he was at the same time working for Hungarian censors. Interviewed by Hall he proposed a preposterous scheme for luring the German fleet into the North Sea, which he would implement, if he was sent to Rotterdam as a double agent. Hall saw straight through Lincoln and told him that he would not employ him under any circumstances. Lincoln then had no compunction in offering himself as an agent to the German Consul in Rotterdam, himself an agent named Gneist. The Consul no more trusted Lincoln than Hall had and sent him back to London with some worthless documents. By the time he had returned to the intelligence division bringing with him these planted papers, Hall had already checked out his background and put the fear of God into the trickster. Fearing arrest, Lincoln fled to New York where he once again took up journalism. He was eventually extradited to Britain on charges of forgery and was sentenced to three years penal servitude and deported to his native Hungary. He is believed to have ended his days as a Buddhist monk in a Tibetan monastery.

Hall and Basil Thomson obtained a confession from the notorious agent Margaret Zeller, a Eurasian professional dancer better known as Mata Hari. While she was working in Madrid in the summer of 1915 naval intelligence had become aware that she was involved with German agents. Early in 1916 while returning to Holland by sea, Special Branch agents had taken her off her ship at Falmouth for interrogation. Although Hall and Thomson knew full well that she was acting as a German courier, they did not have enough evidence to convict her and she was deported to Spain with a strict warning not to continue any Secret Service activities. She foolishly disregarded Hall's advice and resumed her work as an agent. Even more foolishly, she crossed into France and was promptly arrested, tried and executed that October. By one account, she declined to be blindfolded, and even saluted the firing squad as the order to shoot was given. Hall later described Mata Hari to his family – by legend the most glamorous female spy of the 20th century – as 'a fat old hag without attraction'.

The United States

In the same way as the German intelligence chiefs in Washington used the services of activist Irish-Americans, led by John Devoy, Captain Guy Gaunt, the naval attaché in Washington and Hall's principal agent in North America, succeeded in discreetly recruiting a network of German-speaking Czechs and Slovaks, disaffected citizens of Austria-Hungary. Their leader was a remarkable man, named Voska, whom Barbara Tuchman described as the allies' single most valuable secret agent in the United States.[1] Early in his life, he had been expelled from his native Bohemia as a political agitator. Emigrating to the US he had become a prosperous businessman while remaining a staunch patriot. In the summer of 1914, the Czech nationalist leader, Thomas Masaryk, had selected Voska to set up an intelligence operation in the US. He contacted Gaunt and quickly proved his credentials as an opponent of Austria-Hungary. He turned out to be a boon to British intelligence. At one stroke, Voska had remedied one of Gaunt's nagging problems, the lack of reliable transatlantic agents.

At the naval attaché's suggestion, Voska's compatriots succeeded in infiltrating the German and Austrian embassies in Washington and their consulates in New York, as well as the offices of the leading German shipping line, Hamburg Amerika, whose executives were deeply involved in espionage, several German-American newspapers and the transatlantic radio station at Sayville on Long Island. The reach of the Voska organisation, in all about eighty strong, was truly amazing: among its operatives were Bernstorff's chauffeur and his wife's maid, the assistant chief clerk in the Austrian Embassy and four employees of their consulate. Voska ran his network from his house in New York and Gaunt spent much of his time in that city to maintain his contacts with his valued agent.

The information collected by Voska and supplied to Gaunt provided Hall with detailed and authentic evidence of German subversion and their flagrant and repeated breaches of American neutrality. Gaunt cultivated his fellow Australian, the Anglophile John Rathom, editor of the *Providence Journal*, the paper which 'was soon to exhibit a startling and intimate acquaintance with German secrets'. By prearrangement, Rathom's exposés appeared simultaneously in the *New York Times*, whose opening line, 'The *Providence Journal* will say this morning' soon became famous.[2]

The first dividends from the Voska network arrived at the end of August 1915. By this time, a courier with a neutral passport and carrying German and Austrian documents was sailing on every neutral liner leaving New York. The agents discovered that one John J. Archibald, a courier acting for the Austrian Embassy, was booked on the *Rotterdam* which sailed on the last week of the month. A signal using the route Voska-Gaunt-Hall tipped off naval intelligence, and 110 of Archibald's documents – according to Tuchman as full of plums as a fruitcake – were taken off the liner when it was searched at Ramsgate.

When Hall examined these incriminating papers, he found a report from the Austrian Ambassador, Count Constantine Dumba, which implicated his Embassy in fomenting strikes by Hungarian workers in munitions factories, together with progress reports on sabotage by von Papen and Boy-Ed and cancelled cheques and payments made to saboteurs and propagandists.

The Foreign Office, still under the illusion that Britain could fight an enemy as ruthless as Imperial Germany by the rules, initially declined to forward these damning discoveries to the American State Department. Hall never suffered from such qualms. Then and later he had absolutely no reservations about Germans, whom he habitually disparaged as huns. He had every intention of paralysing their suppression and espionage operations in neutral countries.

He bypassed the Foreign Office and showed the documents to Ed Bell, a career diplomat, the Second Secretary and intelligence point man at the American Embassy in London, who enjoyed the full confidence of his Ambassador, Walter Hines Page. Bell was described as 'a man of great tact and discretion with a quiet sense of humour which must have appealed to Englishmen'.[3] He briefed the Ambassador, who lost no time in cabling the information to their contact in the State Department, Leland Harrison, an Old Etonian anglophile. The passing of the documents recovered from Archibald is the first recorded occasion of any contact between Hall and the American Embassy. An extremely close relationship developed between Bell, on the American side, and Hall, Serocold and Herschell on the British. This would mature into full-bodied co-operation during the handling of the Zimmermann telegram and in directing joint intelligence operations after the US had entered the war.

Suspecting that President Wilson might be reluctant to act on these revelations of German ill faith, the British released the most incriminating documents in a Parliamentary White Paper that September. Once published in the US they were the sensation of the month. Slowly but surely American public opinion, angered by the contemptuous way in which Imperial Germany and its agents were behaving, grew more hostile towards the Central Powers. Outflanked by the skilful British gambit initiated by Hall, Wilson promptly ejected the conniving Austrian Ambassador. Anxious to avoid confrontation with Germany, at a time when he was negotiating a settlement for the American lives lost on

Lusitania, Wilson overruled his Secretary of State, Robert Lansing, and refused to expel the two attachés.

Hall's efforts notwithstanding, the German espionage operations in America had already run into difficulties. Dissatisfied with the performance of von Papen and Boy-Ed, the High Command in Berlin decided not to recall them but to send an agent, without diplomatic accreditation, to boost the sabotage campaign and to organise the restoration of the former Mexican President, General Victoriano Huerta, whom Wilson detested, to power. They selected Franz von Rintelen, the self-styled Dark Invader, a Commander in the Naval Reserve, then in his late 30s, who had lived in the US for several years as a representative of a major German bank. He was fluent in English and, unlike so many of his fellow countrymen, knew and understood the country. Unlike von Papen, who never concealed his detestation of Americans, he was a man of considerable charm. He was later to write the story of his life as an intelligence agent. Tuchman wryly described these books as: 'two volumes of memoirs notable for a Munchausen-like quality of stretching the possible into the preposterous.'

A man of many aliases, von Rintelen arrived in New York early in April 1915, travelling on a Swiss passport under the name of Emil Gasche. From the outset the ill-defined command structure caused trouble. Somewhat tactlessly, von Rintelen announced that he was taking over command of all espionage and subversion operations. He only succeeded in earning the resentment of the service attachés and particularly of von Papen. Throughout his long career, the military attaché was a habitual and practised intriguer. A Vicar of Bray character, he generally succeeded in emerging on the winning side. Von Papen and Boy-Ed eventually managed to persuade Bernstorff that von Rintelen should be recalled and he sailed from New York on the Dutch liner *Noordam* on August 3 1915. Once again he was travelling as the Swiss Emil Gasche. Accompanying him on the voyage was one Andrew Meloy, a conniving and disreputable American arms trader, to whom he had entrusted his secret papers.

In only four months in America, he had succeeded in creating and leaving behind him a formidable and effective sabotage operation, which was to cause the Wilson administration considerable trouble, including damage to property, notably the colossal Black Tom explosion in July 1916, and as well as losses to British shipping.

Hall had been tipped off to von Rintelen's enforced departure, either by the Voska network or through a decrypt and Special Branch were waiting when *Noordam* called in at Ramsgate for examination on August 13. Their suspicions multiplied when Meloy tried to put in a word for his companion. The police searched his baggage and discovered the incriminating papers. The two men were taken to London for interrogation by Hall, accompanied by the German-speaking Herschell and by

Thomson. Von Rintelen had been thoroughly rehearsed as to the details of the real-life Gasche and he was so convincing that Hall even agreed that he should be taken to see the Swiss Minister, who also accepted his protestations that he really was Gasche. Hall, sure of his real identity, watched von Rintelen's reactions closely when he suggested that the British Legation in Switzerland be asked to confirm if the real Gasche could possibly be in London. Von Rintelen realised that the crafty Hall had outflanked him and that he was in danger of being shot as a spy. He then admitted his true identity as a naval officer. Despite Meloy's protests that he was an innocent businessman, his papers proved that his objective in visiting Germany was the purchase of arms for one of the rival Mexican factions, not, as Beesly noted, a mission calculated to endear him to the American Government. Ten days later, Hall handed over both men's papers, incriminating each of them in Mexican intrigues and von Rintelen in subversion and espionage, to a grateful Bell.

In a section of his imaginative memoirs filled with patent inaccuracies, von Rintelen describes Hall as an Admiral although he was still a Captain in 1915 and was not promoted to flag rank until 1917. According to his account, he was taken in interrogation into a room occupied by a group of naval officers in gold-encrusted uniforms and that Hall and Herschell were wearing the aiguillettes of royal aides-de-camp. Hall's service record indicates that he only became an aide-de-camp in 1916, whilst Herschell's position was that of a Lord in Waiting. He tells the unlikely story that in the middle of the War Hall and Herschell took him, an admitted agent, to dinner at the Junior United Services Club, where they revealed certain exploits of naval intelligence including the use of deception to entice von Spee to his defeat at the Battle of the Falkland Islands. According to von Rintelen, Herschell invited him to his flat after dinner, where he poured him a whisky and played Wagner on the piano, while waiting for the police to take him into custody. This tale has one indicator of truth, as Herschell was a talented pianist.

Von Rintelen was sent to a POW camp, where he remained until he was extradited to the US after they declared war. He duly served four years for sabotage in a Federal penitentiary in Atlanta. Late in 1920 Wilson commuted his sentence on the condition that he immediately leave the country. Over the next 20 years, his and Hall's paths continued to cross and a remarkable, somewhat wary, friendship developed between the one-time adversaries.

To maintain his advantage, Gaunt continued to feed Rathom of the *Providence Journal* with information discovered in the papers taken from Archibald and von Rintelen. As previously, series of articles were published simultaneously in the *Journal* and the *New York Times*, demanding the expulsion of von Papen and Boy-Ed, once again creating a media sensation. The climax was reached on December 8, when the headlines in the *Times* declared:

> UNCOVER GERMAN PLOT TO EMBROIL US WITH MEXICO
> VON RINTELEN CAME HERE, BACKED BY MILLIONS,
> FOR THAT PURPOSE, GOVERNMENT LEARNS.
> ESPOUSED HUERTA'S CAUSE.
> NEW REVOLUTION WOULD DIVERT FROM ALLIES
> THE FLOW OF MUNITIONS

After the westbound liner *Ancona* was torpedoed in the Mediterranean by U-38 operating from the Austrian naval base at Cattaro in November 1915 with the loss of 200 lives, 20 of them American, Wilson determined to take a stronger line with both Germany and Austria. When both Lansing and Colonel House recommended that the two attachés, whom they described as 'obnoxious underlings' be ejected, the President did not demur.

Sadly, this was not to be the ineffable Franz von Papen's last encounter with history. In June 1932, he became Chancellor of the already decaying Weimar Republic, the unloved successor to Imperial Germany. In his five months in office, he distinguished himself by sacking the elected state government of Prussia, a flagrant breach of the constitution. He was conceited enough to believe that he could control Hitler, helping to pave the way for his rise to power. During the Third Reich, von Papen served as Vice-Chancellor and as Ambassador to Austria; although Hitler had two of his principal aides murdered in the so-called Night of the Long Knives in June 1934. Von Papen used his talent for intrigue and espionage to undermine Austrian independence and prepare for the forcible Nazi takeover in March 1938. During World War II he was Ambassador to Turkey. In 1945 he was arraigned at Nuremberg as a war criminal but was acquitted, later serving two years in prison of an eight-year sentence handed down by a denazification court.

As diplomats, von Papen and Boy-Ed enjoyed immunity from arrest, but Hall believed that such immunity did not include their baggage and any papers. Von Papen had foreseen that his baggage might be searched and believed that he had destroyed any incriminating papers before leaving Washington. When the liner carrying von Papen called in for examination at Falmouth on January 3 1916, Special Branch discovered that he had brought with him the stubs of all the cheques he had written between August 1914 and his expulsion in December 1915. When naval intelligence examined these stubs, they found evidence of payments which he had made to at least four agents, all of whom they already knew to be involved in sabotage and subversion in both the US and Canada. Hall believed that these revelations were so important that he took them directly to Page. The Ambassador immediately cabled this incriminating evidence to Lansing, who was by this time convinced that the inexorable and identifiable movement of Germany towards total war would make American entry inevitable. Despite this verification of ill-faith, Wilson would not move away from his considered position of neutrality and it was only the damning Zimmermann telegram, more than a year in the future, that would cause him to alter his position.

Throughout 1915, Hall and Gaunt had played their cards adroitly and, even if they had only marginally influenced the President's stance, they had quietly gained much influence within the Administration, notably with Lansing and House, who had become close to Gaunt, and with the media. The British cause in the US had been mightily advanced.

Ireland

The episode of the cruise of the *Sayonara* displayed Hall's powers of imagination and craftiness. He and his ally at Special Branch, Basil Thomson, were leery about the activities of the extremist Irish nationalist movement, Sinn Fein, which was tacitly associated with Germany, and decided to supplement the anti-subversion efforts of the Royal Irish Constabulary. He followed up a suggestion made to Thomson by Arthur Shirley Benn, MP for Plymouth. He chartered the yacht *Sayonara*, then in British waters, from her American owner, the staunchly pro-allied Antony Drexel. His objective was for the yacht to sail Irish waters under her American flag to garner information about German subversion and Sinn Fein activities and, more importantly, to intercept Roger Casement, who, as noted earlier, was also collaborating with the German Government. Hall knew through the decrypts that the German espionage chiefs had planned that Casement should be landed in Ireland with a consignment of arms.

Hall installed a hand-picked naval crew who were dressed in American yachting gear, commanded by a Lieutenant F. M. Simon, a Royal Naval Reserve officer who had served under him on HMS *Queen Mary*. Simon had had a varied career. Like many RNR officers, he had been a deck officer for Cunard and in 1910 had been the navigator on the airship *America II*, the first to attempt to cross the Atlantic. Hall recalled that Simon was a skilled mimic and that the lower deck on *Queen Mary* had nicknamed him the Yank, as American accents were his speciality. He was thus ideally cast in the role of American Captain of *Sayonara*. Hall gave Simon a letter confirming his real identity and his credentials to be used in case of emergency. Only a few aboard the yacht, including a courier who would supply Hall with intelligence, knew the real purpose of the cruise. Motivated by Simon's enthusiastic leadership, the crew were delighted to be playing the parts of American sailors – right down to chewing gum!

Hall's choice of Major Wilfred Howell as *Sayonara*'s 'owner' was equally inspired. Patrick Beesly described him as a soldier of fortune. In the past he had been a peripatetic railway engineer. He was a Catholic and his father had been a Chamberlain to the Pope. He had been educated in Austria and was fluent in several languages including German. He had won a Distinguished Service Order during a rising in Sierra Leone and had been wounded in the Boer War. He also had some intelligence experience. On Hall's instructions he had adopted the persona of Colonel McBride, a well-heeled and strongly pro-German American of Irish descent from Los Angeles. Beesly noted that 'with his Homburg hat and up-turned moustache he looked more like a caricature of Kaiser Wilhelm II than the Yankee he was meant to be … It is unlikely that they [the crew] would have deceived any genuine American, but they certainly deceived the rest of the Royal Navy.'[4]

Sayonara sailed from Southampton on December 15 1914. As she neared the Irish coast, the wireless operator discovered that the set aboard was a different model from those in use in the Navy so he could not use it. Confronted with the urgent problem of replacing the operator, they had to put into Queenstown.

Hall's ruse worked. Simon and Howell/'McBride' played their parts so well that the boarding officer reported that the Captain was 'a wealthy Yankee' and the owner 'looked like a hun'. The yacht was placed under guard and Simon and Howell, under some suspicion, were taken before Sir Charles Coke, Vice-Admiral Queenstown and the Senior Naval Officer in Ireland. Simon revealed Hall's letter to the Admiral who was initially displeased as he was totally in the dark as to the operation. However, the audacity of the scheme must have appealed to his sense of humour and he helpfully provided a new wireless operator, smuggled surreptitiously aboard *Sayonara* under cover.

This arranged, Coke invited Simon and Howell to lunch with his staff. Over the meal they gave a bravura performance, Simon remarking that he had formed a very high regard for the efficiency of the Kriegsmarine during a recent visit to Germany and Howell, in rather halting English and stressing his neutrality, expounded his knowledge of Germany and its resources which made her such a formidable enemy. He obligingly added that it would be difficult to beat her. The staff officers, who of course were not aware of the operation, were naturally extremely suspicious of both men. The Navy accordingly placed *Sayonara* under tight surveillance shadowing her at every port of call. Captain Le Mesurier of HMS *Cornwallis*, a battleship on which Hall had served as Commander ten years earlier and an old friend of Hall's, carried out a thorough search of the yacht which did not find either the crew's naval uniforms or the hidden arms. His suspicions were not allayed when he discovered that *Sayonara* had a wireless set concealed aboard, her wireless operator having carelessly raised her aerial in bright moonlight. He promptly placed her and her crew under arrest. Howell, playing his part as McBride to perfection, feigned great irritation and threatened to complain to the American Embassy in London and to his powerful friends in the States. *Sayonara* was only released through Hall's direct intervention, much to Le Mesurier's chagrin.

This scrutiny did not go unnoticed by the Irish rebels, who assumed that the yacht and its crew had come to the West Coast to support and encourage them and were more than ready to contact and befriend Hall's agents. It so happened that the Sinn Fein leader in Westport, County Sligo, was also called McBride, who developed a camaraderie with Howell, eagerly trying to discover whether they were related. In the atmosphere of bonhomie which quickly developed, doubtless fortified by liquid hospitality, tongues surely wagged and useful information was gleaned and passed back to Hall by courier.

One of the shadowing vessels, the Coastguard cutter *Safeguard*, was commanded by Lieutenant Hicks, another of Hall's agents, who was privy to the operation and who had provided Howell with a list of suspected extremists, all of whom Howell succeeded in meeting.

The peppery Marquess of Sligo, one of the largest landowners in the west coast of Ireland who owned Westport and most of the surrounding land, betook himself 'in a paroxysm of patriotic rage' to London where he was sent to see Hall. He indignantly demanded that action be taken against the American troublemakers, who were clearly allied to the extremist nationalists of Sinn Fein, and were doubtless on the German payroll. He announced to the enormously amused Director of Intelligence that he had seen the crew of the yacht with his own eyes laying mines in his own harbour. When he threatened to take his complaint to Churchill and Fisher, Hall turned his charm on the enraged Marquess and let him into the secret.

On January 4 1915 Hall wrote to Simon via the courier:

It is anticipated that C [Casement] will arrive in the Danish steamer, *Mjolnir*, of Copenhagen, 580 tons. She is due to leave Christiansand on 9th and be off the west coast of Ireland between the 13th and 15th. With C will be Adler Christiansen, age 24, height 6 ft, strongly made, clean shaven, fair hair, gap in front teeth, wears thick double-breasted greatcoat and soft dark hat. Speaks English fluently but with Norwegian-American accent ... He is wanted by New York police. I hope to get rendezvous, but it is doubtful, but I feel that you are just about at the best place round the coast from Cashel to Achill.[5]

By early 1915 German intelligence had concluded that the support for an armed uprising in Ireland was much weaker than Devoy and Cohalan, the Fenian leaders in New York, had implied to their contacts in the Washington Embassy. They decided that the operation should be postponed until conditions were more favourable. Hall's intelligence sources confirmed the German change of plan: On January 9 he told Simon that 'we have lost track of C', instructing him to return *Sayonara* to Southampton before her charter expired.[6]

Beesly was sceptical as to whether the cruise produced any effective results, wondering if the Irish really were taken in by the appearance of an American yacht in wartime and in winter, hardly peak yachting season. Hall always insisted that the intelligence collected by Simon and Howell proved its worth during the Easter Rising fifteen months later.

Early in 1916 the German Government returned to the plan to assist an uprising in Ireland, promising to send a consignment of arms to equip the rebels. At the end of March Devoy told a meeting of Irish activists in New York that the British intended to arrest the extremist leaders in Ireland and (a lie) to introduce conscription. He and his colleagues decided that the time was ripe for an armed uprising to start on Easter Saturday and that Casement, accompanying the arms, should land in Ireland on the previous day, Good Friday.

The decrypts revealed the extent of German complicity in the Easter Rising. Beesly noted that between 1914 and 1917 Room 40 intercepted over 30 messages between Bernstorff and Berlin indicating German support for the extremists. Early in April they decoded a signal from Bernstorff informing his Government that the rebellion was planned for Easter Sunday, April 23. He asked that a quantity of between 25,000 and 50,000 rifles together with machine guns and light artillery be supplied to the rebels and confirmed that Casement was to be landed in Ireland on Good Friday. The General Staff agreed that the arms would be sent by steamer and forwarded details of the codewords to be transmitted by Nauen to confirm that the consignment was on its way to Ireland or alternatively that its delivery had once again been postponed. Through the decrypts Hall was fully aware of the main course of the uprising and arranged for necessary counter-measures to be implemented. The naval forces in Ireland commanded by Vice-Admiral Sir Lewis Bayly, VA Western Approaches at Queenstown (who had succeeded Coke after the loss of *Lusitania*), were reinforced and sailors and marines put ashore to guard naval and coastguard stations and to assist the civil power.

On April 9 the gunrunner *Libau*, manned by a crew from the Kriegsmarine but disguised as the Norwegian steamer *Aud* and carrying false Norwegian papers, left Lubeck with a cargo of 20,000 rifles, Russian Mausers captured after Hindenburg's victory at Tannenberg, ten machine guns and a million rounds of ammunition, together with a supply of explosives. On April 15 Room 40 intercepted a Nauen signal, all too typical of the cavalier German use of wireless telegraphy, asking '… whether German auxiliary cruiser which is to bring weapons to Ireland has actually …' Although the decryption was incomplete, the message was fully understood.

On April 12 Casement and two companions left Wilhelmshaven aboard U-20, the submarine which had torpedoed *Lusitania* eleven months before. The U-boat damaged its rudder and had to return to port. Its three passengers were transferred to U-19, which was unable to sail until April 15, thus crucially delaying Casement's arrival in Ireland by three days. The signals that had passed between the U-boats and the submarine command were intercepted by Room 40. *Libau/Aud* reached Tralee Bay on April 20 but owing to navigational errors and faulty planning failed to make any contact with the rebels. She was intercepted by HMS *Bluebell* and ordered to proceed to Queenstown. Her crew, who had by then changed into German uniform, scuttled her. Naval divers later recovered her cargo. Within hours of landing near Tralee, Co. Kerry, on April 21, Casement was arrested, as were his two companions two days later. Hall's initiatives, particularly the interception of the German arms, severely reduced the effectiveness of the Uprising, which broke out on Easter Monday, April 24, later than originally planned. In the event the rebellion was almost entirely confined to Dublin.

In his unpublished 'Recollections', Henry Oliver wrote: 'We knew beforehand that Revolution in Ireland would start on Easter Monday 1916 and we made naval preparations in advance. The Cabinet would not believe the First Lord.'[7] His account makes it clear firstly that Hall, so often accused of keeping information garnered from the decrypts from Ministers, had briefed Balfour about the Easter Rebellion before the event. Secondly, with the strange inertia all too typical of the Asquith Coalition Government, it took no action and the British authorities at Dublin Castle, the Army and the Royal Irish Constabulary (RIC) were never informed of the impending Rebellion. The police force was entirely Irish and was widely suspected, not least by Basil Thomson and Special Branch, of a tendency to leak confidential information and several commentators have suggested that reservations about its security procedures resulted in it being kept in ignorance.

The RIC's own intelligence was surprisingly ineffective. Despite many years experience in watching extremist Republicans, they do not appear to have mounted any surveillance on two of the most active leaders of the rising, James Connolly and Patrick Pearse. In January 1916, Connolly had written an editorial in his paper *The Workers Republic*, declaring that '… the time for Ireland's battle is NOW, the place for Ireland's battle is HERE.' Pearse had given a particularly inflammatory eulogy at a funeral for an old Fenian.

As a result of these intelligence and communications failures, the outbreak of the Rising in Dublin on Easter Monday, April 24, caught the RIC completely unawares and the insurrection was only subdued following forceful intervention by the Army. The inept Chief Secretary for Ireland, Augustine Birrell, who had held the post for far too long (nine years) and who reputedly seldom visited Dublin, lost his job. But Hall, as the de facto coordinator of intelligence and Thomson must share some responsibility for the failure to pass information to the RIC, one of the most serious intelligence breakdowns in British history. In modern intelligence patois, the dots were never connected. Hall would have been totally justified in ignoring the indifference of the Asquith Government and in ensuring that the authorities in Ireland were briefed of the impending uprising.

Casement was taken to London and on the morning of April 23 he was interrogated by both Hall and Thomson. Hall was struck by his strange mixture of idealism and vanity. Casement expressed his disillusion with the Germans for sending only one shipload of arms and no soldiers, accusing them of breaking their agreement to send both. He added that the German spy chiefs had told him that, if he did not accompany the arms, his Irish supporters would assume that he had abandoned them. They eventually agreed that he could travel to Ireland by submarine. Casement alleged that his intention in going in Ireland was to persuade the organisers of the rebellion to call it off. In view of the LIBAU's mission, neither Hall nor Thomson was convinced by this claim. As his guilt was not in doubt, Casement was duly indicted for treason and sent for trial at the Old Bailey, where he was tried, convicted and sentenced to death.

As a result of the international reputation as a campaigner for human rights that Casement had acquired following his revelations about the Congo and the Putumayo, many influential people in Britain, Ireland and the US advocated that his sentence be commuted to life imprisonment. The United States Senate passed a resolution asking the British Government for clemency. Determined that Casement should not escape the gallows, Thomson was chiefly instrumental in orchestrating a campaign aimed at powerful opinion-formers to undermine the movement for clemency. To this end he used his knowledge that Casement, in the prevailing morality of the time, was entirely compromised.

When Hall and Thomson first interrogated Casement, 'A superintendent of the Special Branch entered the room and placed a book on the table. Casement showed no signs of recognizing the book which had been found in his luggage.'[8] When Thomson examined the book he discovered that it was a diary explicitly relating Casement's homosexual activities. At the same time that he had been exposing the terrible ill-treatment of native workers by their employers he had regularly been debauching local boys. Thomson had made the diaries available to the prosecution, led by F. E. Smith, then Attorney-General, and to the defence on the grounds that they constituted evidence for a verdict of guilty but insane. In the event they were not used during the trial. These documents, five in all, which are now in The National Archives at Kew, became widely known as the Casement Black diaries and were for many years a source of considerable controversy. Even in today's more permissive climate, these diaries are astonishingly frank and Thomson had little doubt that targeted circulation of the diaries in a society which regarded homosexuality as taboo (and criminal) would have a devastating effect.

To achieve his objective, Thomson needed access to Hall's formidable networking capability and in particular to Herschell's royal and political connections. With his strong aversion to traitors, Hall was only too willing to help. King George V was among those who were shown the diaries, probably by Herschell. Although the King was no doubt shocked by the treason of a man he had knighted, he was widely understood to be sympathetic to clemency. Some years later, his reaction to the unmasking of a former Liberal Cabinet minister, Lord Beauchamp, as a homosexual was to declare: 'I thought men like that went out and shot themselves.' The monarch, like many of his contemporaries, would have had little comprehension of or sympathy for Casement's sexual orientation and he promptly withdrew any objection to his execution. Once he had seen a copy of the diary, John Redmond, the leader of the Irish Parliamentary Nationalist party, also retracted his support for clemency for his fellow Irishman. The American Ambassador, Walter Hines Page, read an extract and remarked: 'One needs a strong stomach to eat anything after reading this.'[9] Photocopies of the diaries were widely circulated to Members of Parliament and journalists who had expressed some sympathy for Casement and to those who had signed a petition for the commutation of his sentence. Gradually, as Thomson had foreseen, the support for Casement faded away.

Evidence suggests that the campaign waged by Hall and Thomson was unnecessary. On August 1, Page lunched with Asquith, who had the final responsibility for deciding whether Casement should receive clemency. His memorandum on this meeting read:

> ... he [Asquith] confessed that he felt some anxiety about the anti-British feeling in the United States. This led him to tell me he could not in good conscience interfere with Casement's execution, in spite of the shoals of telegrams that he was receiving from the United States. This man, said he, visited Irish prisoners in German camps and tried to seduce them to take up arms against Great Britain – their own country. When they refused, the Germans removed them to the worst places in their Empire and, as a result, some of them died. Then, Casement came to Ireland in a German submarine, accompanied by a ship loaded with guns. In all good conscience to my country and to my responsibilities I cannot interfere.[10]

Page did not record whether he had discussed the diaries with Asquith, who had clearly reached his decision on strict legal criteria. Casement was executed two days later. The underhand methods employed by Hall and Thomson had the effect of arousing suspicions of foul play, particularly in Ireland, and of making Casement into a martyr. W. B. Yeats was particularly active, eulogising him in the poem 'Roger Casement':

> I say that Roger Casement
> Did what he had to do.
> He died upon the gallows,
> But that is nothing new.
>
> Afraid they might be beaten
> Before the bench of time,
> They turned a trick by forgery
> And blackened his good name.

Casement had been very discreet about his sexual orientation and the accusations of his homosexuality were widely disbelieved. Over the years the suspicion that British Intelligence had not only circulated the diaries but had actually fabricated them grew. Their retention by the Home Office, who withheld them from the public domain for more than three-quarters of a century, only increased the suspicion. Interestingly, the Irish Nationalist leader Michael Collins was given access to the diaries when he was negotiating Independence in 1921 and concluded that they were genuine.

Several of Casement's defenders put forward what became known as the Normand Theory. Armando Normand had been one of the most brutal managers of the Peruvian Amazon Rubber Company, whom Casement had exposed during his investigation in the Putumayo. He had obtained one of Normand's diaries, which he had sent to the Foreign Office. The supporters of this theory argued that British intelligence had deliberately attributed this diary to Casement in their efforts to discredit him. The trouble with this swap theory was that Casement had himself identified Armando Normand as a predatory *heterosexual*, who had habitually exercised *droit de seigneur* over the women and girls of the Putumayo.

In 1936 an American doctor, William Maloney, directly accused Hall of fabricating and circulating the diaries, firstly in an article in the *Irish Times* and then in a book *The Forged Casement Diaries*, which had a considerable impact. Although Maloney had not read the diaries, he drew attention to the Normand Theory and to patterns of inconsistency in the accounts of Collins and others who had seen them. The English poet Alfred Noyes, who had been a wartime employee of the News Department of the Foreign Office, had written a denunciation of the Black Diaries, describing them as touching the lowest depths of human degradation.

After he read Maloney's book, Noyes wrote to the Irish Press recanting his earlier work. Maloney noted that Hall had given Ben Allen, a London correspondent of the Associated Press, access to the diaries and had even promised him an exclusive, although this never materialised. Allen deposited a statement detailing his meetings with Hall in the National Library of Ireland. Knowing that the diaries were genuine and having assured the Admiralty that he would not publicly refer in any way to the decrypts, Hall refused to comment on Maloney's charges.

In 2001, the Casement diaries were at long last declassified and placed into the public domain at The National Archives. A forensic examination of the Black Diaries was commissioned by Bill McCormack, Professor of Irish Studies at Goldsmiths College, London and funded by the BBC and its Irish equivalent, RTE, who were co-producing a TV programme, 'The Secrets of the Black Diaries'. This task was entrusted to Dr Audrey Giles, an internationally respected expert in documentary forensics. In March 2002 she reported:

> The unequivocal and confident conclusion, which the Giles Document Laboratory has reached, is that each of the five documents collectively known as the Black Diaries is exclusively the work of Roger Casement's hand, without any reason to suspect either forgery or interpolation by any other hand. The Diaries are genuine throughout, and in each instance.[11]

The charges of fabrication so widely made against Hall and Thomson by Yates and others fail. But did Hall act unethically? Casement was unquestionably guilty of treason on at least two counts, the attempt to suborn Irish POWs in German camps and conspiracy against the Government of the United Kingdom. The argument that he had gone to Ireland to stop the rebellion, which he had put forward to Hall and Thompson and which was later reiterated by some of his defenders, was lame. Before he was executed, he wrote that he was guilty ten times over. The movement to grant him clemency was both powerful and internationally based. Asquith was notoriously loath to take unpleasant decisions and his robust determination not to interfere with the course of the law could not have been foreseen. The use of the diaries, which Hall and Thomson knew to be genuine, was a legitimate weapon against a powerful tide of popular sentiment. In the author's opinion, this charge also fails.

Spain

Hall was pleased enough with the results obtained by *Sayonara* to commission another yacht to undertake a comparable assignment, this time in Spain. He was concerned that Spain, traditionally friendly towards Germany, might turn a blind eye and allow the Kriegsmarine to set up refuelling locations for U-boats on their Atlantic coast, thereby considerably extending their range and increasing the risk of allied shipping losses. On this occasion, the yacht and its skipper and crew would be British. Once again Hall displayed his remarkable talent for selecting the right man for the job. He chose an Anglo-Irish baronet, the splendidly named Sir Hercules Langrishe, described as 'a very astute man ... brilliant at any sports he chose to go in for, a good helmsman, a Master of Foxhounds and a man who seized every opportunity of adventure'. Unlike Simon and Howell he would more or less be playing himself, an affable Anglo-Irish aristocrat who enjoyed the good things in life but was at the same time perceptive and worldly. The yacht *Vergemere* was put at Hall's disposal by the C-in-C Portsmouth and Langrishe was allowed to pick a naval crew. He was given a second mission; to convince the Spaniards that, despite the war and a pervasive German propaganda campaign, Britain was still a land of abundance. To this end Hall arranged that *Vergemere* would sail for Spain with a plentiful supply of the best champagne and instructed Langrishe to entertain lavishly and 'to turn on his full charm when he met Spanish ladies of influence'.[12]

The *Vergemere* mission proved both timely and fruitful. Langrishe discovered that the Germans had also dispatched a yacht to Spain on a similar mission, which he was told dared not put to sea for fear of British submarines. As its entertainment budget could only stretch to beer, Langrishe and his officers became highly popular with their guests winning the battle for Spanish hearts and minds hands down. As a result several influential Spaniards adopted a pro-British position. Langrishe provided Hall with much useful information, in particular confirming his perception that German intelligence was active in Spain and urgently needed to be countered.

In both World Wars, Spain was a happy hunting ground for the rival British and German intelligence services. As a strategically sited neutral country, Spain was a focal point for intelligence and subversion activities. The German embassy in Madrid directed and co-ordinated operations both in Spain and throughout Latin America. The success of the *Vergemere* expedition persuaded Hall to set up a permanent organisation in Spain under the control of the Naval Intelligence Division.

He placed Herschell, a close friend of King Alfonso XIII and his wife Queen Victoria Eugenie, a cousin of King George V, in charge. His contacts were to prove invaluable as his influence far outstripped that of the German Ambassador, Prince Ratibor, a diplomat of the old school who, unlike his colleague in Washington, Bernstorff, was extremely uncomfortable with his involuntary involvement in the world of intelligence and subversion.

To head the operation in Spain, Hall made an inspired appointment. A. E. W. Mason was a successful author who had published 35 books and plays, including the celebrated *The Four Feathers*. He had also been a Liberal Member of Parliament and was a keen mountaineer and yachtsman. From the outbreak of the war, Mason, ever young at heart, had become involved in propaganda; but seeking action and knocking off twelve of his 49 years, he had enlisted as a Captain in the Manchester Regiment. His contemporary, Anthony Hope, described him as a man of wonderful readiness and adaptability both of mind and body. It is not certain how Hall came to select him, but both men were members of the same London clubs, the Garrick and the Beefsteak. Hall quickly realised that Mason's talents were not being fully utilised as an officer in an infantry battalion and that he was better suited to intelligence work.

In his book *The Summons*, Mason has the character Martin Hillyard interviewed by Hall, thinly disguised as Commodore Graham.

> Hillyard entered a room, which surprised him. So greatly did its size and outlook from its windows contrast with the dinginess of its approach. A thin man with the face of a French abbé sat indolently twiddling his thumbs by the side of a big bureau.
> 'You wanted to see me.'
> 'Mr. Hillyard.'
> 'Yes.'
> 'In what way can I help you?'
> 'Bendish tells me that you know something of Spain.'[13]

Hall had Mason transferred to the Royal Marine Light Infantry and within a month of *Vergemere*'s return to Portsmouth, Mason had arrived in Spain as his representative on the ground. He and Hall became and remained close friends and Hall developed a high opinion of Mason's ability, describing him as 'my star-turn'. The two men were both prone to bronchitis and asthma and in later life regularly travelled to warmer climes to avoid the damp British winter.

Under Mason's leadership the organisation in Spain became increasingly effective and scored several coups over their German rivals. Mason produced a regular digest containing detailed information of disaffection among the workforce and of strikes fomented by German agents. Herschell passed this on to the Spanish Government, thus thwarting the German efforts as well as facilitating Spanish co-operation with Hall's network.

Mason never wrote his autobiography, although he left some notes about his intelligence work; his life by Roger Lancelyn Green devotes only one chapter to his service as an agent in Spain and later in Mexico. Mason wrote three short stories about Secret Service activities in Spain and Morocco, largely based on his own experiences and published in the early 1920s.

For the third time, Hall provided an agent with a steam yacht, on which Mason spent some of his time visiting Gibraltar and ports on the Spanish mainland, in the Balearics and in Morocco, playing the part of an eccentric English millionaire to perfection. When Mason asked the Governor of Cadiz why the locals were so unfriendly to the English, the Governor responded politely but with some incredulity: 'Have you forgotten Drake? ... Spain is a country of long memories.'

He discovered that Hall's concern that German submarines were being refuelled in Spanish ports was well-founded. When he complained to the Spanish authorities that a U-boat was being refuelled from a German merchant ship in the harbour of Cartagena, a blatant breach of Spanish neutrality, he was told that he had made the story up as anti-German propaganda. Refusing to be deflected, Mason waited in Cartagena until a second U-boat arrived. At some risk he sailed close to the freighter, and undetected by the Germans, took a photograph of the refuelling in process. The nationality of the freighter and the U-boat could not have been in any doubt. He printed thousands of postcard copies of the damning photograph which he distributed widely throughout Spain, putting a stop to this particular example of German disregard for the rules of war.

In his story *One of Them*, Mason's character Anthony Strange, working with a Secret Service representative, Major Slingsby, followed a German merchant ship in his yacht which had been equipped with a gun disguised as a capstan. The merchant ship was carrying a large number of barrels of 'bicarbonate of soda', which it suspiciously unloaded in a remote bay and then sailed away. Strange and Slingsby went ashore and discovered that the barrels contained diesel fuel. They broached the barrels and waited for the arrival of the U-boat, which they promptly sank with the concealed gun.

Soon after he arrived in Spain, Mason visited French Morocco, where he met with the proconsul, the famous General Lyautey, who was attempting to suppress a tribal rebellion instigated by a German agent named Bartels operating from the adjacent territory of Spanish Morocco. He discovered the methods Bartels was using through agents to keep money flowing into French Morocco and he succeeded in cutting off the funds and intercepting the flow of arms and ammunition to the rebels. He described this winning operation in his book *The Winding Stair*, published in 1923. Mason was the first member of naval intelligence to uncover the German involvement in germ warfare, a function entrusted to their agents in Spain. In his notes, Mason mentions his interception of a quantity of anthrax bacillus concealed in a consignment of shaving brushes. The bacilli were to have been injected into a shipment of mules being transported from South America to Spain by the French Army.

By the end of 1916, Mason's cover was in real danger of being blown. His fictional alter ego, Martin Hillyard wrote: 'The purpose of this yacht was long since known to the Germans. The danger of the torpedo was ever present ... and if she were sunk and he captured, any means would be taken to force him to speak before he was shot ... he carried hidden in a matchbox a little phial, which never left him, to put the sure impediment between himself and a forced confession of his aims and knowledge.'[14] For many years Mason kept the real phial in a drawer in his desk, which he would occasionally show to his friends, telling them it contained a powerful explosive. The phial probably contained cyanide of potassium. Two of Mason's fictional characters used this method to commit suicide.

In January 1917 Hall recalled Mason to London. He had achieved some significant successes and he had frequently thwarted the schemes of his German opposite numbers. He was replaced as head of Hall's operations in Spain by a more conventional but equally effective agent, the Royal Marine Colonel Charles Thoroton – Charles the Bold to his colleagues in Naval Intelligence. He had recruited Juan March, a native of Majorca who had become one of the leading tobacco smugglers in Spain. In later life, March went legitimate, ending up as one of the richest men in the country and one of General Franco's most important supporters. In World War II he once again became a valuable British agent, working for Hall's successor as DNI, Rear-Admiral John Godfrey. In a remarkable tribute to Thoroton, Ed Bell reported from the American Embassy in London to Leland Harrison, his superior in Washington, that Mason's operation

> ... had become immensely powerful and used frequently to get information to the Spanish government of disaffection and strikes in Spain itself, and when a few months ago Admiral Hall started to cut down the organization ... the Spanish Government actually requested him not to do so on the grounds that his organization was to them a far more reliable source of what was going on in the country than their own police and civil authorities.[15]

A later chapter will relate the saga of the *Erri Berro*, the interception at sea of a cargo of wolfram from Bilbao destined for Germany that was attempting to run the allied blockade, a major coup for Hall and his Spanish operation; and Mason's exploits as an agent in Mexico.

Notes

1. Tuchman p.62
2. Ibid. p.64
3. Beesly p.225
4. Ibid p.185
5. Ibid. p.186
6. James p.53
7. NMM OLV 12 *Oliver Recollections* p. 165
8. James p.112
9. Ibid. p.113
10. Hendrick *The Life and Letters of Walter Hines Page* Vol. 2 p. 168
11. *BBC History Magazine* April 2002 'Casement's Diaries Black and Right' by Paul Tizey
12. James pp.54-55
13. Green A.E.W. Mason pp.158-59
14. Ibid p.147
15. Beesly pp.190-91

CHAPTER IX

Jutland – An Intelligence Failure

One of the chapter headings in Hall's abandoned autobiography read: 'Jutland and German fleet out again August 1916'. Sadly he left no notes on the battle and his correspondence with Beatty was unfortunately lost by Ralph Straus, the co-author of his autobiography.

Admiral Hugo von Pohl, the former Chief of the Admiralstab who had succeeded the sacked von Ingenohl as commander of the High Seas Fleet after the Dogger Bank, proved to be as cautious as his predecessor. Constrained by the Kaiser's prohibition of any action that involved risk, the Fleet made only five sorties into the North Sea over the next year, never venturing more than 120 miles from Wilhelmshaven. On January 24 1916, von Pohl, stricken by terminal cancer, was replaced by the much more aggressive Admiral Reinhard Scheer. Scheer succeeded in obtaining permission from the Kaiser to undertake operations that would bring the Grand Fleet to action.

Beginning in March 1916, Scheer planned a series of actions against the east coast of England, intended to draw out the Grand Fleet. In the first of these operations, on April 25, planned to coincide with the Easter Rising in Ireland, his battlecruisers would bombard the East Anglian towns of Lowestoft and Yarmouth. Admiral Friedrich Boedicker, commanding the battlecruisers while Hipper was on sick leave, was instructed to retreat once the bombardment was completed. Scheer was to take the battle fleet to sea to act as a screen and to intervene if the Grand Fleet or Tyrwhitt attempted to attack the battlecruisers. The operation went wrong from the start. Boedicker's flagship, the ever unlucky *Seydlitz*, hit a mine and was holed below the water line. She was forced to return to Wilhelmshaven while the remaining four battlecruisers, screened by six cruisers and two flotillas of destroyers, proceeded towards their targets.

Room 40 had intercepted a number of signals and concluded, correctly, that an operation was in the offing. Hope's note on these signals read: 'HSF under way. "Special state and readiness" ... This implied an attack on Lowestoft as it subsequently turned out.'[1] Oliver was understandably reluctant to send the Grand Fleet to sea until Room 40 could confirm that the High Seas Fleet was out. However, he did not give either Jellicoe or Beatty any advance warning of the German operation until 3.50 pm on April 24 and the Fleet was not ordered to raise steam and put to sea until 7.05 pm, by which time Boedicker had already been at sea for several hours. This unwarranted delay in sending any intelligence to the fleet commanders made it impossible to intercept the German battlecruisers.

Tyrwhitt was, however, ordered to sea and at about 4 am on April 25 he sighted the battlecruisers. As his force was not strong enough to attack them, he turned away and continued to track them. After bombarding both towns, Yarmouth only briefly, Boedicker turned for home. As Tyrwhitt was engaging the German light cruisers, the battlecruisers suddenly emerged from the mists and opened fire at a range of 13,000 yards. Once again he turned away south but his flagship HMS *Conquest* was hit by a 12-inch shell, which killed or wounded 40 of his crew and reduced the cruiser's speech to 20 knots. Boedicker now had an opportunity to destroy Tyrwhitt's force, but, lacking Hipper's aggressive spirit, once again turned away to the east to rejoin Scheer. The Fleet commander had however been warned by the Kriegsmarine's radio station at Norddeich that Jellicoe and Beatty were at sea. Having lost any advantage of surprise, the frustrated Scheer decided to fight another day, and returned to port; Beatty, further delayed by heavy seas, was only 200 miles to the north.

Scheer now started to plan a very much larger operation, which the Royal Navy and the Kriegsmarine were respectively to name Jutland or Skagerrak. With its apparently inconclusive outcome, different opinions about strategy and tactics and the losses suffered by the Grand Fleet, Jutland inevitably became a subject of continued controversy in Britain. Beatty's questionable efforts as First Sea Lord after the war to rewrite the history of the battle in his favour forced Jellicoe and his supporters to respond in an effort to gainsay the revisionism. The disagreement between the two Admirals was exacerbated by the animosity between the capricious Ethel Beatty, no stranger to intrigue, and the 'formidable and peremptory' Gwendoline Jellicoe.[2] As the wags in the service clubs used to say, the disagreement between the Admirals was as nothing in comparison to the feud between their wives.

The claims and counter-claims aside, the battle has been the subject of objective works by authoritative naval historians: notably Arthur Marder in *From Dreadnought to Scapa Flow*, published in the 1960s and more recently Andrew Gordon in his admirable *The Name of the Game* and Robert Massie in *Castles of Steel*, his epic history of the clash between the Royal Navy and the Kriegsmarine in World War I. A review of the battle as a whole is beyond the scope of this chapter, which will concentrate on its intelligence aspects and primarily the Admiralty's handling of raw intelligence.

At Jutland there were lamentable technical and communication failures at all levels. British ordnance was inferior to German. Design flaws, unsafe ammunition handling practices and the instability of the British cordite resulted in the loss of three battlecruisers, including Hall's old command, HMS *Queen Mary*, with a fourth, Beatty's flagship HMS *Lion*, narrowly escaping destruction. The Kriegsmarine had taken corrective action after the near-loss of the battlecruiser *Seydlitz* in the fleet action of the Dogger Bank when a British shell penetrated her armoured deck, resulting in the destruction of her two aft turrets. They had instituted new handling practices, including equipping the battleships and battlecruisers with anti flash protection in the hatches connecting the turrets and the magazines. Although turret fires had broken out on both *Lion* and *Tiger* at the Dogger Bank, no similar action had been taken by the Grand Fleet. After Jutland, Commander Hubert Dannreuther, the surviving gunnery officer of HMS *Invincible*, another of the lost battlecruisers, admitted that, on his ship, the magazine doors had been left open.

The gunnery of the German battlecruisers was far more accurate than that of the British. During the so-called Run to the South, the battlecruiser encounter at the outset of the action, Hipper, who had placed far greater importance on gunnery practice than Beatty, scored 22 hits whilst receiving only six. Three of these were fired by *Queen Mary* before she blew up under concentrated fire from two of Hipper's best gunnery ships, *Derfflinger* and *Seydlitz*. Admittedly, Beatty had led his force in a formation that impeded the ships at the back of his line from opening fire. The smoke interference resulting from Beatty's handling of the approach to the German battlecruisers not only delayed his rear ships from opening fire but also prevented them from taking the target ranges and bearings essential for determining the opening range.

The Grand Fleet's command and control system proved to be a severe disadvantage. In August 1914 the author's father, a graduate of the second course of the War College, who was later to have a distinguished career in World War II, was serving in a triple capacity as Flag Lieutenant, Squadron Signals Officer and War Staff Officer to Vice-Admiral Sir Douglas Gamble, then commanding the Fourth Battle Squadron. Like many contemporary Admirals, Gamble resented the institution of the War Staff and the author's father wrote of him: 'He won't admit that a knowledge of war is the least necessary for any officers until they come to flag rank but how they are to learn it then I don't know ... the old school will not admit that any one junior to them can have any ideas at all.' He noted that the Fleet's command and control system was too rigid and the tactics were too inflexible, adding presciently that: 'I do hope we get a day of good visibility, then I think we shall wipe them off the map. A low visibility is unpleasant and anything may happen.'[3] Jutland was fought in poor visibility and the deficiencies of the Grand Fleet's command system were all too clearly demonstrated.

Communications failures were horribly frequent. Jellicoe was undoubtedly badly served by the uninspired leadership of many of his subordinate admirals and captains, from Beatty downwards, who repeatedly failed to keep him fully informed of German fleet movements. During the initial battlecruiser action, Beatty sent no signals to Jellicoe between 4.45 and 6.05 pm. In an uncanny repeat of the Scarborough Raid incident when Admiral Arbuthnott declined to open fire on German cruisers without orders from the Squadron Commander, Rear-Admiral Arthur Leveson, holding the same appointment commanding the B Division of the 2nd Battle Squadron, did not fire on German capital ships which had blundered into his line of fire during the night action.

When Scheer returned after the disappointing Yarmouth raid, he was informed by Admiral von Holtzendorff, the Chief of the Admiralstab, that the German Government, under American pressure, had abandoned the unrestricted submarine warfare campaign. A furious Scheer, ever a hawk, immediately recalled all the High Seas Fleet's U-boats. As these submarines would now be available to support the surface fleet, he began to plan an ambitious operation. He reckoned that if he could entice the British fleet to sea, he could station his U-boats to attack them once they had left the security of their anchorages.

He proposed that his battlecruisers would bombard Sunderland, a major industrial and shipbuilding town in the north of England, only 100 miles south of Beatty's base at Rosyth. He reckoned that such a challenge would inevitably result in Beatty coming out to attack the German battlecruisers and that his submarines, strategically positioned, might succeed in sinking several of his ships. As he still did not know of Room 40, he made the critical assumption that he had at least six hours in which he could deal with Beatty before Jellicoe and his battle squadrons could intervene. He intended to use his Zeppelin airships for reconnaissance, ordering them to patrol almost the entire North Sea south of a line from the Skagerrak to the Firth of Forth. The Zeppelins relied on clear weather, which was not always forthcoming. The operation, originally planned for May 17, was postponed until May 23, and then until May 31 because several of Scheer's latest battleships of the *Konig* class had problems with their condensers and *Seydlitz* was not released from the dockyard until May 29.

A lengthy spell of bad weather, preventing Zeppelin reconnaissance, forced Scheer to drop his projected bombardment of Sunderland and substitute an alternative plan. He ordered Hipper to patrol off the Norwegian coast and attack British merchant shipping on the trade routes in the Skagerrak, an operation which did not require aerial reconnaissance, reasoning that Beatty would go to sea to protect them.

From the middle of May, Room 40 intercepted a series of signals indicating that the HSF was being prepared for operations. By May 28 their decrypts revealed that a major German sortie into the North Sea was imminent. At 11.02 pm that evening Scheer instructed his fleet to assume a state of special readiness and at midnight warships were ordered to raise steam. His U-boats were told to remain at sea on June 1. At midday on May 30 the Admiralty used the land lines connecting it to Jellicoe's flagship HMS *Iron Duke* at Scapa and to Beatty on *Lion* at Rosyth, warning the fleet commanders that the HSF was assembling in the Jade River, indicating that it was going to sea. At 3:36 pm that afternoon, Room 40 intercepted Scheer's signal 31 GG 2490. The cryptanalysts concluded that 31 referred to an operation to be undertaken on the next day, May 31. At 5:16 pm the Grand Fleet and the battlecruisers were both ordered to raise steam. Twenty-four minutes later the Admiralty signalled both the commanders: 'Germans intend some operations commencing tomorrow morning, leaving via Horn's Reef. You should concentrate to eastward of Long Forties ready for eventualities.'

By 10.30 the entire Grand Fleet and the battlecruisers had left their anchorages. Thanks to excellent Room 40 intelligence, they had sailed three hours earlier than the HSF. The greatest armada in the history of naval warfare was now at sea. Jellicoe had under his command 24 Dreadnoughts, three battlecruisers, which had been sent north for gunnery practice, eight armoured cruisers, 11 light cruisers and 47 destroyers. Beatty's force was made up of six battlecruisers, the four Queen Elizabeth class fast battleships, which had been temporarily transferred to his command while the three battlecruisers were at Scapa, 12 light cruisers, 27 destroyers and one seaplane carrier. They were opposed by Scheer's 16 Dreadnoughts, six pre-Dreadnoughts, six light cruisers and 36 destroyers; and Hipper's five battlecruisers, five light cruisers, and 30 destroyers. So 143 British warships were facing 98 German. (By comparison, in the much more decisive Battle of Midway in 1942, the American task force consisted of 49 warships and the Japanese 71, a total of 120, or half the number of ships that took part at Jutland.) Both fleets were lumbered with obsolete vessels that proved to be a liability during the battle, the Grand Fleet by its armoured cruisers and the HSF by the pre-Dreadnoughts.

Oliver still rigidly controlled the transmission of decrypts to fleet commanders, forwarding intelligence only at his discretion. He was grossly overworked, habitually working a 15- to 18-hour day and unnecessarily overloading himself with routine. Fisher had once reputedly told Churchill that 'AKW (Wilson) and dear Oliver are mules! ... they concentrate for days on some side issues ... Oliver so overburdens himself he is 24 hours behind with his basket of papers.' He had no deputy and was supported by only one Personal Assistant. The inherent deficiencies of this system were to be graphically highlighted during the battle.

Oliver's practice of keeping intelligence at arms-length from operations had already resulted in inaccurate information being passed to

Jellicoe. He had exaggerated the strength of the HSF by stating that two *Bayern* class battleships with a main armament of 15-in guns and the battlecruiser *Hindenberg* had joined the fleet. In fact, Scheer had left *Bayern* behind in Wilhelmshaven as she was not fully worked up. Her sister ship *Baden,* and *Hindenberg* were still under construction and the latter did not join the HSF until 1917. If Oliver had permitted Hope to review the signals sent to Jellicoe and Beatty, this misapprehension would have been rapidly corrected. W. F. Clarke, a senior cryptanalyst who was on duty throughout the battle, pointed out that Room 40 had accurate and detailed information of the exact strength of the HSF, having analysed their call signs, movement of warships between the North Sea and the Baltic, details of exercises and gunnery training and of coaling. This intelligence does not seem to have reached the fleet.

Once at sea, Scheer had observed radio silence with his base for security reasons and to keep the British guessing where he was. He communicated with his squadrons using the effective low power radio developed by Telefunken, which Room 40 could not easily intercept and which was superior to the visual signalling on which the Grand Fleet largely depended, and as a result they had no current knowledge of the HSF's movements.

At about noon on May 31 Captain Thomas Jackson, the Director of the Operations Division, paid a rare visit to Room 40. Although he had held this appointment for more than a year, he had, according to W. F. Clarke, only been there twice previously. Jackson was a particularly narrow-minded naval officer, to whom the usually dispassionate Andrew Gordon attached a collection of choice adjectives, including ridiculous, angry and blustering, portraying him as a buffoon. He had never really grasped the advantages of cryptology. He scarcely bothered to hide his contempt for the talented civilian cryptanalysts, particularly the academics, on the grounds that they were not 'real navy'. He did not believe that they could make any contribution to naval operations: a job reserved solely for naval officers. As Clarke wrote:

> In 1914–18, cryptographers were regarded for a long time as puzzle solvers and not as the experienced intelligence officers which years of training and experience had made them. The room 40 cryptanalysts were well aware of Jackson's prejudice and normally kept well clear of him.[4]

With his habitual arrogance, Jackson asked where the Direction Finding stations placed the call sign DK allotted to Scheer's flagship *Friedrich Der Grosse*. The duty cryptanalyst replied 'In the River Jade'. The supercilious Jackson did not wait for any explanation and without any further ado, he left, unaware that Room 40 had known since the time of the Lowestoft raid that DK was the call sign Scheer used only when he was in harbour. When he went to sea, he used the subterfuge of transferring DK to a shore radio station in the Jade. If Jackson had told the cryptanalysts that he required this information to brief Jellicoe, they would have understood the reasons why he asked the question and would have pointed out that *Friedrich Der Grosse* was not in the River and that her call sign was changed when she was at sea.

Scheer's deception had succeeded in wrongfooting the Admiralty. Reacting to Jackson's misinformation, Oliver signalled Jellicoe and Beatty at 12.30: 'No definite news of enemy. They made all preparations for sailing this morning. It was thought Fleet had sailed but directional wireless placed the flagship in Jade at 11.10 GMT. Apparently, they had been unable to carry out airship reconnaissance which has delayed them.'

Hope, Denniston and Clarke – indeed the entire staff of Room 40 – did not know that this signal had been sent until several hours later. They would become uneasily aware that this grisly intelligence blunder could result in serious consequences. Indeed, as Massie wrote: 'The damage done by Jackson's bungling rippled on disastrously through the day and night.'[5] Firstly, to conserve fuel, Jellicoe was not sailing at top speed. If the Admiralty had informed him that Scheer and his battle squadrons were at sea, he would certainly have increased speed to support Beatty and to engage the HSF in battle while several hours of daylight remained. He was then three hours steaming time from Beatty. As the Admiralty had just informed him that Scheer was still in port, he could reasonably believe that Beatty's force, six battlecruisers and the four Queen Elizabeths, could deal with Hipper and his five battlecruisers. Unknown to either British Admiral, Scheer and his battleships were only 50 miles astern of Hipper. Had Jellicoe received the correct intelligence that Scheer was at sea, his and Beatty's dispositions in the opening phases of the battle would undoubtedly have been very different.

As he had no reason to doubt the accuracy of the intelligence, the signal lulled Jellicoe into a false confidence. His biographer noted: 'Jellicoe concluded that he still had plenty of time. There was no chance of meeting the enemy for hours to come. He eased off speed a little to conserve his destroyers' fuel, always a source of worry to him … It was altogether a most leisurely progress toward the action.' Had Jellicoe not been misinformed: 'He would have had a little more daylight for fighting, perhaps enough to be decisive.'[6] As a result, he was late in making his rendezvous with Beatty and valuable daylight was lost. At 2:10 pm Beatty prepared to make his planned turn to the north to meet Jellicoe. Fifteen minutes later, his scouting cruiser HMS *Galatea* encountered two of Hipper's destroyer escorts and opened fire, triggering the first shots of the Battle of Jutland.

At the outset Scheer was communicating with his squadrons by low powered wireless. The shore stations could not easily intercept this signal traffic although as early as 2.28 pm the battleship HMS *St Vincent* reported to Jellicoe that her alert radio operators were picking up a succession of strong signals on the HSF's normal frequency. Seven minutes later the C-in-C ordered the battle fleet to raise steam to full speed ahead. Although Gordon believed that the false feeling of security caused by Jackson's signal had only marginal consequences, over two hours had been lost before these orders were given. Secondly and far more seriously, Jellicoe's confidence in Admiralty intelligence was shattered when Beatty sent him a signal at 4:40 pm that he had sighted the HSF, which the Admiralty had told him was in the River Jade, 180 miles to the south of Scheer's position. As Beatty noted pointedly to Clarke when he visited him when he was C-in-C: 'What am I to think of the Operations Division when I get that telegram and in three hours time I meet the whole High Seas Fleet well out at sea?'[7]

Worse was to follow. During the battlecruiser actions and later while Scheer was pursuing the retreating Beatty northward Scheer maintained long distance radio silence. At 7.15 pm, Jellicoe crossed Scheer's T for the second time. and once again he subjected the HSF to the full force of his battleships' extremely accurate gunnery. The German C-in-C realised that his fleet, especially his already seriously damaged battlecruisers, was facing potential disaster. He cast around for a way of escaping the Grand Fleet and retreating southward. He decided to return to Wilhelmshaven by the most direct route, the way he had come, via Horn's Reef close to the Danish coast. Sooner or later, he would need to make radio contact with his shore bases and intercepts would flow in to Room 40.

Oliver's over-centralised system was already proving incapable of delivering the prime requirement of intelligence, its rapid dispatch to commanders. During the evening and night of May 31 the Operations Division descended from the merely inept to the downright dysfunctional. As the evening wore on, Oliver, who had been on duty almost continuously for three days, was forced to take a rest. Unbelievably Captain Jackson, as the next senior officer in Operations, was not even in the Admiralty and the responsibility for transmitting the vital decrypts was passed not to Hall, who had the necessary experience of both operations and intelligence, but to Rear-Admiral Allan Everett, Naval Secretary to the First Lord. Although Everett was a distinguished officer who had commanded the Signal School, he had no recent experience of operations and was unfamiliar with the system for handling intelligence. Serious errors were to follow.

On several occasions, delays occurred in the transmission of intelligence. A signal recording the position of the HSF, intercepted at 4:35 pm, was decoded and passed to Oliver at 5 pm. It was not sent to Jellicoe until 5.45 pm. An even worse delay took place two hours later. A Room 40 intercept of a signal from Scheer instructing three destroyer flotillas to attack the Grand Fleet during the night was not radioed to Jellicoe until 9.55 pm – almost 90 minutes after it had been received.

Jellicoe, understandably suspicious of the accuracy of Admiralty information, disregarded two signals, the first with good reason. At 9.58 pm he received a message placing the HSF 10 miles southwest of him. He knew this information to be inaccurate as the German fleet was then to his north-west. His dubiety about the intelligence increased. 'I should not for a moment have relied on Admiralty information of the enemy in preference to reports from the ships, which had actually sighted him to the north-west.'[8]

At 10.41 p.m. Scheer's signal of 9.10 pm finally reached Jellicoe. It read: 'German battle fleet ordered home ... battlecruisers in rear. Course south south east ¾ east. Speed 16 knots.' Although this signal was a clear indication that Scheer was returning to port via Horn's Reef, the already distrustful Jellicoe did not believe this intelligence.

The makeshift organisation within the Admiralty completely failed. Between 10:43 p.m. and 1 am no less than seven signals from Scheer revealing his current position were intercepted by Room 40 but were never transmitted by the Operations Division to Jellicoe. The most serious failure related to a signal from Scheer to his shore base requesting a Zeppelin reconnaissance of Horn's Reef at daybreak of June 1, received in the Admiralty at 10.10 pm. The significance of this intelligence would have been immediately apparent to Hall, had he been present, or indeed any experienced intelligence officer, who would have immediately ordered its transmission to Jellicoe. Instead the report was filed. If Jellicoe had received this intercept, combined with Scheer's previous signal, he would have had direct evidence of his intention to return by Horn's Reef.

> The lamentable part of the whole business is that, had the Admiralty sent all the information ... there would have been little or no doubt in my mind as to the route by which Scheer intended to return to base. As early as 10.10, Scheer's message to the airship detachment ... was in possession of the Admiralty. This was practically a certain indication of his route, but it was not passed to me.[9]

In 1928 Jellicoe wrote to the author's father, who had been his Flag-Commander on his round-the-world voyage to report on a proposed Imperial Navy, and who was then an instructor at the Naval Staff College at Greenwich preparing a lecture on Jutland. He referred to the failure to send him these signals: 'If only they had been passed to me ... how different things might have been, unless the thick weather off Horn's Reef had prevented action.'[10]

Deprived of this vital intelligence, Jellicoe abandoned his original plan to take up station off Horn's Reef at daybreak and turned north in the hope of encountering Scheer and collecting his by now scattered cruisers and destroyers. Some historians, notably Massie, have asserted that a decisive outcome might have been achieved if Jellicoe had been not been so badly served by the intelligence failures in the Admiralty and by the communications failures of his admirals and captains, who had neither reported having seen German battleships passing behind them during the night action, nor had opened fire. Massie believed: 'Nothing could have saved the High Seas Fleet had Jellicoe stood between it and Horn's Reef with eighteen hours of daylight ahead.'

Massie is almost certainly exaggerating. Another Trafalgar or Tsushima would have been improbable on that anniversary of Hood's Glorious First of June. As he admits, visibility was poor, not more than 4,000 yards, and Jellicoe's fleet was widely dispersed. Beatty's battlecruisers and, perhaps as seriously, his light cruiser squadrons, needed for scouting, had become detached. Seven of Jellicoe's battleships were now far to the west. Even without these capital ships, he still had a formidable force, nineteen Dreadnoughts, with which to give battle. Had he been able to encounter the HSF that morning, he would have inflicted serious damage on the Germans and probably finished off the already seriously crippled battlecruisers *Derfflinger* and *Seydlitz* and some of the more heavily damaged battleships such as *Konig*, which was dangerously low in the water. Such an action would have evened up the losses between the British and the Germans in both ships and men, preventing the Admiralstab from claiming a victory and enabling the Grand Fleet to return home with the satisfaction of knowing that they had encountered and succeeded in defeating the HSF.

In her acclaimed biography of her uncle Dillwyn Knox and his three equally accomplished brothers, Penelope Fitzgerald remarked that Room 40 was in disgrace after Jutland. This is an unusual mistake by a normally incisive writer.[11] Room 40 had performed superbly. Under Hope's experienced leadership, the flow of raw intelligence had been successfully analysed and the most important signals transmitted to the Operations Division. Her observation would have been more accurately made of Oliver and Jackson. As Beatty remarked, a system which depended so entirely on the judgment and decision of one man was totally impracticable and unsound. Ironically, Thomas Jackson, who bore considerable responsibility for the failures in the system, was promoted Rear-Admiral shortly after the battle. Nevertheless, he was a marked man and Jellicoe eased him out of the Admiralty soon after he became First Sea Lord in the following December. He was given an appointment as Alexandria, where, with this customary high-handedness, he was soon at odds with his subordinates.

Beatty's biographer, Stephen Roskill, declared that intelligence at Jutland was handled with almost criminal ineptitude. Massie was even more outspoken, remarking that in the Operations Division ignorance and incompetence held firm. The most recent commentator on Jutland, Paul Halpern, noted: '… the lessons were clear, all the intelligence received is of little value if it is not properly interpreted and transmitted to the people who need it.' These criticisms are justified; the Admiralty's failure to take full advantage of the magnificent Room 40 intelligence denied the Grand Fleet any chance of a more decisive victory.[12]

The ultimate responsibility for the breakdown in communications on the night of Jutland can be traced back to Fisher's failure to reform the Navy's command and control structure in his first term as FSL. He remained as opposed to the creation of a naval staff system as the fossil Admirals he loved to deride, preferring to keep all authority over operations in his own hands and, as one historian remarked to the author:

> ... perpetuating the delusion that victory comes from one man with a mass of rings on his sleeve, the Royal Navy and the Admiralty before and during the First World War were still Victorian in their concept of command, staff work and intelligence – unlike the Army, which thanks to the Haldane reforms and forward-looking officers like Haig and Robertson, had fully developed the general-staff system, with the Staff College at Camberley as the school for modern commanders and staff officers.[13]

In the aftermath of the battle, the Admiralty proceeded to add another serious failure in communications to the intelligence bungle during the encounter. On the evening of June 1, the Admiralstab issued a communiqué, which, if not actually mendacious, was certainly economical with the actualité. Declaring a victory they had not achieved, as they had turned for port leaving the Grand Fleet in command of the North Sea, they minimised their losses. They failed to mention that their newest and most powerful battlecruiser *Lutzow*, heavily damaged and in danger of sinking, was abandoned, her crew taken off, and was torpedoed and sunk by her escorting destroyers on the morning of June 1. The sinking of two light cruisers was not reported. The German press was triumphant, banner headlines reading 'Great Victory at Sea' and 'Many English Battleships Destroyed and Damaged'. The news was speedily taken up by Fleet Street: 'Great naval disaster! Five British battleships lost.'

The need for the Admiralty to issue a communiqué to contradict these rumours was urgent. It would be difficult to find four men less suited to the task at hand than the First Lord, Balfour, an Olympian patrician with a lofty disdain for public opinion and the three Admirals, Henry Jackson, Oliver and Wilson, none of whom regarded public relations as being of any importance. Balfour drafted most of what can only be called a maladroit document, released on the evening of June 2:

> On the afternoon of Wednesday, May 31, a naval engagement took place off the coast of Jutland. The British ships on which the brunt of the fighting fell were the Battle Cruiser Fleet and some cruisers and light cruisers

supported by four fast battleships. Among these the losses were heavy ... The battlecruisers *Queen Mary*, *Indefatigable*, and *Invincible* and the cruisers *Defence* and *Black Prince* was sunk. The *Warrior* was disabled ... and had to be abandoned ... no British battleship was sunk ... The enemy's losses are serious. At least one battlecruiser was destroyed; one battleship was reported sunk by our destroyers during a night action: two light cruisers were disabled and probably sunk.

The communiqué did not mention that Jellicoe had twice crossed Scheer's T, each time forcing him to turn away or that he had retreated to port during the night leaving the Grand Fleet in command of the North Sea. Published in the morning newspapers on June 3, the impression was inevitably given of a serious defeat. The Admiralty had seen fit to publish the communiqué without consulting Jellicoe, who was understandably furious. His vehement protests that the document had been misleading resulted in Balfour asking his predecessor Churchill to redress the balance. His report, published in the Sunday newspapers, corrected the misleading impressions given in the original communiqué but led to a new battle with the press, who, with some reason, asked why an out-of-office politician was given information denied to them.

Balfour and the senior Admirals had completely failed to consult Hall and the naval censor, Brownrigg, the only two officers in the Admiralty who had any experience of dealing with the press. By May 1916, Hall had been briefing reporters weekly for almost 18 months, with whom he had built up a good working relationship. His influence and personality was such that even the most hard-bitten reporters were careful not to reveal any confidences. Once again the top civil and professional powers in the Admiralty had insisted on carrying out themselves an important task that should have been delegated to able and experienced subordinates.

Hall's agents soon told him that the Kriegsmarine's losses were heavier than their communiqué had indicated. The admirable Consett reported to Hall that the subsequent revelation of the losses of the battlecruiser *Lutzow* and the cruiser *Elbing*, which had not initially been disclosed, had had a bad effect throughout Germany and that public confidence in any future Admiralstab communiqués had been shaken.[14] Roger Keyes, passing through London on his way from the Mediterranean to take over command of the battleship HMS *Centurion* in the Grand Fleet shortly after the battle, noted that he had studied the records of Jutland with Hall who ' ... assured me that the German Fleet had been sufficiently roughly handled to keep it in harbour for a few weeks.'[15]

Hall's reaction to the chronic failure by Oliver and the Operations Division to take full advantage of the Room 40 intelligence and of the opportunities missed can only have been one of utter frustration He had been out of the loop on 31 May and he was not involved in the fateful

Admiralty decisions. The events at Jutland had convinced him, more than ever, that the interception and interpretation of SIGINT had to be thoroughly integrated and that every aspect of operations and intelligence – two sides of the same coin – had to be equally thoroughly coordinated if the blunders which had marked that day were to be prevented in future. He was also uncomfortably aware that the necessary changes could never be implemented as long as Oliver remained as Chief of the War Staff and that he had to bide his time. The outcome of the battle cannot have improved the already uneasy relationship between the two men.

The loss of his old command, *Queen Mary*, of whom he had been so rightly proud, with all but eighteen of her crew, must have been a devastating blow to Hall. By his leadership and example, he had welded her crew, officers and lower deck alike, into a happy and efficient ship and she had been widely considered to be the champion ship of the Battle Cruiser Fleet. Gordon wrote that: 'sinking her was the Kriegsmarine's greatest single achievement of the 1914-18 war.'[16] Georg von Hase, the gunnery officer of the German battlecruiser *Derfflinger*, wrote a vivid account of her tragic end:

> *Queen Mary* was firing less rapidly than we were but usually full salvos. I could see the shells coming, and I had to admit that they were shooting superbly ... But the poor *Queen Mary* was having a bad time. In addition to *Derfflinger*, she was being engaged by *Seydlitz* ... at 4:26 p.m. [she] met her doom ... First, a vivid red flame shot up from her forepart. Then came an explosion forward, followed by a much heavier explosion amidships. Black debris flew into the air and immediately afterwards the whole ship blew up with a terrific explosion. A gigantic cloud of smoke rose, the masts collapsed inwards, the smoke cloud hid everything and rose higher and higher. Finally, nothing but a thick, black cloud of smoke remained where the ship had been. At its base, the smoke column covered only a small area, but it widened towards the summit and looked like a monstrous pine tree.[17]

In the August action, which Hall had referred to in his chapter heading, Scheer reverted to his plan to bombard Sunderland. From August 15 onwards Room 40 intercepts revealed HSF fleet movements, including a signal that two battle squadrons, together with battlecruisers and light cruisers, were assembling in the Jade River, indicating an imminent sortie into the North Sea. On August 18 further intercepts disclosed that the 3rd Battle Squadron had been instructed to sail from the Jade at 10.30 that evening and that Zeppelins were to proceed to their reconnaissance stations. Acting on this signal, Oliver ordered the Grand Fleet to sea within two hours of its being decoded and Jellicoe and Beatty had both sailed five hours before the HSF had left Wilhelmshaven, as Jellicoe's most recent biographer noted, 'thanks to excellent intelligence, better and more reliable'.[18] With 29 Dreadnoughts and six battlecruisers, the Grand Fleet was overwhelmingly superior to the HSF's 18 battleships and two battlecruisers. Tyrwhitt's Harwich Force was also sent to sea.

At 5.05 am on August 19, the British submarine E-23 torpedoed the battleship *Westfalen*. Her Captain's signal reporting the attack was immediately picked up by one of Room 40's Direction-Finding stations but this important intelligence and Scheer's instruction to the battleship to return to base was not sent to Jellicoe until 7 am. An hour earlier, one of Beatty's scouting cruisers, HMS *Nottingham*, was hit and sunk by three torpedoes from U-52. As no one aboard the cruiser had seen any torpedo tracks, Jellicoe, fearing mines, turned north. Two hours later, he received confirmation that *Nottingham* had in fact been torpedoed and resumed his original course. Although he had lost four hours, he could still have encountered the HSF. A faulty report from one of his Zeppelins saved Scheer from a possible disaster. At 12.35, he was informed that a force of 30 ships, including five battleships, was rapidly approaching the HSF and was only 70 miles to his south. The observers aboard the Zeppelin had mistaken Tyrwhitt's cruisers and destroyers for battleships. Scheer immediately abandoned the raid on Sunderland and altered course to intercept the weaker force coming up from the south. At 2.35 pm U-53, which had previously reported that Jellicoe had turned north after the sinking of *Nottingham*, now informed him that the Grand Fleet was steaming south, only 65 miles to his north. Fearing that he might get cornered in a pincer movement, the victorious Admiral of the Skagerrak wasted no time in turning east-south-east for home. Ninety minutes later Room 40 intercepted his signal that he was heading for Wilhelmshaven. When this intelligence that the HSF had once again declined battle was passed to him, a bitterly disappointed Jellicoe turned back to Scapa. The only consolation Scheer could derive from this abortive action was the loss that afternoon of another British cruiser, HMS *Falmouth*, hit by four torpedoes from U-66.

After Jutland, Jellicoe had never regained confidence in Admiralty intelligence or more precisely the way in which it was received on *Iron Duke*. In November, he wrote to Henry Jackson complaining that the intelligence received in signal form often did not match the details later sent to him in documents. Oliver was asked to draft a reply, which was eventually signed, slightly amended, by Balfour. In briefing Oliver for this reply Hope prepared this compelling justification of Room 40's methods and the care they had taken to maintain security.

> We can be reasonably certain that no naval operation can be undertaken by HSF without our having information of it. Without this knowledge we should be compelled to keep a large proportion of our Scouting Forces constantly at sea with all the liability to damage by torpedo or mine and the consequent wear and tear to personnel and material.

> The possession of these codes being of such great importance, every precaution should be taken by keep secret the fact that we have them.
>
> We know that the Germans have been working at our codes in the same way that we have been working at theirs ... we know this because the results of their investigations are frequently sent by wireless which we are able to intercept and decode. By this means we are able to know which of our codes are compromised.
>
> In order to prevent the Germans knowing their codes are compromised every care should be taken not to send wireless messages (which always run the risk of being intercepted and decoded by the enemy) containing information, which on the face of it, must have been obtained from an intercepted German message.
>
> For this reason it is undesirable to telegraph the C-in-C more information than is absolutely necessary. The risks of compromising the codes ought only to be taken when the results would be worth it.
>
> On really important occasions such as the HSF going to sea it is understood that the fullest information available is always sent to the C-in-C.
>
> On the other hand, there is a great deal of information obtained from the German intercepts which would be of use to the C-in-C and which might reasonably be placed in at his disposal.
>
> It is suggested that a daily summary of this sort of information might be prepared here and forwarded to the C-in-C personally by hand. This would be a more secure method of sending him such information.[19]

The First Lord reminded Jellicoe:

> My approval has been sought as to send you daily information of the proceedings of the Germans, which we derive from our secret method. By unremitting efforts for two years we have prevented the Germans from discovering this method. I have had many anxious moments: but so far the secret seems to have been well kept. If they have had their suspicions, they have not been strong enough to compel a change.

He agreed that a daily summary of intelligence would be sent to the C-in-C on the understanding that only he and his Chief of Staff would read the document, which was then to be burnt. More debatably, Balfour assured Jellicoe that:

> ... the information [sent to the Grand Fleet] is the best and fullest, which we possess. You may (very naturally perhaps) have sometimes supposed that we possess information not supplied to you, and that you are asked to act in ignorance of the relevant facts, which we have withheld from you. I can assure you that this is not so and that we always take you into our fullest confidence.[20]

In drafting this statement, Oliver must have known that he was, to say the very least, stretching the truth. When Jellicoe became First Sea Lord that December he must have been astonished to realise that Room 40 had been reading all the Kriegsmarine's codes daily and that the Operations Division had constantly withheld much of this vital intelligence from him. Although Oliver remained as Chief of the War Staff for several months, Jellicoe began the process of reorganising the management of Room 40 and its co-ordination with Naval Intelligence.

If Waterloo was won on the playing fields of Eton, then it might be said that Jutland was lost in the corridors of the Admiralty. In the last analysis Jutland was not a defeat for the Grand Fleet as Scheer, confronted with destruction, wisely opted to retreat, leaving Jellicoe in possession of the North Sea. Only once in the remaining 29 months of the war did the HSF essay a fleet action and thus it could be argued that, despite the losses and failures, Jutland was a strategic victory for the Grand Fleet.

Notes

[1] Beesly, p.148
[2] Private information relayed to the author regarding Lady Jellicoe's character
[3] Chalmers, *Full Cycle* p.19
[4] CAC CLKE 3
[5] Massie, p.582
[6] Winton, *Jellicoe* p.178
[7] Beesly, p.156
[8] Admiralty Narrative on Jutland p 108
[9] CAC RMSY 4/4
[10] Ibid
[11] Fitzgerald, *The Knox Brothers* p.136
[12] Roskill, *Earl Beatty: The Last Naval Hero* p.194. Massie, pp.640-641. Halpern, 'Battle in one Dimension' *Proceedings* June 2006
[13] Correlli Barnett to the author September 8 2005
[14] NHB Portsmouth, Consett papers Consett to WRH June 29 1916
[15] Keyes, *The Naval Memoirs of Admiral of the Fleet Sir Roger Keyes Scapa Flow to the Dover Straits 1916–1918* p.35
[16] Gordon, *The Name of the Game* p.120
[17] Massie, p.595
[18] Winton p.226
[19] CAC CLKE 1, Hope to Oliver November 8 1916
[20] Ibid Balfour to Jellicoe November 14 1916

CHAPTER X

Hall takes charge of Room 40

In May 1916 Sir Alfred Ewing was approached by his alma mater, Edinburgh University, and offered the post of Principal, the incumbent having recently died. He reluctantly turned down the approach on the grounds that he was involved in highly secret work, which he could not give up in time of war. Later that summer, the offer was renewed. Ewing took the opportunity of consulting Balfour, who was Chancellor of the University. The First Lord pressed him to accept, reminding him that at 61 he was approaching the retirement age for Admiralty civil servants and that the University was offering him tenure well into his seventies. Ewing's first wife had died in 1909; he had remarried and he and his second wife had a young child.

In October 1916, Ewing followed Balfour's advice and accepted the University's offer, relocating to Edinburgh. He retained his position as Director of Naval Education and continued to exercise some authority over Room 40 in what was clearly an unworkable arrangement. Although Hall was effectively responsible for its day-to-day operations from the time that Ewing left for Edinburgh it was not until May 1917 that he took full control. (Ewing had a successful tenure as Principal, eventually retiring in 1929, honoured by all who knew him. He died six years later.)

What did Ewing contribute to the success of Room 40 in the first two years of its existence? He can certainly take the credit for starting the operation from scratch, for establishing, together with Russell-Clarke, the network of Y intercepting stations, a vital component of a cryptology undertaking, and for the initial recruitment of a number of talented cryptanalysts from the universities and particularly from King's College, Cambridge. He picked his recruits well, many of them becoming stalwarts of Room 40. According to his son A.W. Ewing, he was not a hands-on manager:

> In the discovery of enemy ciphers Ewing took little direct part, except during the first year, for as the staff grew from a zero beginning, it came to comprise members whose faculty for that kind of inspired guessing and quick inference was far greater than his own; and it must be remembered

that the problems themselves had by this time become much harder. His chief function now was to collect the staff and organize it, giving it such general direction as was necessary.[1]

He was of course, an academic rather than a manager and, as his son suggested, he had become in effect a coordinator. He never seems to have understood the inherent flaw in the system: that Room 40 was not part of the Naval Intelligence Division, which was all too often unaware of the detailed information derived from the decrypts. He appears to have remained content with Room 40's status as a cryptological bureau and never attempted to develop its skills into an intelligence operation. Indeed, he was far too close to Oliver. The three Admirals responsible for operations, Henry Jackson, Oliver and Wilson, read only the raw intelligence provided from the more important decrypts. Inevitably, they cut themselves off from a much larger and potentially significant flow of intelligence.

There is no record that Ewing ever complained about the mishandling of Room 40 intelligence at the Dogger Bank or more seriously at Jutland, although he cannot have been unaware of the shortcomings of the Operations Division. As we noted in the previous chapter, three of his leading subordinates had been aghast at the misinformation sent to Jellicoe after Thomas Jackson's disastrous visit to Room 40 on the morning of the battle. No doubt that they would have expressed their exasperation most forcibly to Ewing. In fairness to him, he was working under restrictive rules specified by Oliver and Churchill and within these parameters he had been reasonably successful.

W. F. Clarke, who had been particularly frustrated by Jackson's intervention, became a vehement critic of Ewing's management of Room 40, casting doubt on whether he had ever contributed anything important to its success. He later wrote that Ewing never really understood the problems and wasted more of the valuable time of his subordinates than can be imagined.[2] Clarke was a fervent supporter of Hope and Rotter, he regarded them as the real powers of Room 40. His position was extreme but most of his colleagues seem to have been, at best, lukewarm about Ewing. Alastair Denniston barely mentioned him in the detailed notes he wrote of the early days of the operation. Nigel de Grey, the lead cryptographer on the Zimmermann telegram, remarked that Ewing was a chatterbox and thus presumably a security risk.[3]

By 1916, Room 40's outstandingly able cryptanalysts were able to interpret new and re-keyed German codes with remarkable speed. Its predominantly civilian staff were recruited from universities, commerce, the law and banking, representing an exceptional gathering of talent. Yet despite its undoubted efficiency it was still suffering from a lack of direction from the top. After the misuse of raw intelligence during Jutland and, despite Oliver's complacency, Balfour probably concluded that changes needed to be made at Room 40 and that Ewing had no more to contribute. Had the First Lord decided that Ewing was crucial to the continued efficiency of Room 40, he would not have encouraged him to return to academia.

The replacement of Ewing by Hall bears some resemblance to the removal of Denniston, another academic, as Director of GC & CS and its cryptology operations at Bletchley Park in 1942. Denniston had found it increasingly difficult to control the academics, including a number of prima donnas. He was moved sideways to direct the decoding of political signals in London. His successor Edward Travis was a tough-minded naval officer from the Paymaster branch of the service. The effectiveness of both the earlier and later operations improved sharply once a naval officer took charge. Their experience of large-scale organisation meant they could ensure that what was necessarily a complex operation ran more smoothly. As Frank Birch wrote: 'Power must follow knowledge and progressive organisation … becomes more urgent. The machinery must be continuously overhauled and improved in the light of experience and new ideas.'[4]

The strong connection between the Paymaster Branch of the Navy and naval intelligence is notable. Paymasters made a prominent contribution to the success of Room 40/NID in World War I, among them Rotter, Thring – who came back from retirement in 1939 when he was 64 to take charge of the Submarine Tracking Room – and Lloyd Hirst, and others. Hirst, who ran the Latin American section of Room 40/NID, had been the Intelligence Officer on HMS *Glasgow* at both Coronel and the Falklands. Another Fleet Paymaster, H. W. E. Manisty, ran the Anti-Submarine Division's tracking operation, working closely with naval intelligence. In 1913 the intelligence division employed three Paymasters, by December 1918 this number had risen to thirteen.[5]

In World War II two more Paymasters, Edward Travis, a long-standing officer of GC & CS, under whose leadership Bletchley Park achieved its greatest successes, and Norman Denning, who was one of the leading lights in naval intelligence and later became the last DNI before it was integrated into the combined Services Intelligence Divison, retiring as a Vice-Admiral, had especially distinguished records.

Since the days of sail, every ship which set out on a long sea voyage carried an individual who became known as the Purser, or Pusser in naval jargon, who looked after the cash, stores, victualling and such administration that the Captain did not deal with himself. Admirals and captains of larger warships were assisted by a clerk, who acted as their personal secretary. These positions were originally filled by civilians. By the end of the 18th century they had become Warrant Officers and their status continued to improve. In 1843 they received Commissions and the rank of Paymaster was introduced in 1852, instituting the Paymaster branch of the service. Paymasters continued to be known as Pussers.

Paymaster officers served in both Supply and Secretary roles during their careers. In a large warship, the Supply officers reported to the Paymaster-Commander while the Captain's Secretary, known in the service as 'Scratch', worked directly for the Captain. His responsibilities were far greater than merely handling correspondence and he was effectively the Captain's personal adviser. As he was privy to all the Captain's secrets, he inevitably became a figure of influence in every aspect of the ship's affairs, a big job for a young man.

A successful Captain's Secretary often stayed with his chief if the latter became an Admiral and as he took up different appointments. An adroit and experienced Admiral's Secretary wielded substantial authority. A classic case was Ronald Brockman, who over a period of 26 years served as Secretary to only two Admirals, firstly Dudley Pound until he died in harness as First Sea Lord and then Mountbatten, until his retirement as Chief of the Defence Staff in 1965. Like Denning, he retired as a Vice-Admiral. Perhaps the early responsibility and authority, together with the involvement in so many of the complexities of the running of a ship, explain the success of the Pussers in NI; but there is a more straightforward explanation.

The development of wireless in the first decade of the twentieth century resulted in a dramatic increase in signals traffic between ships and ships and shore stations. A sizeable proportion of this traffic was classified as high security and had thus to be transmitted in cipher. Under Naval regulations, only officers could perform the ciphering and deciphering of any coded traffic. Ashore, this function could be entrusted to civilian cipher clerks under the supervision of naval officers. Ships had to find suitable cipher officers from the wardroom. Because of their existing duties, watchkeeping officers could not take on this function, so the opportunity fell to the Paymasters. By the time of World War I, which resulted in a further rise in the flow of secure signals traffic, they had become deeply engaged in the handling of communications.

From this situation, it was a short but logical step for Paymasters to become involved in intelligence. As their experience tended to be more extensive than that of officers of equivalent rank in other branches of the service, they were well equipped to handle the routine of intelligence. In appointing Lloyd Hirst as HMS *Glasgow*'s intelligence officer, Captain Luce was following the procedure of many of his contemporaries. The talented Norman Denning was appointed to the intelligence division at the time it was being expanded in 1936 precisely because he had been a successful Admiral's Secretary and had acquired considerable familiarity with many aspects of the higher direction of the service. In World War II, when the volume of signals traffic made that of the previous War look insignificant, large number of civilians were commissioned as Paymasters RNVR and did yeoman work in ciphering and intelligence, both ashore and afloat. Commander Rodger Winn, a lawyer in civilian life, who succeeded Thring as Head of the Submarine Tracking Room, had a particularly distinguished record. Paymasters can legitimately take pride in the achievements of members of their branch in both World Wars, an accomplishment that seems never been to have been adequately recorded.[6]

In one important area Hall acted quickly and decisively after Ewing's departure to Edinburgh. He built up close contacts with the Army's cryptological operation, M1.1b, which had been broken off in October 1914 apparently because of a petty dispute between the Admiralty and the War Office. The two operations were complementary as Room 40 dealt almost entirely with German diplomatic decrypts while M1.1b concentrated on neutral cable traffic. Earlier in 1916 M1.1b, led by Major Malcolm Hay, a Gordon Highlander who had been wounded earlier in the war and declared unfit for active service, had successfully broken the Greek, Spanish and Swiss codebooks. The Greek decrypts were of special interest as the pro-German King Constantine was regularly sending messages relating to the allied campaign in Salonika to his brother-in-law, the Kaiser, by wireless from Athens to Sofia, the capital of Bulgaria, a German ally. These contacts remained strong for the rest of the war.[7]

Before his departure, Ewing had never attempted to build up a working relationship with the French or Italian navies and with their intercepting stations in the Mediterranean. The entire operation was still understaffed and overworked. Room 40 did not even employ any typists. As a result, the strain on the staff was increasingly showing. Rotter's health broke down. Happily, as one of the operation's stalwarts, he was able to return after a spell of sick leave. Ewing had bequeathed Hall some serious problems. He rose to the challenge with his customary decisiveness and energy.

Dillwyn Knox was probably the most able and by far the most eccentric of Room 40's cryptographers; because he firmly believed that he worked most effectively from his bath, he annexed Room 53, which by some architectural quirk had the only bath in the Old Building. His niece Penelope Fitzgerald described Hall's initial impact on Room 40 and painted a vivid picture of the everyday work:

> Under his hypnotic blue gaze and furious energy, the work was reorganized and redivided, and the modest 50 personnel, keeping two-man watches round the clock, was greatly increased. Hall foresaw the complications that were to come, and imperiously told the Treasury that he must have more money for more codebreakers. Why 'Blinker' Hall made up his mind to recruit university dons for Room 40 is uncertain. Having gone to sea at the age of fourteen, he cannot have met many of them before. Dons are clever, but how did he know that they would be clever in the right way? International business would seem a more promising field, and there were in fact brilliant cryptographers in the department from the City. The French and the Germans recruited serving officers. But Hall wanted dons.

It was no easy matter to 'sell' them to the Treasury and to the Navy. Gilbert Waterhouse, W. H. Bruford and Leonard Willoughby were lecturers in German, and seemed admissible, but John Beazley was an expert on ancient sculpture and pottery; Frank Adcock, the Dean of King's, was a classical historian; Frank Birch, drafted back from active service, was also a historian; and Dilly [her uncle Dillwyn Knox] came straight from the papyri. It was much to Hall's credit that he managed to turn this awkward squad, who muddled up six bells and six o'clock and failed to salute admirals on the street, into a more or less naval department. Once in, however, they settled down well enough. Senior Common Rooms had prepared them for this much stranger room, cut off from the ordinary world. And for accuracy, discretion and secrecy they could be absolutely relied on.

You reached I.D. 25 [as Room 40 was renamed once it had been integrated into the Intelligence Division in May 1917] through two arches in the Old Buildings. The basement acted as a kind of telegraph office. Intercepted messages coming in by land-line were printed out and sent up by pneumatic tube of the kind that still can be seen in some old-fashioned shops. In the enormous Room 40 itself, the shuttles rattled in to wire baskets at the rate of two thousand a day, with a sound like a Maxim gun. 'Tubists' sorted them into their-time groups and put those aside beginning SD (*sehr drigend*, very urgent). The signals were still in the familiar code, but this was superenciphered by rearranging the letters in vertical columns under a keyword. The key, which in 1914, had been changed once every three months, now changed every twenty-four hours. At midnight the watch on duty set to work frantically to find the new key. It was alleged that if they solved it they fell asleep again immediately; if not, they hung their heads in shame as the new watch came on. But Room 40 was only the central cell of the hive-like organization. It was surrounded by rooms, which were all marked NO ADMITTANCE. RING BELL; but there were no bells. In the rooms were specialized units; directional, diplomatic (Desmond MacCarthy worked in this), Baltic Traffic (set up by Frank Birch), the Card Index, on which every signal was registered, and so forth. There was also an administrative staff, though much smaller than in most departments, but no tea ladies, and no cleaners. Room 40 was never dusted until the war was won.[8]

Fitzgerald created a slightly misleading impression about recruitment. While Hall increased staff numbers and recruited a number of specialists, some of whom were dons, he cast his net wide and often outside academia. In addition to those she named, he brought in a number of dons, mostly Professors and lecturers in German studies, the most important of whom was Dr. E. C. Quiggin, lecturer in German at Cambridge. Quiggin in turn recruited two of his colleagues in addition to Bruford, Edward Bullough and C. W. Hardisty. Hall set Quiggin and Bullough to work on breaking Austrian codes, a hitherto untouched area, while

Hardisty assisted Faudel-Philips, nicknamed the Lord Mayor, in Room 40, on the Berlin-Madrid traffic, which became even more important after the US broke off diplomatic relations with Germany.

Like Knox and Birch, Frank (later Sir Frank) Adcock was a Fellow of King's College Cambridge. During his long academic career he served as both its Vice-Provost and Dean and was Professor of Ancient History at Cambridge for more than 25 years. Adcock was a remarkable character, a distinguished classical scholar and the main editor of *Cambridge Ancient History*, published between 1923 and 1939, the clarity, accuracy and lack of ambiguity of which owed much to his superb talent for improving the work of other scholars.

Adcock had been a postgraduate student in Munich and Berlin where he had been tutored by Williamwitz-Moëllendorf, described by one authority as one of the greatest classical scholars of any age. He had complete command not only of written German but of the inflexions of the language, which made him one of Room 40's most effective and successful analysts.

Tam Dalyell, the Labour MP and former Father of the House, got to know Adcock who was his supervisor when he was an undergraduate at King's in the early 1950s. He remembers his delicious wit 'worth a guinea a minute' both as a conversationalist and as a lecturer and his habit of asking his students to go for a walk with him in the afternoons when 'his chunky, rotund figure propelled itself at an amazing pace'. Like other Room 40 veterans, he served at Bletchley Park in World War II where he acquired the enviable reputation of being able to read the thought processes of Admirals Raeder and Doenitz and other German leaders. He was the first cryptanalyst to receive official recognition when he was awarded an OBE in 1917.[9]

Other recruits from academia included Ernest Harrison from Trinity College Cambridge, F. E. Sandbach and C. E. Gough from the Universities of Birmingham and Leeds respectively, and D. L. Savory, Professor of French at Queens University Belfast.

Hall appointed a couple of actors and the musical critic and author, Francis Toye, who was later to write an account of his experiences at Room 40, plus several army officers who had been wounded and declared unfit for active service. Three of these officers, Spencer Leeson, Edward Molyneux and Lionel Fraser were to become distinguished in later life, Leeson becoming Headmaster of Winchester and Bishop of Peterborough, Molyneux a couturier and Fraser a prominent City banker. An older generation was represented by Lord Lytton, son of a Viceroy of India and himself a former Civil Lord of the Admiralty, and by the barrister, Thomas Inskip, a future Attorney General and Minister for the Coordination of Defence, who as Lord Caldecote achieved the remarkable double of becoming both Lord Chancellor and Lord Chief Justice.

Another City figure, Frank Tiarks, a partner in the merchant bankers, Schroders, who had started his career in the Navy, developed a talent for managing the Direction Finding stations. Many of the non-academics were employed in the function described by Fitzgerald as 'Tubists', handling and distributing the ever-increasing flow of intercepted signals discharged from the pneumatic tubes. Others worked as junior watchkeepers, freeing up the cryptographers for their essential work.

The first female member of the Intelligence Division, Ella Lee, from a naval family, had been appointed as early as 1915. Many were to follow. Hall quickly saw that trained secretaries and typists were vitally needed to speed up the transmission of raw intelligence to the Operations Division. He selected Lady Hambro, the wife of the merchant banker Sir Everard Hambro, to manage the secretaries. Ebba Hambro was a formidable and capable lady, who once shocked her male colleagues by smoking a cigar at a Room 40 social function. As security was vital, she recruited the secretaries, many of them university graduates, from a list supplied by members of the staff. Not all of them had typing skills when they came to Room 40 but, under Lady Hambro's ever watchful eye, they soon became competent and valued members of the staff, speeding up the flow of raw intelligence.

The December edition of the 1916 Navy List revealed a substantial increase in the naval and civilian staff of the Intelligence Division and Room 40 during the year. In December 1915 the division had employed nine clerks. A year later, this figure had risen to include one confidential writer and 15 male and, for the first time, 20 female clerks. Among the staff were twelve officers lent by other departments and 25 cryptographers listed under the Naval Education Department. The establishment continued to rise over the next two years. Room 40 eventually employed about 100 people, around 20 of them women. As the male staff included at least 12 Old Etonians, Hall was inevitably accused of snobbery but in reality his attitude to talent was eclectic. He would take it wherever he could find it, regardless of class or background. (In contrast, the bizarre but effective Colonel Claude Dansey, Deputy Chief of MI6 in the Second World War, consistently refused to employ university graduates.)

In 1953 Clarke drew up a list of the remarkable ladies who became known as Blinker's Beauty Chorus:

> Miss Tribe, secretary to Hope, Welsford, who insisted in joining up again in 1939, Jenkin now famous in the BBC programmes, Mrs. Denniston, Spears, Henderson, daughter of Willie (later Admiral Sir Wilfred Henderson and one of the organizers of the convoy system), Mrs. Bailey, who rather upset things with her love affairs, Hudson who came as my secretary and used to embarrass us by her early arrival (when the night watch was still bathing) ... and daughter of the soap king ... Curtiss who in my view was the most

useful of them all, Joan Harvey, daughter of the Secretary to the Bank of England ... Surprisingly there was only one romance ... Miss Roddam, who spent most of her working time in a bathroom, which we had with some difficulty persuaded the authorities to install. She married Dilly Knox (she was his secretary and shared his somewhat bizarre office).[10]

Clarke had forgotten that Denniston also met his future wife in Room 40.

Ebba Hambro's talents included writing passable poetry. She composed an amusing piece of verse which she called 'The Confidential Waste', gently sending up the people of Room 40 and how they dealt with the inexorable flood of paper. No one escaped her pen:

'Captain James has lost his baccy, Mr. Clarke his favourite pipe ... Mr. Knox was missing from the learned Pundit troop. A fit of aberration due to some 3-letter Group. We found him in the Confidential Waste.' The opening and closing verses give some kind of indication of the superlative spirit which embraced everyone who worked at Room 40:

The day I went to work inside Room 40's sacred walls,
the first thing they taught me, and this sentence still appals;
"Put it in the Confidential Waste."

I soon found out the benefits that from the sack accrue.
It swallowed all you gave it and no one ever knew
What things you shoved in Confidential Waste.
And when the war is over, I shall contemplate with glee,
All enemies of England, whosoever they may be.
Burnt up with all the Confidential Waste.[11]

Ella Lee remembered that no one could ever refuse Hall anything he asked for, no matter how tired one was or how inconvenient the request. Although she was well aware of his explosive temper when his staff knew to keep well clear of him, she added that thunder soon gave way to sunshine, noting that Hall's charm resulted in him being quickly forgiven; but his slightest word was law. The spirit Hall had inspired throughout the Intelligence Division and in Room 40, which Ebba Hambro evoked in her verse, was a consistent theme, recalled by so many of its staff as these tributes indicate.

Marjorie Napier (a family friend, who worked in Naval Intelligence in both wars): 'He inspired loyalty and devotion in his staff in whom he took a personal and stimulating interest. Normally friendly, he could be terrifyingly stern. He had a schoolboy delight in pulling off a coup.'

Lionel Fraser: 'Those of us who served Admiral Hall all revered him. We knew we would be his slaves, come what may, such was his magnetism and our blind devotion.'

Clarke (who was not above disparaging some of his colleagues): 'I do not think that anyone who ever served under Blinker will ever forget his keenness, his energy and his kindness to us all, I certainly never shall ... Toward the end of the war when things were very strenuous and conditions exacting, he would come in through our workshop and say "Look here, some of you want a little relaxation, my car is outside ... you and you are to go out in it for a breather" ... When one of our more brilliant cryptographers had solved a very complicated problem, Blinker asked him what he would like as a present and gave him the easy chair from his room, which he asked for.'[12]

Walter Bruford: 'He had become a legend long before I saw him. By the time I was appointed in 1917, a group of people dealing with naval messages in Room 40 proper was quite large and worked round the clock ... He brought great energy, enthusiasm and organising ability to the task of securing adequate funds and staff and to the extension of naval intelligence into all kinds of fields ... [He was] quite small but had great authority. His quick judgment was no respecter of persons and his limitless self-confidence put many backs up. He used his great power as a mystery man autocratically but apparently to great effect ... I think he was generally admired and trusted by his staff, who felt themselves engaged in highly urgent teamwork.'[13]

Francis Toye: 'He was the most stimulating man to work for I have ever known. When, blinking incessantly, exuding vitality and confidence, he spoke to you, you felt that you would do anything, anything at all, to merit his approval. No man, I dare swear, did more to win the war, no man ever loved or served his country better.'

Spencer Leeson: 'He was indeed an admirable chief to work for. He held us all together and kept the peace. He could spot ability and industry and when he had done so, would extend the range of the man's work, showing him thereby that he was trusted. Mistakes he would call attention to, but not in a too heavy-handed fashion ... He had the knack of educating us in our affairs without seeming to. His speech was quick and short and rather elliptical, not always easy to follow; but when reinforced by his twitching features and sparkling eyes, was very stimulating.'

A final word to Ruth Skrine, his confidential secretary:

> He seemed to have all the qualities most essential for the head of such a Department. He was uncannily quick at sizing up a man – of almost seeing into his mind, and I am sure – unknowingly often – he exercised a sort of hypnotism on some of the unfortunate victims who fell into his hands. Jimmy Bone, the London Editor of the *Manchester Guardian*, once said to me: 'Your great little chief is half Machiavelli and half school-boy' and this was true; the Machiavelli in him was cruel ... But the school-boy was always round the corner, and the love of the dangerous game he, and all of us,

were playing would bubble out, and the fun and hazard of it all would fill him with infectious delight. 'Adventures are for the adventurous' he would chant, rubbing his hands and grinning like a crafty little French Abbé.

He was a gambler. One of his favourite sayings was 'Mistakes may be forgiven, but even God himself cannot forgive the hanger-back.' We all followed with a blind devotion the risks he took, because we were sure he was going to win.

He was a born optimist. 'There are no hopeless situations' he would say, 'There are only men who become hopeless about them.'

His charm would carry everything before it at those wonderful weekly meetings with the Press when representatives would throng into his inner room … thirsty for sensational news, and they never went away disappointed, as his task was to trust them absolutely and to tell them so. He would let them into some secrets not for publication, and tell them others they could make use of, and he proudly and rightly boasted that the Press had never once let him down.[14]

Hall's success at Room 40 was an even greater achievement given that so many of the staff were civilians, some of whom, notably the academics, had an irreverent approach to naval discipline.

With the increased staffing and the establishment of the secretarial function Hall was quickly able to introduce a succession of much-needed innovations. From December 1916, a War Diary was produced daily and a copy sent to the Commander-in-Chief of the Grand Fleet, by then Hall's old chief, Beatty. Although the Diary inevitably took at least 24 hours to reach the C-in-C, it provided him with invaluable information to back up the signals sent to him in real time by cable or wireless. Unfortunately the Diary was heavily qualified with such prefaces as 'We believe that the following is going to happen' or 'it is likely that…' which substantially reduced its usefulness. Beatty told Clarke, when he visited the Grand Fleet, that he was often unsure of the reliability of the information he was receiving from the Admiralty. Hall insisted that the decrypts were no longer sent in raw form to the Operations Division, but rather were accompanied by detailed situation-assessments.

Additional sections of Room 40 were set up with specific geographical and technological responsibilities, including direction finding, the U-boat offensive, minesweeping and operations in the Heligoland Bight and in the Baltic; and as mentioned earlier, a number of cryptographers were detailed to work on the breaking of Austrian codes.

Early in 1917 Herbert Hope, who had long wished to return to sea, was promoted Captain and left Room 40 to take over command of the cruiser HMS *Dartmouth* in the Mediterranean Fleet, winning the DSO. He finally retired as a Rear-Admiral. Although he had never really got on with Oliver, he can take credit for Room 40's early successes and in effect he, rather than Ewing, had been its real head. This quiet and self-effacing officer may not have had the status or the seniority to lobby for an extension of Room 40's authority but he was a man of extremely sound judgment. Hope enjoyed the total confidence and loyalty of his talented but mainly civilian team to whom he was their 'beloved chief'. He was not an easy act to follow. Two replacements failed to make the grade and were quickly removed by Hall, who eventually managed to select his own candidate. Fortunately for him, Willie James, his Commander on HMS *Queen Mary* and previously his Gunnery Officer on HMS *Natal*, had left the battlecruiser some three months before Jutland to become Staff Officer Operations to Admiral Sturdee, Vice-Admiral 4th Battle Squadron in the Grand Fleet and the victor of the Falkland Islands. Sturdee and Beatty were very reluctant to lose James but Hall could be extremely persuasive and finally secured his transfer in the face of their determined opposition.

James took command of Room 40 in May 1917. He was an entirely different character to his predecessor. Like Hall he was a gunnery specialist, who had spent most of his career at sea, Fitzgerald describing him as 'a delightful, breezy and efficient sailor'. He took a little time to understand cryptography, and to familiarise itself with his new staff, very different in personality from his subordinates on Sturdee's flagship. After his first tour of the crowded and cramped accommodation collectively known as Room 40 and meeting the academics, he wrote: 'Around me were a number of civilians and RNVR officers, all talking a strange language and doing strange things; it was an astonishing sight.'[15] He took some convincing to believe that his new staff were actually serving in the Navy.

The staff, accustomed to Hope's methods, initially resented their new chief, who not unreasonably believed that those who keep dogs do not have to bark themselves. He regarded himself as an administrator of an exceptionally talented team and not as one of their members. His intuition and approach was correct and he was quick to invest the sureness of touch which he had gained in sea command and as Sturdee's chief staff officer in protecting and increasing Room 40's authority and influence. Although some of them, notably the acidulous Clarke, considered James to be something of a dilettante, they soon came to accept the change in command and appreciate their new chief and the added clout with which he had endowed Room 40.

He soon decided that the influence of the staff would be increased by giving them RNVR commissions. This move was not initially well received by some of the most senior members of staff. The Fighting Padre, William Montgomery, did not go along with his colleagues, writing to Hall that he did not accept that clergymen should not take part in war, adding that he only regretted he could not go to sea and that he was proud to become a naval padre.

Immediately after he took over, James divided Room 40 into three sections: cryptography, direction finding and intelligence. This reorganisation, together with the secretarial staff led by the able Ebba Hambro, considerably increased the operation's effectiveness. At long last, Room 40 was firing on all cylinders.

With the operation's improved efficiency, Hall was able to tackle an important area Ewing had neglected: liaison with the allies. Early in 1917, he had visited the Italian Navy HQ in Rome and the Mediterranean Fleet in Malta and Alexandria. He had discovered that the French and Italian naval cryptographers were having little success in decoding the large volume of German and Austrian signal traffic they were intercepting. After the disaster at Gallipoli, the British Mediterranean Fleet had been severely reduced and its chief responsibility was trade protection and supplying the Army in the Middle East and in the bitter campaign against the Turks and Bulgarians at Salonika, in which the French army was also involved. A fierce rivalry between the French and Italian naval commands, each of whom had been furthering their national interests, was preventing the co-ordination of operations and intelligence. Neither Navy trusted the other. The French Navy's objective was limited to protecting their supply lines to their bases in Algeria and to their army at Salonika. The Italian Navy, motivated by their intention to conserve their battle fleet as a bargaining tool at a peace conference, was strongly opposed to risking it by fighting any sea actions.

During 1917 an inter-allied agreement placed a British Commander-in-Chief in the Mediterranean, initially Admiral Sir Rosslyn Wemyss, and later Admiral Sir Somerset Gough-Calthorpe, empowered to direct antisubmarine operations. The scale of shipping losses in the Mediterranean had become considerable. In April 1917 German and Austrian submarines sank a total of 258,000 tons of shipping.

Following his visit to the Mediterranean, Hall sent a team of Room 40 veterans, headed by Nigel de Grey – fresh from his success in deciphering the Zimmermann telegram – to Italy where they set up an intelligence centre, first at the naval base at Taranto and then in Rome. They were accompanied by a naval party, trained by Russell Clarke. The objective was to install an additional chain of both direction finding and intercepting stations, which were desperately required. With his team de Grey developed a close relationship with the Italian Director of Naval Intelligence, working successfully on the breaking of Austrian codes.

As a result of Hall's initiative, intelligence on German and Austrian movements and in particular on the activities of U-boats in the Mediterranean, Adriatic and Aegean seas had improved sharply by December 1917. The decrypts and the, by now, extensive chain of direction finding stations permitted the allies to establish an effective tracking system and thus divert convoys away from the known positions of the U-boats. The co-ordination of allied intelligence, which could admittedly have been implemented at least a year earlier, helped to counteract the ongoing German and Austrian submarine campaign. In January 1918, the allied navies sank two U-boats, as many as in the entire previous year, several more being destroyed during that year. Together with better convoy protection, intelligence played a considerable part in the steady reduction of shipping losses, which by January 1918 had dropped to 103,738 tons. In the last full month of the war losses had fallen as low as 28,007 tons, a tribute to this effective co-ordination of operations and intelligence.

Co-operation between Room 40 and the French military and naval cryptographers had been minimal until Hall and James took full charge in May 1917. They provided technical know-how to the French authorities, which enabled them to intercept the Austrian codes, although Hall declined their request for information about the German naval codes. He was presumably reluctant to provide full access to Room 40's cryptological knowledge in view of the French Navy's minimal involvement in operations outside the Mediterranean, unless they could provide any SIGINT to which Room 40 had no access. With this proviso, he arranged for a regular transmission of information to their Naval staff on a similar basis to the War Diary being sent daily to Beatty. Hall built up good relations with the French Naval C-in-C, Admiral De Bon, and the pipeline of information which ran between the two Admiralties was handled by Serocold, fluent in French, and by Commodore Heaton Ellis, the British naval attaché in Paris and a former Deputy DNI. By the end of 1917 the co-operation between the naval intelligence divisions in both countries had been greatly improved.

By contrast, relations between Room 40 and the Imperial Russian Navy had always been cordial and the two services had freely shared intelligence in gratitude for the Russian Navy's generosity in providing a copy of the SKM codebook, captured on *Magdeburg*. Expertise in breaking new keys was regularly supplied to the intelligence staff in St. Petersburg along with information on HSF movements, particularly in the Baltic. Room 40 had intercepted German signals concerning Operation Fall Albion, the attack on the Gulf of Riga. Birch and Clarke noted that: 'Every step in the preparations, every movement of the squadron was known at once in the Admiralty, whence the information was loyally forwarded to the Russians.'[16]

In December 1916, a commander in the Russian Navy had visited Room 40, apparently the first allied naval officer to be given this privilege. He relayed the benefits his service had derived from their access to Room 40's SIGINT, the advance information on German operations and the routes taken by their warships. The Russian Navy was consequently able to reduce the number of ships they used as scouts. The Imperial Navy, unlike the Kriegsmarine, rarely broke wireless-silence and had pioneered the use of one-time pads, which, if used properly, were virtually undetectable. The co-operation between the two navies was mutually advantageous but particularly to the British, as German operations against the Russians in the Baltic reduced the number of their warships available for actions in the North Sea against the Grand Fleet.

Hall continued this excellent co-operation with the Russian Navy after the March Revolution, which had overthrown the Tsar, until Lenin staged his coup d'état against the Kerensky regime and seized power in the October Revolution. Hall then entreated their head of intelligence to burn all documents relating to their co-operation. In the event, the Kriegsmarine does not seem to have learned from any Russian source that their codes had been broken. Hall was understandably exercised about the safety of his old allies, who had rendered such valuable help, suggesting to St. Petersburg:

> Am perturbed as to safety of Russian officers in the event of the Revolutionary Committee surrendering ships to Germans. Suggest you consider proposition of officers, bringing all latest types of destroyers to South end of Sound on given date and time. Arrangements could be made to have forces to distract enemy and to assist vessels through Sound to England.[17]

He signed this signal Your Friend. Unfortunately, nothing came of Hall's characteristically bold and imaginative suggestion. In that ominous silence lay the origins of his intense dislike and suspicion of Soviet Russia.

One senior Russian naval intelligence officer, Ernst Fetterlein, managed, after some hair-raising adventures, to escape from the Bolsheviks after the October Revolution and reach England. He had once been Imperial Russia's most successful cryptanalyst, solving not just German and Austrian codes but also, with evident even-handedness, those of the British. His proudest possession was a large ruby ring given him by Tsar Nicolas in thanks for his many code-breaking achievements. On arrival in London, now penniless except for his ruby ring, which he certainly did not intend to sell, he offered his services to the highest bidder. Without hesitation Denniston recruited him for Room 40. Fetterlein may have had an eye for the main chance but one of his colleagues, who worked closely with him, remembered him as a brilliant code breaker, in the same class and almost as great a character as Dillwyn Knox, writing of him:

> Fetty [as he quickly became known in Room 40] would arrive precisely at 9.30 and read his *Times* until 10 when he would adjust a pair of thick-lensed glasses and look to us expecting work to be given to him. On book cipher and anything where insight was vital he was quite the best. He was a fine linguist and he would usually get an answer no matter the language. When he deposited his first cheque at a London bank, he was asked for his references, to which he replied 'Pardon me? It is my money. Where are your references?'[18]

Like many of his colleagues, Fetterlein stayed on as a cryptologist after the War and became a key member of staff at Bletchley Park in World War II.

In May 1917 First Sea Lord Jellicoe implemented a far-reaching reorganisation of the War Staff, introducing a welcome degree of decentralisation. (These reforms and their consequences for naval intelligence will be discussed in greater detail in chapter 13.) For the previous seven months Hall had been head of Room 40 in all but name and under the reorganisation its operations were at last fully integrated into the Naval Intelligence Division under the title ID 25. Under Hall's and James's inspired leadership, it was now able to develop its full potential. By November 1918 it had become an effective Intelligence centre, working closely with the Operations and Anti-Submarine Divisions and the forerunner of the Operational Intelligence Centre in World War II, which played such a key role in winning the Battle of the Atlantic.

Notes

[1] Quoted in Beesly p.170
[2] TNA HW 3/6
[3] TNA HW 3/177
[4] TNA HW 3/8
[5] Navy List Dec. 1918
[6] I am grateful to Captain David Garstin for this brief history of the Paymaster Branch of the RN and its connection with Naval Intelligence.
[7] Freeman Draft Article 'M1.1b and the Origins of British Diplomatic Cryptology'
[8] Fitzgerald pp.126-127
[9] Information from Tam Dalyell to the author, January 19 2005
[10] Quoted in Beesly p.174
[11] TNA HW 3/6
[12] Beesly (Fraser, Napier and Clarke tributes) p.175
[13] CAC MISC 20
[14] James (Toye, Leeson and Skrine tributes) pp.201-203
[15] Fitzgerald pp.128-129
[16] Beesly p.181
[17] Ibid. p.182
[18] Smith pp.259-261

CHAPTER XI

Arthur Zimmermann Sends a Telegram

In his unpublished autobiography, Hall described how he first read Arthur Zimmermann's infamous telegram:

> I am not likely to forget that Wednesday morning, 17 January 1917. There was the usual docket of papers to be gone through on my arrival at the office, and Claud Serocold and I were still at work on them when at about half past 10 de Grey came in. He seemed excited. DID, he began, do you want to bring America into the war? Yes, my boy, I answered. Why? 'I have got something here which –well, it is a rather astonishing message which might do the trick if we could use it. It isn't very clear, I'm afraid, but I'm sure I've got most of the important points right. It's from the German Foreign Office to Bernstorff.'[1]

The German Foreign Office had intended to send the telegram to the US by the cargo submarine *Deutschland*, due to sail on January 15. Her departure was cancelled at the last minute, possibly resulting from the imminent reversion to unrestricted submarine warfare. Zimmermann, who had been Foreign Minister for only two months, was forced to use cable. Before 1914, the main German transmitter at Nauen had been connected with two receiving stations at Sayville on Long Island and Tuckerton, New Jersey. The stations had been partly financed by French capital, and in August 1914 the French shareholders objected to their being used for German government traffic. They were then closed and eventually taken over by the US government. The German Embassy in Washington was allowed to send messages from Sayville and Tuckerton provided that a text copy of each signal was given in advance to the State Department. This network could not therefore be used for confidential or ciphered traffic.

To overcome this problem, the German Foreign Office sought and obtained the permission of the Swedish government to send sensitive traffic by their wireless system direct from Stockholm to Washington. Although Sweden was neutral, the King and the government were unashamedly pro-German and Swedish industry was making super-profits from meeting the ever-increasing demands of their war effort. The indignation which had swept the country following the sinking of *Lusitania* had soon subsided and it was business as usual. The Swedes had no compunction in committing such a flagrant breach of neutrality. Room 40 quickly discovered this unethical agreement and under pressure the Swedish government agreed to stop sending German diplomatic traffic direct to Washington. It is probable that this pressure was applied on the Swedes without Hall's agreement.

The Swedes then resorted to subterfuge to avoid the assurances they had given London. They restarted the network, routing it through their legation in Argentina. The signals were then handed to the German Ambassador in Buenos Aires, Count Karl Luxburg, who transmitted them to Washington. Luxburg, like Bernstorff, was active in sponsoring espionage and subversion on behalf of his government. It did not take Room 40 long to discover the existence of this route. In May 1916 Hall told Gaunt that he had concluded that the signals were being sent to Buenos Aires and thence to Valparaiso in Chile. Definite proof of the Swedish involvement in the traffic was soon in his hands. At the end of that month Nigel de Grey, the lead cryptologist in Room 40's political section, showed Hall an intercepted letter, written in code 13040, from Heinrich von Eckardt, the German Minister in Mexico, to the Imperial Chancellor, Bethmann Hollwegg, dated March 8:

> The Swedish Chargé d'affaires here, Herr F. Cronholm, has ... made no concealment of his sympathies with Germany and has placed himself in close connection with this legation ... he is the only neutral diplomat through whom information from the enemy camp can be obtained. Further, he arranges the conditions for the official telegraphic traffic with your Excellency.

Because of its circuitous route, this arrangement became known in Room 40 as the Swedish Roundabout. Hall wrote of this incident:

> ... it was clear that steps would have to be taken to have all Swedish Foreign Office cipher telegrams brought to us for examination ... In many cases it was found that after a few Swedish groups our old friend 13040 would appear. Our excitement, moreover, may be imagined, when through this means we discovered the route by which Bernstorff was communicating with his government ... Now we knew which Legation was responsible and as a result we were in a short time reading all the essential parts of Bernstorff's dispatches and the replies of his Government. In this way, we found ourselves in full possession ... of the enemy's every move in the diplomatic game of the moment, and knew from the Ambassador's admirably clear dispatches the points of greatest importance in Mr. Wilson's

fluctuating policy ... in addition it afforded us an insight into some of the devious ways of German agents all over the American continent.[2]

Eckardt's objective in writing to the Chancellor had been to obtain a German declaration for the helpful Folke Cronholm. Although the latter never received the honour he evidently craved, his vanity was, ironically, to prove an almost priceless windfall for British Naval Intelligence. In Hall's view, the British national interest was best served by tolerating the Swedish Roundabout as an invaluable source of intelligence, while, at the same time, lulling the enemy into a false sense of security. Rather than inform the politicians of his discovery and risk having the system closed down for a second time, he kept its existence a jealously guarded secret within the Intelligence Division.

Cronholm's collusion with the German Legation had not gone unnoticed. His vigilant British counterpart, Tom (later Sir Thomas) Hohler had become suspicious of his frequent visits to the telegraph office in Mexico City, which he believed could not be justified by the volume of communications with the Swedish government. He passed on this concern to the Foreign Office, which complacently ignored him. The determined Hohler then alerted Hall, who asked him to supply any further intelligence. Among his friends in the British community in the city were two brothers, one of whom ran a printing business and the other worked for the telegraph company. Not without some difficulty, Hohler managed to rescue the printing brother from the firing squad after he had falsely been accused of forging banknotes. Understandably, the brothers were extremely grateful to Hohler for his timely action and there was little that they would not do for him. The brother in the telegraph office was only too pleased to supply the diplomat with a copy of every cable received and transmitted by von Eckardt and Cronholm. In turn Hohler passed these cables on to Gaunt, who forwarded them to Hall. (In the books by James and Tuchman, both published in the late 1950s, Hohler is referred to only as Mr. H.: an example of the British establishment's obsession about secrecy long after the event.)

Bernstorff worried about the circuitous nature of this network. After the sinking of *Lusitania* and in an effort to speed up the transmission of wireless traffic, he succeeded in persuading Colonel House, Wilson's gullible adviser on Foreign Affairs, that his ability to communicate with his government was being compromised by British interference and that he should be permitted to use the State Department's private network, which connected Washington and Berlin via Copenhagen. At the very least Wilson and House had been blasé in permitting this concession to the Embassy, which Lansing had opposed. Page, Ambassador in London, far more realistic than the President or his adviser, had long considered that the suave Bernstorff, arguably the most effective ambassador of a major power in Washington, held too strong an influence over House and had urged the President to have him recalled. The American naïveté, which so concerned Page, allowed Germany to use this privilege to undermine US national security.

By the autumn of 1916, Room 40 had correctly deduced that the German Foreign Office was using yet another route for its cable traffic with the Washington Embassy. On September 21 de Grey told Hall:

> It is now abundantly clear that telegrams are passing to Washington not intercepted by us [as postal mail] and not transmitted via Buenos Aires [the Swedish Roundabout]. Neither can the telegrams omitted from our series be fitted into the wireless messages from Sayville or Tuckerton – their number is by no means large enough. I consider it likely that they are sent via the State Dept. and the USA embassy and might consequently be interceptable there.[3]

Room 40 had thus been reading traffic sent by the State Department network for four months before Zimmerman had sent his telegram.

Previous writers including Tuchman, Friedman and Beesly have suggested that the telegram was sent by more than one route. More recent research reveals conclusive evidence that it was dispatched to Washington solely via the State Department network. Dr. Otto Göppert, the senior German civil servant bought in to investigate how the telegram got into the hands of the American Administration, reported that it had been delivered to the American embassy in Berlin at around 3 pm local time, on January 16. At that time Berlin was using both the State Department network and the Swedish Roundabout to transmit messages to Bernstorff, sending him six telegrams by the Roundabout between January 16 and 27, which might explain these misunderstandings.

The actual telegram (numbered 158) was attached to instructions to Bernstorff (numbered 157) on how to inform the State Department of the resumption of unrestricted submarine warfare and to ensure that the German merchant ships in American ports be rendered inoperative if the US declared war. The combined documents consisted of more than one thousand coded groups – an unusually long message.

James Gerard, the American Ambassador in Berlin, wary of the German use of the network, only authorised the transmission of the message when the Foreign Office emissary assured him that it contained instructions relating to President Wilson's recent peace initiatives. With this lie, the fateful message was sent on its way to Washington. It was logged through Copenhagen at 7.50 that evening and then passed through London, where it was intercepted by Room 40.

In Washington the Secretary of State, Robert Lansing, received the coded message on the morning of January 18. Uneasy both at the concession Wilson and House had made and by the unusual length, Lansing sat on the message for 24 hours, declining to hand it over to Bernstorff until he received a direct order to this effect from Colonel House, who never suspected that he was being manipulated by the Germans.

By the time that Bernstorff finally received the telegram on the morning of January 19 Washington time, it had already been in Room 40's possession for more than 48 hours. The Ambassador returned to the Embassy and decoded the document with growing incredulity, fully realising its sinister implications. For some unfathomable reason he had only been supplied with one copy of code 7500. As he could only communicate with the other Embassies and Legations in Latin America by code 13040, he was forced to rewrite the message in the older code and send it to von Eckardt in Mexico City via Western Union. As the message was sent in groups of digital code and not by commercial code, Western Union charged the Embassy the high price of $85.27 for the service. The telegram was received and acknowledged later the same day.[4]

Hall described Lieutenant Commander Nigel de Grey as 'one of our best decypherers'.[4] In January 1936 Hall wrote to Chatfield, then FSL, who with Willie James, his DCNS, was giving the NID a new lease of life, indicating his great admiration for de Grey:

> In case a man is wanted for Y method, [radio interception stations] I venture to tell you that Nigel de Grey who can be found at the Medici Galleries in Grafton Street was the man who had charge of and ran the Intelligence work of that type in Italy during the latter part of the war; brilliant man and absolutely trustworthy.

He is remembered by his family as a talented actor, writer and painter. He had joined the political section of Room 40 on its formation in June 1915 and had since worked almost exclusively on the German diplomatic code 13040. Before the War his work as a publisher had not led him to pay any attention to cryptography, but once in Room 40, in Hall's words, he had almost immediately shown a remarkable flair for the work. 'By this time [January 1917] de Grey was rapidly reaching the stage when he could understand at any rate the general sense of nearly all dispatches sent in the 13040 code.'[5]

The telegram had been sent in the newly introduced diplomatic code 7500, with which Room 40 was not familiar. The codebook had probably been sent to Bernstorff on board the cargo-carrying submarine *Deutschland* on its voyage to America in November 1916. In their history of the Zimmermann telegram and its cryptographic background, Friedman and Mendelsohn traced the first use of 7500 to that November. In his account of the telegram, written in 1945, de Grey mentioned that it had been introduced too recently for Rotter, Room 40's acknowledged expert in breaking

German codes, to have progressed far in its solution. He was able to read enough groups to appreciate the telegram's potential significance. In his account of how he deciphered the telegram, de Grey wrote:

> ... He [Dillwyn Knox] and I worked solidly all morning upon it. With our crude methods and lack of staff, no elaborate indexing of groups had been developed –only constantly recurring groups were noted in the working copies of the code as our fancy dictated. Work was therefore slow and laborious but by about midday, we had got a skeleton version, sweating with excitement as we went on, because neither of us doubted the importance of what we had in our hands. Was not the American-German situation our daily bread?
>
> As soon as I felt sufficiently secure in our version even with all its gaps, I took it down to Admiral Hall ... although Ewing was nominally our head, Blinker had made a compact with a few of the 'research party' that if ever we dug out anything of real importance we were to take it direct to him without showing it to Ewing whom he distrusted as a chattter-box (and rightly). Blinker was always accessible to the lads of Room 40, at least he always was to me at that time because I was getting him all the news from Diplomatic Germany. I was young and excited and I ran all the way to his room, found Serocold ... alone and Blinker free. Then came the job of convincing a man who knew no German with a half readable text. And Blinker was no sort of a fool. But he was patient with me and was convinced. Then the three of us talked out all the implications and as I was daily decoding the messages, I knew the position between Wilson, Lansing, Bernstorff and Bethmann Holwegg pretty well. I remember urging DID to give it to America. Finally, he naturally said that he was thinking it over and sent me off saying: 'But before I do anything I'll tell you what I'm going to do.' That was why we all loved Blinker, he always played fair by us.[6]

Beesly noted: 'It is very doubtful if any single intelligence coup has ever had such profound consequences.'[7] The partly decoded message, which de Grey showed Hall read as follows:

> Berlin to Washington W.158 16 January 1917
> Most Secret for Your Excellency's personal information and to be handed on to the Imperial Minister in (?) Mexico with ... by a safe route.
> We propose to begin on 1 February unrestricted submarine warfare. In doing so, however, we shall endeavour to keep America, neutral ... (?) If we should not (succeed in doing so) we propose to (? Mexico) an alliance on the following basis:
> (joint) conduct of war
> (joint) conclusion of peace
> Your Excellency should for the present inform the President (of Mexico)

> secretly (that we expect) war with the USA (possibly ... Japan) and that at the same time, negotiate between us and Japan ... (indecipherable sentence meaning Please tell the President) that ... our submarines ... will compel England to peace within a few months. Acknowledge receipt
> Zimmermann.

Hall immediately saw the lethal significance of the telegram even in its abbreviated form and intuitively knew that it had to be handled with considerable care.

> At the moment, nothing was to be done except to take all possible precautions to keep the news to our three selves. I thanked de Grey, and asked him to bring me the original telegraph in cipher. This, I told him, is a case where standing orders must be suspended. All copies of this message both those in cipher and your own transcripts, are to be bought straight to me. Nothing is to be put on the files. This may be a very big thing, possibly the biggest thing in the war. For the present not a soul outside this room is to be told anything at all. A little later the original message was locked away in my desk, and I sat down by myself to evolve a plan of campaign.[8]

The prescient Hall had long expected the Kriegsmarine to resume unrestricted submarine warfare. As early as January 1916 Consett advised him that the Germans had by then only lost 20 submarines and that they would have 100 ready by early summer. Continuous training had taken place throughout the winter. He expected that by the summer every available U-boat would be instructed to attack merchant shipping off the coast of the UK simultaneously and at the greatest number of points with as little warning as possible. In September 1916 Hall wrote to Gaunt: 'The Germans, I think, will start the submarine warfare within the next few weeks. They have tried for armistice with the neutrals and failed. I think they're not trying to secure an armistice direct, and will fail again, and when convinced that we mean war they will go all out.'[9]

Serocold, who had worked with him for more than two years, watched his chief admiringly as he summed up this exceedingly difficult situation with his usual clarity, his ability to think laterally and calculate the motives which had led the Germans to take this extraordinary action. Another man might have shouted Eureka or echoed the Philistines after the capture of Samson: 'O Lord thou hast delivered mine enemy into my hands.' The power to alter history is given to few men: Washington led his raggle-taggle army across the Delaware on Christmas night 1776 and inflicted a stunning defeat on the British at Trenton that changed the course of that war. Churchill's iron determination to fight on against the might of Nazi Germany, whatever the odds, in May 1940, saved Western civilization. The telegram gave Hall the ability to change the course of the war in favour of Britain and her allies. Its downside was equally clear to him. He would have to handle the message with the greatest discretion. Hall's dilemma was adroitly summed up by Ed Bell: 'Blinker was torn between reluctance to give away the fact that he could read the Bosh [sic] signals and the desire to pin something good right on them.'[10] Hall expressed his purpose with his usual clarity in the affidavit he swore for the Mixed Claims Commission in December 1926:

> Owing to the paramount importance of our having for the use of the British Navy the information contained in the messages regarding the movement of German ships it was imperative that we should avoid, if possible, disclosing to the Germans the fact that we were reading their communications to this extent. Hence it was impossible for us at the time to make full use of all the information which was before us. The American Ambassador in London, Mr. Page, was in our constant confidence, however, regarding the German communications affecting America during the war, but it was necessary for all of us to exercise the greatest caution regarding the messages.

On the following day, Hall sent for de Grey, who wrote:

> … He asked for the best version that we could produce – in fact, we had got only a little further with the help … of Rotter … He then discussed with me again the pros and cons. Obviously we had two fears. The first and by far the greatest was that we should 'blow' Room 40 – a crazy risk to run when it is remembered that we read the German Naval codes operationally and always currently … Secondly we did not want to risk the fact that we took drop copies in London off the cables or reveal that we had bowled out the Swedes in a non-neutral act. The first would have lost us an invaluable source of intelligence if the coup with America failed, the second would have created an unpleasant situation at a pretty critical moment of the war … I remember his saying to me 'Our first job would be to convince the Americans that it's true – how we can do that? Who would they believe? Is there any Englishman, whom they will believe? I've been thinking and the only person I think they would believe is Balfour … To all Englishman at that time Balfour stood head and shoulders above the politicians as the wise man, the elder statesman … Indeed I have … always thought that Blinker's use of Balfour as his mouthpiece was a stroke of genius (such as he used to exhibit from time to time). Balfour had been First Lord and knew all about Room 40 and was then Foreign Secretary. 'I shall go and see him at once' and he there and then telephoned for an appointment. As I went out Blinker said to me 'You boys think you do a very difficult job, but don't forget that I have to make use of all the intelligence you give me and that's more difficult.'[11]

De Grey's account belies the allegation made by some writers, most recently by Diana Preston in her book on *Lusitania*, that Hall somehow conspired with Page and Bell to conceal the existence of the telegram from the politicians.

Hall had to make a value judgment on the likely reaction of President Wilson to the revelation that Germany had reverted to unrestricted submarine warfare. Wilson was one of the most complex men ever to sit in the White House and his thought processes were by no means easy to read. Three days after *Lusitania* had been torpedoed, he went to Philadelphia to address a meeting of recently naturalised citizens in what became known as 'the too proud to fight' speech. On the spur of the moment, he made some off-the-cuff remarks which he immediately regretted:

> The example of America must be a special example ... not merely of peace because it will not fight but of peace because peace is the healing and elevating influence of the world and strife is not. There is such a thing as a man being too proud to fight. There is such thing as a nation being so right that it does not need to convince others that it is right.

This speech has been described as one of the biggest errors of his Presidency. More recently, the President had adopted a stance that might today be described as moral equivalency. By the end of 1916 he had become somewhat disenchanted with the allies and especially with the British. He had been offended by the *Baralong i*ncident when the crew of a Royal Navy decoy ship had machine-gunned U-boat survivors in the water, by the severity of the sentences handed out to the ringleaders of the Easter Rising and by the heavy loss of life on the Somme. In this mood he had conceived the unrealistic concept of peace without victory, which he expounded in a speech on 22 January 1917, five days after Room 40 had first decoded the telegram, lecturing both sides to renounce their ambitions. His finger wagging went down badly in London and Paris, with the British, who had gone to war to defend the integrity of Belgium, being understandably exasperated. Theodore Roosevelt, always an incisive critic of the President, declared that Wilson's belief that there was little difference in morality between the allies and Germany was 'wickedly false'.

The agreement, which he and Lansing had negotiated with the German Foreign Office after the torpedo attack on the cross-channel ferry *Sussex*, had followed an ultimatum that the US would break off diplomatic relations in the event of another attack on a passenger ship.

> If it is still the purpose of the Imperial Government to prosecute an indiscriminate warfare against vessels of commerce by the use of submarines

without regard to what the government of the United States must consider the sacred and indisputable rules of international law ... the Government of the United States is at last forced to the conclusion that there is but one course to pursue. Unless the Imperial Government should now immediately declare and effect an abandonment of its present methods of submarine warfare against passenger and freight-carrying vessels, the Government of the United States can have no choice but to sever diplomatic relations with the German Empire altogether.[12]

In the light of this vigorous and unambiguous language, Wilson would certainly be bound to cut all ties with Germany. A decision to go to war was less probable. If the President did ask Congress to declare war, the lethal telegram could safely rest in the Intelligence Division's safe to be discovered by historians half a century into the future.

The origins of the telegram lay in events of the previous year. By the spring of 1916 Wilson and Lansing had succeeded in achieving a diplomatic solution to the acrimonious dispute with Germany that followed the sinkings of *Lusitania* and three other passenger liners and the attack on *Sussex*. Matters might well have rested there in the absence of three seemingly unrelated events which occurred later in 1916: Jutland, a significant change in the power structure inside Imperial Germany, and the poor harvest worldwide.

Five days after the battle, the Kaiser went to Wilhelmshaven to congratulate the Kriegsmarine, extravagantly declaring that the spell of Trafalgar had been broken. Scheer pointedly reminded Wilhelm that he had only 10 Dreadnoughts and a single battlecruiser ready for sea and that despite the loss of three battlecruisers the British had more than twenty Dreadnoughts and six battlecruisers. A month later, reporting to the Kaiser on the battle, he stressed that: '... there can be no doubt that even the most successful result of a high sea battle will not compel England to make peace. A victorious end to the war at not too distant a date can only be sought by the crushing of English economic life through U-boat action against English commerce.'[13] The star of the submarine hawks was rising once again.

Wilhelm was meanwhile losing faith in the Chief of the General Staff, Erich von Falkenhayn. In August 1916 he was made a scapegoat for the costly failure at Verdun and demoted to a field command in the Balkans. He was replaced by the formidable combination of Hindenburg and Ludendorff, formerly C-in-C and Chief of Staff on the Eastern Front. Both men were uncompromising hawks. Citing the exigencies of war, the duo demanded and received extensive powers over all aspects of national life and economic activity and Imperial Germany gradually drifted into military dictatorship.

In October 1916, Holtzendorff, the Chief of the Admiralstab, intensified the submarine warfare campaign against commercial targets. As a result of the priority given to submarine construction, he now had 87 U-boats available for operations out of a total fleet of 119, as against only 25 when the previous offensive began in February 1915. Many of the newer U-boats had a long range and some could even cross the Atlantic. In October 1916 U-53 had appeared off Newport, Rhode Island, creating a considerable stir, and torpedoed five ships, two of them neutral, on one occasion asking the captain of an American destroyer to move out of the way so that she could get a better shot at her target! From a German point of view the results were impressive. Although the Kriegsmarine was still observing cruiser rules, over the four months to the end of January 1917, 757 ships, with an average monthly tonnage of 326,000, were sunk, more than double the figure achieved in May 1915, including *Lusitania*.

In November, Wilson won a second term, campaigning on the slogan 'He kept us out of war', which his diplomatic manoeuvrings had made possible. In the same month the P & O liner *Arabia* was sunk in the Mediterranean without warning. An explosion in her boiler room killed 11 of her crew. Good seamanship and the prompt arrival of rescue ships allowed her 439 passengers including a large number of women and children to be saved. This action was a flagrant breach both of the Kaiser's instructions that unarmed passenger liners were not to be attacked and of the agreements Wilson and Lansing had so painstakingly achieved with Berlin earlier in the year. Lansing protested strongly to Bernstorff but in return the Germans prevaricated and offered excuses. Their recalcitrance indicated the growing influence of the hawks within the German command and control structure.

By December 1916 the once-sceptical Holtzendorff had become a convert to unrestricted submarine warfare. Despite the successes of the autumn campaign, he had accepted the arguments forcefully presented by Scheer and his Chief of Staff, the bellicose Adolf von Trotha. They reasoned that if the Navy continued to operate under cruiser rules, the submarine would never become a decisive weapon and that Britain could not be defeated. Trotha maintained that the Admiralstab had deferred to American diplomatic pressure for too long and that it was time that the sharp end of the sword should be presented to the enemy. Holtzendorff and his economic advisers concluded that Britain, with her extensive overseas resources, was effectively maintaining her allies and that if she was knocked out of the war, France and Italy would be forced to sue for peace.

They argued that the failure of the 1916 harvest throughout Europe and in the chief cereal-producing areas in North America and Argentina provided an unrepeatable opportunity for decisive action. Holtzendorff's experts concluded that Britain would not be able to buy their full requirement of wheat and other grains from the United States and Canada after February 1917. They asserted that Britain would have to make good this deficiency by importing wheat from Australia, which would entail the diversion of 750,000 tons of much-needed shipping. With 100 submarines available in January 1917 and a return to unrestricted submarine warfare, the Admiralstab reasoned that they could sink in excess of 600,000 tons per month, or double the current level. With the allied merchant navies suffering such heavy losses and believing that neutral ship owners would react to unrestricted warfare by keeping their fleets in port, they considered that they could force Britain into submission in six months. They urged that the unrestricted campaign should start no later than 1 February so as to achieve its objective before the 1917 harvest could provide the British with any relief.

On 9 January 1917, an Imperial Conference met at Pless in Silesia ostensibly to consider Holtzendorff's plan. In reality the outcome was a foregone conclusion. As early as August 1916, Hindenburg and Ludendorff had advised the Kaiser to revert to unrestricted submarine warfare. By Christmas they had decided to support the Kriegsmarine even at the cost of risking an American declaration of war. Once Holtzendorff had expounded on the scheme, Bethmann-Hollweg objected, arguing that American entry into the war would strongly reinforce the allies and would be greatly to Germany's disadvantage. He made the mistake of rambling on for nearly an hour, thoroughly irritating the Kaiser, who was noted for his remarkably short attention span. Holtzendorff, inflated to bursting point by hubris, retorted: 'I will give Your Majesty my word as a naval officer that not one American will set foot on the Continent.' Hindenburg told Wilhelm: 'We can take care of America.' Ignorance of and contempt for the Americans coloured everything at Pless. Holtzendorff's attitude is particularly surprising as he was presumably aware of the strength of the American Navy, whose 12 Dreadnoughts, 56 destroyers and 50 submarines made it a force to be reckoned with.

The Chancellor no longer carried much weight and within a few months was to be pushed out of office by Ludendorff. No one took any notice of him and eventually he caved in. Alfred von Valentini, Chief of the Kaiser's Civil Cabinet, overheard the distraught Bethmann-Hollweg mutter *Finis Germaniae*. So the die was cast, the agreement reached with Washington the previous spring was unilaterally torn up and Holtzendorff was authorised to resume unrestricted submarine warfare on 1 February. The US and the other neutral countries were not to be told of the decision until the evening before. It was a massive gamble and one which came shockingly close to succeeding.[14]

In November 1916, the relatively moderate Foreign Minister, von Jagow, who had shared Bernstorff's objections to unrestricted submarine warfare, was replaced by his deputy, Arthur Zimmermann, a hard drinking and blustering warmonger and an archetypal Prussian bully. Unlike most of his contemporaries in the diplomatic service, he was of middle-class origin. Fiercely ambitious, he had realised that his advancement would be aided firstly by adopting the characteristics of his Junkers colleagues, becoming more regal than the Kaiser himself, and secondly by habitually agreeing with his superiors. In 1902 he transferred from the consular service to the Foreign Ministry and nine years later was appointed Under-Secretary. Although Zimmermann had only ever spent ten days in the US, crossing the country by rail from San Francisco to New York on his return from a consular posting in the Far East, he considered himself an expert on all matters American.

He had handled the detailed negotiations with the US following the sinking of *Lusitania* in an aggressive style which would today be called megaphone diplomacy. At one meeting with Ambassador Gerard, he worked himself into a fury and declared: 'The United States does not dare to do anything against Germany because we have 500,000 German reservists in America, who will rise in arms against your Government if [it] should dare to take any action against Germany.' Gerard's reply had a certain icy charm: 'We have 500,001 lampposts in America and that is where the German reservists would find themselves if they tried any uprising.'[15]

Zimmermann had originally opposed the decision to resume unrestricted submarine warfare. In so doing he had incurred the wrath of Ludendorff, who peremptorily summoned him to his headquarters early in January and gave him a severe dressing down. True to form, Zimmermann, recognizing that Hindenburg and Ludendorff were the real powers in Germany, saved his own skin by reversing his position and supporting the submarine campaign. He found it necessary to demonstrate his loyalty to the military by following through on a powerful policy initiative.

He no longer played the German fifth column card with which he had threatened Gerard after the sinking of *Lusitania*. He believed that he had a better card to put on the table, one which would be considerably to Germany's advantage. Since the revolution of 1910, relations between Mexico and the United States had been fraught. Wilson's ham-fisted intervention in the internecine world of Mexican politics had made matters worse. In April 1914 he had ordered the Marines to forcibly occupy the port of Veracruz to prevent a German cargo liner landing guns and ammunition for the then President, Huerta, whom he detested. Later that year Huerta was driven out by one of his rivals, Venustiano Carranza, Don Venus to his detractors. The new President was not in complete control of the country. In March 1916, the warlord Pancho Villa crossed the border and torched the town of Columbus, New Mexico, killing some 20 people. It is possible that German agents, who had been actively interfering in Mexican affairs since the revolution, had incited this action. In response, Wilson had sent an expeditionary force, commanded by General J. J. (Black Jack) Pershing, in what proved a futile effort to hunt Villa down.

Pershing's troops had only recently been recalled and an uneasy peace now prevailed between the two governments. Zimmermann pointed out the strained relations between the US and Mexico, noting that Carranza was openly pro-German and antagonistic towards the States. He had been infuriated by the Pershing expedition, conveniently overlooking Villa's incursion. Heinrich von Eckardt, the Minister in Mexico City, had successfully exploited Carranza's partiality, enjoying such unusually close relations with him that he was almost a de facto member of his Cabinet.

The initiative, which became known as the Zimmermann telegram, had originated with the Foreign Office's Counsellor on Latin American and East Asian affairs, Hans Arthur von Kemnitz – as he himself later admitted. Kemnitz's influence and his position as Counsellor on East Asian affairs can also be detected in the approach made to Japan. His proposal was eagerly accepted by Zimmermann who saw it as a way to restore his standing with Ludendorff.

Immediately after the decision made at Pless the new Foreign Minister travelled to Supreme Headquarters, where he proposed von Kemnitz's scheme to Hindenburg and Ludendorff, believing that it would inveigle America into trouble in her own backyard, making her entry into war with Germany even less likely. The Foreign Minister had little difficulty in convincing the bellicose military rulers of Imperial Germany that the Mexican President could be encouraged to resume hostilities against the US and proposed an alliance with Mexico. They could offer Carranza the incentive of recovering the territories lost after the Mexican American war almost 70 years earlier. The opportunity Zimmermann had placed before Hindenburg and Ludendorff was too promising for them to overlook. With his standing restored, they instructed him to proceed with the initiative and he returned post-haste to Berlin to make the necessary arrangements.

Hall wrote of the telegram:

> … I know of no other incident in my experience as an intelligence officer, which better illustrates at once the difficulties of using to the best advantage such information as is obtained and the great and sometimes grave risks which have to be taken to bring about the desired end. Our exposure of the Zimmermann telegram was in the nature of a huge gamble. Luckily, it came off. The steps we took in point of fact, turned out to be about the best we could have taken: what is equally important, they were taken at the right moment. But very easily indeed this gamble might not have come off and in that case, I do not care to think of what might have happened …
>
> It was the most anxious time, and from my point of view, a peculiar time, for to the study of the enemy movements, which was our primary duty,

was added the necessity for an intensive study of American politics ... The one question of paramount importance was this: at what date would the Germans open their campaign of unrestricted submarine warfare? That it must come sooner or later, we were fairly certain. We knew, of course, the reason why their submarine attacks had almost stopped earlier in the year. It was not, as they alleged, in deference to American opinion, but because their existing submarines were being refitted and new crews trained, but by October they had about 200 submarines ready, some of which had crossed the Atlantic and were operating very close to American waters. On October 7, U-53 had appeared at Newport Rhode Island and during the next two days had sunk no less than nine merchant ships ... in circumstances which led us to hope that American patience might be nearing its end ... President Wilson had been re-elected. We knew that he would never declare war unless he was convinced that all the States, and not only those in the East, desired it.

At home the position was exceedingly difficult. There was not only a shortage of men, but a shortage of food as well. There were distinct signs of war-weariness, and criticism was being directed against most Government Departments. In particular, the Admiralty was singled out for the fiercest attacks. Complaints were made, and not only in the press, that the Board had become 'stale'. There were angry meetings in the City, and demands for a more forthright policy to deal with the submarine menace ... By the end of December we could not say at what precise date unrestricted submarine warfare would begin and there was nothing to do but to wait and prepare.[16]

Knowing that, within two weeks, Bernstorff would inform the State Department that the Kriegsmarine was resuming unrestricted submarine warfare on February 1, Hall cogitated, calculated, then merely ordered Room 40 to continue working towards completing the decryption of the telegram. In effect, he locked the menacing communication away while he waited for events in Washington to unfold.

During the ensuing two weeks, Hall closely scrutinized Bernstorff's decrypts in which he sought valiantly but unavailingly to convince his government not to proceed with the unrestricted submarine warfare campaign or at least to postpone it to allow him further time to negotiate with Wilson. However, Holtzendorff's U-boats were already at sea and the prevailing mood in Berlin was to proceed with the campaign.

On January 28 Hall might have had time for a wry smile amidst the making of history when he read the embattled Ambassador's suggestion that Berlin reply to his signal by wireless, complaining that cables always take several days. Room 40's efficiency was such that he was scanning Zimmermann's messages two days before they reached Bernstorff.

Nor was Hall surprised by Zimmermann's playing the Mexican card, as the regular flow of cables intercepted by Hohler's contact in the Mexico City telegraph office produced strong indications of German intrigue. One decrypt sent by von Eckardt mentioned that 'Carranza [is] openly friendly to Germany [and] willing to support if necessary German submarines in Mexican waters to the best of his ability.' On November 12 1916 an even more valuable signal from Bernstorff to Eckardt was intercepted:

> The Imperial Government proposes to employ the most efficacious means to annihilate its criminal enemy, and since it designs to carry its operations to America with the object of destroying its enemy's commerce, it will be very valuable to have certain bases to assist with the work of its submarines both in South America and in Mexico, as, for example in the State of Tamaulipas [the most northeasterly coastal state in Mexico, bordering Texas]. Accordingly the Imperial Government would see with the greatest pleasure the Mexican Government's consent to cede the necessary permission for the establishment of the base in its territory.[17]

Hall immediately took this disturbing intelligence to Ed Bell at the American Embassy. They had been working closely together since Hall had turned over the incriminating documents his agents had seized from the courier Archibald at Falmouth a year earlier. Despite the bad blood persisting between Washington and Mexico City since Carranza had taken power, American pressure was sufficient to persuade the Mexican Government to forbid any submarine bases to the Germans.

At four o'clock Washington time on the afternoon of January 31, Bernstorff called on Lansing at the State Department to break the news that on the following day Germany was resuming unrestricted submarine warfare. The normally reserved Lansing suppressed his anger at the extremely short notice the Administration had been given. In a gesture of sympathy, he escorted the disconsolate Ambassador to his car with his arm round his shoulder. The overt part of Bernstorff's mission, to keep the US neutral, had ended in failure.

Wilson vacillated. He had a genuine aversion to conflict, resulting from his memories of the American Civil War, when as a small boy he had tended wounded Confederate soldiers in his father's church in Augusta, Georgia. He could not bring himself to believe that the European belligerents had no interest in his efforts to mediate between them. He was loath to break with neutrality and he still clung to his unworkable concept of peace without victory. He was still dithering when his Cabinet met on February 2, when the majority, headed by Lansing, told him there was no option but to ask Congress to declare war. Wilson even told the

Blinker Hall as Captain of HMS *Queen Mary*, 1914. (*Timothy Stubbs/Churchill Archives Centre*)

HMS *Queen Mary*. (*Imperial War Museum Q 39898*)

Lusitania at speed. (*Imperial War Museum Q 43227*)

Winston Churchill as First Lord of the Admiralty 1911–1915. (*Imperial War Museum Q 93275*)

Jacky Fisher as First Sea Lord. (*Churchill Archives Centre*)

Henry Oliver as Admiral of the Fleet by G. Blair Leighton, 1935. This portrait hangs in the Royal Navy's School of Maritime Operations. HMS *Collingwood*, Fareham, Hampshire.
(*The Royal Navy Trophy Fund/Churchill Archives Centre*)

Admiral Jellicoe on HMS *Iron Duke*. (*Imperial War Museum Q 55499*)

The German cruiser *Dresden* flying the white flag, March 1915. Her discovery was one of Room 40's earliest successes. (*Imperial War Museum Q 46201*)

The destruction of Hall's old command, HMS *Queen Mary*, at Jutland. (*Imperial War Museum SP 1708*)

The German battlecruiser *Seydlitz* heavily damaged after Jutland: a vivid illustration of Hall's statement that the German Fleet had been sufficiently roughly handled to keep it in harbour for a few weeks. (*Imperial War Museum SP 2157*)

Kaiser Wilhelm II with Hindenburg and Ludendorff, the real rulers of Imperial Germany from August 1916. (*Imperial War Museum Q 25746*)

Arthur Zimmermann, German Foreign Minister 1916–17. (*Press Portrait Bureau/Churchill Archives Centre*)

Hall as Director of Naval Intelligence, in a sketch by Louis Raemaker. (*Timothy Stubbs/Churchill Archives Centre*)

Alastair Denniston, one of Room 40's earliest recruits, as Director-General of GC & CS, 1941. (*Polperro Heritage Press*)

Claud Serocold, Hall's PA from 1914 to 1919. (*Cazenove & Co/Churchill Archives Centre*)

Nigel de Grey, the lead cryptanalyst on the Zimmermann telegram. (*Anthony de Grey/Churchill Archives Centre*)

Captain (later Admiral Sir) William 'Bubbles' James, Deputy Director of Naval Intelligence and Head of Room 40, 1917–1919. (*Arthur Marder*, From Dreadnought to Scapa Flow, OUP, 1969/ *Churchill Archives Centre*)

Sir Maurice (later Lord) Hankey, Secretary of the Committee of Imperial Defence and Cabinet Secretary from 1916, a staunch Hall ally, with Lloyd George in France, 1919. (*Hankey Papers, Churchill Archives Centre*)

Lloyd George and Arthur Balfour in Paris, 1917. (*Imperial War Museum Q 57038*)

Admiral Duff with Sir Eric Geddes and the American Secretary of the Navy and CNO Washington, 1918. (*Imperial War Museum 19398*)

Beatty with King George V on HMS *Queen Elizabeth*, Scapa Flow, July 1918. (*Imperial War Museum Q 19840*)

Robert Lansing, US Secretary of State, 1915–1920. (*National Archives and Records Administration/Double Delta Industries 111-SC-63344*)

Walter Hines Page, US Ambassador in London 1913–1918, by Philip de Laszlo. Page was a great admirer of Hall's, who worked closely with him over the handling of the Zimmermann telegram and other intelligence issues. (© *The de Laszlo Foundation*)

Admiral William S. Sims, Commander-in-Chief of the US Navy in Europe, 1917–19, and a staunch ally of Hall's (first on the left, front row), and Admiral Sir Rosslyn Wemyss, First Sea Lord 1917–1919 (third from the left, front row), at the Inter-Allied Naval Committee in Paris, November 1918. M. Georges Leygues, the French Minister of Marine, is second from the left, front row. (*National Archives and Records Administration/Double Delta Industries 165-WW-400A-17*)

Woodrow Wilson is greeted by the Mayor, Mr E. W. G. Farley, on his arrival at Dover, 26 December 1918, the first occasion that a President of the United States had set foot on British soil. (*Imperial War Museum Q 58364*)

The surrender of the German High Seas Fleet, November 1918. (*Imperial War Museum Q 19284*)

German U-boats, which had brought Britain close to defeat in 1917, surrendered at Harwich in November 1918. (*Imperial War Museum Q 19328*)

The cover of the ID 25 (Room 40) Concert Programme, December 1918. Hall is depicted enjoying himself as he eavesdrops on two quarrelling German Admirals. (*Robin Denniston/Churchill Archives Centre*)

Admiral John Godfrey, Director of Naval Intelligence 1939–43. Hall was in many ways Godfrey's mentor and he once remarked that when in doubt he often asked himself what Hall would have done. (*Penguin Books/Churchill Archives Centre*)

Secretary of Agriculture, David Houston, that he did not want either side in the conflict to win.

On the following day, Wilson finally made his mind up. He took the line of least resistance telling Congress that 'I refuse to believe that it is the intention of the German authorities to do in fact what they have warned us they feel at liberty to do ... Only overt acts on their part can make me believe it even now.' He did not declare war but merely broke off diplomatic relations with Germany, handed Bernstorff his passports and stationed armed guards on American merchant ships.

Colonel House, whom Gaunt had taken care to befriend, told the British naval attaché of the President's decision two hours in advance. Gaunt immediately cabled Hall, using their personal code in which Wilson was referred to as Aaron, House as Beverly and Bernstorff as the Barber after Mozart's Barber of Seville. With some salty naval language the cable read 'The Barber gets his papers at 2 p.m. today. I will probably get soused.'[18] Armed with this information, Hall rushed round to the American Embassy where Ambassador Page and his staff were eagerly awaiting the President's announcement. With, in retrospect, undue optimism, Page broke out a bottle of champagne to toast the outcome. They soon realised that Wilson had not asked Congress to declare war. Hall and Page shared their bitter disappointment over what both men felt was Wilson's lack of leadership.

Unwittingly the President of the United States had put the lethal telegram back into play. Hall had played the waiting game. The time had come for him to up the ante. He would now face the greatest challenge of his career, one which would entail the full use of all his talents. In the days that followed, he would be tested but he would not fail.

Notes

[1] CAC HALL 3/6 p.10
[2] Ibid pp.5-6
[3] TNA HW 3/184 Quoted by Freeman. Unpublished draft article 'M1.1b and the origins of British Diplomatic Cryptology'
[4] Freeman *The Zimmermann Telegram Revisited* pp.114-130
[5] CAC HALL 3/6 p. 4. NMM CHT/3/1 Hall to Chatfield Jan 6 1936
[6] TNA HW 3/177 Nigel De Grey Zimmermann Telegram p.2
[7] Beesly p.204
[8] CAC HALL 3/6 pp.11-12
[9] Ibid p.2
[10] NARA Bell to Hurley July 13 1921
[11] TNA HW 3/177 p.2
[12] Quoted in Gerard *My Four Years in Germany* p.178

13. Halpern pp.326-328
14. Gilbert *First World War* p.306. The Pless Conference is described in Tuchman pp.137-141
15. Gerard p.165
16. CAC HALL 3/6 pp.2-4
17. Ibid p.9
18. Gaunt p.256

CHAPTER XII
War comes to America: 'Alone I did it'

Once Wilson's decision not to go to war had been confirmed, Hall set about devising a battle plan to exploit the telegram with his customary precision, as if he had been directing a naval operation from the bridge of a battlecruiser. He had a number of cardinal objectives. He had to work closely with the Foreign Office and resume the brief discussion he had had with Balfour after he had originally seen the incomplete telegram. He had to brief the American Embassy and indicate the seriousness of the situation in which the Wilson administration now found itself. Anticipating that certain people in the US would charge that the telegram was a hoax, forged by the crafty British to entice the US to join the allies and improve their position in a war that had deteriorated into a stalemate, he had to convince Wilson and the American people that the telegram was genuine. Knowing that cryptology was a closed book to most Americans, he mulled over his dilemma:

> Even if somebody whom he implicitly trusted like Mr. Balfour were to give his personal assurance that the telegram was genuine, the President might not unreasonably ask if the message really bore the meaning we ascribed to it, and how could that be done without our giving to the Americans information of the most secret nature?[1]

Hall never lost sight of the vital necessity of protecting SIGINT. Some commentators, notably the American cryptographer Friedman, have criticised Hall for not having revealed the telegram to the American Embassy immediately after it had been intercepted. They overlook Hall's determination to shield the advantage the Admiralty obtained through their knowledge of German naval movements, particularly with the renewed threat of unrestricted submarine warfare from a much larger U-boat force:

> Publication of this particular telegram would almost certainly rouse the whole of the United States and might well force the President to declare

war, but it would be at the cost of hazarding the most vital part of our Intelligence system. It was imperative that we ran no risk of the Germans learning the secret of 40 OB [Hall's term for Room 40] therefore the 'intercept' already in our hands must in no circumstances whatsoever be exposed.[2]

In 1921 Ed Bell described the choice simply: 'Blinker was torn between reluctance to give away the fact that he could read the Bosh [sic] signals and the desire to pin something good right on them. He took me into his confidence and I pressed for the latter.'[3] Hall had to prevent the Americans from discovering that Room 40 was intercepting their diplomatic communications – although the NID's actions in reading these transmissions were of course a far less serious transgression than the German misuse of the facility to send a message advocating the invasion of a neutral nation! Understandably he did not refer to this issue in his autobiography and it suited his objectives to insinuate that the telegram had been sent via the Swedish Roundabout.

Although de Grey had made some progress towards breaking 7500, the original telegram which Room 40 had intercepted had by no means been totally decrypted. Hall determined to obtain a copy of the version of the telegram Bernstorff had cabled to Eckardt.

If Hall and Page had been disappointed by Wilson's failure to go to war, Zimmermann was elated. He boasted that his prediction that Wilson would not open hostilities over the resumption of unrestricted warfare had proved correct. He now decided to ratchet up the pressure on Carranza. On February 8 he sent a telegram to Eckardt:

> Most Secret. Decipher personally. Provided there is no danger of secret being betrayed to USA you are desired without further delay to broach the question of an Alliance to the President [Carranza]. The definite conclusion of an alliance, however, is dependent on the outbreak of war between Germany and USA. The President might, even now, on his own account, sound Japan. If the President declines from fear of subsequent revenge, you are empowered to offer him a definitive alliance after conclusion of peace, providing Mexico succeeds in drawing Japan into the alliance.

Carranza had originally been asked to approach Japan only after an American declaration of war on Germany. As the German Embassy in Washington had now been shut down, Zimmermann was forced to send the message directly to Mexico City by the Swedish Roundabout using 13040. The telegraph was therefore intercepted by Room 40 and instantly decoded. With this damning decrypt in his possession, Hall now had indisputable evidence of German hostility towards the US to place before his friends in the London Embassy.

On Monday February 5, the first working day after Wilson decided to break off diplomatic relations with Germany, Hall went to see Lord Hardinge, the Permanent Under-Secretary at the Foreign Office. Hardinge was a star in the British diplomatic service. Early in his reign, King Edward VII, a shrewd judge of character, had picked him to be his personal adviser on foreign policy and a member of what might be called his Kitchen Cabinet, together with Jacky Fisher among others. His advance had been swift. He had become Ambassador to Russia and then Permanent Under-Secretary before he had turned 50. He had been reappointed to his former position in June 1916 following his return from India at the end of his time as Viceroy. Hardinge was to become one of Hall's staunchest supporters and admirers. At this meeting, Hall described him as being 'his usual cool self, interested but cautious'.[4] Despite his understandable wariness, Hardinge immediately authorised the proposal Hall put before him and to which he attached considerable importance – the acquisition of a copy of the telegram Bernstorff had recoded in 13040 and sent by Western Union to Eckardt in Mexico City.

In December 1916 Tom Hohler had been promoted to a post in the Washington Embassy. His successor, Edward Thurston, had previously been Consul General in Mexico City and had been involved in securing the release of the unfortunate printer. He was thus fully in the loop as to the procedure for recovering copies of German and Swedish cables from the telegraph office. On February 6 Hall ordered Thurstan to obtain copies of every cable received and sent by Eckardt since January 18 and forward them to Gaunt in New York, who would dispatch them to the Intelligence Division in London.

Hall's next priority was to exploit the excellent relationship he had built up with both Ambassador Page and Ed Bell. Page had been a friend of Wilson's for over 30 years. Both men were Southerners, Wilson from Virginia and Page from North Carolina. When they first met, Wilson was a rising academic and Page an ambitious and successful journalist. He had been the editor of the prestigious *Atlantic Monthly* and had then formed a successful partnership with the publisher Frank Doubleday. He had founded and edited their magazine *World's Work*, which had commissioned many of Wilson's articles. Page had encouraged Wilson to leave academia and enter politics, promoting him as a coming man and backing him when he ran for Governor of New Jersey. He had long believed that the Democratic Party's perennial Presidential candidate, William Jennings Bryan, was unelectable and had consistently advocated Wilson as a viable alternative. His magazine had strongly supported his nomination and his campaign for the Presidency in 1912. Wilson was thus considerably in Page's debt and rewarded him with the prestigious appointment to the London Embassy. An outgoing man of considerable charm he enjoyed the respect, to the point of admiration, of his staff, becoming as popular a personality in London society as Bernstorff was in Washington.

Ed Bell was a career diplomat, who had been posted to the Embassy as Second Secretary in September 1913, a few months after Page had arrived in London. He had been a Harvard contemporary of Franklin D. Roosevelt. The two men remained close friends. Bell had quickly won the confidence of the Ambassador, who had put him in charge of intelligence issues and of liaising with Naval Intelligence. Page's friendship with the President had begun to fray after *Lusitania* had been torpedoed and he had become increasingly critical of Wilson's insistence on neutrality. He had recognised that German aggression would, sooner or later, drag the US into the conflict. The information Hall had supplied to him and to Bell, following his interception of the Archibald and von Papen documents and the interrogations of von Rintelen and von der Goltz, had alerted him to the uncomfortable reality that Imperial Germany was far exceeding the restraints that a belligerent would normally have displayed towards a neutral country. Page had repeatedly but unavailingly warned the President about German subversion in the States.

Wilson shared one trait with the Kaiser, both men being utterly incapable of accepting unwelcome advice. Rather than listening to his Ambassadors, he preferred to accept the counsel of House, who generally told him what he wanted to hear. Page was well aware that the President disregarded his advice and listened to those in Washington, who took the line that he had become unduly Anglophile, had 'gone native'. When he returned to Washington for consultations with the State Department in the summer of 1916, only with great difficulty could he arrange a meeting with the President. The two men, once so close, could not find any common ground. Page was astonished and depressed to discover that while Wilson was irritated by the British, he was surprisingly tolerant of the Germans. As he said good-bye, he noticed tears come into the President's eyes. His conscience must have been troubled at his cavalier treatment of an old friend. They were never to meet again.

After Wilson had won re-election in November, Page honourably tendered his resignation, believing that he had lost the President's confidence. Although his letter was not answered for several months and until Page insisted on a reply, Wilson went behind his back and offered the London Embassy to Cleveland H. Dodge, an industrialist, who had been the largest single contributor to each of his Presidential campaigns. Wilson made this offer on February 6 1917, three days after he had broken off diplomatic relations with Germany, a powerful indication of his determination to get rid of Page and remain neutral. Dodge declined the position and Page stayed on in London, increasingly at odds with the President.

Hall was by now meeting Hardinge and his Private Secretary, Ronald Campbell, the future Ambassador to France and Portugal in World War

II, almost daily to discuss how they should deal with the telegram and in particular how the American Embassy would be informed. They were initially reluctant to give the impression that their objective was to influence a neutral government. An increasingly worried Hall knew only too well that time was of the essence. On 14 February a coup d'état had installed a pro-German regime in Cuba. Germany had clearly been involved in the coup and a number of agents who were about to be evicted from the US were speedily transferred to Havana.

Thurstan had reported from Mexico City that German reservists resident in the country, who had been prevented from returning home to join the army by the British blockade, were mobilising. Other groups of reservists were believed to be moving into Mexico from Central and South America. His information suggested that their intention was to seize control of the oilfields in the State of Tampico and deny their output to British and American oil companies. Hall took this threat extremely seriously, as the British-owned Mexican Eagle Company had a contract to supply the Navy with 200,000 tons of oil annually. Throughout his tenure as Director of Naval Intelligence, the adequacy and security of the Navy's oil supply was a subject of continual anxiety to him.

His apprehension was increased by the Japanese connection. He was inherently distrustful of Japanese ambitions. Japan was bound to Great Britain by the Anglo-Japanese alliance of 1902 and under its terms had declared war on Germany in August 1914. Their Navy had played a part in clearing the Kriegsmarine from the Pacific and Indian Oceans and in escorting Allied troop convoys. Hall had observed the rapidity with which Japan had seized control of the German possessions in Micronesia, the Caroline, Mariana and Marshall Islands, thus extending their territory deep into the Central Pacific.

The Admiralty had been infuriated by the Japanese refusal to lease them one of their British-designed battlecruisers for the duration of the war to replace one of the three similar ships lost at Jutland. As the German East Asiatic Squadron had long since been driven from the Pacific, the only possible adversary for such modern and powerful ships would have been the American Pacific Fleet. Hall's intelligence contacts in Mexico had reported previous Japanese interest in securing a naval base on the country's Pacific Coast. More recently and in contravention of an agreement to supply armaments only to Britain and her allies, a quantity of rifles and machine-guns had been sold to the Mexican army. In October 1916, Room 40 intercepted a telegram from Admiral von Hintze, the German Ambassador in Peking, to Berlin, reporting his recent discussions with his Japanese opposite number: illicit, since both countries were at war. His clear intention was to induce Japan to break off her alliance with Britain. He noted that at a minimum the Japanese would stop delivering munitions to the allies and that they were angling to get Germany to give them a free hand in China, including political and economic co-operation. Hintze observed that Britain would not grant Japan any further territorial concessions in China.[5]

Hall had privately told Ed Bell that he was in possession of information which might profoundly alter the attitude of both the American government and American public opinion. He asked Bell to wait until he had obtained the full details, which he expected in a few days time.

On February 19 he received from Gaunt the full text of Bernstorff's cable to Eckardt, which he had sent to him reciphered in a British code. De Grey immediately decoded it. Room 40 was now able fully to compare the two codes, 7500 and 13040. They had the complete Rosetta Stone. 7500 was now broken.

Its contents, now revealed in full to Hall and his cryptanalysts for the first time, were dramatic:

> WE SHALL COMMENCE UNRESTRICTED SUBMARINE WARFARE ON FEBRUARY 1ST. WE SHALL ENDEAVOUR IN SPITE OF THIS TO KEEP THE UNITED STATES NEUTRAL. IN THE EVENT OF THIS NOT SUCCEEDING, WE MAKE MEXICO A PROPOSAL OF ALLIANCE ON THE FOLLOWING BASIS: MAKE WAR TOGETHER, MAKE PEACE TOGETHER, GENEROUS FINANCIAL SUPPORT AND AN UNDERSTANDING ON OUR PART THAT MEXICO IS TO RECONQUER THE LOST TERRITORIES IN TEXAS, NEW MEXICO AND ARIZONA.
>
> YOU WILL INFORM THE PRESIDENT OF MEXICO OF THE ABOVE MOST SECRETLY AS SOON AS THE OUTBREAK OF WAR WITH THE UNITED STATES IS CERTAIN AND ADD THE SUGGESTION THAT HE SHOULD, ON HIS OWN INITIATIVE, INVITE JAPAN TO IMMEDIATE ADHERENCE AND AT THE SAME TIME MEDIATE BETWEEN JAPAN AND OURSELVES. PLEASE CALL THE PRESIDENT'S ATTENTION TO THE FACT THAT THE UNRESTRICTED EMPLOYMENT OF OUR SUBMARINES NOW OFFERS THE PROSPECT OF COMPELLING ENGLAND TO MAKE PEACE WITHIN A FEW MONTHS

As soon as de Grey had decrypted the telegram in the familiar 13040, he brought it to Hall and Serocold. The three men looked at the document with a kind of awe. In its complete form it was even more lethal than they could have believed. Zimmermann's brazen effrontery and total lack of realism stood exposed for all to see; the German Government had absolutely no ability to deliver on the promises it had so rashly made to Carranza.

Under the Treaty of Guadalupe Hidalgo at the end of the Mexican-American war in 1848, the Mexican provinces of Alta California, the present-day California and Nevada, and Nuevo Mexico, contemporary Arizona and New Mexico as far south as the Gila River, had been ceded to the United States and Mexico accepted the US annexation of Texas, with the Rio Grande River recognized as its southern border. The land south of the Gila River in Arizona and New Mexico had been acquired from Mexico in 1853 in the Gadsden Purchase for the building of a US transcontinental railroad.

The text of the Zimmermann telegram specifically mentioned only Texas, New Mexico and Arizona but also referred to 'lost territory', which may also have included California. The cryptographer William Friedman speculated that Zimmermann might have earmarked California as an incentive to be offered to Japan, had it formed an alliance with Mexico.

Less than sixty years earlier, Abraham Lincoln had fought a bloody civil war, which had resulted in more casualties than any other conflict in American history, in order to preserve the Union. Hall reasoned that no administration in Washington could possibly tolerate the invasion of three American states by a foreign power, an incursion which would in any case have been fiercely resisted by their residents. Don't Mess with Texas would have be been the battle cry in the Lone Star State. Since their incorporation into the Union almost seventy years earlier, the population of these states was now predominantly of American stock. Their Hispanic populations, notably the Tejano community in Texas and the descendents of Spanish settlers in New Mexico, had no particular love for their neighbours south of the border. This hostility had been exacerbated by the brutal revolution of 1910 and the subsequent disorder, which had led to widespread emigration into the US. Cession of these states to Mexico in any peace treaty would have been politically impossible.

Hall saw at once that the telegram provided the necessary ammunition to sway American public opinion in the hitherto isolationist Midwest and South-west towards supporting entry into the War. He picked up the telephone and called the Embassy. Within thirty minutes, Bell was sitting opposite Hall and his colleagues as he read the telegram with incredulity. His initial reaction was to remark: 'Why not offer them Illinois and New York while they were about it?' Once he had recovered from the shock, he found it difficult to believe Zimmermann could seriously advocate carving large slices of territory out of the United States and handing it over to its troubled southern neighbour and he refused to accept that the telegram was not a hoax. Patiently Hall led him through the process he had overseen since the first discovery of the document; stressing the importance he had placed on ensuring that it was indeed genuine. He did not take long to convince the diplomat. Bell responded. 'But, DID, this means war.'[6] Hall agreed, adding the caveat 'If it is published' and reminding him that he had to obtain the agreement of the Foreign Office to pass on the telegram to the Embassy before it could be transmitted to Washington. He asked Bell to show the telegram to Page on the understanding that he should take no action until Balfour and Harding had decided how to proceed. Bell replied that his Ambassador would accept Hall's proviso given that there was no delay.

Bell returned to the Embassy and broke the news to Page. As soon as Hall had briefed Hardinge, setting off a debate inside the Foreign Office as to how the Embassy should be told officially, he and Bell went to see the Ambassador. Page quickly saw the significance of the telegram and unhesitatingly accepted its authenticity. He did not record this event in his diary, possibly because Hall insisted on maximum secrecy. Joined by the First Secretary at the Embassy, Irwin Loughlin, the four men spent the rest of the day working out the best method of revealing the telegram to Washington and of establishing its validity without compromising Room 40's operations. They concluded that Balfour should summon Page to the Foreign Office and hand him the telegram. Page noted 'that would be the British Government giving it to our Government' and that Balfour was effectively assuring Washington that the telegram was genuine. Bell put it more bluntly: 'Finally it was agreed that Mr. Balfour ... could give a translation to Mr. Page with assurances that it was the goods, as being a stronger move than Reggie's giving it to me.'[7]

The Ambassador would then cable the telegram to the State Department. The four men pondered how they would counter Wilson, who would almost certainly demand proof of the document's authenticity and thus salve his conscience at having to descend into the sometimes murky world of secret intelligence. Hall remembered that Bernstorff had recoded the telegram and sent it to Eckardt by Western Union. They eventually decided that the State Department should recover the cable from Western Union and send it to Bell in London. De Grey would then bring the 13040 codebook to the Embassy, allowing Bell to decode the telegram. This strategem would permit the Administration to deflect any criticism by announcing that the document had been decoded by an American diplomat in the presence of his Ambassador on what was technically American property.

The next day, February 20, Campbell reported to Hardinge on his meeting with Hall:

> ... Captain Hall submitted the following considerations: assuming that the Cabinet are anxious to see America's entry into the war as a belligerent (a view which he personally concurs from an Admiralty standpoint) he submits that such a consummation could be hastened by a judicious use of this information. He would suggest that he be authorized to give the substance to Mr. Bell of the United States Embassy, who after informing the Ambassador would see that it reached the President. This might be a better plan than that the information should be given the ambassador from the Foreign Office ... which might have the appearance that HM Government were trying to bring America in. Captain Hall has given the Embassy a

considerable amount of information useful to them in this way and they place reliance on it. Or, if it be desired to give the matter more publicity and consequently to produce more effect on the American people, for whose unanimity President Wilson is waiting, Captain Hall could arrange for it to come out in the American press without any indication that HM Government ... was at the bottom of the exposure. Whatever plan is adopted, Captain Hall is confident that he could arrange things without any risk of the source of this information being compromised.

Publication in the American press might create a furore of indignation.[8]

At this juncture, Balfour intervened. His experience of foreign affairs stretched back nearly forty years, to the Congress of Berlin in 1878 where he had served as Secretary to his uncle, Lord Salisbury. Beneath a languid manner he possessed a formidable intellect and an ability to act decisively should the need arise. Not for nothing had he been known as 'Bloody Balfour' when he was Chief Secretary of Ireland in the late 1880s. His realism was displayed in his reply to Wilson's peace note.

Though the people of this country share to the full the desire of the President for peace, they do not believe that peace can be durable if it is not based on the success of the Allied cause. For a durable peace can hardly be expected unless three conditions are fulfilled. The first is that the existing causes of international unrest should be as far as possible removed or weakened. The second is that the aggressive aims and the unscrupulous methods of the Central Powers should fall into disrepute among their own peoples. The third is that behind international law, and ... treaty arrangements ... some form of international sanction should be devised, which would give pause to the hardiest aggressor.[9]

Like Hall and Page, Balfour had become convinced that the US would eventually be forced into the war by German intransigence. Hall's intelligence of German intrigues in Mexico and Cuba, about which he had briefed Hardinge earlier that day, persuaded him that the time had come to take the bull by the horns. His niece and biographer, Blanche (Baffy) Dugdale, described his reaction:

Ever since the middle of January ... a piece of information had been in the possession of the British Government, which would move, if anything could, the populations behind the Atlantic seaboard States, who still read of the European War with as much attachment as if it be raging in the moon. This was the famous telegram from Zimmermann ... The method by which this information had reached the British Intelligence Service had made it impossible for some time to communicate it to the United States Government. Therefore for over a month Balfour read in his despatches from Washington of the slow awakening of the American will to war, but could do nothing to hasten the process. Till – at last – information about the Mexican plot reached London through channels which enabled the Intelligence Service to cover up the traces of how it had first been got.[10]

Dugdale had been close to her uncle and her comment confirms de Grey's account that Hall had revealed the contents of the initial telegram intercepted by Room 40 to Balfour without delay, rather than waiting several days as some commentators, including Diana Preston, have alleged. She was the first and for many years the only author to imply that Room 40 had been intercepting American diplomatic traffic.

Later that day, Balfour told Hardinge: 'I think that Captain Hall may be left to clinch this problem as he knows the ropes better than anyone.'[11] He was giving Hall a free hand – a testament to the degree to which the Director of Naval Intelligence had gained the confidence of one of Britain's most experienced and distinguished statesmen. Armed with this support, Hall decided that Balfour should ask Page to visit him at the Foreign Office where he would formally give him the telegram. On the afternoon of February 23, Page called on Balfour, who presented him with the coded and uncoded versions of the telegram. Dugdale described the historic occasion: 'Delight was unbounded in Whitehall and the Foreign Secretary himself was unusually excited. As dramatic a moment as I remember in all my life, he once said … By the ceremony of this act the British Government gave its pledge that the communication was authentic.'[12]

Bell noted: 'Mr. Page came back from his interview with Balfour with a translation in his hand and blood in his eye.'[13] The Ambassador, Loughlin, Bell and his personal secretary, Eugene Shoecraft, sat up all night engaged in the difficult task of drafting a telegram for Wilson. They had to reconcile Hall's security requirements with the language which could persuade the President that he was dealing with a ruthless government in Berlin which would shrink from nothing that could advance their objective of subverting the United States and rendering it impotent.

At 8 am London time on the morning of Saturday February 24, Page advised the State Department that in three hours time he would be sending a cable of great importance to the President and the Secretary of State. By the time he had finally drafted the cable to his and his staff's satisfaction and it had been encoded, a further five hours had passed. The final message read:

London, February 24, 1917- 1 p.m.
5747 … For the President and the Secretary of State.

Balfour has handed me the text of a cipher telegram from Zimmermann, German Secretary of State for Foreign Affairs, to the German Minister to

Mexico, which was sent via Washington and was relayed by Bernstorff on January 19. You can probably obtain a copy of the text relayed by Bernstorff from the cable office in Washington. The first group is the number of the telegram, 130, and the second is one of 13042, indicating the number of the code used. The last group but two is 97 556, which is Zimmermann's signature. I shall send you by mail a copy of the cipher text and of the decode into German and meanwhile I give you the English translation as follows: [Page inserted here the English text of the telegram.]

The receipt of this information has so greatly exercised the British Government that they have lost no time in communicating it to me to transmit to you, in order that our government may be able without delay to make such disposition as may be necessary in view of the threatened invasion of our territory.

Early in the war, the British Government obtained a copy of the German cipher code used in the above message and have made it their business to obtain copies of Bernstorff's cipher telegrams to Mexico, among others, which are sent back to London and deciphered here. This accounts for their being able to decipher this telegram from the German Government to their representative in Mexico, and also for the delay from January 19 until now in their receiving this information. This has hitherto been a jealously guarded secret and is only divulged to you now by the British Government in view of the extraordinary circumstances and their friendly feeling toward the United States. They earnestly request that you will keep the source of your information and the British Government's method of obtaining it profoundly secret, but they put no prohibition on the publication of Zimmermann's telegram itself.

The copies of this and other telegrams were not obtained in Washington but were bought in Mexico.

I have thanked Balfour for the service his Government has rendered us and suggest that a private official message of thanks from our Government to him would be beneficial.

I am informed that this information has not yet been given to the Japanese Government, but I think it not unlikely that when it reaches them they may make a public statement on it in order to clear up their position regarding the United States and prove their good faith to their Allies.

Throughout that day the senior staff of the State Department eagerly awaited the arrival of Page's cable. Lansing had taken the weekend off, leaving his Under-Secretary, Frank Polk, in charge. Polk read the document with growing amazement and anger. Realising that he could not wait for Lansing's return, he called the White House. Within minutes, the President received him in the Oval Office. Wilson was badly shaken and Polk eventually persuaded him to take no immediate action until Lansing could brief him once he had returned on the following Tuesday,

February 27. Polk went back to the State Department to research the facts Lansing would require to communicate to the President.

As the drama unfolded in Washington, Bernstorff was enduring a miserable journey back to Germany. The ejected Ambassador, his wife and his staff, 200-strong, found passage on the Danish liner, *Frederik VIII*, which sailed from New York on February 15. The British had granted Bernstorff safe passage on the condition that the liner should call at Halifax, Nova Scotia for a detailed search. This diversion had been instigated by the Admiralty at Hall's request. Having studied his intercepted messages over a period of two-and-a-half years, he had developed a high regard for Bernstorff's powers of persuasion and worried that, even at this late hour, he might be able to argue Berlin out of a confrontation with the US. In reality Bernstorff had no influence with the military rulers of Germany and their ultranationalist allies. Taking no chances, the Navy held *Frederik VIII* in Halifax for no less than 12 days, only authorising the liner's departure after the telegram had safely been in the hands of the State Department for 72 hours. The Canadian customs agents were thorough: every passenger, every cabin and every piece of luggage was searched. To their fury, Bernstorff and his party were not allowed to go ashore.

The agents discovered a trunk the Swedish Minister in Washington had entrusted to Bernstorff to deliver to the Foreign Ministry in Stockholm. With the Swedish Roundabout in mind Hall ordered the trunk seized. After the publication of the Zimmermann telegram, he cunningly leaked a story to the press that the Canadian customs had discovered that the seals of the trunk had been broken before the liner had arrived at Halifax, implying that an American undercover agent had discovered and removed a copy of the telegram concealed in the Swedish papers.

Wilson had to deal with another problem. The bill to authorise arming merchant ships passed the House by a majority of 402 to 13 but had become bogged down by a filibuster in the Senate, led by a group of antiwar senators. With Congress due to adjourn on March 4, the President intended to put pressure on the Senate by personally appearing on Capitol Hill on Monday February 26 and demanding that the bill be passed. His efforts proved fruitless.

The well-informed Gaunt had his ear close to the ground. On the same day, he cabled Hall, using their personal code:

> Aaron [Wilson] has got hold of a cable to Barber [Bernstorff] from his employer directing him in the event of a break at once to include an alliance with Mexico. This information will most likely become public property by Wednesday morning. Can you send me any information, which would make information fuller and more decisive?

Hall replied:

> Germany guarantees assistance to Mexico if they will reconquer Texas, New Mexico and Arizona: also proposes alliance with Mexico to make war together. Do not use this till Aaron announces it ... Premature disclosure fatal. Full details in possession of Aaron. Alone I did it.

Although Hall was by then reasonably sure that his plan had succeeded, secrecy remained one of his prime objectives. He reminded Gaunt: 'It is imperative that knowledge of this affair shall never be traced to British sources.'[14]

Western Union had given Polk three other coded telegrams sent out by the German Embassy. Anxious to discover their contents, Lansing wired Page on February 28:

> Please endeavour to obtain copy of German code from Mr. Balfour ... Effort will be made to secure copies of all German code messages as far back as possible and if the Department were in possession of the code, it could be a great saving of time and expense. Contents of messages decoded here would of course be communicated to the British Government.[15]

Hall had anticipated that the State Department might ask for the code-books and he was not prepared to agree. He noted that Page and Bell privately agreed with him, but felt that they 'had to press the point'. On the next day, March 1, Page replied to Lansing:

> The three messages were deciphered today and are practically identical. They contain instructions to use a certain variation of the cipher book when communicating with Berlin. The question of our having a copy of the code has been taken up, but there appeared to be difficulties. I am told that the actual code would be of no use to us as it was never used straight, but with a great number of variations, which are known to only one or two experts here. They cannot be spared to go to America. If you will send me copies of B's cipher telegrams the British authorities will gladly decipher them as quickly as possible giving me copies as fast as deciphered.[16]

On the morning of February 27, Lansing returned from his weekend break to be briefed by Polk on the telegram and the circumstances in which it had arrived in Washington. An approach to Western Union to hand over the incriminating cable from Bernstorff to Eckardt was initially rejected as undue interference by the Administration in the business of a commercial undertaking. Polk was continuing his efforts at a higher level. Lansing had long harboured no illusions about Imperial Germany and had always believed that sooner or later a German blunder would lead to war. He was not surprised by this denouement or by Zimmermann's effrontery in using the State Department network to transmit a message suggesting the dismemberment of the Union.

At eleven-thirty that morning Lansing went to the White House and spent an hour with the President discussing the telegram and how best to use it. Wilson was perplexed as to how Bernstorff had received the message from Berlin, remarking that the closing of the Ambassador's secret lines of communication with his Government made him a little uncertain as to its authenticity. Lansing told the President that its legitimacy could be easily confirmed. Early in January, Bernstorff, at Colonel House's request, had been attempting to obtain concrete terms of peace from his Government. The Ambassador had complained of his inability to communicate secretly and therefore freely with Berlin, which he considered essential to achieve this objective. The State Department had reluctantly consented to send messages for him through the US Embassy in Berlin in a cipher for which they did not have the key. Several telegrams had been exchanged with the German Foreign Office by this method. On January 17 an exceptionally long message (some one thousand groups) was received from Berlin and delivered to the Ambassador the next day. On the 19th the telegram from Bernstorff to Mexico was filed. From these facts Lansing concluded that the long secret message delivered on the 18th was intended for the German Minister in Mexico as well as other instructions to be implemented, should diplomatic relations be severed.

An increasingly uneasy Wilson exclaimed 'Good Lord' several times during Lansing's briefing, accepting his explanation of how Bernstorff had received his orders. He expressed his anger at the German Government's action in using the Administration to advance a conspiracy against the US.

The scales had at last dropped from Wilson's eyes. Not only was he incensed by the German duplicity, he was angry with himself for having been duped by the suave Bernstorff into allowing him to use the State Department network to America's disadvantage. He must also have been uncomfortably aware that the British Government knew of his naïveté. On the following day, February 28, the strength of his feelings about the German betrayal became evident, when he met a delegation of Quakers and other peace activists. The Quaker leader, William Hull, noted:

> Wilson stressed repeatedly his conviction that it was impossible to deal any further in a peaceful method with the German Government ... I recall with great vividness his tone ... a mixture of great indignation and determination – when he said: '... if you knew what I know at this present moment, and what you will see reported in tomorrow morning's newspapers, you would not ask me to attempt further peaceful dealings with the Germans.'[17]

Whatever his reservations about Page, Wilson never doubted the authenticity of the telegram. Lansing persuaded him to wait until Polk could obtain the copy telegram from Western Union, thus providing some useful confirmation to overcome the incredulity which he knew would be widely felt on Capitol Hill. Wilson instructed Lansing to cable Page and ask him to thank Balfour for providing information of such inestimable value. Page immediately passed this message to Hall. Neutrality had begun to fade.

Lansing returned to the State Department highly relieved by his talk with Wilson to find that Polk had finally persuaded the President of Western Union, Newcomb Carlton, to hand over a copy of the telegram. The remaining pieces of the jigsaw were falling into place. Faced with the continuing intransigence of the antiwar senators, the President decided to play the trump card that Room 40 had discovered and which Hall, Balfour and Page had placed in his hands.

On the morning of February 28 Wilson told Lansing to show the telegram to one of the recalcitrant senators, Hitchcock of Nebraska. The dumbfounded Senator promptly changed his position on the bill. Lansing released the telegram unofficially to the Associated Press correspondent, E. M. Hood, at 6 pm that evening in time to catch the next morning's newspapers. Playing a cautious game, he confirmed its validity while being careful not to reveal how it had come into the hands of the Administration.

On the morning of 1 March every newspaper in America led with the sensational story. The banner headlines of the *New York Times* thundered:

> GERMANY SEEKS ALLIANCE AGAINST U.S.
> ASKS JAPAN AND MEXICO TO JOIN HER
> FULL TEXT OF PROPOSALS MADE PUBLIC

There were many in the US who could not believe what they read. Like Hall and Page before him, Lansing had faced the quandary of how many details he could safely release without disclosing how the telegram had been obtained. The story contained one serious error – Hood had inadvertently stated that Wilson had received the telegram on February 3, the day that he had severed diplomatic relations, three weeks before he had actually seen it.

Fully aware that their Minister in Mexico had actually discussed the telegram's contents with the Mexican Foreign Minister, the Japanese Government, as Page had forecast, quickly repudiated any connection with Zimmermann's scheme and loudly declared their loyalty to the Western alliance. The Vice-Minister for Foreign Affairs, Shidehara, stated:

> We are greatly surprised to hear of the German proposal. We cannot imagine what Germany is thinking about to conceive that she could possibly involve us in war with the United States merely by asking Mexico. It is too ridiculous for words. Needless to say, Japan remains faithful to the Allies.[18]

On March 2, Room 40 had intercepted a cable from Eckardt to Zimmermann, informing him of the meeting between the Japanese Minister and the Mexican Foreign Minister. This intelligence, which Hall certainly would have passed on to the Foreign Office and the American Embassy, can have done nothing to allay mistrust of Japanese intentions.

As Hall had predicted, a small number of isolationists in the Senate asserted that the telegram was a forgery, initiated by the devious British to force the US into the war. The Irish-American Senator O'Gorman of New York asserted that it was all a plot set up by perfidious Albion. His colleague, Smith of Michigan, (who had shown himself up as an ignorant landlubber during the inquiry into the loss of *Titanic* five years earlier), went even further, calling it 'a forgery and a sham born in the brain of a scoundrel and a fool'. True to form, George Sylvester Viereck rushed into print in *The Fatherland*, declaring that the telegram 'had been planted by British agents – a preposterous document, obviously faked'.

On the evening of March 2 Gaunt had dined with the Round Table Club in New York, whose members included Elihu Root, Secretary of State in the Theodore Roosevelt Administration, and Joseph Choate, a former Ambassador to Great Britain; a group of eighteen distinguished men, who were by no means pro-German. The telegram was the chief topic of conversation. He wrote to Hall: 'After dinner they all drew their chairs up around the fire and went for me. Choate openly said that the telegram was a forgery, an assertion which was practically unanimously supported by the whole bunch.'[19] Gaunt retorted that both Wilson and Lansing had given their word that it was authentic. When Choate suggested that proof should be shown to a select group from Congress, he objected forcefully, pointing out that men's lives were involved and it would be most unwise to give any details to the leaders of the antiwar group in the Senate. Root and Choate asked Gaunt pointedly whether he thought the telegram was genuine and even whether he knew anything about it. Although he astutely parried the question, his intuition told him that they believed he was well aware of the message. Eventually he closed the argument by saying that he had received details of the telegram from the Administration and that he was satisfied that it was correct.

As Balfour and Hall had foreseen, the Prussian Invasion Plot, as the media rapidly christened the telegram, crystallized opinion across the US against Germany; particularly among the majority of Americans, who did not live on the Eastern Seaboard and to whom the war had hitherto been remote and the issues far from clear. The sinking of *Lusitania* had alerted Americans to German frightfulness and left them with a deeply rooted aversion to their war machine's ruthless disregard for human life. Nevertheless the diplomatic war of paper bullets which had followed her torpedoing and the later losses like *Arabic, Sussex, Ancona* or *Laconia*, sunk only a few days earlier with the loss of two American lives, had not greatly aroused their interest. Zimmermann and his telegram had all but eradicated this apathy. Tuchman summed up the situation:

> This was different. This was Germany proposing to attack the United States, conspiring with America's neighbour to snatch American territory: worse, conspiring to set an Oriental foe on America's back. This was a direct threat upon the body of America, which most Americans had never dreamt was a German intention.

The Washington correspondent of *The Times* reported that the Mexican revelations had aroused the public:

> ... more than anything else since the outbreak of war ... it was worth a dozen *Laconia* outrages ... the West had never been touched by the submarine issue but ... the Mexican plot and Bernstorff's complicity had touched everybody ... to the quick.

The isolationist *Chicago Tribune* was typical, asking its readers to realise 'without delay that Germany recognizes us as an enemy' and that the country could no longer avoid 'active participation in the present conflict'. In Chicago and Minneapolis, Omaha and St. Louis and a thousand other cities throughout the Midwest irate Americans reluctantly accepted that Imperial Germany's cynical machinations would involve them in war. Their sentiments were mild in comparison to their contemporaries in Texas or on the West Coast. The *El Paso Times* derided Prussian militarism as 'writhing in the slime of intrigue' and the *Sacramento Bee* denounced Germany for its 'treacherous enmity, [and] underhanded, nasty intriguing'.[20]

The minority in the Senate continued to press Lansing to disclose his sources. The Secretary of State was determined to outflank them. Late on March 1 he cabled Page:

> Some members of Congress are attempting to discredit Zimmermann message, charging that message was furnished to this Government by one of belligerents. This Government has not the slightest doubt as to its authenticity but it would be of the greatest service if the British Government would permit someone in the embassy to personally decode the original message which we secured from the manager of the telegraph office and then cable

to Department German text. Assure Mr. Balfour that the Department hesitated to make this request but feels that this course will materially strengthen its position and make it possible for the Department to state that it had secured the Z note from our own people …[21]

Once again Hall had foreseen this development and as neither he nor Page thought it necessary for the telegram to be decoded in the Embassy, he asked Bell to visit the Admiralty. De Grey, thrilled that he had so successfully deciphered the message, came to Hall's room to coach Bell in deciphering it. In his excitement he accidentally forgot to take his 13040 codebook. He quickly realised his error, but as by this time he knew both 13040 and the telegram by heart, he was able to guide Bell through the decoding process without the latter suspecting that anything was wrong. Armed with both the German and the English texts of the telegram, the diplomat sped back to the Embassy.

These urgently undertaken moves were soon to prove unnecessary. Washington and London were to receive assistance from a most unexpected quarter, which would resolve the authenticity of the telegram beyond any doubt. On the morning of March 2, Zimmermann gave a press conference. Replying to a question from William Bayard Hale, the Hearst correspondent in Berlin and a covert German agent, asking him whether the telegram was fake, he revealed that he had indeed sent it. Gaunt told Hall:

> … had not Zimmermann come out with his statement on Saturday, I think it would have done us a great deal of harm. As it was, it was a complete success, because Viereck … and all the rest of the inkslingers just had time to get their yarn into the papers, pointing out how obviously it was a British fake, when Zimmermann's statement knocked the bottom out of everything.[22]

Interestingly, Hall never agreed with the conventional wisdom regarding Zimmermann's revelation, that it was a colossal error. With his customary insight into the German mindset, or his ability to see to the heart of the matter at least, he reasoned:

> Zimmermann's speedily published admission was by no means the stupid move that some people held it to be. As yet he had no definite information with regard to the 'treachery', but he was not to be blamed for believing that it had been committed on American territory, and he knew that a denial would only mean the production of the original telegram, and possibly others with it, from the Washington cable-office. And if a copy of their code-book had been produced, he would be helpless. He took what in my opinion was the wisest course, though it led to his downfall.[23]

In Washington many people now fervently wished that they had kept their mouths shut. Viereck readily recognised that at a stroke Zimmermann's admission had destroyed the political influence of the German-American community. It is difficult to have much sympathy for him but it is ironic that he should have been betrayed by the very men in Berlin in whose cause he had so loyally propagated such flagrant lies. German-owned papers in the Midwest, which had followed Viereck in denouncing the telegram as a forgery, either lapsed into a sheepish silence or rapidly announced that they and their readers were and always had been loyal Americans. After Hitler came to power, Viereck showed his true allegiance, becoming a leading light in the German-American Bund, the local offshoot of the Nazi Party.

In investigating the leak of the telegram, Dr. Göppert had not overlooked the possibility that code 13040 had been compromised. His task had been made more difficult by Hall's guile in overseeing the process by which the American government had been made aware of the telegram. Hall had thrown him off the scent. Although Eckardt had been advised as early as March 4 that 13040 might have been broken and should not be used in future, Göppert reported on March 12 that the code was believed to be secure and could still be used in communications between Berlin and the Legations in Latin America. He believed that the telegram had been discovered as a result of American rather than British action.

Noting that the American Administration had been surprised by Bernstorff's announcement on January 31 of the resumption of unrestricted submarine warfare, Göppert argued that they could not then have known of the telegram's contents. He concluded that the Administration must have received a plain text copy of the document as a result of either negligence or treachery within the Washington Embassy. He refused to believe that any of the German codes could be broken and placed the blame firmly on spies and traitors. It apparently never occurred to him that 13040 could have been intercepted before it ever reached Washington. Even after a detailed investigation, he was making the same error as the Admiralstab had in 1914, when they refused to believe that the SKB might have come into allied possession. Hall rightly judged the flaw in the German character that could never accept the possibility that the advanced technology built into German cryptology could ever be solved by mere foreigners, who had not enjoyed the benefits of a German technical education. In World War II, the German military establishment did not learn from the lessons of the earlier conflict, refusing to believe that the highly sophisticated Enigma technology could be broken by the British. In the lecture he gave on Room 40 in Edinburgh in 1927, Alfred Ewing described this purblind confidence: 'The assumed stupidity of the British was the most valuable asset, and it was not, apparently, till the war was over that the Germans became aware how completely that confidential channels of communication had been compromised.'[24] In the only newspaper interview he ever gave, in 1925, Hall made more or less the same point:

> This one thing shows the difference between the British and German mentality. I am sure, if the position was to be reversed, the British would never have been so stupid as not to have suspected that the messages were being deciphered. If I had disclosed the actual wording of the Zimmermann telegram the Germans would have suspected something at once … The Germans actually thought that there had been a leakage between Bernstorff and Mexico, which is what I wanted. Right until the end of the war, I do not think that the Germans suspected that we knew as much as we did about their intelligence service.[25]

True to character, the infuriated Zimmermann cast around for someone to blame. He took the opportunity of settling old scores. There never had been much love lost between him and Bernstorff and he proceeded to castigate the Ambassador for allowing his papers to be opened by American agents aboard *Frederik VIII* between New York and Halifax. Unwittingly, he was falling for Hall's ruse in spreading disinformation about the Swedish trunk. He also suspected that security in the Legation in Mexico City had become excessively lax, chastising Eckardt and his secretary, Magnus, for negligence. A succession of angry telegrams passed between the Foreign Minister and the Legation.

> Zimmermann to Eckardt, March 7 1917
> Please learn compromising instructions. Entirely approve your attitude. We have openly acknowledged cable Dispatch No. 1 [the original telegram]. In connection with this, emphasise that instructions were only to be carried out after Declaration of War by America.
> Cable dispatch No.11 (the telegram dated February 8 is of course being kept strictly secret here.)

On March 21, Stumm, one of Zimmermann's assistants, cabled Eckardt:

> Please cable to same cipher, who deciphered Cable Dispatches I and II, how the originals and decodes were kept, and, in particular whether both dispatches were kept in the same place.

Six days later Eckardt received another cable from Berlin:

> Various indications suggest that the treachery was committed in Mexico. The greatest caution is indicated.

Once again, Eckardt was told to burn all compromising material. Beesly sarcastically noted that this was a classic occasion of slamming the stable door after the horse had bolted. Realizing that he was being set up as a scapegoat, Eckardt fired off a furious reply:

> Eckardt to Zimmerman , March 27, 1917
> Both dispatches were deciphered, in accordance with my special instructions, by Magnus. Both, as is the case with everything of a politically secret nature, were kept from the knowledge of the Chancery officials.
> Telegram No. I was received here in cipher 13040, while Kinkel [a diplomat, who been transferred from Washington to Mexico City after the Embassy had been closed down] ... thinks he remembers that it was sent off by the Washington Embassy, like all telegrams sent here in cipher, from Cape Cod. The originals in both cases were burned by Magnus and the ashes scattered. Both dispatches were kept in an absolutely secure steel safe, procured especially for the purpose and installed in the Chancery Building, in Magnus's bedroom, up to the time when they were burned ...

On March 30 Eckardt sent a follow-up cable to Zimmermann. He did not hesitate to shift blame to the now-defunct Washington Embassy.

> Greater caution than is always exercised here would be impossible. The text of telegrams which have arrived is read to me at night in my dwelling house by Magnus, in a low voice. My servant, who does not understand German, sleeps in an annex. Apart from this, the text is never anywhere but in Magnus's hand or in the steel safe, the method of opening which is known only to him and myself. According to Kinkel, in Washington even secret telegrams were known to the whole Chancery. Two copies were regularly made for the Embassy records. Here there can be no question of carbon copies or waste paper.
> Please inform me at once as soon as we are exculpated, as we doubtless shall be; otherwise, I insist, as does Magnus also, on a judicial investigation, if necessary, by Consul Grunow ...

Eckardt's feisty and strongly argued defence forced Zimmermann to back down.

> Foreign Office to Eckardt, No.28 April 4 1917.
> After your telegram it is hardly conceivable that betrayal took place in Mexico. In face of it the indications which point in that direction lose their force. No blame rests on either you or Magnus.[26]

As these exchanges were all transmitted by 13040, Hall and his cryptographers in Room 40 were highly amused by Zimmermann's frantic and unavailing attempts to discover someone he could hold responsible for the fiasco. That the telegram had been discovered in both Washington and Mexico City certainly did not escape them. Fleet Paymaster Lloyd Hirst, the head of the NID's Latin American section, remarked that the Germans were living in a fool's paradise.[27] As Page's biographer noted, tongue-in-cheek:

> ... These [messages] were passed around at the time among a select few in the American Embassy and the British Foreign Office and were the occasion of much hilarity. Page, with his alert sense of fun and with his well-known love of everything German, found these telegraphic manifestations of Teutonic woe an endless delight.[28]

Carranza may not have been an intellectual heavyweight, but he had been shrewd enough to pick his way through the minefield of Mexican politics to power and the disclosure of the telegram had enraged him. He may have realised that Zimmermann was using him as a catspaw and that, as Hall knew through the decrypts, the Germans were intriguing with his rival Villa, supplying him with munitions. The recent withdrawal of the Pershing expedition allowed him to declare victory over American arms. On April 14 Eckardt cabled Zimmermann that Carranza intended to remain neutral, stating that: 'The alliance ... had been wrecked by [the telegram's] premature publication but might become necessary at a later stage.' The telegram not only brought America into the war but kept Mexico out.[29] In the mid 1970s Professor Larry Hill of the Texas A & M University was researching President Wilson's relations with various leaders of the Mexican Revolution in the Secretariat of Foreign Affairs in Mexico City. He encountered considerable difficulty in gaining access to the relevant archives. One index card referred to the 'alleged Zimmermann telegram'. He was eventually given the relevant folder only to discover that it was completely empty. When he showed the staff that its contents were missing he was greeted with complete indifference, indicating they had not the slightest knowledge of their importance. When he later told Berta Ulloa, a prominent historian at the Colegio de Mexico, about his experience, she replied that she was not surprised. She apologized for the difficulties foreign scholars faced when attempting to research in some of her nation's archives, especially those dealing with foreign affairs or the military. It is difficult to escape the conclusion that that the Mexican authorities regard their involvement in the Zimmermann telegram as an embarrassing incident, best forgotten.

When the anti-war Senators filibustered out his bill to arm merchant ships, Wilson issued an executive order putting the guards aboard. German U-boats had meanwhile sunk five American ships without warning, three of them on one day, 18 March, with the loss of 36 lives, further inflaming anti-German feelings. By the middle of March the neutralists were in total disarray and public opinion had run ahead of the President. When Americans of such different political views as Theodore Roosevelt, who had once been in a small minority in advocating war, and the pacifist Josephus Daniels, whom Wilson had made Secretary of the Navy (a most unsuitable appointment) agreed that conflict was now inevitable, he had to act. The March revolution in Russia, ousting the Czar, was helpful to Wilson's volte-face. He could reasonably justify his complete change of position by claiming that the US would be fighting a war to save democracy.

On 21 March, Wilson summoned a special session of Congress for the evening of 2 April to receive a message about 'grave matters of national policy'. Despite the late hour and a steady spring drizzle, a large crowd had gathered to watch Wilson drive down Pennsylvania Avenue with a cavalry escort on his way to Capitol Hill. Inside the great chamber of the House of Representatives, not a seat was to be had. Washington society had dined early and flocked to Capitol Hill to hear the historic announcement. Many Congressmen were wearing miniature Stars and Stripes in their buttonholes. The Justices of the Supreme Court in their black robes, Lansing and other Cabinet members and the Chiefs of Staff of the Army and Navy were in the audience. Nearby were the Allied Ambassadors, relief almost perceptible on their faces.

On the stroke of 8.30 pm, the Sergeant-at-Arms appeared on the floor of the House and announced the President. Wilson strode to the rostrum and began his address, asking Congress to: 'declare the recent course of the Imperial German Government to be in fact nothing less than war against the government and people of the United States'. He described the submarines as outlaws and referring to the Zimmermann telegram, he reminded the legislators that Germany 'means to stir enemies against us at our very doors'. When he declared that 'there is one choice we cannot make ... we will not choose the path of submission', the venerable Chief Justice, Edward White, who had fought in the Confederate Army during the Civil War, was so moved that tears ran down his cheeks. By Colonel House's calculation, Wilson reached the climax of his eloquent peroration after speaking for 32 minutes, asserting:

> ... that the German Government was a natural foe of liberty ... that the world must be made safe for democracy ... that America must fight for the principles that gave her birth. To such a task we can dedicate our lives and our fortunes, everything we are and everything we have, with the pride of those who know that the day has come when America is privileged to spend her blood and her might for the principles which gave her birth and happiness and the peace which she has treasured. God helping her, she can do no else.[30]

It was probably Wilson's finest moment. The continual provocation Germany had offered America had led him reluctantly and dangerously late in the day to propose war to Congress with the support of a united nation. His most implacable adversary, Theodore Roosevelt, conceded: 'The President's great message was literally unanswerable. Of course when a war is on, all minor considerations, including all partisan considerations, vanish at once. All good Americans will back the President with single minded loyalty.'[31]

Congress and the gallery gave Wilson a standing ovation which one reporter called 'a roar like a storm'. The Senate voted for war by 82 to 6, the House by 373 to 50. At noon Washington time on 6 April 1917, Wilson signed the formal declaration. To borrow the words of Admiral Yamamoto after Pearl Harbor, Imperial Germany had recklessly awoken the slumbering giant against her and had thereby sealed her fate.

In London Hall breathed a hearty sigh of relief. The game, which he had begun nearly three months earlier when de Grey had first shown him the incomplete decrypt of the telegram, and which he had pursued with such tenacity, had ended in personal triumph. John W. Davis, Page's successor as Ambassador in London, who had been close to both Wilson and Lansing, told Bell that '... no single event contributed more directly to the ultimate declaration of war'.[32]

Zimmermann's ambitious gambit had failed and he had committed one of the major unforced errors in history, with catastrophic consequences for Imperial Germany. When Ludendorff finally succeeded in driving Bethmann Hollweg from office that July, Zimmermann fell with him, never to hold office again.

In contrast Hall's star was rising. On 27 April he was promoted Rear Admiral and that October, on the recommendation of the Foreign Office, he was knighted. In his letter of congratulation, one of many Hall received, Page passed on a message from Wilson, who had asked him '... to assure Admiral Hall of my very great appreciation of what he has done and of the spirit in which he has done it'.[33] In his reply Hall told Page how greatly he valued the President's words. Writing to Wilson in March 1918, Page displayed his talent for words and his publisher's touch for a story in this vivid pen-portrait:

> Hall is one genius that the war has developed. Neither in fiction nor in fact can you find any such man to match him. Of the wonderful things I know he has done, there are several that it would take an exciting volume to tell. The man is a genius – a clear case of genius. All other secret service men are amateurs by comparison. If there be any life left me after this war, and if Hall's abnormal activity and ingenuity have not caused him to become translated, I wish to spend a week with him at some quiet place and then spend a year in writing out what he will have told me. That's the shortest

cut to immortality for him and for me that has yet occurred to me. I shall never meet another man like him: that were too much to expect.

And (whether it becomes me to say so or not) Bell and I have his complete confidence and that fact entitles us to some special consideration in the esteem of our friends. For Hall can look through you and see the very muscular movements of your immortal soul while he is talking to you. Such eyes as the man has! My Lord! I do study these men here most diligently, who have this vast and appalling War-Job. There are most uncommon creatures among them – men about whom our great-grandchildren will read in school histories; but, of them all, the most extraordinary is this naval officer – of whom, probably, they'll never hear. He locks up certain documents 'not to be opened until 20 years after this date'. I've made up my mind to live twenty years more. I shall be present at the opening of that safe![34]

Sadly, Page was not to live for even one of these twenty years. In August 1918 his health broke and, to almost universal regret in British official circles, he was forced to resign. He lived long enough to see the Armistice, dying in his native North Carolina on December 21 1918. This admirable man had worked himself into his grave in the service of both the US and Britain. He was remembered in a plaque in Westminster Abbey, one of only three Americans to be so honoured. Its inscription reads:

THE FRIEND OF BRITAIN IN HER SOREST NEED

If the Zimmermann telegram had been the catalyst to bring the United States into the conflict, Hall was the master player, the right man in the right place at the right time, who had steered his project to success, overcoming the complex difficulties which he had encountered and achieving his cardinal objective of protecting his sources. The process of deception, on which he had so rigorously insisted, had succeeded. Zimmermann never suspected that British Naval Intelligence had broken Germany's main diplomatic codes. The revelation of the Zimmermann telegram is one of the biggest and most far-reaching coups in the history of intelligence. As Ed Bell noted 'We gave Reggie the cards to play. He played his cards in his own way, and he played them damned well.'

Two charges have been laid against Hall over his handling of the telegram. Firstly, that he had delayed revealing it to the American Embassy for over a month after its initial interception. He would have had no reason for disclosing it if Wilson had declared war in retaliation for the German resumption of unrestricted submarine warfare. Only nineteen days passed between the decision taken on February 5 to obtain the text of the message from Mexico City and Page passing it to Washington. It took fourteen days to brief Thurstan and for him to extract the telegram from the Mexican telegraphic authorities and send it to London via New York, where it was reciphered. He lost little time in executing his orders. As Hall and the Foreign Office had acted decisively and in a remarkably short period of time after the complete telegram had been deciphered, the accusation of delay does not stand up.

Secondly, Hall has been attacked for misleading Page and Bell by telling them that Room 40 had acquired a copy of the 13040 codebook earlier in the war. In his unpublished 1933 autobiography, he candidly admitted this deception:

> This, of course, was not so: but it was the official explanation which we had decided to give to the American Government. It was thought to be a better safeguard for 40 O.B. than the actual truth. A codebook was always liable to reach enemy hands. It might be recovered from a sunken ship or from a Zeppelin brought down or even on a field of battle [The NID's success in retrieving codebooks from U-boats and Zeppelins is described in Chapter 14] ... it would be much better from our point of view, for the Germans to suppose that a copy of their 13040 codebook had come into our hands than that without any such assistance we were able to read their most secret dispatches.
>
> Actually, I understand, in German official circles, it was generally held that we had obtained our information from a stolen copy of the deciphered dispatch.[35]

Although Hall may have lied to an ally, he was surely justified in his determination to safeguard Room 40 and to prevent the Germans from discovering the extent to which it was intercepting its signal traffic.

In April 1917, the month in which the US entered the war, Holtzendorff's U-boats sank a record total of 860,000 tons of allied shipping – 237,000 tons in the last week of the month alone. As the Admiralstab had foreseen, the unrestricted submarine campaign was threatening to cut off the sea-lanes on which Great Britain depended for its survival. The clock was ticking dangerously close to midnight when the Admiralty belatedly introduced convoy at the end of April and the losses started to fall. Its Anti-Submarine Division had estimated that seventy destroyers were required to act as convoy escorts but the hard-pressed Royal Navy could only allocate forty to the task. For the first time in its long history as a maritime power Britain was facing the possibility of losing a war at sea. Had she been forced to sue for peace, her allies in the West, France and Italy, would almost inevitably have had to follow suit.

Robert Lansing's strongly held belief that Imperial Germany would sooner or later perpetrate an act of folly of such magnitude that the United States would be drawn into the conflict proved justified. The timing of the telegram was critically significant, indeed providential, for the allies. Admiral W. S. Sims, sent by Washington to London before the declaration of war, quickly grasped the danger to the allied cause and persuaded his superiors to dispatch a strong force of vitally needed destroyers to reinforce the Royal Navy and provide the necessary number of escorts. Indeed, the availability of United States Navy destroyers to act as convoy escorts was the deciding factor in the Admiralty dropping its opposition to convoy in the last week of April 1917. On April 30 Hankey drafted a memo which Lloyd George sent to the War Cabinet:

> I was gratified to learn from Admiral Duff [Director of the Anti-Submarine Division] that he had completely altered his view in regard to the adoption of a system of convoy, and I gather that the First Sea Lord shared his views … Admiral Duff is not enamoured with the system, but a number of circumstances have combined to bring him to the view … that … at any rate an experiment in this direction should be made. One of these reasons is that now that the United States of America have entered the War, he thinks it should be possible to find escorts which were formerly impracticable.[36]

By the summer of 1917 34 USN destroyers were serving in European waters. The combined strength of the RN and USN working together in the aptly named and highly effective Operation Pull Together, directed by Admiral Bayly from Queenstown, succeeded by the end of 1917 in reducing the losses from U-boat attack to sustainable proportions. Without the active participation of the USN, the operation would not have been so successful.

The German Government's decision to facilitate Lenin's return to Russia after the March revolution was a significant factor in enabling the Bolsheviks to seize power in November 1917. Under the Treaty of Brest-Litovsk they withdrew from the war. The General Staff were thus free to transfer their armies from the East to the Western Front and mount the so-called Kaiserschlacht, a series of offensives beginning in March 1918, which came close to breaking the stalemate which had lasted since October 1914. In the previous autumn, the British Expeditionary Force had suffered extremely heavy losses at Passchendaele, an operation fought to take pressure off the French Army, and had no reserves of manpower. Only the build up of the American armies in France, made possible by the increasingly effective campaign in the Atlantic against the U-boats, eventually swung the balance on the Western Front to the allies from the summer of 1918 and led to the crushing military defeat of Imperial Germany that autumn. Holtzendorff's boast that 'not one American soldier would land in Europe' had been belied. In the last analysis American strength both at sea and on land secured the allied victory.

Conversely, had the US entered the war at any time later than the spring of 1917, her impact on the conflict would have been less decisive and its outcome very different. Had the reinforced German Army on the Western front defeated the allies in France between March and June 1918, Germany would have won the war.

Wellington famously described Waterloo as '…the nearest run thing you ever saw in your life', adding with justification, ' By God I don't think it would have done if I had not been there.'[37] The same could be said about the Zimmermann telegram and the man who exploited it. Hall had almost single-handedly influenced the course of history, averting the spectre of defeat and setting in place the developments which led 19 months later to victory over Imperial Germany on land and at sea. Echoing Wellington, Hall could well justify his claim to Gaunt: 'Alone I did it.'

Notes

[1] CAC HALL 3/6 p.14
[2] Ibid p.12
[3] NARA State Department papers Ed Bell to W.L.Hurley July 13 1921
[4] CAC HALL 3/1 p.17
[5] TNA ADM 223/778
[6] CAC HALL 3/6 p.19
[7] NARA Bell to Hurley
[8] CAC HALL 3/6 p.21
[9] Dugdale *Arthur James Balfour 1906-1930* p.135-137
[10] Ibid p.137-138
[11] CAC HALL 3/6 p.21
[12] Dugdale p.138
[13] NARA Bell to Hurley
[14] Beesly p.221
[15] Ibid p.223
[16] Ibid p.222
[17] Nickles *Under the Wire* p.151
[18] Hendrick Vol 3 pp.351-352
[19] CAC HALL 3/6 p.30
[20] Tuchman pp.159-160
[21] Beesly p.223
[22] CAC HALL 3/6 p.30
[23] Ibid p.31
[24] The *Scotsman* December 14 1927
[25] *Daily Mail* October 31 1925
[26] Hendrick Cables between Berlin and Mexico City pp.352-360

27 CAC MLBE 5/1
28 Hendrick Vol 3 pp.356-357
29 Desmond Young in *Member for Mexico*, his life of Lord Cowdray, the founder of the Mexican Eagle Oil Co. and who had many other interests in Mexico. The information regarding the empty 'alleged Zimmermann Telegram' folder was provided to the author by Professor Hill, March 7 2008.
30 Seymour *The Papers of Col. House* Vol 2 p.469
31 Miller *Theodore Roosevelt* p.544
32 NARA Bell to Hurley
33 Hendrick Vol 3 pp.362-363
34 Page to Wilson March 17 1918 Hendrick Vol 3. p.361
35 CAC HALL 3/6 p.25
36 Marder Vol 4 p.163
37 Longford *Wellington: The Years of the Sword* pp.489-490

CHAPTER XIII

All Change at the Admiralty

Arthur Balfour was one of the few British political figures who, before August 1914, had recognized the submarine's potential as an offensive weapon. Primed by Hall's intelligence that Germany intended to intensify submarine warfare and alarmed by a sharp rise in merchant shipping losses after Holtzendorff had directed his U-boats to attack allied merchant ships in October 1916, he decided that in an increasingly critical situation he had to change First Sea Lords.

Henry Jackson had not been a success in the post. His expertise lay in technology and he had had little experience of sea command. In November 1916 Balfour decided that Jellicoe, the obvious candidate because of his experience and the prestige he enjoyed throughout the service, should succeed Jackson. On November 24th Jellicoe reluctantly accepted the post. Balfour had no hesitation in appointing Beatty as the new C-in-C Grand Fleet. At forty-five he was the Navy's youngest fleet commander since Nelson.

Twenty-eight arduous months in command of the Fleet had left their toll on Jellicoe. His health had suffered and the bullet which had lodged in his lung during a shore action in the Boxer Rebellion sixteen years earlier cannot have helped. He was a tired man. He had hardly taken any leave during his time in command and, perhaps unwisely, as Jackson and Oliver could have held the fort for a couple of weeks, he did not have a break between the two appointments. As Gordon noted '... the wisdom of replacing a lacklustre First Sea Lord with an exhausted one was not, at the time, an issue.'[1] Marder put his finger on the difficulties which Jellicoe encountered at the Admiralty: 'Commanding an intensely loyal and admiring fleet was one thing – operating in the jungles of Whitehall during the most critical years of a war was something else again. Overtired men are never at their best, for excessive fatigue has an adverse effect on judgment.'[2] Jellicoe had an intuition of the Greek tragedy which lay ahead of him, telling a friend that he would be lucky to last twelve months.[3]

Within two weeks of Jellicoe's appointment, the ineffective Asquith Government had fallen. In the first week in December, Lloyd George united with the Conservative leaders, Bonar Law and Curzon, to overthrow him. In the resultant political crisis, Hall was close enough to the action to write that he had had breakfast with Carson, lunch with Asquith and tea with Balfour.

On December 7 Lloyd George became Prime Minister and Balfour Foreign Secretary. He was succeeded at the Admiralty by Sir Edward Carson, one of the most formidable lawyers in the land. He was best known as the leader of the hard-fought Ulster Unionist opposition to Home Rule for Ireland. Unlike his predecessor, he had little knowledge or experience of defence. Nevertheless, Carson was able to establish good relations with Jellicoe and the other Sea Lords.

Marder wrote of Jellicoe, who was well-known in the service as a centraliser: 'A serious shortcoming was his inclination to do too much himself – he became overwhelmed with work – he never understood that there was but one way for a high war administrator not to be worn-out before his time and that was to concentrate on policy and leave the details to his subordinates.'[4] His normally supportive biographer, John Winton, commented: 'One of the great flaws of Jellicoe's career in command remained his unwillingness to delegate.'[5]

Fisher observed that Jellicoe was 'not the man to stand up against a pack of lawyers clothed with Cabinet garments and possessed of tongues that have put them where they are'.[6] It was Jellicoe's supreme misfortune that his arrival at the Admiralty coincided with Lloyd George's at Downing Street and that he had to face a serpentine Welsh lawyer far more devious than the general run of politicians. To stretch the metaphor to breaking point, the new Prime Minister developed a venomous dislike of the Admiralty in general and of Jellicoe in particular. As early as September 1916 Hall had noted that the Admiralty had become the subject of fierce criticism. This constant disparagement intensified after the change of government, the two newspapers controlled by Lord Northcliffe, *The Times* and the *Daily Mail*, subjecting the Admiralty to a constant stream of criticism.

Jellicoe brought with him from the Grand Fleet a number of senior officers, the most important of whom was Rear-Admiral Alexander Duff, previously Second-in-Command of the Fourth Battle Squadron, whom Marder named as one of the five outstanding Admirals of the war. He appointed Duff to head a new Anti-Submarine Division to direct operations against the U-boats along the lines he (and Beatty) had unsuccessfully advocated after the sinking of *Lusitania*.

After the mishandling of intelligence by the Operations Division at Jutland, and despite Oliver's complacent reassurances, Jellicoe was far from satisfied with the present arrangements. He took a personal interest in Room 40 and its staff. Before going back to Admiralty House at the end of the working day, he would drop in and ask the watchkeepers, in his habitually friendly way, 'Can I count on a quiet night, gentlemen?'[7] According to Clarke, he was the only one of the wartime First Sea Lords ever to set foot in Room 40.[8]

The war against the submarines; and downing the Zeppelins

In May 1917 Jellicoe implemented a far-reaching reorganisation of the War Staff, which clipped Oliver's wings and resulted in at least some easing of the over-centralised command structure. He merged the post of Chief of Staff with that of First Sea Lord, thus taking overall responsibility for Operations. Oliver became Deputy Chief of the Naval Staff (DCNS) responsible for surface warfare and Duff was promoted to the new position of Assistant Chief of the Naval Staff (ACNS) with overall charge of the campaign against the U-boats. He was succeeded at the Anti-Submarine Division by Captain W. W. Fisher, another highly capable officer transferred from the Grand Fleet, where he had commanded the battleship HMS *St Vincent*. He was affectionately known in the service as The Great Agrippa as he was immensely tall.

Ideally, Oliver, who had served for two-and-a-half years in the War Staff, should have been relieved and given a sea command. At that time, Jellicoe was reluctant to let him leave the Admiralty in view of his considerable experience. Oliver was not going to alter his methods and he continued to transmit information from the decrypts to Beatty and Tyrwhitt with minimal interface with the Intelligence Division. The drawbacks of this system became evident later in the year.

As part of this reorganisation, Ewing finally left the Admiralty. Room 40 was at last fully integrated into the Intelligence Division and was officially renamed ID 25. For the previous seven months, Hall had been its chief in all but name and he now possessed the untrammled authority to reshape it along the lines he had long advocated. He and James acted quickly to restructure the operation into three sections, cryptography, direction-finding, and intelligence.

They quickly broke down the almost water-tight division between Room 40, the Holy of Holies as it was sometimes called, and the intelligence subdivisions, particularly the German section, which compiled information on the Kriegsmarine and its organisation and the Enemy Submarine section E.1, whose staff now had full access to the decrypts. The Naval Staff Appreciation of Jutland indicted the previous system:

> Co-operation with the German Section would have been enormously useful to Room 40, and Room 40 could have supplied the German section with priceless information, but they were not allowed to work in conjunction ... The case of E.1 Section was precisely similar ... All reports (from British

and neutral sources) of ships attacked and reports of sighting and attacking German submarines came to E.1 and were duly plotted and recorded there. Room 40, on the other hand, obtained their information from German sources, and knew nothing of British reports. It took in the submarines' signals and knew their identity and time of departure. E.1 followed their track across the ocean so far as British reports could give it, but the two sections were not allowed to work in conjunction.[9]

By the time the reorganisation had been implemented, the consequences of Holtzendorff's resumption of unrestricted submarine warfare had become all too evident. Sinkings of allied and neutral shipping rose from 328,391 tons in January to 520,412 in February, 564,397 in March and a catastrophic 860,334 tons in April. Inside the Admiralty, Jellicoe and even the normally astute Duff had, wrongly, opposed the introduction of convoy, although the Navy had successfully pioneered the system in the Napoleonic wars. Beatty had believed the Navy should immediately resort to convoy. Sir Joseph Maclay, a tough-minded Glasgow shipowner appointed as Shipping Controller in Lloyd George's Government in December 1916, strongly supported convoy and told the Admiralty very forcefully that the alternative was 'starvation and defeat'. To put this disaster into perspective, the level of losses was never exceeded in World War II, even at the peak of the Battle of the Atlantic in March and April of 1943, when the Kriegsmarine had deployed a force of over 100 U-boats at sea, some of them operating in wolfpacks, more than twice as many as they could muster in 1917.

On April 27th, confronted with these unacceptable losses and with Great Britain facing Armageddon, Duff persuaded Jellicoe that the Admiralty had no alternative but to institute convoy. Lloyd George's claim that he had descended on the Admiralty in person on April 30 and dragooned Jellicoe and the War Staff into accepting convoy against their judgment was utterly fallacious. In reality, however belatedly, the decision had been taken several days earlier. This episode only served to increase the already existing mutual animosity between Lloyd George and other members of the War Cabinet and the Admiralty; although Carson, at some degree of risk to himself, loyally supported Jellicoe and the War Staff. Fortunately, Duff did not share Oliver's obdurate resistance to the development of positive co-operation between operations and intelligence. Duff and Hall, who had been promoted Rear-Admiral in April 1917, worked harmoniously together to counter the U-boat menace, establishing an effective and durable working relationship between the Intelligence, Trade and Anti-Submarine divisions.

On two counts, James was particularly well placed to work with Duff. Not only had they served together in the Fourth Battle Squadron, Duff as RA and James as Staff Officer Operations (SOO), but James was also his son-in-law. According to Hall, James had met his future wife, Robin, at a dinner party at Hall's London house.

If Hall and James were strongly supported by the naval and civilian staff of Room 40, now operating close to peak efficiency, Duff and Fisher were similarly extremely well served by their highly efficient SOO, Commander Reginald Henderson and by Admiral Sir Lewis Bayly, the C-in-C Western Approaches and operational commander of the anti-submarine campaign based at Queenstown. Jellicoe's biographer wrote an acute pen-portrait of Bayly: 'One of the ablest Admirals in the Navy; a tough man, hard-working, no sufferer of fools or temperer of winds to any shorn lamb. He had a rough tongue in conversation, and in signals.'[10] Jellicoe had inherited Hall and Bayly. His selection of Duff and Fisher put in place a team of outstanding ability to deal with such a critical situation.

The close co-operation which Hall and Duff developed was focussed on a newly instituted Submarine Tracking Centre. The Convoy Section headed by Fleet Paymaster H. W. E. Manisty, previously on the staff of the Trade Division, reported directly to Duff, providing for the first time unified authority over the convoys. The new Centre was housed in the West Front of the Admiralty, looking over Horse Guards Parade. It included an invaluable innovation, the Chart Room, set up to plot the courses of both convoys and U-boats, connected with Room 40 by its effective pneumatic tube system, enabling it to receive the most up-to-date information from the DF network, run by Frank Tiarks, which had by then grown to 40 stations employing 800 men; and from the Submarine Section, headed by Fleet Paymaster E. W. C. Thring, the NID's acknowledged authority on U-boats. One of his colleagues wrote of Thring:

> By hard work and persistence, he amassed a huge amount of information, which proved later to be of untold value, and in time, he developed what I can only call an uncanny 'feel' for what the enemy was doing. From a chart of plotted sinkings he would say '…that … and that and that are the work of Submarine U-: she will have so and so many torpedoes and so much fuel left.' The various Captains acquired recognized characteristics in his mind. (I kept a gallery of the photographs with notes on their careers for him) and his forecasts were of uncanny accuracy. A lot of his information came from Room 40 but there was a great deal more to it than that.[11]

Room 40 intercepts and NID analyses were now made available to the Convoy Section with minimal delay and were plotted on their charts and to the German and Enemy Submarine Sections of the NID. For the first time, it was possible to see the latest information about enemy submarines, side by side with the track of a convoy, and also, as the Commodore's ship was always equipped with wireless, it was possible at once to divert a convoy from a dangerous area.

Hall kept a watchful eye on the progress of the war against the submarines and when he heard that a U-boat had been destroyed, he used to order one of his staff, Leonard Willoughby, a young RNVR Lieutenant, 'Willoughby, go and fetch the rum!'[12]

By July a daily U-boat situation report was being sent to both Beatty and Bayly. James, who was directly responsible for Room 40, described how vitally important the intelligence gained from intercepts of the German signal traffic became to the entire anti-submarine campaign.

> We kept a careful watch on all the movements of the High Sea Fleet. The submarines talked a lot when they were at sea, and the interesting thing is that it was we who made them talk. We were continuously laying mines at the end of the swept channels out of Wilhelmshaven and Brünsbuttel. Every submarine returning from the Atlantic made a wireless signal reporting the tonnage she had sunk and the position she would be at the time and date at the end of a swept channel, so that she could be met by minesweepers or told to arrive at some other position. If they did not report their arrival, they might blunder into a minefield. Then when we laid that mine barrage from North of Scotland to Norway (1918) they reported on their outward journey that they had safely passed it. To concentrate for an attack in the Atlantic necessitated quite a lot of signals, and with our numerous stations round the coast, including the Shetlands and Ireland (about forty wireless stations, direction-finding and intercepting) we were able to fix to them by bearings and usually read their signals. We had our bad periods when the Germans brought in a new signal book, but we had great luck picking up a book from a crashed Zeppelin and a sunken submarine, so these blank periods did not last long. Our men were brilliant at reconstructing a signal book, but it was a slow process, as the Germans never used the groups in the book but always encyphered them. The cipher the Germans used was the Playfair type and paper with numbered columns, writing the groups down and reading them across. If we had the book, the job was to find the key word which gave the order for numbering the columns.
>
> But what was even more important than warning the Anti-Submarine Division when submarines would be expected on the trade routes and when they had left and when they returned was that the submarines often used wireless when in the Atlantic. The method of attack they developed was concentrated attack on one convoy by several U-boats, but to do this they had to interchange signals. These were picked up by D.F. [direction-finding] and intercepting stations and we were able to warn the Anti-Submarine Division, who ordered the convoys to avoid the area by a large alteration of course. Several valuable convoys escaped attack by avoiding the concentrations of submarines. Geddes [appointed First Lord in July 1917] was so pleased with the safe arrival of these convoys that he sent for me and R.G.

Henderson [Duff's Assistant] and told us that we had been promoted to Captain [October 1917]. Promotions were made half-yearly and his immediate promotion of two Commanders was, I think, a unique occurrence.

James's comment 'I think it is true to say that without the Room 40 information the defeat of the submarines would have been far more difficult and more prolonged' was entirely justified.[13] Vice-Admiral Sir Arthur Hezlet, the historian of the electron in naval warfare and himself a submariner, noted that radio intelligence was the most important factor in the defeat of the U-boats, giving the Admiralty a fairly complete picture of where the U-boats were, what they were doing and where they were going.[14]

Hall dearly loved a ruse and never more so when he could wreak havoc on the detested huns. By mid-1917 he strongly suspected that the relatively unsophisticated naval minelaying code was compromised. He and Bayly decided to use disinformation to lure a Kriegsmarine minelayer to its destruction. Knowing through the decrypts that UC-42 had laid mines in Waterford Harbour, they sent out a signal claiming that the Harbour had been cleared. Bayly meanwhile suspended all minesweeping operations in its vicinity and closed the harbour to all shipping for two weeks. The U-boat command fell for the deception. On August 4 UC-44 appeared in the harbour to lay new mines and was promptly blown up by one of the mines laid by her sister ship. Hall was highly amused when her commander, KapitanLeutnant Teben-Johans, complained bitterly to him during his interrogation about the incompetence of the British minesweepers! Bayly's divers quickly recovered her codebooks and charts and on September 26 the U-boat was raised to the surface and towed to a nearby beach. NID's SIGINT team were able to examine her radio and established that it operated on eight pre-set frequencies ranging from 300 to 820 metres – the exact range Room 40's interception stations had been monitoring.[15] A month later UC-42 herself sank after striking a mine off Queenstown. Knowing that the Kriegsmarine had recently changed their call signs, Hall asked Bayly to recover her signal books and a further haul of documents made its way to Room 40.

During 1916 the Kriegsmarine's Naval Air Division stepped up its Zeppelin raids over southern England. The Zeppelins were highly vulnerable to both antiaircraft guns and fighters. Three Zeppelins had been shot down in 1915 and a further eight in 1916. They had been issued with naval call signs and were required to report hourly to the Fleet flagship in Wilhelmshaven. This needless procedure enabled Room 40's direction finding stations to fix on to their position and alert the antiaircraft forces and the fighter squadrons.

Early in 1916, Hall launched an initiative which was to yield the NID a handsome dividend, not least in the field of ASW. He appointed Major

Bernard Trench of the NID's German section to take charge of a team to interrogate survivors and to recover codebooks and any other documents from the shot-down Zeppelins. Trench had had been one of Hall's officers on HMS *Cornwall* at the time of his intelligence coup in Kiel in 1908. He and a fellow-officer, Lieutenant Vivian Brandon, had secured some useful information whilst ashore in the German naval base, for which they had received an Admiralty commendation.

Two years later Brandon and Trench had been sent by NID on a mission to examine German sea defences in the Frisian Islands and were arrested while photographing a newly installed battery, part of the fortifications at Borkum controlling the access to the naval base at Emden. They were sentenced to four years imprisonment but were released in 1913 under an amnesty ordered by the Kaiser on the occasion of his daughter's wedding, which was attended by King George V and Queen Mary. Hall had been concerned by their arrest and by what he believed to be have been the inequitable treatment they had received from the NID after their release, particularly the failure to compensate them for the heavy financial loss they had suffered, including having to pay the prison costs the Germans had demanded. After he had become DNI he arranged for them to be reimbursed and to rejoin the NID. Trench was an experienced and effective interrogator and his time in a German prison had made him a hard man with no love for his former captors.

After Jutland, the Admiralstab had introduced a new code, the AFB, for their Air Division, which Room 40 was having difficulty breaking. Towards the end of September the NID had another stroke of fortune. On September 24 one of the Royal Flying Corps's aces, Lieutenant Frederick Sowrey, shot down Zeppelin L32 over Essex on its way home after bombing London, with the loss of all her crew. By the following morning, Trench and his team were trawling through the wreckage. They discovered a copy of the AFB. Although it had been singed in the crash, it enabled Room 40 to read the code in full. With this knowledge they were able to predict the routes of future Zeppelin raids well in advance and with almost pinpoint accuracy.[16]

Following its success in recovering the airship codes, the NID began to examine the wrecks of U-boats in British coastal waters. Hall and Trench put together an experienced team of naval divers, headed by Shipwright E. C. Miller. As the work was strenuous and not without danger, a bounty of £100 (£3,000 in today's money) was awarded for any documents recovered. Miller later rather dramatically described to an American journalist, Richard Rowan, how he found

> ... huge salt-water eels and other voracious creatures of the deep feasting on the bodies of the German crew ... and that he had forced his way into ... the captain's cabin. There caught in a kind of strong room, he discovered

a stout metal box, dragged it out of the hull and attached it to a line to be hauled to the surface.[17]

The first U-boat wreck to be inspected by the NID team was UC-32, which had been blown up by one of her own mines off Sunderland on February 23 1917. Three days later they dived, recovering a complete torpedo and some useful equipment. On July 26 UC-61 went aground off Cap Gris Nez and was captured before her crew could destroy her together with the latest Channel charts and up-to-date codebooks. Under interrogation by Trench, her wireless operator revealed his procedures and details of the Admiralstab's system for communicating with the U-boats. In all, the transmitters at Bruges, Nauen and Emden broadcast to them seven times each day between 0100 and 2300 GMT. Other members of the crew provided valuable intelligence that enabled the NID to establish the order of battle of the U-boat fleet based in the Belgian harbours of Ostend and Zeebrugge.

One of the four Zeppelins brought down over southern England in 1917 provided valuable information to the NID. On the night of June 17 two Zeppelins, L42 and L48, attacked the port of Harwich. L42's compass jammed and her commander tried desperately to get a fix on her position from the German wireless stations. Meanwhile he drifted inland and before he could be provided with his bearings, the airship was shot down. Although all but three of her crew were killed, her wireless cabin survived the crash. Trench's investigators discovered that L42 had been carrying a cipher table for the AFB and three lists of newly introduced code-words, thus breaching Admiralstab standing orders. L48 managed to escape and reported that her sister-airship had not been completely destroyed. Scheer was sufficiently alarmed by the security implications that five days later he asked Holtzendorff to replace the current cipher tables.[18]

The Kriegsmarine's advantage was short-lived. That October two more Zeppelins, L49 and L50, suffering from engine and wireless failures, strayed badly off course after an unsuccessful raid on Norwich. Their crews were suffering seriously from the effects of altitude sickness and the commander of L49 decided to abort his mission after being attacked by French fighters. He landed near Dijon. His attempts to set the craft on fire failed and he and his disoriented crew were quickly arrested by a Frenchman, out hunting boars. Meanwhile L50 was rapidly losing altitude and finally crashed into a wood in central France.

French and American intelligence officers inspected both wrecks but in their initial examination found no documents. Colonel Richard Williams, a senior intelligence officer on General Pershing's staff, took charge of the investigation and searched the path of destruction left by L50 before she finally crashed, recovering two maps from a tree and a swamp. He then discovered that before the intelligence teams had arrived on the scene, two misguided American officers had removed L48's codebook as a souvenir. They were quickly forced to hand over their ill-gotten gains and on Colonel Williams's orders, the recovered documents were driven posthaste to NID in London.

Trench discovered that the maps included the latest Admiralstab grids not only for the North Sea but for the Irish Sea, the Skagerrak and the Kattegat. The NID could now read the current Zeppelin codebook, regaining the advantage it had held prior to the changes implemented after the loss of L42. The NID had received an invaluable treasure-trove of information. An appreciative Hall wrote to Pershing's staff:

> I hasten to express to you my most grateful thanks for your kindness and promptitude in sending me this most valuable document ... You may rely on it that any information therein which will be of value to the United States Forces will at once be communicated to them.[19]

After three years of war, these gratuitous breaches in German naval security, in both the U-boat and Zeppelin commands were still providing NID with a detailed knowledge of their operating procedures as well as such priceless information as the ocean grids. In particular, the commanders of Zeppelins operating over hostile territory were habitually provided with information that greatly exceeded their 'need to know'.

By the end of 1917 Room 40 was operating at peak efficiency. Convoy and effective anti-submarine warfare, backed up by effective use of intelligence, reduced shipping losses to 400,000 tons in December 1917. By the end of that year, losses of convoyed ships and dropped to one half of one per cent. They remained under 300,000 tons per month throughout 1918. In September 1918 they were only 188,000 tons. (Though the word 'only' is a terrible diminution of the freezing hell faced by so many merchantmen.) An eloquent tribute to the effectiveness of convoy was provided by a German U-boat commander with no axe to grind. KaptainLeutnant Saalwachter of U 94 wrote in his war diary as early as August 1917, before convoy was fully operational:

> The convoys with their strong and efficient escorts making an attack extremely difficult, are in my view quite capable of drastically reducing shipping losses. The chances of sighting a convoy of seven ships is less than fighting seven individual ships. In the case of a convoy it is mostly possible to fire on only one ship.[20]

Jellicoe's downfall

At a high level meeting in June 1917, chaired by Lloyd George, Haig noted the extent of Jellicoe's pessimism: 'Admiral Jellicoe ... stated that adding to the great shortage of shipping, due to German submarines, it would be impossible for Great Britain to continue the war in 1918. This was a bombshell for the Cabinet and all present.'[21]

Believing that he was incurably defeatist, Lloyd George now determined to remove Jellicoe. To achieve this, Lloyd George had firstly to get rid of Carson, who had flatly refused to carry out the Prime Minister's instruction to dismiss Jellicoe. Lloyd George had to act with discretion as Carson was an influential political figure, whom he wished to keep in his government. His colleague, Lord Milner, suggested that he could solve the problem by effectively kicking Carson upstairs to the War Cabinet.

He replaced him by Sir Eric Geddes, an able technocrat with a considerable reputation. A member of a talented Scottish family – his brother Auckland also served in the Lloyd George government as Minister of National Service – he had been a tearaway as a boy. He had been sent to the US where he had gained his initial experience of railways working for Andrew Carnegie on the Baltimore & Ohio. He had then run a railway system for a consortium of plantations in India.

Returning to Britain in 1904, he had joined the North Eastern Railway at the invitation of the then General Manager, Sir George Gibb, one of the foremost railway executives of the day, who was renowned for selecting talent. On January 1907, when he was only 31, Geddes became the NER's Chief Goods Manager. He was an advocate of the then recently introduced system of Statistical Analysis. Applying this technique to the railway's goods traffic, he secured impressive gains in productivity, which significantly boosted profitability. Gibb's successor, Alexander Butterworth, described him as a man of 'exuberant vitality accompanied by acute mental activity and clear judgment. His energy and power of concentrating on important matters ... marked him out as an ideal executive'.[22] He was not without his flaws. A rapid and tireless worker, he was relentless in his demands on his staff and, as Jellicoe was to discover, he was not always personally considerate.[23]

Geddes had been one of the businessmen recruited by the Push and Go Committee, the forerunner of the Ministry of Munitions formed in the winter of 1914–15 to increase the volume of armaments for the Army. Here he attracted the attention of Lloyd George. Transport remained his first love and in September 1916, he had been appointed Director-General of Military Railways and Transportation in France with the rank of Major-General, reporting directly to Haig. He inherited a shambles and turned it into a going concern, building over 1,000 miles of track, at a rate as high as 50 miles per week.[24] When he left to become Controller of the Navy in May 1917, Haig, who admired him for his drive and energy wrote: 'Geddes left me today. Such a good fellow, and has been of the greatest help to the Army in matters of railways, roads and docks. He is very sorry to go.'[25]

Geddes had been appointed Controller, an appointment traditionally held by a naval officer, with the rank of Vice-Admiral, at Lloyd George's instigation. His terms of reference were to coordinate the shipbuilding and ship repairing industries, mercantile as well as naval, along the lines which had proved so successful with armaments production at the Ministry of Munitions.

While Jellicoe was pleased to find that Geddes 'got things done', he was not popular with the more narrow-minded officers inside the Admiralty, notably Oliver, who sarcastically complained: 'We have been upside down here ever since the North Eastern Railway took over the management.' Marder castigated Oliver for his dismissive it-can't-work-here attitude towards the introduction of Statistical Analysis, which showed quantitatively for the first time what was happening in the submarine war, commenting that 'Oliver's inability to see that foresight must be based on sound knowledge of the past ... goes a long way towards explaining why the Admiralty were so dilatory in adopting and extending the convoy system.'[26] Carson had been well liked and his removal was resented. The Service was prepared to give Geddes the benefit of the doubt and Admiral Hugh Evan-Thomas, who had commanded the 5th Battle Squadron at Jutland, wrote:

> We have made the great Enrico Geddes ... First Lord of the Admiralty – the other day, assistant manager of a Railway – a bullet-headed sort of a cove, who anyway looks you straight in the face, which is more than those confounded Politicians will do. So perhaps he will suit us quite well.[27]

To his credit, Geddes told Lloyd George that he had accepted the post of First Lord on the specific understanding that Jellicoe would not immediately be removed. Lloyd George also instructed Jellicoe to sack Oliver, who had annoyed the PM by arguing at a War Cabinet meeting. By threatening resignation and insisting that with his considerable experience Oliver was indispensable, Geddes succeeded in making Lloyd George back down. The Prime Minister was ready to bide his time.

At the end of September, at Geddes's instigation, Admiral Sir Rosslyn Wemyss, Second Sea Lord and former C in-C in the Mediterranean, was appointed Deputy First Sea Lord to ease Jellicoe's burden. Nevertheless the First Sea Lord remained reluctant to delegate any of his responsibilities to Wemyss.

The Norwegian Convoys

On the morning of 17 October 1917, two German minelaying cruisers *Brummer* and *Bremse* (4,835 tons, four 6-in guns) attacked a westbound Norwegian convoy, 12 merchant ships, escorted by the destroyers HMS *Mary Rose* and HMS *Strongbow* and two trawlers, approximately 70 miles east of the Shetlands. The cruisers, the profiles of which resembled similar British ships, achieved total surprise. Recognition procedures failed and *Brummer* succeeded in jamming *Strongbow*'s signals. Although the two destroyers fought valiantly, enabling two of the merchantmen to escape, they were sunk with the loss of most of their crew along with the remaining ten merchant ships. The German cruisers then turned for home at their top speed of 34 knots. News of the disaster did not reach the Admiral Commanding in the Orkneys and Shetlands until 3.50 pm, when any hope of the Grand Fleet intercepting the cruisers was long gone. *Brummer* only broke wireless silence announcing the success of the mission at 6 am the following morning, when she was nearing port. Her signal was intercepted by Room 40.

Although the carefully planned German operation had been carried out with ruthless efficiency, it should never have achieved such success. As early as 4.23 pm on October 15, Room 40 cryptanalysts had intercepted a signal from *Brummer* reporting the postponement of Most Secret Order 71950 until the following day, providing details of her course and requesting minesweeping. Before 6 pm, Oliver cabled Beatty: 'Minelayer *Brummer* leaves via Norman Deep tomorrow 16 probably for minelaying. She should be intercepted.'

Several later decodes that should have indicated *Brummer*'s objective was not minelaying were never passed on. Detailed analysis of the German signal traffic should have indicated that an important operation was in progress and should have set off alarm bells for the War Staff. The Kriegsmarine radio station at Norddeich imposed firm restrictions on wireless transmissions and a U-boat reported a heavy convoy at sea off the Shetlands. On the evening of October 16 the cruiser *Regensberg* reported that she and her escorting destroyers were in position to comply with *Brummer*'s signal of the previous day and U-boats were specifically ordered not to attack light cruisers, unless they were positively identified as British. Not until 2.20 pm on October 17, eight hours after the convoy had been destroyed, did Oliver send Beatty an appreciation suggesting that the German cruisers' intention might be to strike at a convoy. Although Beatty had sent two cruiser squadrons to sea, the inadequate Admiralty intelligence prevented him from giving them the information which might have enabled them to intercept *Brummer* and *Bremse*. James recalled this incident from Room 40's perspective:

> We knew the call signs of the two ships and by D/F we in Room 40 knew that they had moved north from Wilhelmshaven to Lister Tief [north of Sylt] and so were obviously about to carry out some operation. I remember Keyes, the Director of Plans, coming into our chart room and speculating on what these two ships were going to do. We did not of course have on our charts the position of any British ships: they were all shown in the

charts in Operations Division. If the convoys had been shown in our charts, it is probable that Keyes or someone else would have seen the possibility that the *Brummer* and *Bremse* objective was a convoy. My recollection is that Operations did not tell Beatty about these ships. But I do remember there was a devil of a row about this and Beatty came to the Admiralty for a meeting. I think these two ships were fitted as minelayers [they were] and so it did not occur to anyone in Operations that they might be going to attack a convoy. There is no doubt that the Admiralty were at fault in not warning Beatty about these two ships.[28]

Hankey, who missed very little, noted sardonically: 'The Admiralty ... had been fully warned by highly secret but absolutely reliable information [Room 40] of the probability of an attack on the Norwegian convoy and had failed to act. Geddes regards this as an example of Jellicoe's lack of energy, if not timidity, and wants to replace him by Admiral Wemyss.'[29]

On October 31, James, doubtless at Hall's request, wrote to Wemyss about the attack on the convoy. He contrasted the position in the Anti-Submarine Division where the latest known position of the U-boats and the routes of each convoy were plotted on the same chart with the lack of any similar charts in the Operations Division, responsible for surface warfare. He pointed out that the efficient system in the ASWD provided Duff with an accurate and up-to-date situation report, enabling him to direct convoys away from the U-boats. He argued that the lack of liaison between Operations and Intelligence had played a significant part in the disaster.

Marder blamed the loss, at least in part, on excessive Admiralty secrecy. Once again Oliver had been responsible for a monumental failure to act on Room 40 intelligence. He had not only delayed the transmission of intelligence to Beatty but had failed to send vital information of German movements or any interpretation of their intentions. As James had told Wemyss, the very real progress in integrating operations and the interception and analysis of intelligence in the anti-submarine campaign had not been matched in surface warfare. More than a year later, the lessons of Jutland had still not been learned.

As James had noted, the Grand Fleet had been extending its minelaying operations to trap U-boats returning to the North Sea. In response the Kriegsmarine had been sweeping newly laid British minefields as far as 150 miles from the Jade River. Relying on extensive Room 40 intelligence of their movements, Beatty, maddened by the recent attack on the convoy, planned an operation to trap the minesweepers and their screening forces.

When Room 40 intelligence indicated that the Kriegsmarine was planning a minesweeping operation on November 17, Beatty assembled a substantial force, far superior to the four German light cruisers screening their minesweepers. Vice-Admiral Trevylyan Napier, an old shipmate of Hall's, commanded the First Cruiser Squadron, Jackie Fisher's controversial light battlecruisers HMS *Courageous* and HMS *Glorious* (four 15-in guns) with a top speed of 32 knots but extremely lightly armoured. (They were irreverently known in the Fleet as *Outrageous* and *Spurious*). He was supported by two light cruiser squadrons (eight cruisers and six destroyers) and by five battlecruisers. Napier's force sailed from Rosyth at 4.30 pm on November 16 and sighted German ships at around 7.30 am the following morning. Although Napier promptly opened fire, the German commander von Reuter took evasive action including setting smoke screens and zigzagging in the hope of luring the British within range of his two supporting Dreadnoughts *Kaiser* and *Kaiserin*. Surprisingly, Napier, an Admiral who seems to have lacked the offensive spirit, did not call for the full 32 knots *Courageous* and *Glorious* could achieve to cut off von Reuter, who managed to make his escape almost unscathed. The British force only succeeded in hitting the German cruisers five times, although a shell from the battlecruiser HMS *Repulse* caused serious damage to the cruiser *Konigsberg*. Geddes and Jellicoe were both highly critical of Napier and the German official report noted:

> Minesweeping forces, closely supported only by light cruisers, found themselves in a situation which should have ended in the destruction of both minesweepers and light cruisers: if the enemy had acted with vigour ... weak and hesitant attack by far superior British forces provided the essentials for this unexpected outcome.[30]

Although Room 40 intelligence was both up-to-date and complete, including the position of the German cruisers and the fact that the two Dreadnoughts were at sea, their detailed knowledge of the location of the German minefields had never been made available to Napier. He was understandably loath to commit his ships to action in waters he thought to be dangerous. The Operations Division's habitual reluctance to provide commanders at sea with the full intelligence in their possession had contributed to this unnecessary failure.

On December 12 four German destroyers attacked a westbound convoy off the Norwegian coast, destroying all six merchantmen and three out of the six escorts. For once Room 40 had no advance intelligence of this bold and well-planned attack but a court of inquiry found serious failures in the organisation of North Sea convoys and in recognition and reporting systems.

Early in December Beatty asked Jellicoe to appoint Rear-Admiral Lionel Halsey, then Third Sea Lord, to command the First Battlecruiser Squadron. Jellicoe turned him down on the grounds that he could not spare Halsey from the Admiralty, but he agreed to appoint Oliver. Jellicoe, who in July had considered Oliver to be indispensable, now took a different line, telling Beatty that Wemyss and Everett, the Naval Secretary, who had both served with Oliver '… entirely share my views. I don't want to keep him here and ruin his future career. Hope [Captain George Hope, Jackson's successor as Director of Operations] has been at the work for some time now and the advent of Wemyss and Keyes makes it possible to let Oliver go.[31] Jellicoe appears to have appreciated that Oliver had become superfluous, and that a change in the direction of surface warfare at the top was desirable. In September, Roger Keyes, one of the service's foremost advocates of offensive action, was brought to the Admiralty from the Grand Fleet to fill the new post of Director of Plans. He reported to Wemyss – the two men were old allies, having been the service's leading supporters of the Dardanelles operation.

For some time Hall had been regularly submitting reports to the War Staff obtained from decrypts from both outgoing and incoming U-boats indicating that a large number of submarines – estimated to be as many as 30 each month – had been passing through the anti-submarine barrage in the Straits of Dover. Alarmed by these reports, Geddes asked Keyes to chair the Channel Barrage Committee, tasked with improving the effectiveness of this obstacle to submarines. As the former head of the Navy's submarine branch, he was well placed to act as poacher turned gamekeeper. Keyes later wrote:

> I had made up my mind … to devote my energies to stop submarines streaming through the Straits of Dover. Hall assured me they were passing through at the rate of over 30 a month; notwithstanding the assertion of the Admiral [Bacon] that the Straits were closed by his anti-submarine nets, and that nothing was getting through. … During the period, November 1–December 9, it was definitely known by the NID that 55 German submarines had passed through the Straits and from the evidence in their possession, they consider that another 15 submarines had made the passage.[32]

An instruction to submarine captains passing through the Straits had been found among the documents captured from UC-44. 'It is best to pass this [the Dover net defence] on the surface; if forced to dive, go down to 40 metres. As far as possible, pass through the area between Hoofden and Cherbourg without being observed and without stopping … the boats which in exceptional cases pass round Scotland are to let themselves be seen as freely as possible, in order to mislead the English.'[33] Armed with this intelligence, Keyes's committee recommended that searchlights mounted on drifters and trawlers should sweep the Channel at night with the objective of forcing submarines to dive and get entangled in the barrage's nets or get blown up in the minefields.

Sir Reginald Bacon, Vice-Admiral Dover, like Jellicoe, a Fisher protégé, was notoriously obstinate. Despite the detailed intelligence reports, he refused to believe that U-boats were regularly evading the barrage. It took a direct order from Jellicoe on December 18 to make Bacon illuminate the barrage. On the following night, UB-56, confronted by the searchlights, was compelled to dive and was destroyed in a minefield.

The convoy disasters in the North Sea, dissatisfaction with the November 17 operation and the setbacks in the Dover Patrol, all of which had been in large measure intelligence failures, sealed Jellicoe's fate. Geddes was now faced with a situation where his two principal naval advisers were at loggerheads. Wemyss was convinced that Hall's intelligence reports were correct and that Keyes' recommendations should be implemented: 'The Intelligence Department satisfactorily proved to me that the enemy did pass the Straits successfully and almost unchallenged.'[34] He concluded that Bacon should be relieved, but Jellicoe, loyal as ever to his subordinates, refused to remove him.

Geddes backed Wemyss. He decided that Jellicoe was no longer up to the post of First Sea Lord and that he had no option but to replace him. Wemyss, who had been on the point of resigning out of frustration at having so little to do, accepted his invitation to succeed Jellicoe, reluctantly in the circumstances.

Geddes' appreciation was correct. Jellicoe had been much less successful as First Sea Lord than he had been as C-in-C and the pressure of the post had become too much for him. One Admiral in the War Staff noted 'he could not be ruthless'[35] and it was time for a change. Jellicoe had lost the confidence not only of Lloyd George and Geddes but of a significant element of service opinion, both inside the Admiralty and at sea. Whatever the justification, the manner in which he was removed was discourteous in the extreme – Marder called it 'squalid'. Geddes dismissed him in a terse letter, which he received at 6 pm on December 24 as he was about to leave to spend Christmas with Gwendoline, who was six months pregnant, and his family. He barely thanked Jellicoe, whom one of his staff officers on HMS *Iron Duke* had described 'as a man whose whole heart is wrapped up in his country' for his wartime services.[36] His part in reorganising the Admiralty in the twelve months since his appointment was never mentioned. This was Geddes at his very worst. Incredibly, he seems to have believed that he had treated Jellicoe with consideration.

Hall left no known record of these events and James, ever discreet, only mentions that 'He had not disguised the fact that he would welcome a change at the head of affairs.'[37] Hall has been accused, notably by Oliver, of being part of a conspiracy to remove Jellicoe. In his unpublished Recollections, Oliver wrote:

> In December 1917 there was evidence to me that there was underground work going on. One evening about 10:30 pm some officers were talking in my room about Admiralty affairs, and one of them referred to someone as 'Judas Iscariot', and I asked him who he was and was told it was Hall who was mixed up with political people in high places and didn't support Jellicoe.[38]

The author can find no confirmation for this piece of hearsay. Oliver had no liking for Hall, although he acknowledged that he had made a great reputation at the Intelligence Division. Some of his other comments on Hall damn him with faint praise. Duff and Captain Frederic Dreyer, the Director of Naval Ordnance, who had been his Flag-Captain at Jutland, were Jellicoe's two strongest supporters inside the Admiralty. They wrote a paper in which they attributed the entire blame for his sacking to Lloyd George and they do not mention that any naval officer was implicated in his downfall.[39] Hall's successor as DNI in World War II, Godfrey, wrote of him:

> He was a Beatty-ite, didn't like Jellicoe whose attitude he found defeatist and was prone not to appreciate and act on the fruits of NID intelligence. [The latter part of this statement is incorrect, Godfrey's criticism would have been more fairly directed at Oliver.] He certainly did not restrain the national papers that criticised Jellicoe and when he came to the Admiralty as First Sea Lord their relations were strained.[40]

This last statement has some validity as Hall had excellent relations with the press, whom he briefed weekly. A quiet word from Hall might have succeeded in toning down their assaults.

Hall habitually judged Admirals by the yardsticks of his and his father's hero, St Vincent, the apostle of offensive action, who believed that only officers of approved firmness should be employed, and of Nelson, whose instinct was to attack. A Beatty, a Keyes, a Tyrwhitt met this criterion, as did Andrew Cunningham in World War II, whom Hall described as 'a real thruster … How Jellicoe and Madden would have hated him.'[41] By contrast, as his biographer noted, Balfour had left the supreme command of the service to a man who as he well knew was by temperament and conviction ultra-cautious.[42] In accusing him of a lack of offensive action, Hall was being less than fair to Jellicoe. As C-in-C Beatty was to prove as cautious as his predecessor. Hall's old ally, Richmond, who was constantly advocating the offensive, had written:

> The destruction of the German Fleet is a means to an end and not an end in itself. If in endeavouring to destroy the German Fleet we run risks which may prejudice our success in the greater object of the destruction of

Germany, those risks are too great ... Take no risks with the Grand Fleet. The whole of operations all over the world depend on it.[43]

Hall was a friend to some of the so-called Young Turks of the Grand Fleet, who, like many of their fellow-officers, did not have a high regard for the current regime in the Admiralty. In particular he was close to Richmond, who was now commanding the battleship HMS *Conqueror*, and Plunkett, his former torpedo officer on HMS *Natal*, now transformed into the quadruple-barrelled Plunkett-Ernle-Erle-Drax, Beatty's Flag-Commander. Richmond and Drax, knowing that Hall was no friend of Jellicoe's, doubtless pressed their opinion on him during his regular visits to the Grand Fleet. Hall habitually played his cards close to his chest and, unlike Richmond, he did not lobby aggressively.

Marder noted that the Young Turks had the sympathy of a number of senior officers, including Beatty, Tyrwhitt and Keyes, as well as Hall and that man of many secrets and considerable influence, Hankey, now Secretary to the War Cabinet. Richmond was an inveterate lobbyist, who had no compunction in advocating Jellicoe's departure. He worked through his father-in-law, Sir Hugh Bell, a prominent North of England industrialist with strong Liberal Party connections, who, as a Director of the North Eastern Railway, knew Geddes well. Shortly after his appointment as First Lord, Geddes had told Bell of his astonishment 'at the lack of any method in conducting Board meetings, the vagueness, the lack of preparation, the lack of any minutes, the amateurishness of the whole concern'. Bell lost no time in passing these comments on to Richmond.[44]

Geddes's biographer, Keith Grieve, believes that Geddes personally took the decision that Jellicoe should leave the Admiralty, although he took the precaution of securing the approval of both Lloyd George and Bonar Law in advance. Lloyd George seems to been strangely reluctant to dismiss Jellicoe himself. The King, who was more disturbed about the ruthless way in which Jellicoe had been treated than by his actual dismissal, told Beatty that Lloyd George had had his knife into Jellicoe as early as April 1917. As we have seen, in July 1917 he actually backed down when the First Sea Lord threatened to resign after he instructed him to sack Oliver. It is at least arguable that Lloyd George appointed Geddes as First Lord believing that his approach and Jellicoe's were so totally incompatible that sooner or later Geddes would seek to remove him. He had perhaps cynically calculated that Geddes would be the target of all the opprobrium from the service for dismissing such an admired figure and that he would achieve his objective without harming his own reputation.

A firestorm ensued in the service. The Sea Lords, headed by Duff, threatened to resign in support. Although he had been dismayed by his dismissal, Jellicoe convinced them to back down, reminding them that the First Lord had the prerogative of appointing and dismissing a First Sea Lord and that the interests of the service, particularly in time of war, required them to stay in office and support his successor.

Wemyss proved to be the most effective of the five wartime First Sea Lords. The son of a Scottish laird, he was descended from royalty, albeit on the wrong side of the blanket. He was once heard to make the throwaway remark 'I am going down to Windsor to see my cousin George.' His slightly foppish attitude, exemplified by the monocle he always wore, belied his considerable ability, moral courage, sound judgment and common sense. With his great charm, he was widely liked in the service, not least for his skill as a raconteur. Although Wemyss had never commanded a major fleet, he was an experienced operator and an adroit diplomat, who had managed to keep on good terms with both Fisher and Beresford throughout their acrimonious feud. His support for the Dardanelles campaign indicated that he was no stranger to risk-taking and offensive action. As a man of the world, he knew how to deal with politicians, for whom, like Hall, he had little use, and how to keep them off the service's back. He was the man for the moment.

Geddes and Wemyss, both Scotsmen, worked amicably together. Geddes's brother wrote: 'The mutual relations established between the First Lord and the new First Sea Lord were almost ideal ...'[45] Wemyss and Beatty developed an equally strong rapport and relations inside the Admiralty and between the Admiralty and the Grand Fleet quickly improved. As a result, the war at sea went better in 1918 than in the previous year.

Godfrey, who has served on his staff, noted that Wemyss was no centraliser and he delegated extensive responsibilities to his Deputy and to the DCNS and ACNS. James recalled that Wemyss instituted and presided over a daily Staff meeting attended by Duff, Sir Sydney Fremantle – Oliver's successor as DCNS – Hall and Sims, representing the US Navy, at which he was often present to present a resumé of the most recent Room 40 intercepts. In a tribute after Sims died, Dreyer noted: 'All of us who attended the daily staff conference presided over by the First Sea Lord greatly admired the pithy and valuable comments made by Admiral Sims.'[46]

Hall's star was once again ascending. The Intelligence Division had been vindicated over the Channel Barrage. Wemyss was an old friend and he got on well with Geddes, who, as a man noted for his energy and drive, respected the same qualities in Hall. Under Wemyss's Staff reorganisation, Hall now reported directly to the First Sea Lord. He was close to Beatty, whom he always called 'my old chief'. His old antagonist, Oliver, had gone from the Admiralty at last and his replacement, Fremantle, a great-grandson of one of Nelson's captains, (known in the service as My Boy Syd because his father, also an Admiral, had often referred to him thus), did not take the same line as Oliver had toward the treatment of intelligence. Cordial relations grew up between NID and the operations division, who were responsible for the surface war.

The Royal Navy was now on course for victory.

Notes

1. Marder, Vol 4, p.268
2. Marder, Vol 4 p.350
3. Jellicoe to Sir Douglas Brownrigg December 1916. Winton, p.236
4. Marder, Vol 4 p.367
5. Winton, pp.123-4
6. Fisher to E.G. Pretyman December 27 1916 Quoted in Marder, Vol 4. p.58
7. Fitzgerald, p.128
8. Beesly, p.168
9. Naval Staff Appreciation 1922 pp.132-3
10. Winton, p.165
11. Mrs. Mary Carrington to Marder May 21 1965 Marder, Vol 4 p.267
12. Naval Staff Monograph Home Waters May-July 1917. Marder, Vol 4 p.267
13. James to Marder December 19 1962, May 22 1965, Marder, Vol 4 pp.265-66
14. Hezlet, *Electron and Sea Power* p.143
15. Ibid, p.146
16. Nigel West, *GCHQ* pp.52-3
17. Ibid, p.55
18. Ibid, p.57
19. Ibid, pp.57-58
20. Marder, Vol 4 p.285
21. Haig diary June 20 1917. Quoted in Marder, Vol 4 pp.203-4
22. Grieve, *Eric Geddes* p.5
23. R. J. Irving, *Dictionary of Business Biography* pp.507-514
24. Grieve, p.33
25. Haig to Lady Haig May 8 1917. Quoted in Grieve, p.47
26. Marder, Vol 4 p.176n
27. Grieve, p.46. Marder, Vol 4 p.214
28. James to Marder, May 31 1966 & March 19 1968 Marder, Vol 4 p.295
29. Hankey diary October 26 1917. Quoted in Marder, Vol 4 p.334
30. Quoted in Marder, Vol 4 p.307n.
31. Jellicoe to Beatty December 11 1917. Quoted in Marder, Vol 4 p.347
32. Keyes, Vol 2 pp.115 & 137

33. Ibid, Vol 2 p.117
34. Wemyss's unpublished memoirs: Quoted in Marder Vol 4 p.338
35. Admiral Sir Lionel Preston to Marder January 8 1963. Marder, Vol 4 p.58
36. Commander M. R. Best diary Quoted in Marder, Vol 3 p.338
37. James, p.176
38. Oliver *Recollections* Vol 2 NMM OLV 12
39. CAC DRYR 6/13 Dreyer Papers
40. CAC MLBE 1/2 The Hall Tradition
41. CAC HALL 7/2/59 WRH to May Templar February 9 1941
42. Dugdale p.105
43. Richmond to K. G. Dewar January 6 1917 quoted in Marder Vol 4 p.171
44. Grieve p.47. Richmond Diary August 16 1917 quoted in Marder Vol 4 p.214
45. Quoted in Marder Vol 5 p.10
46. *The Times* October 3 1936

CHAPTER XIV

The Great Game II

Spain

With the US now in the war, Spain became increasingly important to the German espionage operatives as a staging ground for their agents in Latin America. By 1917 they were actively involved in biological warfare and used their Embassy in Madrid as a clearing house for the supplies of anthrax and glanders bacillus with which they intended to infect cereals for human consumption and mules for military use, both of which the allies were purchasing in Argentina. They dispatched the supplies by U-boat from the Austrian Adriatic bases at Pola and Cattaro to the Spanish port of Cartagena. Once collected by German agents, these lethal cargoes were shipped to Argentina on Spanish liners. Hall's operatives in Spain, now led by Charles Thoroton and briefed by Room 40 decrypts, kept an extremely watchful eye on their adversaries and often managed to thwart their schemes.

In the 1930s Thoroton destroyed his records other than those he considered useful in defending himself against what he himself referred to as some of his more questionable activities. One of his more dramatic exploits, which became known as the *Erri Berro* affair, was, however, documented. The German Government was determined to counter the increasingly effective British blockade denying them access to vitally required raw materials, including wolfram, the ore used to make tungsten, which was mined in the Basque region of Spain. Maurice Mitchell, a Commander RNR and Thoroton's agent in the Basque capital of Bilbao, headed a small group who kept the mines under a close if discreet watch. He was in close touch with another RNR officer, Lieutenant-Commander G. H. Pierce, who operated from St. Jean de Luz on the French side of the border. He in turn reported to Commodore Edward Heaton-Ellis, the Naval Attaché in Paris and to Herschell and Paymaster Lloyd Hirst, the former Intelligence Officer on HMS *Glasgow* and now the head of the Intelligence Division's Latin American section.

On September 15 1917, Mitchell wrote to Herschell on the wolfram issue, expressing his distrust of one Lauriano Diaz, formerly Krupps's representative in Bilbao, and another recognized agent named Pasch. Mitchell told Herschell that he and Thoroton would readily uncover any German efforts to ship the wolfram out of Spain and run the blockade, possibly by one of their merchant ships currently interned in Spanish ports. Thus alerted, on October 2, the intelligence division was not surprised when Room 40 intercepted a signal to the Naval Attaché in Madrid, Korvettenkapitan Krohn, who had already attracted the attention of the Spanish authorities for his involvement in espionage: 'The Ambassador informed me recently that there is a possibility of shipping wolfram ore in a submarine. The execution of the plan is perhaps possible in November in the neighbourhood of the Canary Islands...'[1]

Ambassador Ratibor knew nothing about the project but the hyperactive Attaché decided to go ahead anyway, informing Berlin on October 16 that a transshipment of the wolfram could be arranged either in the Bay of Biscay or in the Mediterranean. This signal was also intercepted by Room 40. By the end of October Mitchell had told London that he had located the warehouse in Bilbao where the wolfram was being stored – allegedly one of his agents had been able to enter the warehouse on the pretext that he was searching for a guide dog that had run away from its blind owner! Hall instructed Mitchell to prevent the ore being shipped out of the port at all costs and to keep him posted about all developments.

On November 7 Room 40 intercepted a further signal from Berlin to Krohn: 'U-cruisers 156 and 157 [cargo-carrying submarines] can be at the Canaries on November 24. Each can take about 40 tons of wolfram ore. If you are still certain that the plan can be carried out safely, please report details and meeting place can then be settled.'[2]

Hall quickly recognised the double opportunity afforded of seizing the valuable wolfram consignment and destroying two cargo-carrying U-boats capable of running the blockade. He immediately cancelled the existing instructions, ordering Mitchell to keep the German agents and the consignment under close surveillance.

Jellicoe and the War Staff promptly agreed with Hall's proposal to stage what the Navy had always called a cutting-out operation. Detailed plans were drawn up, indicating the importance the Admiralty attached to thwarting the German intention to run the blockade. The Commander-in-Chief of the French Navy was consulted and agreed that the operation would be controlled by the British. Four E-class submarines, detached from Bayly's command and from the Mediterranean Fleet, were transferred to Gibraltar with the objective of destroying the U-boats. The ocean boarding ship HMS *Duke of Clarence*, complete with a prize crew of naval reservists who were skilled in handling small ships, was dispatched to the French port of St. Jean de Luz, with orders to intercept the consignment once it was at sea. Mitchell reported that the consignment would probably be shipped in 'a staunch wooden brig' named *San Jose* with a capacity for 400 tons of cargo. Meanwhile, Room 40 was carefully listening in to the signal traffic between Krohn and the Admiralstab. On November 15 he told Berlin:

> The carrying out of the plan is assured. The sailing vessel will receive sealed instructions concerning recognition signals. When sighting a U-boat at the rendezvous she will lower and furl her sails and hoist a Spanish flag as well as blue and yellow pennants under one another. At night she will show a blue and yellow light ... Request immediate instructions concerning the rendezvous and whether further particulars are necessary.[3]

The first of a series of delays then occurred. The *San Jose* sailed without the wolfram and Krohn substituted a second vessel, telegraphing Berlin on November 19:

> The sailing vessel is a brigantine of 170 tons, both mast heads of equal height painted white. Fore and aft the Spanish flag is painted on both sides and between it the ship's name *Erri Berro*. In front of the main mast a large red water tank. I propose if necessary the further distinguishing mark; a Spanish flag sewn on the schooner's sails. Vessel will put to sea about 26 November.[4]

In two signals sent in the following week the Admiralstab helpfully provided Room 40 with the details of the rendezvous, codenamed U.Platz 30. Two U-cruisers would arrive at about 25 December on the south-west coast of Hierro in the Canary Islands. Two of the RN submarines patrolled the Canary Islands while the remaining pair refuelled and provisioned in Gibraltar. Mitchell had discovered that *Erri Berro* had sailed from Corunna bound for Bilbao on November 30 and the the stevedore instructed to load her with 115 sacks of 'cement' was being paid more than the going rate. Additional delays were caused, firstly, by the German decision to replace her captain and put aboard as supercargo Johann Haberstock, the First Officer on the Hamburg-Amerika cargo liner *Phoenicia*, which had been interned in Bilbao since the outbreak of war and who gratefully seized the opportunity of getting back to Hamburg and his family, whom he had not seen for more than three years. The Kriegsmarine, desperate to get its hands on as much wolfram as was available, ordered the purchase and loading of an additional 60 tons.

Mitchell was of course anxious that *Erri Berro*'s departure be promptly reported to *Duke of Clarence*. His fellow agent in San Sebastian, a resourceful Newcastle shipowner named Dawson, kept in touch by telegram and arranged that any news of her sailing be rushed across the border to St. Jean de Luz. To take no chances, and concerned that she might be at sea at the time, Dawson detained a British merchant ship, *William Bull*, with instructions to send a prearranged coded message 'All's well' to *Duke of Clarence* once her prey had sailed from Bilbao. This shrewd precaution so irritated the owners of *William Bull* that they complained to the Admiralty, who asked Dawson to explain his actions in writing.

By mid-December loading the wolfram was in progress. Unbeknownst to the Germans, their every move was being watched by the vigilant Mitchell and his agents. On December 15 he signalled Hall that he expected the loading to be completed by midday and that *Erri Berro* would sail later that day:

> No reliance can be placed on the original description of her painting. Also she may cross a foreyard after leaving here. Up-to-date the flag has disappeared and the hull is black. Two narrow white lines above and below letters of name ... Grey paint either side of stern.[5]

Once again, delay ensued. Mitchell discovered that defects had been found in her rigging and that repairs were necessary. *Erri Berro* was evidently far from being a well found ship. He concluded from these repairs that the rendezvous was to be some distance from Bilbao. He even suggested to Hall that equipment should be thrown overboard after she was intercepted to suggest that she had foundered. Hall emphatically disagreed, telling Mitchell to take no action as it was important that the Germans should believe the ship had sailed safely with every expectation that she would reach her destination.

Bad weather intervened and it was not until 4 pm on December 31 that *Erri Berro* finally left Bilbao. Within two hours Mitchell and Dawson had informed the Navy at St. Jean de Luz of her departure and *Duke of Clarence* had put to sea in hot pursuit. At 12.30 on New Year's Day she intercepted and boarded the brigantine. Her crew was taken off, a naval crew put aboard and she was taken in tow. With her prize successfully secured, *Duke of Clarence* set course for Devonport.

In London, Hall had stayed late in his office, waiting eagerly for news of the outcome of his initiative. Delighted by the success of such a major coup engineered by his Spanish operation, he arranged with the War Staff that four destroyers should escort *Erri Berro* into Devonport under top security. With such an important New Year's present triumphantly in the bag, he went home to bed.

Just then, things went wrong. When she was securing the tow line, *Duke of Clarence* had bumped *Erri Berro*, neither unusual nor generally of great consequence when two ships came into contact at sea. As already mentioned, the brigantine was not well found and began to ship water at an alarming rate. By the evening of January 1, the prize crew had to be taken off and *Erri Berro* sunk by gunfire. Hall was bitterly disappointed by the news. Although his action had prevented the valuable cargo from reaching Germany, he had hoped to hand the much needed wolfram over to the Ministry of Munitions to assist the British war effort.

As the operation against the U-boats still had to take place, Haberstock and the five members of *Erri Berro*'s Spanish crew had to be held incommunicado for several weeks. As the brigantine had not been equipped with wireless, neither the crew's families nor, more importantly, the German authorities would have expected to have heard from them during that time. At Hall's instruction, the Spaniards were transferred to a POW detention centre in South Kensington where he arranged for them to be especially well treated.

At the beginning of January, the two British submarines, E-35 and E-48, left Gibraltar for the Canaries. One submarine stayed on patrol and the other remained out to sea, recharging its batteries. Meanwhile U-156, which had sailed from Germany in mid-November, while waiting for *Erri Berro* to arrive had been occupied in bombarding Madeira and Funchal (Portugal had entered the war on the allied side). She reached the rendezvous at U.Platz 30 on January 17 where E-48 fired three torpedoes at her. Two missed and the third hit but failed to explode. The U-boat crash dived, leaving several of her crew on deck, two of whom succeeded in swimming ashore. The first news of this encounter was received in a dispatch from *The Times*'s local correspondent, noting an engagement between a British warship and three German U-boats. Only when E-48 returned to Gibraltar on February 4 did Hall learn the of the disappointing outcome of this encounter. U-156 eventually returned empty-handed to Germany in March and U-157, which had never been spotted, a month later.

Family legend has it that on this occasion Hall's renowned hot temper, which he habitually kept tightly under control, manifested itself. Returning home from the Admiralty, intending to let off steam to his wife Essie, who often acted as a kind of safety valve, he found her entertaining several of her bridge-playing lady friends to a tea party, an event he generally enjoyed. In a moment of frustration at the disappointing outcome to his carefully planned coup, Hall's customary charm deserted him. He knocked over one of her tea tables, turned on his heels and stormed out. The devoted Essie, who well knew the pressure under which he was working and that her husband's infrequent bouts of ill-temper were a thunderbolt soon passed, was left to placate her astonished guests.[6]

The loose ends had to be dealt with. The submarines were quickly returned to their former stations and Hall had to take care to avoid any international repercussions and to prevent the Germans discovering that they had been so thoroughly outplayed by his agents in Spain. Fortunately

Krohn, either remarkably ill-informed or anxious to play down his own failure, told his superiors in Berlin that *Erri Berro* had been stopped by the Navy after she had left the rendezvous and that her crew had scuttled her before she could be searched.

Hall's talent for lateral thinking led him to anticipate and forestall any hostile reaction in Spain and ensure that any fall-out descended on German heads. When news of *Erri Berro*'s sinking first appeared in Spanish newspapers, some anti-British feeling arose and the Foreign Office had started to ask the Admiralty some questions. Hall's officers had closely interrogated her crew and her captain had helpfully testified that he had been employed by German agents to run the blockade with a cargo of contraband. Hall succeeded in mollifying Hardinge by passing on this information, adding that the intelligence which had resulted in her interception had been provided by his operatives in Bilbao.

Once he had discovered that the U-boats had escaped he could safely arrange for the crew's return to Spain, advising the Spanish Consul-General in London that the Navy had rescued them from the sinking *Erri Berro* and had since been holding them at the Government's expense. As the Admiralty now wished to repatriate them, he offered the Consul General a cheque for £50 to cover their fares from London to the Spanish frontier. The offer was gratefully accepted, particularly as Hall had thoughtfully provided sufficient funds to cover the crew's return home.

Once in Spain, they told the press how and why they had been captured and how well they had been treated in England. The newspapers quickly changed their tune, criticizing the Germans for a flagrant breach of Spanish neutrality. Once again Hall's devices had worked to the disadvantage of Krohn, who by this time had outstayed his welcome in Spain as well as becoming a liability both to the Ambassador and to the Admiralstab. The authorities promptly expelled him. Ed Bell could not resist sending a cable to Harrison, his superior in Washington:

> I understand that at the Spanish frontier an anti-German demonstration took place when he passed through. My friends of the Admiralty cannot understand how this occurred, and deplore such an outburst of popular feeling against a worthy and gallant officer (Oh Yes, they do!)[7]

Krohn had long been a thorn in the side of naval intelligence and his enforced departure was particularly welcome. As early as June 1916, he had proposed contaminating the rivers Douro and Tagus at the frontier between Spain and Portugal with the cholera bacillus in an effort to close the border and disrupt communications between Portugal and the allies, requesting that he be supplied two vials of bacilli for the purpose. This hare-brained suggestion was too much for Berlin who promptly refused to supply any cultures. Although Berlin had vetoed biological warfare against humans, they did not scruple to use it against animals. On two occasions later in 1916 a U-boat, probably U-35, called at Cartagena to deliver a personal letter from the Kaiser to King Alfonso and to collect the future World War II intelligence chief, Wilhelm Canaris, who had managed to escape from the cruiser *Dresden* after she had been destroyed by the Navy and had succeeded in reaching Spain. On one of these visits Krohn did receive a supply of bacillus.

Krohn persuaded his mistress, Marthe Regnier, who although French, seems to have been extremely loyal to her German lover, to take the consignment to Argentina on a Spanish liner and hand it over to Julio Arnold, one of Germany most effective agents in Latin America. Hall had been informed of Krohn's scheme by a Room 40 decrypt, which revealed Mlle. Regnier's itinerary and details of the trunk in which the lethal vials had been packed. The cruiser HMS *Newcastle* was detailed to board the liner and sieze the vials. Unfortunately *Newcastle* missed the liner in fog and the consignment was duly delivered to Arnold, who used it to devastating effect. Four hundred mules were poisoned.

In February 1918, U-35 once again called in at Cartagena to land two agents with a consignment of twelve cases, among which were anthrax and glanders bacilli concealed in lumps of sugar. Through Room 40 intercepts Hall was aware of this lethal shipment. Thoroton tipped off the strongly pro-allied Chief of Police in Cartagena, who seized the cargo and sent it by train to his superiors in Madrid. By arrangement with Thoroton one of the cases was removed from the train, handed over to one of his agents and sent to Hall in London, who, judging that the time was ripe to strike a blow at German espionage and close down the deadly traffic, sent Herschell to Madrid. He showed the ampoule concealed in sugar to King Alfonso. Infuriated by the German involvement in biological warfare, the King ordered the expulsion of the luckless Ratibor. The use of the Madrid Embassy as a clearing house had effectively been terminated.

At Hall's instigation, the Foreign Office sent a sample sugar cube containing the bacillus to the British Minister in Buenos Aires, Sir Reginald Tower, who dissolved the cube, revealing the ampoule to the President of Argentina, Hipolito Irigoyen. The President was much less impressed with this demonstration than King Alfonso had been and refused to take any action, on the specious grounds that the mules might have been infected at sea.

Latin America

When Hall eventually cleared the liner *Frederik VIII*, on which the ejected Ambassador Bernstorff and his staff were returning to Germany, to leave Halifax, she encountered a severe Atlantic gale, which can only have increased the misery of their journey. When the storm-battered *Frederik VIII* called in at Christiania (now Oslo) on March 13, Bernstorff was interviewed by the Editor of the *Hamburger Fremdenblatt*. He went on record:

> But if they talk of German intrigues in American countries, I must insist that we have always absolutely refused to meddle with the politics of the American Continent. All American statements about German intrigues in Haiti, Cuba and Colombia are fairy tales. In the whole of Central and South America and particularly in Mexico, we have always followed exclusively economic aims.[8]

Bernstorff's statement, particularly astonishing from a diplomat who was by German standards a liberal, was such a shameless fabrication it is hardly surprising that in the chapter headings for his unpublished autobiography, Hall had him listed as the world's champion liar.

German agents had been meddling in Latin America and particularly in Mexico since the revolution of 1910 where von Papen had been especially active in fomenting trouble. In April 1914, the Hamburg-Amerika cargo liner *Ypiranga* had landed ammunition at the Mexican port of Veracruz destined for the then President, Huerta, who had seized power in a coup during which he had murdered his predecessor. Albert Ballin, the line's Managing Director and a close adviser to the Kaiser, had been personally involved in organising this consignment. Wilson reacted by sending in the Marines to occupy the port. Nineteen Americans and over a hundred Mexicans were killed in this futile operation. Later that year Huerta was driven out by his rival, Carranza. The German secret service and their Washington Embassy continued to back Huerta until he died in American captivity in Texas in March 1916. They then transferred their support to Carranza.

After their Washington Embassy had been closed down, the German Government had become even more dependent on the Swedish Roundabout for communicating with its Embassies in Latin America, principally those in Mexico and Argentina, who were deeply involved in running their extensive subversion operation throughout the continent. With Bernstorff's departure, Count Luxburg, their Ambassador in Buenos Aires became the de facto head of their operations.

Harrison had obtained copies of Bernstorff's extensive cable traffic with German diplomats and agents in a number of Latin American countries, sent in January and February 1917 before diplomatic relations had been broken off. He sent these to Bell in London requesting that they be decoded by Room 40; a task completed by Montgomery, under Herschell's or Serocold's supervision and one which caused him few problems as they had been sent in the ubiquitous 13040. Bell's letters include several references to 'the Padre'.

Relations between Hall, Herschell and Serocold, and Bell, supported by Harrison in Washington, were now extremely close. With the US in the war Hall now had access to information sources relating to Latin America previously unavailable to naval intelligence. Even with the expansion of the division, its resources had been severely stretched and its coverage of Latin America had not been particularly effective. With a high degree of co-operation between the intelligence officers in London and Washington, the American government would be able to implement the desirable countermeasures against German activities throughout the continent. With the assistance of naval intelligence in London, Washington could take the lead in undermining the German position, without revealing the extensive British involvement. Hall could now effectively strike at German subversion, leaving the necessary disclosures to be leaked by the Americans. He took considerable care to retain control over cryptology, which he repeatedly declined to share with the Americans even after their chief cryptanalyst, Herbert Yardley, visited London for this purpose. With this degree of control, he was able to exert substantial leverage over the State Department and influence their handling of the information he gave to Bell to pass to them.

Bernstorff's messages highlighted the extent of the German propaganda and subversion activities in the Americas, which had been intensified after US entry into the war. They were now actively placing bombs on merchant ships carrying supplies for the allies and infecting crops, cattle, horses and mules with anthrax bacillus. Despite the revelations of the Zimmermann telegram, Carranza remained unfriendly to the US and tolerated German subversion operations based in Mexico. Opinion in Brazil and Argentina, where German influence had been powerful, shifted markedly to a more pro-allied position following the reintroduction of Unrestricted Submarine Warfare and – in the case of Argentina – Luxburg's consistently tactless and overbearing behaviour.

As it had proved to be an invaluable listening post for Room 40 Hall had never attempted to destroy the Swedish Roundabout. He now began to consider whether its existence could more advantageously be leaked, in order to strike a blow at the German espionage operations in Latin America and boosting allied interests. He decided that the consequences of these revelations – including possibly the declaration of war on Germany by Argentina – would outweigh Berlin realising that their codes and their transmission system were being compromised. He started by revealing to Page the extent to which the German government had been using the Roundabout to further their objectives in the Americas. On August 31 Page cabled President Wilson:

> Most Secret. Admiral Hall ... has given me a number of documents comprising German cipher messages between German diplomatic officers and the

Berlin Foreign Office, chiefly relating to the Argentine and definitely implicating the Swedish Government. In view of the negotiations now going on between Germany and the Argentine, the British government hope that you will immediately publish these telegrams asking that their origin be kept secret as in the case of the Zimmermann telegram. I have the cipher originals and am sending them to you by a trustworthy messenger [William Wiseman, a leading British intelligence agent based in Washington] who will deliver them into your hands about 12–15 September. These telegrams also prove that Sweden has continuously used her legations and pouches and her code to transmit official information between Berlin and German diplomatic officers ...[9]

Page enclosed extracts from several of Luxburg's telegrams, in one of which he had clearly expressed his contempt for Argentinians, calling them 'under a thin veneer, Indians.' As nonsensical as it was despicable; the population of Argentina was predominantly of European descent. Luxburg had been attempting to get Berlin to exclude Argentinian shipping from being sunk under the unrestricted submarine warfare campaign and had been pressing for compensation for the loss of an Argentinian merchant ship, *Toro*. Berlin replied: 'The proposed sparing of ships must remain secret otherwise submarine war would be endangered. Full compensation is guaranteed for *Toro* but ... this is to be attributed, not to liberality but to ... circumstances.' On May 19 Luxburg cabled Berlin: 'This Government has now released German and Austrian ships in which hitherto a guard has been placed. Government will in future only clear Argentine ships as far as Las Palmas, I beg that the small steamers *Oran* and *Guazo* ... which are now nearing Bordeaux ... may be spared if possible, or else sunk without a trace' (in the original German *spurlos versenkt*). Two more telegrams provided by Hall to Bell were equally incriminating. On July 3 Luxburg had told the Foreign Office:

> I learn from a reliable source that the Acting Minister of Foreign Affairs, who is a notorious ass and an Anglophile, declared in a secret session of the Senate that Argentina would demand from Berlin a promise not to sink more Argentine ships. If not agreed to, relations would be broken off. I recommend refusal, and, if necessary, calling in the mediation of Spain.

On July 19 Luxburg returned to this issue:

> Without showing any tendency to make concessions postpone reply to Argentine Note until receipt of further reports. A change of Ministers is probable. As regards Argentine steamers, I recommend either compelling them to turn back, sinking them without leaving any trace, or letting them through. They are all quite small.[10]

(He was covering quite a few bases.) In briefing Page, Hall had provided him with a paper comprehensively describing how the German Foreign Office had used the Swedish Roundabout with Stockholm's full connivance almost since the outset of the war. He set out his objectives with his habitual clarity:

> Nothing but the most urgent Allied reasons can justify the exposure of this system and the loss of supremely valuable intelligence thereby entailed. At the present time, the immediate objectives to be achieved are:
> 1. Entry of Argentina into the war on the side of the Allies, or at least severance of diplomatic relations with Germany.
> 2. Discrediting the pro-German party in Sweden, and thereby aiding in the election of Mr. Branting to power at the forthcoming general election.
> 3. Effect upon Austria at the exposure of German methods which would be greatly accentuated if Argentina joins the allies.
> 4. Effect in the remaining neutral countries – Spain, in particular.
> 5. Effect in Bulgaria and Turkey at the further exhibition of German clumsiness.
> 6. Effect in Germany at the advent of further enemies, should Argentina break with Germany.[11]

Page had little difficulty in convincing Wilson and Lansing to leak these telegrams to the American press as they had leaked the Zimmermann telegram, once again protecting Hall's decrypts and implying that the information had originated in the US. The results were devastating, both in the States and in Argentina, where the Embassy found the cynical reference 'spurlos versenkt' impossible to explain away. Argentina expelled Luxburg and broke off diplomatic relations with Germany. Before he was evicted, the Ambassador had cabled the Foreign Office: 'Whether it is a case of theft of documents or betrayal of a cipher I am unable to say with certainty.'[12]

Rather late in the day Berlin finally decided that 13040 had been compromised and they fell back on the VB code, never realizing that Room 40 had been reading it for nearly three years.

Hall's initiative had been remarkably successful. Not only had Argentina broken off relations with Berlin but Brazil declared war on Germany. As he had forecast to Page, the Swedish electorate took an unfavourable view of the pro-German government's breach of neutrality in allowing Berlin to use its official communications network. The government was soundly defeated at the general election and replaced by a pro-allied coalition headed by the Socialist leader, Hjalmar Branting.

Hall knew well that the German espionage machine in Mexico, now headed by Kurt Jahnke, a German-American who had been widely engaged in sabotage in the US (including the Black Tom Affair) and who had crossed the border after the declaration of war, was still extremely active. An American intelligence report described Jahnke as one of Germany's star-agents, who had been detailed to foment a mutiny in the US Army. It listed some of his other tasks:

> Jahnke also has taken under his wing the general supervision of sabotage in the U.S., the Panama Canal and American possessions generally ... especially sabotage of ships transporting war material and material for ship construction.
> His program ... has been approved by the German Government, with an available credit of 100,000 marks per month, and an additional large commission on results accomplished ... he has already had some experience in the control of German agitators, defeatists ... in this country, and is regarded as an ideal man for the job.[13]

His objectives included involving Mexico in a war against the US as well as sabotaging the oilfields in Tampico. Room 40 had been intercepting a considerable volume of signal traffic between Berlin and their Embassy in Madrid relating to subversion operations in Mexico. The signals were transmitted in the VB code which, after the fiasco of the Zimmermann telegram, they erroneously continued to believe was safe.

In the summer of 1917 Hall's intelligence network in Spain had intercepted a German order for audion valves, technology which had been developed by Dr. Lee De Forest, a leading if controversial American inventor in the field of radio and electronic equipment. These were in effect high-powered valves used to receive radio signals, amplify long distance wired communications and as an oscillator for transmission. In 1914 the patent had been acquired by AT&T for use in developing their transcontinental telephone network. Only AT&T's manufacturing arm and a licensee in Britain had rights to produce the valves. As early as 1915 the management of the American terminal of the German-controlled wireless system at Tuckerton had attempted unsuccessfully to purchase a supply of the valves and consequently their sale was – or should have been – severely restricted.

The intelligence division kept a close eye on the shipments of the valves, which they believed were destined for use in a wireless station to be set up in a neutral country. Their investigations revealed that the valves had been sent not to Spain or Morocco as they had originally believed but had been shipped under conditions of great secrecy to Mexico.

To deal with the German operation, Hall sent his 'star-turn' A. E. W. Mason to Mexico. Mason, now a Major in the Royal Marines, left London in mid-October on a diplomatic passport signed by Balfour and countersigned by the British embassy in Washington. This gave him the authority to proceed to the West Indies and Mexico, charged with dispatches, and to pass freely without let or hindrance, affording him every assistance and protection.

With this cover and disguising himself as an eccentric lepidopterist (although he freely admitted that he neither liked or knew anything about butterflies) Mason rapidly made an ominous discovery. After the loss of the Swedish Roundabout, the German espionage service in Mexico, determined to maintain communications with Berlin, had succeeded in effectively gaining control of the main wireless station at Ixtapalapa, outside Mexico City. Every night at 11 pm, a group of merchant navy officers whose ships had been interned in the port of Veracruz took over the station and were able to transmit and also to receive wireless messages from Nauen, utilising the station's thirteen audion valves. Mason returned to London at Christmas and obtained Hall's authority to immobilise the Ixtapalapa facility, although the British Government, if ever asked, would deny any knowledge of the incident.

By February 1918, he was back in Mexico City. Carefully working through intermediaries, he succeeded in buying up the eleven spare audion valves in the country and set about infiltrating the wireless station. By July he had recruited three Mexicans with appropriate skills, two of them having been senior police officers under previous presidents. The third he described as 'a young fellow with a great charm of manner who held one of the highest positions as a burglar in Mexico'. He discovered that the wireless station was guarded round-the-clock by forty soldiers of the Mexican army, commanded by a Captain. He enlisted the support of a neighbouring landowner, who invited the Captain to dinner, where he met Mason's three agents and invited them to view the facility before the German officers arrived. They were shown the receiving apparatus, including the audion valves, and decided that they could easily be put out of action and that they could readily make their escape. As Mason succinctly noted: 'The destruction of the audion valves ... would, while doing no permanent harm to the wireless installation, preserve the neutrality of Mexico ... within more scrupulous precision than her government was prepared to observe.'[14]

A few nights later, the helpful landowner invited the Captain of the guard to dinner, this time alone. As soon as he had left, Mason's agents arrived at the station with an ample supply of beer. The noncommissioned officers had been induced to riot, believing that the burglar wished to work out a grudge against some of the soldiers. Under the influence of the beer, a brawl broke out and the agents were able to enter the receiving room, smash four audion lamps, remove the remainder and then escape in the confusion. Ed Bell told his superior Harrison that as a result of Mason's successful coup, Jahnke had now no means of communicating with his masters in Berlin.

Although the scope of the German espionage machine in Mexico had been substantially reduced, their most effective agent in Latin America, Julio Arnold, based in Argentina, remained lethally active. Bell portrayed Arnold as 'a nice quiet fellow who for the past two years has been engaged in the Argentine; introducing fungus in stored grain; inoculation of mules with glanders; and the promotion of strikes hostile to Allied interests ... Arnold is one of the cleverest of all the German agents in the Western Hemisphere, and he has such large sums of money at his disposal he is able to go ahead with his plans without referring them ... to Berlin for approval.'[15]

Through Room 40 decrypts, Hall had detected German attempts to start biological warfare, using the anthrax cultures, which the courier, Marthe Regnier, had brought from Spain to Argentina. Arnold used these cultures to infect mules, which had been bought in Argentina by the allied purchasing commission and which were urgently needed by the British and French Armies. In all, some 40 cables dealing with the infection of mules were intercepted. One decrypt in February 1918 read: 'The person in question [presumably Arnold] reports that owing to his work the export of horses to France and Italy has for the time being completely ceased. Since September four ships with 5400 mules started for Mesopotamia; all were thoroughly treated.' In the same month the General Staff cabled the Military Attaché in Madrid: 'Please instruct Arnold to continue his successful activity against cattle. His work directed against grain is to be suppressed as it promises little success.'[16]

The concerns of the British and US governments about Arnold's operations mounted at the end of February when Room 40 intercepted a telegram from the German Embassy in Buenos Aires to Berlin: 'Arnold has dispatched a confidential agent, Julio Rico, to the States.' Another cable reported that agents in the States had been instructed to use anthrax cultures against horses, mules and cattle where 'there was comparative freedom of risk of detection' but that other operations in meatpacking plants were being discontinued.[17]

As he had succeeded in killing a considerable number of mules with anthrax and glanders cultures and he had become a major thorn in the allied side, Arnold's operations clearly had to be terminated. Combined British and American pressure on the Irrigoyen administration finally succeeded in closing down his activities in Argentina. Arnold's extensive financial resources enabled him to continue his operations even after Hall had succeeded in shutting the Swedish Roundabout down. As Bell told Harrison as late as September 1918:

> It is ... rather hard to keep tabs on him. I have just been informed by the Admiralty that there seems very good reason to believe that he is about to institute a campaign of sabotage in Cuba against the sugar crop. This of course would be a very serious matter to all the Allies ... I believe that

Admiral Hall intends to send to Washington a Naval Reserve officer named Arnold to confer with our authorities and then to proceed to the British Legation in Havana as Assistant Naval Attaché ... in order to work with our people to try to keep an eye on the sabotage situation, which Hall regards as very serious.[18]

At the time of the Armistice in November 1918 Britain had less than three weeks supply of sugar. Fortunately, the war ended before Arnold could wreak havoc on the Cuban sugar crop.

The American connection: France

Following the mutiny in the French army in the summer of 1917, the veteran Georges Clemenceau was appointed Prime Minister with a mandate to tackle defeatism, which was all too rife, and remove potential traitors. He acted ruthlessly and among those he arrested were two former ministers, including a former Prime Minister, Joseph Caillaux, and a mendacious and suspect Egyptian citizen known as Bolo Pasha, whom French intelligence believed, with some reason, to be a German agent.

Hall correctly believed that Clemenceau's drive against defeatism and treachery was vital to the success of the allied cause. Room 40's by now vast records produced damning evidence of Bolo's treachery. In February 1915, presumably at Caillaux's instigation, Bolo had asked Bernstorff to advance him a loan of $1.7 million to secure peace on terms favourable to Germany. Hall knew that this intelligence would be invaluable to the Clemenceau government. Fearing poor security Hall had never supplied any Room 40 decrypts to French intelligence and he was, as always, extremely reluctant to risk disclosing NID's knowledge of the German codes. Rather than give the compromising intelligence directly to the French Government he again used the American Embassy in London as his intermediary, as he had in the Zimmermann and Luxburg cases. Bell and Page were only too ready to assist.

In October 2 Bell sent the decrypts to Harrison in Washington and Page reported to Wilson:

> The British authorities have not communicated these telegrams to the French as to do so would divulge the source of information which ... they wish to avoid. They would however be glad if you would do so. As it is quite possible that, for internal political reasons, the French may not find it desirable to make public the contents of the telegrams ... the British authorities ask that they may be informed when the telegrams are handed to the French government so that they may know for certain that the French have the information.[19]

Washington was happy to oblige and on the basis of Hall's intelligence, Bolo was sentenced to death in January 1918.

In January 1918, Hall revealed to Bell several telegrams from Luxburg to Berlin, which had presumably been sent via the Swedish Roundabout, indicating that Caillaux had engaged in treasonous behaviour when he had visited Argentina in February 1915. Bell immediately sent this incriminating intelligence to Harrison, who passed it to Paris as he had in the Bolo case. The telegrams were made available to the prosecutor when Caillaux was brought to trial. After the end of the War he was eventually sentenced to a short spell in prison and 10 years loss of his civil rights.

The American connection: Ireland

After the Easter Uprising and the execution of its leaders by firing squad, Sinn Fein became the dominant political force in Southern Ireland. As early as June 1916 Bernstorff had noted that as a result of the harsh measures taken by the British authorities: '… we now have two friends for every one before the rebellion'. In May 1918 the British decided to arrest the Sinn Fein leaders. In an effort to forestall any difficulty between London and Washington, given the influence of the Irish-American lobby, the British Government decided to publish details of German involvement in stirring up disaffection in Ireland. On May 10 1918 Page wrote to Lansing enclosing copies of

> … thirty-two important communications … exchanged between Bernstorff and his government in the years 1914 to 1917 … establishing connection between Sinn Feiners and German Government and showing conclusively that the latter was involved both in the insurrection of Easter 1916 and in a similar outbreak planned for February last year and later postponed. These documents I obtained from Admiral Hall and I have myself compared the documents with the originals. The Prime Minister, who knows of the existence of the information … now wishes it to be made public in the interest of the Allied cause and consequently this will be done at an early date. In order to give the appearance of consistency in respect of previous disclosures of German telegrams all of which have been made by our government Hall would, in communicating the documents to higher authority for publication, have to intimate that after interchanging information with the American Secret Service for a period of over a year he is now in a position to decipher German messages himself.[20]

Lansing had his doubts. Although he had no sympathy with Sinn Fein, declaring '… their present willingness to co-operate with the Germans shows a blindness to the great issues of the war and a willingness to sacrifice democracy to their own selfish ends', he told the President:

> ... it would be impolitic at the present time for us to assume the responsibility for the publication of these papers. The Irish situation is very delicate and anything which we might do to aid either side in the controversy would, I said, involve us in all sorts of difficulties with the Irish in this country ... While I am not unmindful of the usefulness of the publication to the British Government in the endeavors to discredit the Sinn Fein movement, which is undoubtedly in the interest of Germany and, therefore, hostile to us as well as to Great Britain, I am loath to involve this country in the quarrel.[21]

Wilson backed Lansing and overrode Page, stating that Washington: 'was not prepared to publish these documents at this time'.[22] The incriminating papers were never published and the connection between Sinn Fein and the German Embassy in Washington remained unknown to the public for many years. Hall had suffered a serious defeat and any hope of limiting Sinn Fein's influence over the Irish people had been irretrievably lost.

By the end of the War the co-operation between Hall and Bell had become extremely close. He provided Bell with intelligence of German agents in the US that frequently led to their arrest and conviction. On one occasion he lobbied Bell to request the death sentence for a naturalised American named Bode, a known bomb expert and a deserter from the American army who had been arrested for spying. Bell wrote to Harrison supporting Hall's demand and paying tribute to the valuable intelligence which he had provided: 'It is largely on the information he has been able to supply that we have kept track of Bode and others ... The other authorities in the US have no idea to what extent our Government is indebted to Hall.'[23] Bode never faced a death sentence and was fortunate to serve only ten years hard labour for desertion.

Ed Bell had served his country skilfully. His hard work and outgoing personality were largely responsible for the successful relationship the American Embassy developed with the NID. He was well supported by Leland Harrison and credit is due both to Harrison and to Robert Lansing for the discreet way in which the Room 40 Intelligence was treated in Washington. Sadly, Bell died in 1924 as a result of a fall when he was serving as Counselor of the American Embassy in China. Had he survived he would have undoubtedly reached the highest ranks in the diplomatic service. Harrison went on to serve as Secretary to the American delegation at Versailles and as Minister to Switzerland throughout the Second World War. After his death the Secretary of State, Dean Acheson, wrote admiringly of his ability to make important decisions on his own responsibility and paid tribute to his good judgment, which had enabled him to render valuable services to his country. Hall had been fortunate to have had colleagues of such calibre in their common struggle against Imperial Germany.

Notes

[1] Beesly p.192
[2] Ibid p.192
[3] Ibid p.183
[4] Ibid p.194
[5] Ibid p.196
[6] Ibid p.198
[7] Ibid p.199
[8] TNA HW 1/180
[9] Beesly p.239
[10] Ibid p.238 Cables between Berlin and Buenos Aires
[11] Ibid pp.239-240
[12] Ibid p.241
[13] Jules Witcover *Sabotage at Black Tom* p.242
[14] Green p.151
[15] Beesly p.245 NARA State Dept. papers Bell to Harrison September 11 1918
[16] James p.189
[17] Ibid p.190
[18] NARA State Dept. papers Bell to Harrison September 11 1918
[19] Beesly p.243
[20] NARA State Dept. papers Page to Lansing
[21] Ibid Lansing to Wilson May 19 1918
[22] Beesly p.244
[23] Ibid p.245

CHAPTER XV

On Course for Victory

Four days after Wemyss succeeded Jellicoe, he sacked Bacon as Admiral commanding the Dover Patrol and replaced him by Hall's old ally Keyes, who immediately took steps to close the Straits of Dover to the U-boats. To buy Keyes time to complete his plans, Hall mounted another exercise in deception. He concocted details of an imaginary barrage across the Straits equipped with electric devices to destroy any submarine which might get entangled in it. This misinformation was bought by a known German agent for the not inconsiderable sum of £2,000. Whilst the precise effect of the deception is not clear, there is some evidence that the German U-boats based in Belgium ceased using the Straits in favour of the longer route round the North of Scotland. By March the Dover Patrol had gained total control of the Straits, successfully barring the passage of U-boats. In February 1918 U-55 became the last submarine to negotiate the Straits and between his appointment and the Armistice, Keyes' force had sunk no less than 14 U-boats.

Zeebrugge

On the night of February 15 seven German destroyers, operating in two groups, successfully attacked the illuminated barrage, sinking twelve drifters, two trawlers and a minesweeper. The northern group returned to Zeebrugge without encountering any of Keyes's patrols. The southern group, steaming East after completing its attack, passed within two cables length of the Eastern Barrage Patrol of four destroyers. Although they did not respond to the challenge from HMS *Amazon*, bringing up the rear of the patrol, her commanding officer mistakenly believed the destroyers to be British, despite the repeated gunfire which must have been audible to him, and reported that 'three of our destroyers had passed'. By the time the patrol's Senior Officer had decided that the ships were not British, half an hour had passed and it was too late to pursue the German ships. A furious Keyes ordered that 'Suspicious vessels are to be regarded as enemy ... if the challenge is made and not immediately answered, offensive action is be taken without further delay.'[1]

The German naval command was delighted with this action but strangely enough never mounted another attack on the barrage. On March 6 the War Cabinet expressed dissatisfaction with a number of recent naval actions, including the events of the night of February 15. With his unwavering belief in offensive action, Keyes revived Bacon's plan to block the German naval bases at Zeebrugge and Ostend, making it impossible for them to stage another attack on the barrage. The main German force of destroyers and U-boats was based in the inland harbour at Bruges, which was connected by canals with Zeebrugge and Ostend. The main access to the sea was via Zeebrugge as the Bruges-Ostend canal could only be used by the smaller U-boats. Keyes's objective was to deny the Germans access to the sea by blocking the entrance to both Zeebrugge and Ostend, thus sealing up the Bruges Canal, as well as rendering maximum damage to both ports.

The operation, postponed on two occasions, was carefully planned and implemented with precision and gallantry on the night of April 22/23. Keyes, a charismatic and hands-on commander, directed the action on board the destroyer HMS *Warwick*. Despite relentless fire from the German batteries on the Zeebrugge mole, two of the three blockships, obsolete cruisers loaded with cement, were scuttled inside the port and an old submarine, loaded with five tons of high explosive, was rammed into the pier of a railway viaduct linking the mole to the shore, The crew set the fuses and were picked up by patrol boats before the submarine blew up with a deafening roar, leaving a breach of a hundred yards in the viaduct, preventing reinforcements from reaching the mole. Unfortunately the attack on Ostend failed: in hazy weather the blockships missed the harbour entrance and were thus unable to get into place.

The Zeebrugge operation was a massive boost for morale both in the Navy, where the inactivity in the Grand Fleet enforced by the HSF's consistent avoidance of offensive action had inevitably engendered a sense of frustration, and in the Army, who had experienced the costly stalemate at Passchendaele and the hammer blow of the March offensive. The press was ecstatic, hailing the operation, which had taken place on St. George's Day, as a rebirth of the offensive spirit of Nelson and Drake. Popular opinion was powerfully aroused by the Navy's skill and daring. Keyes received an immediate knighthood, becoming a national hero overnight, and no fewer than eleven Victoria Crosses were awarded. (For the most complete account of this extraordinary action, see Paul Kendall's *The Zeebrugge Raid 1918: 'The Finest Feat of Arms'*.)

Whilst the propaganda effect of Zeebrugge was significant and probably justified the effort and the huge percentage of casualties (170 killed, approximately 400 wounded and 40 missing from something over a thousand effectively in the firing line) despite Keyes firmly believing that the German forces had been penned in at Bruges, the strategic gain was minimal. The Zeebrugge harbour had not actually been completely blocked as the NID soon became aware. James wrote: 'At the Admiralty we knew five hours after the attempt from an intercepted signal that the canal had not been blocked, but no good purpose would be served by publishing this.'[2] Although the German Official History admitted that Zeebrugge had been 'a well-planned ... and bravely executed attempt to eliminate a strongly defended enemy base', it continued 'Close examination of the situation very soon showed that the conduct of the war from Zeebrugge had suffered only minor and temporary restrictions.'[3] In a report in February 1919, the NID confirmed that 'Ostend was never blocked and the submarines from Bruges could always go to sea that way. Zeebrugge was only blocked to submarines for a few days.'[4]

Austria tries to sue for peace

The venerable Emperor Franz Josef of Austria-Hungary had died in November 1916. His successor, his great nephew Karl, firmly believed that an early peace was vital to the survival of the Austro-Hungarian Empire. Throughout 1917 he had made a number of unsuccessful approaches to both the British and the French. When he read President Wilson's Fourteen Points, published in January 1918, he seized the opportunity to attempt to extricate his country from a war which he feared would end in total catastrophe.

Late in 1917, the US had declared war on Austria-Hungary and the persistent Karl decided to make a direct approach to Wilson using King Alfonso XIII of Spain as an intermediary. On February 20, 1918, Room 40's Austrian specialist, E. C. Quiggin, intercepted and decoded a telegram from the Austrian Foreign Minister, Count Czernin, to his Ambassador in Madrid requesting him to ask King Alfonso to pass a message to the President. Quiggin was surprised to read this telegram as most of the Austrian signal traffic, which they were regularly intercepting, was of a routine nature. Karl's message was so important that he took it directly to Hall, whose eyebrows rose when he read:

> The European situation has been materially cleared by President Wilson's speech. ... hence the time seems to have come when a direct discussion between one of my representatives and one representing Mr. Wilson might clear up the situation in such an extent that no further obstacles would stand in the way of a world peace congress.

> Your magnanimous desire to pronounce proposals for peace prompts me to request you to forward the following message through a secret channel to President Wilson …
>
> If you will be kind enough to forward this to the President, I believe that you will render the cause of peace in general and the whole human race the greatest service.

Hall grasped the significance of this, a peace initiative by Germany's principal European ally, and immediately took it to Geddes. Chartering a special train they rushed on what Hall later called their 'mad journey' to Manchester where Lloyd George was speaking. Before leaving he had given a copy of the Emperor's message to Bell for Page to inform Wilson. It was a measure of Room 40's efficiency and dominance over the airwaves that both Lloyd George and Wilson knew the contents of the message before the Spanish Ambassador in Washington could deliver it to the White House. As Colonel House reported to Balfour: 'This afternoon the Spanish Ambassador … handed the President the note from the Emperor of Austria. The President said he had difficulty in composing his face and in trying to look surprised.'[4]

Despite the drama in London and Washington, Karl's initiative failed. Balfour was doubtful from the outset, reminding Page that the 'regrettable' Anglo-French Treaty, negotiated for Britain by the Asquith Government had promised Italy that the Austrian province of the South Tyrol together with Trieste and its hinterland would be ceded to her at any Peace Conference. As Italy had recently suffered a catastrophic defeat at Caporetto, he feared that she might 'quit the war' if she believed that she would not now receive these promised territorial gains. Wilson, hell-bent on self-determination, had no desire to preserve the integrity of Austria-Hungary. Hall gleaned from further Room 40 intercepts of the Berlin-Madrid signal traffic that Germany had soon discovered her ally's peace bid and had never believed that it would succeed. The Austrian desire for peace had waned following the initial successes of the German March offensive on the Western Front.

A Power ploy thwarted

Early in 1918 Hall fought hard and in the event successfully to defeat a challenge to his authority from a man who at first sight might be considered an unlikely opponent, but who was determined to usurp his functions. In February that year Lloyd George appointed Lord Beaverbrook, who in the previous year had bought the *Daily Express* and had served as head of a Government propaganda committee, as the first Minister of Information. As he was widely regarded as a man who totally lacked scruples and loved power for power's sake, the appointment was widely criticised. Evelyn Waugh, often an incisive critic, noted 'the deep malevolence of the man'.

Beaverbrook advocated using the concentrated power of the press as a potent means of promoting the British and allied cause. He proposed setting up his own intelligence division, encountering strong opposition from a powerful trio of Ministers: Balfour, Geddes and Derby, the Secretary of State for War.

On March 16 Hall reported to Geddes on a meeting which had discussed this contentious suggestion. The South African General Jan Smuts, then a member of the War Cabinet, presided and Hardinge and Hall attended together with a representative of the Director of Military Intelligence (DMI). Beaverbrook demanded that his proposed intelligence department be given direct access to the DMI and NID; a proposal which was totally unacceptable both to the Admiralty and War Office. Hall and the War Office representative argued that the present arrangement by which all political intelligence was sent to the Foreign Office should continue. They were backed up by Hardinge who sharply reminded Beaverbrook that the political intelligence department headed by the novelist John Buchan had recently been transferred to the Foreign Office and he would go no further than offering to prepare a digest of intelligence for the Ministry of Information's use.

Following one of his cardinal tenets and emphasising that he had Geddes's complete support, Hall insisted that it would be impossible to hand over any information received from NID agents overseas to a Propaganda Department as the lives of these agents would thereby be endangered. He was ready to supply the Foreign Office with all political information received by his department on the direct understanding that the Foreign Office would ensure that the sources could never be traced.

When Smuts suggested that Buchan's Department be transferred to Beaverbrook's Ministry, Hall vigorously objected and asked Smuts to discuss the proposal with Geddes. His robust opposition to this power ploy had clearly disconcerted Beaverbrook, a man used to getting his own way, who had not expected to meet such determined resistance. He then attempted to threaten the DNI by telling him that unless within a month he had got the Admiralty (by which he meant Hall) into a better frame of mind he would 'have to chuck the whole show or something else would happen'. Hall told Geddes he had the impression that Beaverbrook would spare no trouble to get rid of him. In the event no more was heard of Beaverbrook's ploy.[5]

In August 1918, to the relief of Hall and the intelligence world, Beaverbrook was forced to resign following the publication of a *Daily Express* leader in which the newspaper had threatened to withdraw its support for the Lloyd George Government unless it adopted tariff reform, a cause which he consistently advocated. His biographer noted that his term as Minister may have been brief but it had not been happy.

In May 1941, Churchill transferred Beaverbrook from the Ministry of Aircraft Production to the newly created position of Minister of State without any executive function. Hall wrote to his sister May:

> Beaverbrook without portfolio is simply going to intrigue hard; I know what he wants and that is to take charge of all secret service work and intelligence services: he tried to do it in the last war but I defeated him and he has never liked me since!!

Three weeks later he returned to the charge:

> I am still wondering what roguery Beaverbrook is up to; he wont [sic] sit still and do steady work; that is not his métier but I suppose Churchill prefers to have him under his own eye than acting as a free lance!! I know that at one time he intended to get entire control of the intelligence services: the result would be of course that they will be valueless as no one will believe a word of his reports!![6]

Fortunately for Hall and many others, who regarded Beaverbrook with well-founded mistrust, Churchill moved him once again at the end of June 1941, giving him executive authority as Minister of Supply. Hall and the intelligence community were able to breathe a hearty sigh of relief that he had once again been entrusted with a full-time responsibility which effectively prevented him from meddling in issues well beyond his brief and his competence.

Building on success

By early 1918 the co-operation which had been successfully established between ASWD and NID was extended to include the Royal Naval Air Service operations against submarines. Addressing the RAF Staff College in 1924, Squadron-Leader C. H. Keith, a former RNAS officer noted that:

> The whole system of the AS offensive was a highly organized one, which co-ordinated the activities of every kind of aircraft, ship and submarine, each performing the allotted task within prescribed areas at prescribed times. The aircraft operational orders were framed to fit in with the latest intelligence, movement of convoys and the C-in-C's disposition of naval forces. ... Efficient operations were dependent on a good intelligence service.[7]

Another former RNAS officer, Flight-Lieutenant J. P. Coleman, wrote:

Intelligence Centres were formed in each RNAS Group HQ adjacent to the Naval Operations Centre. A system of plotting movements of enemy submarines from reports of sightings and of ships attacked was instituted. When supplemented by information received from the Intelligence Division in the Admiralty and from other commands, this enabled valuable deductions of the methods of the enemy to be drawn.[8]

These officers were describing a remarkable development which could not have taken place in the era of rigid centralisation: the establishment of integrated operations and intelligence centres not only at command level but also at RNAS group HQs. In April 1918 Hall reported that information about minelaying submarines was being sent directly to Intelligence officers at Portsmouth, Devonport, Queenstown and at Dover.

The HSF sortie, April 1918

In early 1918, Beatty and the Naval Staff were increasingly worried that the HSF would strike again at the Scandinavian convoys. Hall was concerned that the Staff could no longer totally rely on the Room 40 intelligence which, for more than three years, had proved so effective. The HSF, at long last, had understood the advantages of maintaining wireless silence during the run-up to an operation and even more importantly once they were at sea. Important alterations were now being made to the AFB and FFB codes at intervals of seven to ten days, which were taking Room 40 from two to three days to master. U-boats at sea were now kept informed of surface operations by short bursts of code, known in Room 40 as 'catchwords', which gave the cryptanalysts no indication of what operations were being planned. Although four RN submarines, equipped with powerful transmitters whose signals could reach England, maintained a continuous patrol in the Heligoland Bight, they could not automatically be relied on to detect every HSF movement. Beatty thus remained critically dependent on SIGINT to warn him of any possible attacks on the convoys.

By April Scheer was receiving intelligence from his submarines that convoys were running on a twice-weekly schedule and that the number of merchant ships in each convoy had increased. Using this intelligence, he chose the date of April 24 to send Hipper's battlecruisers to strike at a convoy, with his battleships in support. The HSF sailed for Norwegian waters at 5 am on April 23 but at around 10 am was forced to anchor off Heligoland for several hours due to fog and did not get under way again until late that afternoon. Incredibly, the commander of the submarine J-6, on patrol off Horn's Reef, failed to report, firstly, that at around

8 pm he had sighted the light cruisers and destroyers in the HSF van and then half an hour later Hipper's five battlecruisers, the four who had fought at Jutland and the newer *Hindenberg*. He evidently believed that he had sighted British warships. Beatty was understandably furious; but the naval historian, John Creswell wrote, in a serious indictment of a faulty command-and-control system that still plagued the Navy after more than three years of war:

> ... it is not so easy to judge to what extent it was the personal fault of the Captain of J-6, and how much may be attributed to the Higher Command failing to make it quite clear to subordinates – junior flag officers and captains of detached ships – what was required of them.[9]

At about 5 am on April 24, when Hipper's force was 40 miles WSW of the Norwegian port of Stavanger, the battlecruiser *Moltke* lost her starboard inner propeller. Before her engineers could stop the turbine, a gear wheel disintegrated, piercing a condenser and causing severe flooding, which put two of her engines out of action. Contacted by a visual signal, Hipper ordered her to rejoin the main battle fleet. As salt water had penetrated her boilers, she was barely under way. At 6.43 am the battlecruiser broke wireless silence, reporting to Scheer 'break down serious, speed 4 knots'. The C-in-C ordered the battleship *Oldenburg* to take her in tow and his fleet made course for Wilhelmshaven, steaming at only 10 knots.

These two signals were intercepted by Room 40's D/F stations but as they had been sent by low power transmitters it was not possible to make a totally accurate fix and the recent change in call signs did not make it easy to identify the sender or to decode the signals. At 7.58 am the War Staff signalled Beatty: 'Call sign believed to be *Moltke* also unknown call sign located by directional in 58 degrees 30 North 6 degrees East at 7 am.' Beatty disregarded the signal as it had evidently reported the incapacitated battlecruiser's position as some 12 miles *inside* Norway. Two hours elapsed before the War Staff and Beatty managed to sort out this error.

At 9.40 am Beatty received a further Room 40 report: 'Enemy W/T procedure shows important operation in progress. Neümunster reports British unaware that German forces are at sea.' This signal convinced him that a major HSF sortie was afoot and. at 9.58 am he ordered the Battle Cruiser Force to raise steam and half an hour later sent similar instructions to the entire Grand Fleet. At 10.47 the War Staff ordered Beatty to take the Fleet to sea. By early that afternoon Beatty's Armada – 31 battleships, four battlecruisers, 26 cruisers and 85 destroyers – had cleared the Firth of Forth in a pea soup fog (a considerable feat of seamanship) and was steaming due east at full speed.

Meanwhile Hipper, resuming the operation, sailed along the Norwegian coast as far as Bergen searching for the expected westbound convoy. Finding the seas empty, he turned for home at 2.10 pm, rejoining Scheer later that day. Beatty was too late to intercept the HSF, which crossed his line of advance during the night of April 24 approximately 150 miles ahead of him. At 11.30 am on April 25 he ordered the Grand Fleet home.

At around 4 am that day the luckless J-6 sighted the returning HSF. Her Captain neither attacked the Germans, nor reported the sighting until 6.30 am, by which time he had lost sight of them. At 6.37 about 40 miles north of Heligoland another submarine, E-42, torpedoed *Moltke*, flooding her engine room, *Oldenburg* having cast off the tow an hour earlier. Although her crew reported that she was out of control, the battlecruiser managed to reach the Jade under her own power – evidence of the resilience of German warships. By the evening of April 25 the HSF was back in Wilhelmshaven, never, in the event, to go to sea again during the war. The last chance of an engagement between the two fleets had passed.

Beatty shared the Grand Fleet's frustration that once again they had been unable to bring the HSF to action. He wrote to Wemyss:

> We have just returned once again disappointed ... we must reconsider the outlook which permits apparently considerable Forces *indeed the High Seas Fleet* to get out without our knowledge – otherwise we might meet with disaster of some magnitude to this cursed convoy supporting Force.[10]

Room 40 held an inquiry into whether its intelligence had failed. Between 10 am and 11 pm on April 23 five HSF signals were intercepted although it was not possible to decode them. The DF station at Hunstanton reported a change in German W/T control, an indication that an important operation was in progress. Shortly after midnight on April 23/24, Beatty was informed of a Room 40 intercept advising that Zeppelin reconnaissance had been ordered for the North Sea, which might have indicated an attack on the East Coast, although a second signal sent at 4.20 am informed him that reconnaissance had been cancelled owing to heavy winds. On the basis of this intelligence the Harwich Force was brought to one hour's readiness to go to sea.

James concluded that Room 40 had failed to appreciate the significance of a 'catchword' sent out by a HSF submarine depot ship on April 23, which might have indicated that a major operation was in progress. He added that although Room 40 'could not make head or tail of it' they had told the Operations Division of this unusual message. In 1936 James told Chatfield, referring to this sortie and insisting on the superiority of line of-sight intelligence: 'These wonderful modern inventions, the plane, wireless, cryptography, *may* assist, but *nothing* can give the same *assurance* as the 'frigate' off the enemy coast.'[11]

According to Beesly 'Room 40 ... must at least share some of the blame, because they were now being consulted and Operations were beginning to pay attention to their opinions.'[12] This was perhaps a 'damned if you do and damned if you don't' kind of judgment and Operations, who were in the last analysis responsible for sending orders to Beatty, were theoretically equally to blame. Until *Moltke* broke wireless silence, intelligence of the HSF movements was sketchy to say the least and the DCNS, Fremantle, responsible for surface warfare, might have considered it insufficient to order the Fleet to sea.

Marder acidly described Fremantle as 'a flag officer of no extraordinary abilities upon whom Fortune smiled beyond his deserts.'[13] It is difficult to understand why he did not advise Beatty earlier that the HSF might be at sea and why the Grand Fleet was not brought to one hour's readiness at the same time as the Harwich Force. If Beatty was to intercept the HSF, he would have had to have sailed before midnight on April 23 in extremely unsatisfactory weather conditions, in heavy fog at night, and with the Admiralty having no firm indication of Scheer's position.

There had certainly been an intelligence failure in the HSF. Scheer chose the date of the operation on the basis of faulty intelligence from his submarines. Throughout the war German intelligence had continually been inept. The classic instance, often quoted, was their complete failure to discover the serious mutiny in the French Army in the summer of 1917. The Admiralstab never seems to have enlisted the services of German Consuls in neutral countries as Hall had done with considerable success, notably in Holland. The German Consuls in Norway could have provided the Admiralstab with accurate details of the departures of westbound, and the arrivals of eastbound, convoys in Norwegian ports. With this intelligence he could have timed his operation either a day earlier or a day later to coincide with the actual convoy movements and could have inflicted serious losses in consequence. He appears not to have known that the Grand Fleet had moved from Scapa to join the battlecruisers in the Firth of Forth on April 12, less than 10 days before his sortie and consequently that Beatty could have been in position to cut off his retreat. Subsequent knowledge of this move may have been one reason why the HSF never attempted another sortie against the convoys.

In his biography James was highly critical of the HSF's lack of enterprise and in particular its failure to use its fast and modern battlecruisers effectively as commerce-raiders – a role for which they were ideally suited. The Grand Fleet was indeed fortunate that the HSF let these opportunities slip.[14]

Naval oil supplies

As Assistant to the Controller of the Navy, Hall had been involved in the radical decision (strongly supported by Churchill) that the Queen Elizabeth class of fast battleships, then on the Admiralty drawing boards, should be oil-fuelled, unlike all previous capital ships, which had been coal-fuelled. The Queen Elizabeths, a technical tour de force and a mainstay of the Navy in both world wars, could never have achieved their top speed of 25 knots unless they had been oil-powered. Their Kriegsmarine contemporaries, the *Bayern* class, with a similar displacement and main armament, could only achieve 22 knots. As a forward-looking naval officer, Hall was well aware of the superiority of oil over coal as fuel for warships.

This decision was extremely controversial, as unlike the US, whose Navy had already ordered two oil-powered battleships, Britain had no indigenous oil (that she could extract) and ample supplies of coal. Powerful figures inside and outside the Admiralty fervently opposed any switch from coal to oil for the new battleships. To build support, Churchill set up a Royal Commission on Oil Supplies, chaired by Jacky Fisher, an enthusiast for oil. The commission reported in December 1912, supporting the decision that the Queen Elizabeths should be oil-powered and recommending the creation of a massive oil reserve for the Navy. In 1914 the Admiralty purchased a 51% interest in the British-owned Anglo-Persian Oil Company (APOC), with the objective of safeguarding naval oil supplies.

As DNI, Hall was acutely conscious of the importance of oil supply, notably British control over the Navy's oil supplies and their adequacy and security. In July 1916, he wrote: 'It should be a cardinal principal that under no circumstances should any oil bearing territory in British possessions fall into the control of a foreign or quasi-foreign oil company'[15] He had reason to worry. In 1915 German agents had cut the main APOC pipeline and at one time in 1917, at the peak of the U-boat offensive, the Navy's oil reserve fell as low as three weeks supply. To make matters worse, APOC proved an unreliable contractor, frequently failing to meet the Admiralty's oil specifications even as late as 1918. As a result the Admiralty threatened to stop buying APOC's oil unless its quality improved.

As the war continued Hall became extremely suspicious of the international oil companies, notably the American-owned Standard Oil and Shell, 60% owned by Royal Dutch. Room 40 had intercepted a telegram from Bernstorff to Berlin, dated January 1915 noting that 'The Standard Oil Company seeks to show itself obliging to us and desires to rescind the veto on the supply of kerosene from Holland or Sweden to Germany.' On one occasion the vigilant Captain Consett reported attempts by American oil interests in collusion with a Danish trading company to run the blockade.[16]

Hall had an anti-Semitic streak, not unusual among his contemporaries. In 1930 he wrote to his American friend, Percy Madeira, about a visit he and his brother Clifford intended to make to Canada: 'We mean to come over in a cabin ship … I myself prefer a smaller ship than these great leviathans and we're not likely to meet any Jews on board.'[17] He developed an unreasoning hatred for Sir Marcus Samuel, the head of Shell in London, and his right-hand man, Robert Waley Cohen. His distrust of Shell was totally unwarranted as its dominating force was not Samuel but the resolutely pro-allied Dutchman Henri Deterding, who was later awarded an honorary knighthood for his services to the allied cause. As Geoffrey Jones, the historian of the British oil industry wrote: 'Shell's impressive contribution to the war effort had provided a clear demonstration of the company's expertise and power, and of its devotion to Britain.'[18]

Hall's suspicion of Shell was shared by Rear-Admiral Edmund Slade, one of his predecessors as DNI, who after retiring from the Service had become a director of APOC representing the Admiralty's interest. At the same time, in a blatant conflict of interest, he had acted as the Admiralty's oil adviser. The two men worked closely together to promote the concept of a single British-owned oil company, excluding Shell, which would control all oil reserves within the Empire as well as those in Persia and Mesopotamia (now Iraq), at that time the largest undeveloped oil resources in the world. Slade embodied this concept in a paper, 'The Petroleum Situation in the British Empire'. The Fourth Sea Lord, Rear-Admiral Hugh Tothill, whose department was responsible for the Navy's oil supplies, took a contrary position, favouring Shell. The Admiralty's Assistant Director of Contracts had described the company in February 1916 as one of the 'most efficient and indeed indispensable contractors'. Hall and the NID were thus at loggerheads with the staff officers and Admiralty civil servants who had direct responsibility for oil procurement.

In August 1918 Slade succeeded in persuading Wemyss to place the paper, 'The Petroleum Situation in the British Empire', before the War Cabinet, together with a supporting note written by Hall:

> The importance of all-British controlled supply and distribution of fuel oil can hardly be overestimated and I view with some alarm the possibility of the Royal Dutch through their subsidiary company – Shell – having any interest in British oilfields.[19]

Slade's initiative resulted in a major row inside the Admiralty. He had managed to bypass not only Geddes but the Fourth Sea Lord and the Civil Lord, E. G. Pretyman, who represented the Admiralty on the Petroleum Imperial Policy Committee, set up to devise a long-term oil strategy for the Government. Both men were infuriated at Slade's efforts and protested strongly at the lack of consultation, Pretyman describing many of his claims as 'exaggerated or inaccurate'. On September 18 Geddes formally dissociated the Admiralty from Slade and his paper, supporting only '… the contention that the oil bearing districts of Mesopotamia and Persia are of very great national importance to us'. Reprimanding Hall for his excessive support for Slade, Geddes wrote 'DNI's interest in this matter is right and proper but must not exceed the function with which his office is charged.'[20] Hall and Slade had both overplayed their hands and this incident must have contributed towards the allegations, which were soon to surface, that Hall had developed a pronounced taste for intrigue.

Mutiny in the HSF

In the summer of 1918 the balance of the war altered decisively in the allies' favour. Their armies on the Western Front attacked on a wide front in August, grinding the Germans back. Ludendorff described August 4 as the 'darkest day in the history of the German Army'. By October the allies had forced the Germans back to the Belgian frontier and they had evacuated both Zeebrugge and Ostend. One by one, Germany's allies threw in the towel. Bulgaria asked for an armistice on September 30. Allenby's armies had cleared the Turks out of Palestine and, advancing into Syria, captured Damascus. On October 20th the Turkish Government sued for peace. Ten days later Gough-Calthorpe signed an armistice with their representatives on board the battleship HMS *Agamemnon* off the island of Mudros. On the same day Austria-Hungary signed a peace agreement with Italy.

The German General Staff, realising that they had lost the war, advised the Kaiser to seek an armistice. Room 40, reading the signal traffic between Berlin and Madrid and between the General Staff and the Army commanders in German-controlled territory in Russia, was closely following these developments. On October 5 Bell, briefed by Hall, sent a signal to Harrison: 'I learn from the usual unimpeachable source that the new German government intends making a peace offer to the President.'[21] Informed by Harrison, Wilson was not surprised when later that day the new Imperial Chancellor, Prince Max of Baden, using the Berlin-Madrid wireless link, approached him asking for terms; the second time that Room 40 intelligence had given him prior notice of an enemy peace bid.

As a precondition, the President insisted that all submarine attacks against merchant ships should cease immediately. On October 20 the Chancellor accepted this demand and that day Scheer, Chief of the Admiralstab since August when Holtzendorff had retired, recalled all the U-boats operating against merchant shipping. This order freed the entire submarine force for action against the Grand Fleet.

Two days later Scheer ordered Hipper, who had succeeded him as C-in-C of the HSF: 'The Forces of the High Seas Fleet are to be employed to strike a blow against the English Fleet.' He strongly believed that the HSF should attack the Grand Fleet one last time, regardless of cost. 'Even a Pyrrhic victory might alleviate the increasingly stringent demands which the Allies were now making.'[21]

Although the German call signs had again been changed in mid-September, Room 40 was able to correctly interpret the HSF and submarine movements. On October 22 the Admiralty briefed Beatty that the U-boats had been instructed to assemble in the middle of the North Sea and to attack warships by day. An Admiralty appreciation concluded that the recent British mining of the German-swept channels necessitated the U-boats waiting out at sea and that their dispositions had been selected to provide maximum opportunity to strike at the Grand Fleet. A large-scale operation by the HSF was clearly being planned. Two days later the War Staff expressed concern at: 'an unusually large number of messages in the most secret cipher on the night of 23–24 October but no purport.' On October 28, signals ordering five U-boats to take patrol positions, and to one of Hipper's Battle Squadrons to coal at Wilhelmshaven, were intercepted. Hall, like Wemyss, believed that the HSF would make one final attack on the Grand Fleet before peace terms were concluded. He feared that their surface forces might attempt to cut the protective nets in the Firth of Forth, thus allowing the U-boats to attack the Fleet at anchor. Around midnight on October 28, Hall and Fremantle jointly drafted this situation-assessment for Beatty:

> Dispositions of enemy submarines combined with position of their large minefield recently laid ... constitutes fairly decisive evidence of his desire to draw the Grand Fleet out ... no evidence as to how he proposes to achieve his object but evidence that no move of battlefleet can take place before ... tomorrow night. No enemy objective is apparent which will not involve great risk to him. Therefore he may confine himself to emerging from the Bight and returning after making us aware of his exit by W/T signals. Unlikely that enemy will risk fleet action until Armistice negotiations are settled one way or another. Press reports of German submarines proceeding home via the Norwegian coast probably emanate from Germany and are intended to conceal the existence of submarine trap.[22]

This analysis underrated the daring of the HSF in a situation approaching desperation. Hall and Fremantle had been influenced by the consistent caution and determination to avoid unnecessary risks the HSF had demonstrated throughout the War. The dispatch of this assessment highlights the extent to which the handling of intelligence inside the Admiralty and the extent to which the C-in-C was being kept informed had improved. At long last the days of the Chinese wall dividing Operations and Intelligence were over. The staffs of the two divisions were now working effectively together and NID's situation-analysis was being taken fully into account by the FSL and DCNS before Operations took their final decisions. Hall could take considerable satisfaction from this development, for which he had been in large measure responsible.

Hipper's intention was to take the entire HSF to sea and concentrate his cruisers and destroyers into two groups to attack British and allied warships in the Thames estuary and off the Belgian coast. They would be screened by his battleships and battlecruisers. His objective was to lure the Grand Fleet south into the path of his submarine patrols and the newly laid minefields as Hall and Fremantle had correctly predicted. The operation was planned for October 30. It never took place. Hipper ordered the HSF to assemble in Schilig Roads outside Wilhelmshaven on the afternoon of October 29.

The order resulted in considerable insubordination among the crews of the battleships and battlecruisers, which intensified into a mutiny during the night. A huge gulf separated the belief of the officer corps as expressed by Scheer – 'It is impossible for the fleet to remain inactive in any final battle that may … precede an Armistice. … it is a question of the honour and existence of the Navy to have done its utmost in the last battle'[23] – and the seamen who knew only too well the superiority of the British fleet and feared that they were to be sacrificed in a needless battle in a war Germany had already lost. The crew of the battleship *Markgraf* assembled on the forecastle, noisily shouting for peace and cheering Wilson. Although the mutiny had taken Hipper completely by surprise, he quickly came to terms with reality, cancelling the operation on the morning of October 30. He dispersed his three Battle Squadrons to Wilhelmshaven, Kiel and the Elbe, thus fortuitously spreading the mutiny to all the main German naval bases. By November 4 they were all flying the red flag.

At 8.33 am on October 30 Room 40 intercepted a signal stating that the HSF would remain at anchor until further notice and at 1 pm they learned that the operation had been postponed until the following day. Later that day the War Staff told Beatty that all submarine operations set for November 4 and 5 had also been cancelled, evidence that the sortie had been postponed for several days at least.

On the same day Hall warned Ed Bell that a source in Berlin, probably the Swedish Minister, had told his government that the termination of U-boat attacks on passenger ships was dependent on an armistice and that they would restart if the negotiations failed. He told Bell that the U-boats had not been recalled to their bases and they were being massed in the North Sea. In turn Bell reported to Harrison: 'Admiral Hall informs me that he had learned from an absolutely sure source that at a recent

Council in Berlin the German Emperor said: "During the peace negotiations or even after peace my U-boats will find an opportunity to destroy the English Fleet." Hall asked to be excused from divulging the source of this astonishing information but he assures me that it is as certain as the wireless to Madrid and he dictated what I have quoted as the exact words used by the Emperor.'[24]

Room 40 was well aware of the mutiny. As the situation deteriorated, the HSF abandoned any attempt at wireless silence and from November 1 onwards the cryptographers, shocked at the evidence that the officers were losing control, intercepted a succession of signals detailing courts martial and listing deserters. By November 4 the situation was almost beyond redemption and on the next day Hipper ordered all codebooks and ciphers locked up and that signals should only be decoded by officers. During the evening Wemyss told Beatty of 'indications of a revolution at Kiel. … Submarine HQ has not yet been affected'. At 2.30 am on November 6, Captain Andreas Michelsen, commanding the U-boats, ordered his submarines in the Baltic 'to fire without warning on all ships flying the red flag. The whole of Kiel is hostile. Occupy exit from Kiel harbour'. He instructed his U-boats to allow no ship to proceed. Later that day Hipper attempted to restore order, signalling his Admirals and Captains: 'Admiralstab in conjunction with the Government has ordered the resistance to be broken with all available forces. Red Flag is to be treated as enemy.'[25]

Meanwhile Hall was using the mutiny to exercise his talent for deception one last time. He prepared bogus photographs of British warships flying the Red Flag, which his agents in Holland and Denmark smuggled across the German frontier and circulated in Kiel and Wilhelmshaven, announcing that the Royal Navy had also mutinied and would unite with their German colleagues in overthrowing the old order. This ruse resulted in the fire-eating Michelsen telling his U-boat commanders on November 6 that a British squadron flying the red flag would arrive in Kiel later that day, which he would greet with a salvo of torpedoes.

By November 7 the mutiny was rapidly spreading to the cruisers that had previously remained loyal and Soldiers and Sailors Councils were in the driving seat at most German ports. On the following day Beatty was told that the Admiralstab had effectively caved in and was working with the Councils. The mutiny which had started in the Navy had turned into Red Revolution, which swept across all Germany from Schleswig-Holstein to Bavaria and from Silesia to the Rhineland. On November 10 the Kaiser abdicated and on the next day the Armistice was signed. On the Eleventh Hour of the Eleventh Day of the Eleventh Month, the fighting ceased.

Under the terms of the Armistice, the naval terms of which had been negotiated by Wemyss, the entire U-boat force would be surrendered to

Tyrwhitt at Harwich and the surface fleet was to be interned in British waters under the control of the Royal Navy. Beatty and his officers were bitterly disappointed that the HSF had not come out to fight. As he wrote to a friend on the day after the armistice: 'The Fleet, my Fleet is broken-hearted ... All suffering from a feeling of something far greater than disappointment, depressed beyond measure.' Marder commented: 'The feeling of incompleteness was undoubtedly caused by the fact that the fruits of victory at sea had been won without a latter-day Trafalgar.'[26]

On the day the HSF surrendered, November 21, Beatty staged a veritable coup de theatre. Alastair Denniston was sent to Rosyth to represent NID and Room 40 and to act as the C-in-C's interpreter. He quickly formed the opinion that 'Sir David Beatty is a very wilful man, and has no mercy on a man or nation he despises.' Denniston graphically described the events of that memorable day:

> ... at 7 a.m. I went on deck and was much surprised to find that we were now outside May Island, in fact at sea ... when action stations was sounded at 9 a.m ... I found myself on the signaling bridge where the Admiral had his sea cabin ... At 9:30 a.m. the Hun ships were first spotted about 5 miles away and then the thrills began. The first lot (the battlecruisers, who had fought so well at Jutland) were the Admiral's particular pets for he had been close to them, but never had enough time to examine them so closely. Everyone was pointing out features in the ships they had noted ... As the rest of the fleet came along the C-in-C dictated his signal to the Admiralty that he had taken over the German Fleet. It was a dramatic signal but he wished he could have wired he'd sunk the lot in fair fight, and he said so, and a lot of other unpleasant things about them. Then the whole British fleet turned round which made the Q.E the leading ship, and we proceeded towards the Forth. Once inside the Q.E. stopped, and the climax of the day arrived. Close on the south side of us the Germans passed, in very good order, but silent and sullen, hardly a man to be seen on deck, their flags flying for the last time, for the C-in-C now made his second signal that the German flag had to come down at sunset, and not to be hoisted till further orders. On the North side of us ship by ship went the British Fleet including the American squadron. ... Every ship was dressed, the bands were playing, and as they passed cheered Beatty who stood greeting them from the bridge. The First Battle Squadron rounded up the Huns ... leading them to the fixed anchorage. ... Then the Q.E. put on full speed, and once again passed the English Fleet full of beans and cheering ... after mooring the Admiral came down and this time his crew rushed to cheer him ... acknowledging the cheers he cried 'I always told you they'd have to come out.'
>
> At 6 in the evening we had the thanksgiving service on the quarterdeck under the huge 15 in. guns. It was quite dark ... the deck was lit by two arc lamps and there about 1000 men, leaving their work for about half an

hour assembled, and did really the most English thing that could be done – the thing I doubt whether any other nation would have done. And that ended 'der tag', the toast of the German Navy since its beginning.[27]

Victory at sea

Despite the setbacks and the frustration so keenly felt in the Grand Fleet at their failure to win a decisive battle over the HSF, the Royal Navy had won the war at sea. While the Kriegsmarine had descended into the slough of disgrace, the officers and men of the Navy, to quote the words of the wise medieval Bishop, had once again 'kept the sea which is the walle of England' as their forebears had in the days of Drake and Nelson and as their successors, who were to be tested to the full, were to do in World War II.

The Service's greatest triumph had been the defeat of the U-boats, a dangerous challenge to the very survival of Britain. Their success resulted from a combination of anti-submarine measures including convoy, the development of effective anti-submarine weaponry, notably hydrophones and first-generation sonar, vigorous minelaying and excellent intelligence. The successful integration of operations and intelligence in the ASWD had established what, was in effect, a new frontier, the forerunner of the hugely successful Operational Intelligence Centre in World War II. Hall, Room 40 and the Naval Intelligence Division had played a vital role in this achievement. Hall told his sister in 1941: 'It is by sea and sea alone that our salvation depends; the army will finish off the matter with the air force but neither can do anything unless we are successful at sea.'[28]

The importance of intelligence in anti-submarine operations was demonstrated anew in World War II. After Bletchley Park broke the naval ENIGMA in the spring of 1941, merchant shipping losses fell sharply from an average of almost 300,000 tons January to June to 105,000 tons in July to December. Pressed by Donitz, the German cryptographers added a fourth rotor to ENIGMA in February 1942 and it took Bletchley until December to crack the new system. Average monthly losses, which had risen to 456,000 tons in 1942, fell to 138,000 in 1943, through improved intelligence, the creation of the Escort Groups, the elimination of the air gap in the Mid-Atlantic and the provision of effective radar to Coastal Command and the US Naval Air Force.

Three of the greatest tributes to Hall came from Americans. Ed Bell put it in a nutshell: 'We gave the cards to Reggie to play and he played the hand at his own time and in his own way but damned well ...'[29] Marder named him one of the five outstanding Naval figures of the war, '... a genius in his own sphere and brilliantly successful' and one of only three Admirals of whom he was entirely uncritical, the others being

Wemyss, the master administrator, and Tyrwhitt, the outstanding sea commander of the war.[30] In March 1932 Admiral Sims, who had worked so closely with Hall, wrote regretfully declining an invitation to a dinner to be given in Hall's honour in New York

> ...I should dearly love to ... greet the Admiral to whom we owe so much for the wonderful success, during the Great War, of these unique services.
>
> Though the very nature of these services renders it impossible to estimate their full importance, we naval men know that they were of incalculable value to the cause of the Allies in blocking and defeating the very dangerous submarine campaign against the wholly essential lines of supply.
> It is unpleasant to reflect upon what might have been the result but for the uncanny ability of this great Sherlock Holmes.
> Please ... express to him my profound admiration for him as a man and as a naval officer, and the gratitude of all the Yankee sailors whose efforts in co-operating with John Bull's Navy were so greatly aided by his vision and advice, and by his secret knowledge of enemy intentions ...[31]

In one other less dramatic but equally important respect, Hall's insistence on maintaining a high level of security and in protecting his sources including the all-important decrypts had been totally vindicated. The Kriegsmarine and the German Foreign Office had never realised that, day in and day out for most of the war, Room 40 had been intercepting and decoding their signal traffic. Their successors would repeat the same mistake with ENIGMA in World War II. In a remarkable expression of loyalty to their country, to their service and to their chief, no one in the NID, naval officer and civilian alike, from the most important member of staff to the most junior secretary, had ever betrayed security. During his visit to the Grand Fleet, Denniston had been pleasantly surprised to find that Room 40 had managed to keep its activities such a tightly-guarded secret:

> ... for the last four years I had considered myself, and the department in which I worked, a very important cog in the machine; now for the first time I ran across the 'business end' of the weapon and I realised most strongly what a little cog we were. Practically no one I met had any idea of the existence of such a cog, which was satisfactory to know, as we had tried to conceal our identity. I had to keep a straight face and lie right well to many an old friend ... who wanted to know what my job was.[32]

Hall's contribution to the political and diplomatic outcome of the war, notably by, but certainly not limited to, his adroit handling of the Zimmermann telegram, was equally significant. Eloquent tributes to his achievements came from the Foreign Office. Hardinge, the Permanent Under-Secretary, wrote when he retired:

> I would like to express our appreciation of the ever-willing and invaluable help which he has always given me. It goes without saying over so wide a field as that in which foreign relations and naval intelligence have a common denominator, there have been differences of opinion, but it is due to the DNI's personal charm and loyalty that they have left no ill feeling on either side; in the far more numerous matters in which there has been complete agreement his advice and co-operation have been as useful as his resourcefulness and energy have been encouraging. He will be a great loss to the many friends he now counts within these walls. I have written these few words because they voice not only my own feelings but those of the Foreign Office as a whole.[33]

Three days after the Armistice, Sir Rennell Rodd, the Ambassador to Italy, told Balfour:

> At moments like the present when one is rejoicing at the great results and must think of those who have assisted in bringing them about, I feel an impulse to record an unsolicited testimonial to the valuable work which Sir Reginald Hall did here in organizing with the Italian Naval Authorities a special secret information service. During the last week or two it has been a great value for us to obtain rapid and sure information of what was going on on the other side of the Adriatic, and I don't think either we or the Italians should have had much of it if it had not been for the system which he devised and induced the Italians to work. Probably very few people know of this or would give him credit for all he did.[34]

Ernest Maxse, the Consul-General in Rotterdam, who had been one of Hall's most effective agents and who had hoped that he would one of the naval representatives at the Peace Conference, wrote on learning of his retirement:

> … I hope you will allow me to say that I think your departure from the Admiralty almost a national disaster … It is my genuine and honest conviction, after more than three years work in connection with your Department, that your personality is practically irreplaceable … However I cannot let the opportunity pass without thanking you most heartily and most warmly for the strong and permanent support you have afforded me … and I feel that I'm losing, not only a friend, but a very strong support by your departure.[35]

Hall's retirement from the Navy at the very height of his fame and in the hour of the victory to which he had made such a signal contribution has been interpreted as a decision by his superiors to dispense with his services. A number of reasons have been put forward. W. F. Clarke maintained that Wemyss had discovered Hall's part in getting rid of Jellicoe and that he had decided that he too had to go. Clarke, often acid about his colleagues in NID and Room 40, is an unreliable witness. At different times, he had described Ewing as a 'first-class brain' and 'a stupid and conceited little man'; his story is manifestly unlikely. Wemyss had brought Richmond to the Admiralty to fill the new appointment of Director of Training and Staff Duties, although it was common knowledge in the Service that he had consistently advocated Jellicoe's removal. Even after Richmond had tactlessly offended a large number of officers in the Admiralty, Wemyss had given him the command of the battleship HMS *Erin* as compensation for removing him from this post.

James, who was as close to Hall as any man, wrote: 'He had openly expressed his opinion that Beatty should take Wemyss's place as one of the British representatives at the Peace Conference and this proved his undoing.'[36] The wording is ambiguous and the author can find no corroborating evidence.

Relations between Wemyss and Beatty had deteriorated in the last weeks of the war as Beatty, wrongly in the view of many naval historians, had tried to usurp some of the FSL's prerogatives, notably in deciding the future of the German fleet. Wemyss had succeeded in restoring at least the semblance of an agreement on these contentious issues but as Hall was Beatty's most senior and prominent supporter inside the Admiralty, he was inevitably caught in the crossfire.

On January 20 1919 Wemyss wrote to Hall on his retirement:

> I cannot let you leave the Admiralty without letting you know how much I appreciate all the good work you have done during my short reign as CNS. I have not always agreed with your views but I have always realised your breadth of view and I have much benefited by our many talks together. I have no recollection of any interview during the last 18 months that wasn't altogether pleasant.[37]

Rumours had circulated in the Admiralty and the Service clubs of some serious disagreement between the two and Wemyss's last sentence was presumably meant to squash these. But Wemyss was not the type who could have been as devious as to write such an amicable letter to a man whose career in the service he had just terminated and not mean it.

Hall had hoped to attend the Peace Conference as its expert on intelligence, a post for which he had credentials which no one else could even approach. His intuitive mistrust of the Germans and his extraordinary ability to read the German leadership's mindset would clearly have been extremely valuable assets to the allied delegations. His influence and experience might have helped avoid some of the errors made at Versailles, which Franklin Roosevelt believed in the 1920s 'had been both too hard, burdening Germany ... with obligations it ... could never fulfill, and too soft, because it could not do enough to keep Germans from wishing for war and being able to wage it'.[38]

Wemyss, 'that very rare bird among British naval officers, a First Sea Lord who could deal with his own and other Services and with kings, presidents and prime ministers',[39] had used his diplomatic skills to conduct the naval negotiations leading up to the Armistice. He had determined, not entirely unreasonably, that he and he alone, would represent the Navy at Versailles. It is possible he did not want Hall, who had won the admiration as well as the friendship of many of the principal allied leaders, to steal any of his thunder and he did not include him in the delegation.

The powerful Admiralty civil servants surely cannot have been sorry to see the back of Hall. He once wrote: 'The civilians strongly resent their loss of control of the Navy and hate to see it passing into naval hands – so we are always here engaged in a mimic trench warfare. It keeps one's hands in but is wearing.' He told another friend: 'The only place I can't get assistance is here and the Secretariat who know nothing of Intelligence work block everything. I shall go up in a blue flame shortly.'[39]

His unorthodox methods, his bypassing of accepted procedures to bring additional wireless stations into commission and his constant demands to increase the establishment of the NID had brought him into conflict with the civil servants. Such unprecedented ventures as the chartering of yachts for covert intelligence operations, the purchase of a large quantity of the best champagne to win influence in Spain and the payment of bounties to the NID divers for recovering code and cipher books from U-boats and Zeppelins must have infuriated the Secretariat beyond belief at a time when they were trying to extract increased budgets from the always reluctant Treasury. The Admiralty supply departments would have taken his support for Slade's over-ambitious initiative as evidence that he was exceeding his authority. Jellicoe supporters inside the Admiralty must still have resented Hall's advocacy that a change of First Sea Lord was desirable.

The real reasons for Hall's retirement are much more prosaic than the conspiracy theorists suggest. He had never held a sea command as an Admiral and indeed he was medically unfit to go to sea. After four years as DNI he was due for relief and, with the size of the Navy and particularly of the NID, which no longer had to monitor the now interned HSF, reducing following the Armistice, he could not expect to stay on the active list for more than a short time.

Three days after the armistice, Bell wrote to Harrison:

Hall expects to be on the job and doing his present work for some months at least after peace is declared. His staff will be cut down as the German Fleet will not need his kindly intentions as it has done in the past but the work in which we are particularly interested will go on as usual. Once he has cleared it up which will be, I suppose, sometime within a year, he intends to retire from the Navy and go into Parliament. The Board of Admiralty have extracted a promise from him that he shall not do so as long as he is DNI on the grounds that he knows too much and they are not far wrong at that.[40]

On January 11, 1919 Geddes, who left the Admiralty to become Britain's first Minister of Transport, wrote to Hall:

It has been a great pleasure to work with you and to experience your great mental acumen.

Everyone in the country owes you a great debt of gratitude in my opinion for what you have done in the war, so little of which can be told.

I am happy in the belief that had I remained longer you would have delayed taking the step which you have and which deprives the Navy of the services of such outstanding ability.

Hall replied on the following day: 'Had you remained I would not have gone, at least not for a year or two. I will always look back on your time as First Lord as one of the great periods of naval administration.'[41]

In a later letter to Hall, Geddes added this tribute:

As your Chief at the Admiralty during the time that the submarine campaign ... was at its height, and during the anxious days which passed until the Navy eventually got it under, I had the closest touch with you, and I can say with perfect confidence that without the magnificent system of intelligence which you organised and ran, we could never have overcome the greatest menace ever launched against the Empire.[42]

These letters demonstrate that Hall's decision to retire was entirely voluntary. His friends in the City, notably Claud Serocold and Everard Hambro, had enabled him to achieve financial independence and enter the House of Commons, where he could continue to work in the best interests of both his country and his Service.

The erroneous opinion that the Admiralty had summarily dispensed with Hall's services was formed when his name did not appear in the Victory Honours List, although the Director of Military Intelligence and his predecessors all received the KCB. It was an omission which James called 'scurvy'.[43] His remark needs some qualification. Hall's service record shows that on February 13 1919: 'Their Lordships expressed appreciation of his valuable services as DID.' Wemyss may well have reasoned that, as few Rear-Admirals received knighthoods, this commendation together with the KCMG Hall had received in 1917 constituted sufficient recognition for his services and his contribution to the victory. He may have decided to use the Ks at his disposal to reward other deserving flag officers. As knighthoods required political approval, it is possible that some powerful figure outside the Admiralty, whom he had offended, objected to him receiving a further honour.

Beesly somewhat unreasonably criticised Beatty for not rectifying this oversight when he succeeded Wemyss as FSL later in 1919. In reality it would have been difficult for him to have written a retrospective citation for Hall's wartime achievements. Beatty seems to have been determined to make some amends to his 'old friend and colleague' by promoting him to the rank of Vice-Admiral and then to Admiral on the retired list during his tenure of office, appointments which were very largely in his prerogative as FSL.

The British Government has too often displayed ingratitude towards its intelligence chiefs. Hall at least did receive a knighthood unlike John Godfrey, his distinguished successor in World War II, who was kicked upstairs in 1942 and appointed Flag Officer Royal Indian Navy. Godfrey – made a scapegoat for the mutiny in the RIN in 1946, which he had quickly and effectively suppressed – was one of only two Vice-Admirals who served in World War II not to be knighted. Bill Cavendish-Bentinck, the extremely capable Chairman of the Joint Intelligence Committee in World War II, fared even worse. In 1947 the then Foreign Secretary, Ernest Bevin, vindictively dismissed him from the diplomatic service and confiscated his pension rights because he wanted to divorce his tiresome wife, who had deserted him before the war.

Although Hall did not receive any official recognition in 1919, academia gratefully acknowledged Hall's achievements. Amid distinguished company he received a DCL from Oxford and an LLD from Cambridge, the highest honour which either university could bestow. Beatty appears to have been the only other man to be so honoured by both Oxford and Cambridge that year. Hall received his degree at a Congregation held in October 1919. In accordance with tradition the Orator, John Edwin Sandys, described his achievements in Latin. The English translation read:

> The shrewdest ancient writer on war declared more than once that almost all the fortunes of war are unforeseen and doubtful; that he will be most successful who watches for an enemy's weak moment, who grasps it and holds it fast, who most swiftly detects his plans and forestalls them.
>
> Even schoolboys, I believe, are familiar with these words. But in war at sea, how hard it is to discover everything only one who has tried will judge.

How great then are the benefits we derived from him who, during so many years, always found out what the Fleets of the Germans were contriving, tracking down the size and objectives of their forces, who planted his own spies throughout all the world and thwarted those of the enemy, who passed on to our commanders that intelligence in reliance of which they finally achieved victory? In this activity, I believe, he who has kept himself unseen, has guided his life aright. But to-day we at long last do not leave his merit to remain obscure, and we salute it in his presence;
I bring before you WILLIAM REGINALD HALL, Knight.

Hall and Essie were deeply moved by this eloquent address, which so adroitly summed up his achievements at the NID in less than two hundred words.

The curtain falls

With the coming of peace, the Admiralty charladies, with their mops and brooms, were at long last allowed to give Room 40 a thorough cleaning. Many of its staff said their goodbyes as they prepared to take up their former lives and return to the House of Lords, academia, the City, the law, publishing, the church and a host of other occupations, all of them leaving with a sense of pride in a vital job well done. A select few, Denniston, Knox and Clarke, kept the torch of cryptology burning throughout the years between the wars.

On December 11 1918, Francis Birch organised a Room 40 victory and farewell concert. The cover of the programme depicted Blinker Hall with a happy smile on his face, listening behind a screen to two furiously arguing German Admirals (see picture section). A verse from one of the songs Birch composed read:

> While some say that the Boche was not beaten by Foch
> But by Winston or Ramsay Macdonald
> There are others who claim that the *coup de grace* came
> From the Knoxes (our Dilly and Ronald)
> It was Tiarks and Thring who with charts and with string
> Gave the U-boats their oily quietus
> Yet without the Lord Mayor in his Diplomats' lair
> The Huns *might* have managed to beat us
> Peace, Peace, who gave us peace?
> And how was our victory won?
> I know scores who aver it's through him (or through her)
> On the strictest QT it's entirely through me
> That the war is all over and done

On January 18, 1919 Captain Hugh Sinclair, 'a very strange and original character, a clever man who shone in command of men',[44] who had been one of Hall's Deputies, relieved him as DNI. Before he left the Intelligence Division for the last time, Hall demonstrated his remarkable capacity for foresight. Recalling the opportunism they had displayed on several occasions during the war, he warned the War Staff against Japanese expansionism, at that time a threat with scarcely the presence of a cloud on the horizon. Summoning his staff he thanked them for all that they had done and after discussing the successes and the disappointments they had shared together, he made a short speech wishing them well, ending with these words:

> Above all we must thank God for our victory over the German nation; and I want to give you all a word of warning. Hard and bitter as the battle has been, we now have to face a far, far more ruthless foe, a foe that is hydra-headed, and whose evil power will spread over the whole world, and that foe is Russia.[45]

Notes

1. Marder Vol 5 pp.43-45
2. Ibid p.60
3. Ibid p.63
4. James pp.166-167
5. TNA Geddes papers ADM 116/1808 A 290
6. CAC HALL 7/ 2/69 & 7/2/72 WRH to May Templar May 3 & 24 1941
7. TNA AIR 1/2387
8. Ibid
9. Marder Vol 5 p.150. Lecture to RN Staff College 1931
10. Ibid p.155 Beatty to Wemyss
11. Ibid pp.155-156 James to Chatfield March 12 1936
12. Beesly p.289
13. Marder Vol. 5 p.284
14. James *The Sky Was Always Blue* p.110
15. Jones *The Emergence of the British Oil Industry* p.186
16. NHB Portsmouth Consett Papers Consett to WRH Jan 25 1916
17. CAC HALL 1/6 WRH to Madeira June 28 1930
18. Jones p.189
19. TNA ADM 1/8537/240 July 30 1918. Quoted in Jones p.199
20. Jones pp.199-200
21. Beesly p.293

22 Ibid pp.294-295
23 Marder Vol 5 p.173
24 Beesly p.296
25 Ibid p.298
26 Marder Vol 5 p.188
27 CAC DENN 4/2 Denniston *Thirty Secret Years* pp.39-41
28 CAC HALL 7/ 2/60 WRH to May Templar Feb 16 1941
29 Beesly p.315
30 Marder Vol 5 p.322
31 Hall & Peaslee *Three Wars Against Germany* Sims to Peaslee pp.150-151
32 CAC DENN 4/2 Denniston p.39
33 James p.175
34 Beesly p.305
35 CAC HALL 1/1 Maxse to WRH December 6 1918 James pp.176-177
36 James pp.176-177
37 CAC HALL 1/1 Wemyss to WRH Jan 20 1919
38 Quoted in Michael Beschloss *The Conquerors* p.12
39 James p.176
40 NARA State Dept. papers Bell to Harrison Nov 14 1918
41 TNA ADM 116/1810 Geddes papers
42 Quoted in James p.179
43 James *The Sky Was Always Blue* p.112
44 Marder Vol 5 pp.201-202
45 James p.177

CHAPTER XVI
1919–43

In March 1919, Hall was elected to the House of Commons as the Conservative Member for the West Derby division of Liverpool. When he was Captain of HMS *Natal,* Hall had successfully shepherded the seriously damaged Liverpool sailing ship *Celtic Race* into Milford Haven during a fierce gale. His action had earned him a considerable reputation in the city, especially within its shipping community.

Hall's objective was to act as a voice at Westminster for the Navy and the Merchant Marine and he spoke frequently on naval issues. He voiced his opposition to the restrictions introduced under the Washington Naval Treaty, which he firmly believed were against the Navy's interests. He strongly advocated that the Navy should regain control of its air arm which had been lost with the formation of the RAF in April 1918 with disastrous consequences for British naval aviation. He was always listened to with considerable respect on all sides of the house.

Hall had stood for Parliament as a supporter of the Lloyd George coalition but like many Conservative MPs he had become disillusioned with the Prime Minister. He was one of the MPs who voted in October 1922 to break with Lloyd George. In March 1923 Andrew Bonar Law, Lloyd George's successor as Prime Minister, offered him the appointment of Principal Agent of the Conservative Party. He accepted against his own better judgment and the advice of many of his friends. His terms of reference were to control the Party's Central Office, to co-ordinate public relations and to oversee the selection of candidates.

Although the Conservatives had a comfortable majority in Parliament, Law's successor, Stanley Baldwin, called a snap election held on December 6 on the issue of protection. Hall was one of 88 Conservative MPs who were defeated. Although the Conservatives remained the largest party at Westminster, they lost their overall majority.

On January 1 1924 the Baldwin Government was defeated in a vote of confidence and Ramsay Macdonald became Britain's first Labour Prime Minister, whose minority Government was dependent on Liberal party support. Hall was unjustly made one of the scapegoats for the electoral defeat and he resigned in March 1924 from what was the only unsuccessful appointment of his career.

In August 1924 the Liberal party withdrew its support from the Macdonald Government over its decision to guarantee a loan to Russia. On October 8 it was defeated in a vote of no confidence in the House of Commons: Parliament was dissolved and a General Election set for October 29.

On September 15, Gregori Zinoviev, the leader of the Communist International, the Comintern, had written to the British Communist Party using inflammatory language and advocating an armed uprising in working-class districts. The letter was in the hands of MI6 by October 9 and Macdonald protested strongly to the Soviet *chargé d'affaires* in London. Hall's detractors have alleged that he was involved in leaking the Zinoviev letter to the *Daily Mail*, which published it on October 25, four days before the election. He had maintained close connections with the intelligence services and like many serving and former intelligence officers, he was deeply suspicious of Soviet intentions. Hall and Thomas Marlowe, the Editor of the *Mail*, had repeatedly co-operated in circulating disinformation during the war. Marlowe later wrote that he had originally learnt about the Zinoviev letter on the morning of October 23 in a telephone message from 'an old and trusted friend' who may well have been Hall. Marlowe never revealed the identity of his sources and the involvement of Hall or any other member of the intelligence services remains a conjecture.

Whenever any communication from the Comintern to their agents in Britain was published, they inevitably reacted by declaring that it was a forgery cooked up by British intelligence and the Zinoviev letter, in particular, has long been a staple of Communist demonology. However the letter reflected known Comintern policy and on balance it was probably genuine.

Hall was determined to return to Parliament should the opportunity arise. In June 1925 he returned at a by-election for the safe seat of Eastbourne. Essie Hall got a round of applause when she told the voters that they had chosen as good a man as she had years before. Over the next year, the crisis in the coal mining industry became a major political issue. The Baldwin Government attempted to deflect the dispute between the owners and the union by instituting a subsidy and by appointing a Royal Commission, whose report, advocating a small cut in wage rates, was unacceptable to the union. As the Government was unwilling to continue the subsidy indefinitely, deadlock had been reached. On May 1 1926 the coal owners effectively locked the miners out.

The Trade Union Congress (TUC) called out other unions in a General Strike from midnight on May 3. The evidence suggests that the TUC deliberately positioned the print, rail and transport unions in the frontline of the strike with the objective of severing the Government's communications with the public. On the evening of May 2, the *Daily Mail* compositors refused to set up a lead editorial criticizing the TUC, a breach of a tacit understanding between the publishers and the printing unions. The TUC refused the Government's demand that they disown this action, making the General Strike inevitable.

H. A. Gwynne, the editor of the right-wing *Morning Post*, reminded the Government that the *Daily Herald*, owned by the Labour party, had already undertaken to publish a TUC-oriented news sheet and that with the national newspapers on strike the Government's case was in danger of going by default. When Gwynne offered the Government the use of the *Post*'s printing presses, Baldwin quickly accepted, appointing Churchill Editor-in-Chief of the proposed news sheet. That night, Churchill commandeered the newspaper's facilities for the production of what he christened the *British Gazette*. In a night of brilliant improvisation 230,000 copies of the *Gazette*'s first issue had been printed and distributed by 6 am.

Hall was approached during the night to take charge of personnel. Implacably opposed to the strike and aware that Russia had advanced £2 million to the miners union, he accepted with alacrity, like an old warhorse called back from retirement to take up arms once again. Early the next morning, Hall was busy interviewing the legion of volunteers who had offered their services to the *Gazette*. His old chief, Beatty, provided 30 Engineering Room Artificers, who literally proved to be worth their wealth in gold.

Hall allocated those who had technical experience to production and those who either owned or had access to cars or vans as drivers to deliver the *Gazette* to newspaper wholesalers. His rapid powers of thought, his talent for man-management and for organising large numbers of men made him a focal figure in the *Gazette*'s operations. His electrifying presence, his blue eyes blazing as he toured the printing rooms and packing halls encouraging the staff to go that one yard further, was a vital factor in what proved to be a remarkably successful venture, run with energy like an operation of war.

Night after night the *Gazette*'s makeshift management team rose to the challenge. The circulation of its second issue more than doubled to 507,000. On May 10, when Hall became Chief of Staff of the British Gazette Organisation, the circulation broke through the million copy level and on the last night it was published (May 12) it had risen to a remarkable 2,209,000. In every issue the *Gazette* painted a vivid picture of a country successfully and cheerfully coping with the strike.

On May 11, the *Gazette* published an article headlined 'Triumph of Distribution', a glowing testament to its management and particularly the personnel function so adroitly directed by Hall:

> More than one million copies of the *British Gazette* were printed last night and distributed in all parts of the country. It is expected that this number will be exceeded tonight ... an achievement which is the best tribute to the success of the organization, which had to be so hastily improvised on Tuesday in countering the attempt to keep the nation in the dark by suppressing the newspapers ... it has been possible to produce the *British Gazette* day by day as a four-page paper giving a synopsis of the news for all parts of the country, and every day more difficulties have been overcome and production has gone more smoothly ... Distribution has been a task calling for no less ingenuity and resource than printing ...

On May 12 the TUC, recognizing that its effort had failed, called off the strike. The *Gazette* had enabled the Baldwin Government to decisively win the propaganda war and defend the principle of freedom of the press. Its success has generally been attributed to Churchill. The reality is more complex. A successful newspaper requires two ingredients: editorial excellence, which Churchill had provided in full measure, and effective and timely distribution, for which Hall must bear much of the credit. Once again, he had played a considerable part in a great affair. He and his colleagues had played vital roles in ensuring that the *Gazette* saw the light of day. They had carried on the great tradition of the press: the news must get out.

Gwynne had no reservations about Hall's contribution to its success. He wrote to congratulate him:

> I wish to tender to you and all those who helped you in the organization of the personnel of this office while we were bringing out the *British Gazette*, our warmest thanks for the splendid manner in which you brought order out of chaos, and secured the smooth working of an emergency organization. But for you, I am quite sure that the difficulties of bringing out the *British Gazette*, would have been almost insuperable ... We shall never forget what you have done and already the tradition in the office is to talk of our Admiral.[1]

Following a serious operation, Hall decided not to run again in the 1929 General Election. Baldwin, who was greatly in his debt following his contribution to the success of the *Gazette*, offered him a peerage. He reluctantly decided to decline as the honour would be awarded for his political services and not for his achievements in the war.

In August 1925 Amos Peaslee, an American lawyer met Hall. Peaslee was the lead attorney, acting for both major plaintiffs in the famous Black Tom Case which dated back to July 1916 when the freight terminal of the LeHigh Valley Railroad in New York Harbor, including thirty-seven railcars packed with explosives, was blown up. Six months later, the assembly plant of the Canadian Car & Foundry Company in Kingsland, New Jersey, where munitions for Russia were being packed for shipment, was also totally destroyed. Black Tom and Kingsland were the most spectacular of nearly 200 acts of espionage executed by German agents between 1914 and 1917 at a time when America was still neutral.

Under the terms of the Peace Treaty between the US and Germany a Mixed Claims Commission (MCC) was set up to adjudicate on each country's war claims. The MCC was comprised of two Commissioners, one each from the US and Germany, and an American Umpire, whose decision was to be final.

Peaslee found that the German Foreign Office, despite their Treaty obligations, was unwilling to assist in a case which highlighted their repeated breaches of American neutrality. Aware of the existence of the Room 40 decrypts, he contacted Hall through an introduction from Admiral Sims, Hall's old ally in 1917-18. Hall obtained the Admiralty's agreement for Peaslee to use the documents he needed. He selected 264 intercepts, relating to German involvement in sabotage in America, directly incriminating several known agents in the Black Tom and Kingsland cases and revealing the involvement of top German diplomats, including Bernstorff, Eckardt and Luxburg.

Under the rules of discovery the existence of the decrypts had to be disclosed to the German Government. Their first reaction was to contest their authenticity. The Foreign Office did not in the event, react to this threat, realising that the testimony of Hall, Serocold, de Grey and others would enable the American plaintiffs to destroy their case. Conceding that the statements of Admiral Hall would not be disputed, the Germans then attempted to claim that the sabotage at Black Tom and Kingsland had been the result of unauthorised actions committed by individuals. The MCC ruled that America had to demonstrate exactly who had been responsible for Black Tom and Kingsland as the decrypts did not specifically incriminate any German agents.

In January 1929 Peaslee told Hall that he had interviewed two important German witnesses: 'A more humiliating and crushing collection of evidence I can hardly imagine, but I wonder if the Commission, in its solicitude for the underdog, will see it that way.' Peaslee was putting his finger on one of the difficulties under which he and his team were working. Hall recounted that when a prominent German was asked: 'What will you to do if you lose the war?' he replied 'We will organise sympathy.'[2] Throughout the case, the German lawyers consistently played the sympathy card with telling effect.

From the inception, they resorted to downright fraud. In effect, the Americans were forced to contest the case on what was not a level playing field. Twice, in 1930 and 1932, despite Peaslee's compelling evidence, the Commission inexplicably ruled in Germany's favour. As a result the case dragged on for nearly fifteen years.

In 1938, the Umpire, Supreme Court Justice Owen Roberts and a newly appointed American Commissioner, Christopher Garnett, agreed that the Commission's earlier decisions were invalid and that the action should be reopened. The Commission met in Washington in January 1939 to hear the case for the US, presented by a former Attorney-General, William D. Mitchell. On June 15 1939 the Commission handed down its decision in a masterly 480-page judgment written by Garnett. He found Germany guilty of sabotage at both Black Tom and Kingsland and also of presenting a fraudulent defence at the earlier hearings. The marathon endeavour had finally ended in total victory for the Americans.

Hall cabled Peaslee: 'Heartiest congratulations to you Greatheart. Triumphant vindication and justification of your many years work.'[3] The access to the decrypts, which Hall had provided, had been essential to the success of the case. His constant encouragement and participation in preparation, his unparalleled knowledge of the world of intelligence and espionage and his remarkable insight into the German approach had been invaluable. On October 30 1939, the plaintiffs were awarded the then unprecedented damages of $55m, including accrued interest.

Hall received a fee for his services of at least $120,000 (approximately £30,000 at the then rate of exchange and equivalent to at least £750,000 in today's currency), which he used to set up a fund for the widows and children of naval officers. It is fitting that a small portion of the proceeds extracted as compensation for German crimes should have been used to help the dependents of naval officers who had perished in the struggle against Nazi Germany and her allies.

After he left Parliament, Hall moved to the New Forest where he lived for the rest of his life. He became a passionate gardener and his grandson recalled that he would retire to his study at nine o'clock every morning to deal with a mass of correspondence, much of it from his old naval colleagues.

In December 1932 Essie Hall died suddenly from a heart attack when playing bridge. Her death after 38 years of an exceptionally happy marriage was totally unexpected and for Hall, a devastating blow from which he never fully recovered.

The deep-seated distrust of Germans, which Hall had developed as DNI, had been reinforced by his experience of their duplicitous behaviour during the Black Tom case. He wholeheartedly detested both Nazism and Communism, seeing them as two sides of the same dangerous totalitarian coin.

He was always opposed to appeasement and he persistently argued for rearmament, believing that a strong Britain was the best guarantee for continued peace in Europe. Nor did Hall harbour any illusions about

Japanese militarism, to which he had alerted the Admiralty in 1918. He correctly forecast that they would move south to take over the Dutch East Indies and Malaya for their abundant raw materials.

After the outbreak of war in 1939, Hall was active behind the scenes and, with his strategic insight and considerable experience of intelligence, his advice was keenly sought both in London and Washington. In November 1941 he told his sister: 'I had a very busy time in Town ... I had a number of quite unexpected conferences and found myself still at work when midnight struck one night – and this is something quite new for me, but I hope the result will be good: anyhow they were good enough to consider my proposals as being the only decent ones. I can't tell you the subject but you can guess that it was something on my old lines of the last war.'[4] Despite his health, he joined the local Home Guard, serving, suitably, as their Intelligence Officer.

In July 1943, his always questionable health broke down when he was in London. Too frail to be moved home to Hampshire, Claud Serocold, ever loyal and ever generous, rendered one last service to his old Chief. As a Director of the hotel he put him up in a suite in Claridge's where, looked after by a devoted Irish nurse, his strength ebbed away.

In the last hours of his life, something went wrong with the plumbing and a plumber arrived to put matters right. He proved to be a tall lugubrious individual, clad, as it was Claridge's, in an impeccable black suit, white shirt and black tie. He was somewhat startled to hear the voice, which in his prime had struck the fear of God into defaulters and which had been listened to with respect by the most powerful men in the land, intone: 'If you're the undertaker, my man, you're too early.' The old Admiral's renowned sense of humour had never deserted him.

Death finally came for Hall quietly and almost with respect for such a redoubtable adversary shortly before midnight on October 22. It was his body which had failed, not his mind, nor his formidable fighting spirit, which had remained unbroken to the end. His obituary in the *Manchester Guardian* included this vivid pen-portrait of Hall at the height of his career:

> It was in October 1914 that Admiral Hall began the historic period of service as Director of Naval Intelligence ... He had a flair for the work that could only be described as genius. He was a man of contradictions and could assume any personality. In appearance white haired, tiny and benevolent even at the early age of 47 ... He was both frail and tireless. To save a few minutes necessary to get to a car, if he was wanted at the Admiralty during the night he had a motor-scooter on which he used to dash through the deserted streets to his office when he was called. He could be, in conversation, a simple unassuming country gentleman or as dictatorial as a

Prussian sergeant major. His cross examinations of certain German submarine prisoners in the privacy of his room at the Admiralty were as ruthless as anything the Old Bailey has ever seen ...[5]

Before the war Hall had spent every winter outside England seeking warmer and drier climates for the sake of his health. In December 1939 he told Peaslee: '...the idea of warm sun and dry air goes very near to making me throw up everything and come over.' And four months later, 'My doctors insist on my not spending another winter in England.'[6] As the war intensified his reluctance to leave the country increased. Like the old warhorse he was and knowing the sacrifices that would be demanded of younger men and women in the services he was determined to stay on the bridge until the bitter end.

He had once jokingly remarked: 'I could not have my grandchildren asking: "What did you do in the war?" and have had to reply that I went to America when trouble came.'[7]

In making this altruistic decision, Hall had, in effect, signed his own death-warrant and in retrospect his achievement in surviving four successive English winters was a remarkable tribute to his determination and his powers of endurance.

He was laid to rest alongside Essie, who had gone nearly eleven years before him.

Home is the Sailor, Home from the Sea.

Notes

[1] James, p.186
[2] Hall & Peaslee pp.110 & 293
[3] Ibid. p.187
[4] CAC HALL 7/3/92 WRH to May Templar November 9 1942
[5] *Manchester Guardian*, October 23 1943, reproduced by kind permission of Guardian Newspapers.
[6] Hall & Peaslee pp.306 & 311
[7] CAC HALL 1/6 WRH to Madeira February 17 1941

CHAPTER XVII

The Hall Legacy

Hall's contacts in the intelligence world remained extremely close throughout the interwar years, particularly after his old friend and shipmate, Hugh 'Quex' Sinclair, was appointed Director-General of SIS in 1923 following the death of Mansfield Cumming. In 1922 the control of the Government Code and Cipher School, known by its initials GC & CS, the successor to Room 40, by then principally involved in reading diplomatic signal traffic, passed from the Admiralty to the Foreign Office. In practice GC & CS operated under the aegis of SIS and reported to Sinclair. The Room 40 veteran, Alastair Denniston remained its Director until 1942 and worked wonders in keeping the organisation operating despite the severe budgetary cuts enforced by an unsympathetic Treasury.

Of those who followed Hall as DNI, only Sinclair came anywhere near to matching his ability and influence. Many of the Directors who had followed W. H. Hall had gone on to fill top positions in the service, and one of them, Battenberg, had served as FSL. In contrast, after 1918 the appointment of DNI was too often given to flag officers as a pleasant prelude to retirement, Donald Maclachlan, who served in the NID in World War II and who wrote the acclaimed *Room 39*, the history of naval intelligence in that war, noted when reviewing Willie James's biography of Hall, that this practice even continued after 1945.

The Division's significance inevitably declined. In 1924 its establishment had fallen to only 46 and it became but a shadow of what it had once been. Its days of glory in World War I when Hall had made it a focal point in the intelligence world and as Roger Keyes wrote, 'one met every kind of interesting person in his room'[1] were no more.

As a result few senior officers had any knowledge of or insight into intelligence. In October 1935 one Admiral, who did understand intelligence and who had served as one of Hall's key subordinates, was appointed DCNS. Willie James's career had prospered in the intervening years; he had commanded the cruiser HMS *Curlew* and the battleship HMS *Royal Sovereign* and he had served as Chief of Staff on the China Station to his father-in-law, Admiral Duff. (During his time in the Far

East he had, like so many naval officers, grown to distrust the Japanese.) He had been Admiral-President of the Naval War College and he had been closely associated with the then FSL, Chatfield, serving as his Chief of Staff in both the Atlantic and Mediterranean Fleets. Before coming to the Admiralty he had a successful period in command of the prestigious Battlecruiser Squadron.

Disturbed by the decline of the NID, especially following the aggressive actions of the Italian government in the Abyssinian crisis, James set about its regeneration to enable it to meet the challenges of a new war. After the outbreak of the Civil War, Spanish Nationalist (and possibly German and Italian) submarines had been sinking merchant ships in the Mediterranean and the Admiralty needed to secure proof of their identity. The NID's existing resources proved inadequate for this task.

Remembering the successful co-operation between the Intelligence and the Anti-Submarine Warfare Divisions in which he had been closely involved in 1917–18, in June 1937 he appointed Paymaster-Lieutenant Commander Norman Denning, an officer of considerable ability, to set up what became the Operational Intelligence Centre (OIC). When he was stationed in Singapore in the early 1930s Denning had noticed a large number of Japanese fishing boats anchored in the harbour. In a remarkable display of lateral thinking, a quality he shared with Hall, he concluded that these craft were too numerous to constitute a viable fishing fleet and that they must therefore be engaged in intelligence work, preparing the ground for an invasion of Malaya from the land. NID's reaction was dismissive: 'This officer has too vivid an imagination.'[2] Imagination is a desirable quality in an intelligence officer, and subsequent events justified Denning's supposition.

Denning made a detailed study of the history of naval intelligence in World War I, particularly the achievements of Room 40. The disastrous consequences of the separation of operation and intelligence, most notably at Jutland, were fully apparent to him. He understood the imperative of integrating every aspect of intelligence, both cryptography and analysis, with operations at sea. Under Denning's superlative direction, the OIC, encompassing both surface and anti-submarine warfare and combining intelligence and operations, took shape, extending the scope of its predecessor organisation twenty years earlier. Growing from an original staff of five to seventy-five, it played an invaluable role in many naval operations, most notably during the pursuit of *Bismarck* in 1941 and in the victory of the Battle of the Atlantic in 1943. This extremely successful initiative owed much to and was inspired by Hall's pioneering work in developing an effective interface between intelligence and operations. Once again following in Hall's footsteps, James reinvigorated the Direction Finding and Y interception networks that had played such a useful part in World War I.

James's hand could also be seen in the invitation to Hall to address the Naval War College at Greenwich on Intelligence in Wartime. Speaking to a large audience, including representatives of the other services and the Foreign Office in March 1936, Hall summarized his principles of intelligence, which were to guide his successors during and after World War II and which remain valid today:

1. The acquisition of information about the enemy.
2. The double process of sifting truth from what is probably or demonstrably false – knitting together information to produce a balanced picture, which he added was not so easy.
3. Those in authority have to decide to use information to their best possible advantage, which he described as a troublesome task.
4. The necessity of covering up one's tracks when one is using information in order to prevent the enemy finding out how this information is being obtained.

Repeatedly referring to successful operations in World War I including the Zimmermann telegram, he stressed the importance of never breaking the lines of enemy communication: once you come across the line let it run on, adding that this was far safer than breaking it as then one has to find a new line and that is not so easy.

Hall addressed the importance of propaganda, noting that it could be used for a number of objectives:

1. To deceive the enemy in order to lead him to take a course of action for which you are prepared or to relieve pressure on a planned operation by inducing him to move his forces to resist an imaginary movement. He specifically quoted the instance of the Falkland Islands (see Chapter 5).
2. To destabilize enemy morale by undermining the confidence of the civilian population.
3. To induce neutral countries either to keep quiet or give assistance when required.
4. To counter enemy war aims by demonstrating what would happen if they were to win. He noted that this gambit had considerable effect on American opinion.[3]

Deception of the enemy, along lines which would have delighted Hall, was used to significant effect in World War II, notably in two spectacular confidence tricks. Firstly Operation Mincemeat, planned and executed by NID when the body of a dead man dressed in the uniform of a Major, Royal Marines, was dropped from a submarine off the Spanish coast and washed ashore under the nose of a particularly active German agent. The body was carrying forged documents which totally misled the German High Command into concluding that the projected invasion of Sicily would in fact take place in Sardinia and in Greece. (See *The Man who Never Was* by Ewen Montagu for the full story.) Secondly, Operation Fortitude, the misinformation disseminated before the Normandy invasion which misled the Germans as to its chosen location (see Chapter 8).

When Hall was giving evidence before the Dardanelles Commission in October 1916, he was questioned by one of its members, the former CIGS Field Marshal Lord Nicholson on an issue which has long plagued intelligence chiefs – the reliability of agents – to which he had clearly given much thought, notably when an agent's reports were uncorroborated.

> Nicholson: With regard to those agents you employ on secret service, of course they are paid. Are they not rather inclined to prophesy things which they think would please you rather than the other things?
> Hall: That is a danger we are always up against.
> Nicholson: When you get very good ones, of course the danger is less?
> Hall: If you can get an agent in a high position, you can generally get a cross-cut on him. One of the principal duties we have is to put together all the reports on a certain subject; and in fact the system really is this. You have an agent ... you take all his reports for a month; you check them through, and if out of 20 statements he makes 18 are correct and two wrong you count him as a 90 per cent man.[4]

1936 also saw the setting up of the organisation which by 1939 had developed into the Joint Intelligence Committee (JIC) whose objective was to co-ordinate the various British intelligence agencies. The initiative which created the organisation had originated with the Deputy Chiefs of Staff Committee on which James had represented the Admiralty. James and his opposite numbers had concluded that an ad hoc network of the type which Hall had ran in World War I, would no longer be effective and that it should be replaced by a more formal body. By September 1939 it included representatives of the three service intelligence divisions, the Foreign Office and the newly-formed Ministry of Economic Warfare, reporting directly to the Chiefs of Staff. Under its Chairman, the urbane and highly capable Bill Bentinck, seconded from the Foreign Office, the JIC performed a co-ordinating role strikingly similar to the one which Hall had pioneered in World War I. The JIC provided the War Cabinet and the Chiefs of Staff with a significant advantage with their analysis of intelligence on an inter-service basis over the German High Command, who lacked a similar organisation. Among his successes, Bentinck forecast almost to the exact day the timing of Hitler's invasion of Russia.

In February 1939 the DNI, Admiral Troup, retired and the then FSL, Sir Roger Backhouse, appointed Rear-Admiral John Godfrey to replace him. The choice proved inspired as Godfrey was the first DNI since Sinclair whose ability and dynamism was equal to Hall's. He had an outstanding record both in sea-going command and in staff appointments and had served as Deputy Director both of the Naval Staff College and of the Plans Division of the Admiralty. Like Hall before him, his last appointment before becoming DNI had been the command of a battle-cruiser, HMS *Repulse*, a happy and efficient ship in the Mediterranean Fleet. His successful tenure had been recognized both by Dudley Pound, then C-in-C in the Mediterranean, and by Andrew Cunningham, who as Vice-Admiral Battlecruiser Squadron had been his immediate superior. Cunningham wrote to him: 'I was sorry not to have seen *Repulse* again … I should have liked to say a few words to your ship's company to tell them what a high opinion I have of *Repulse*. It has been a great pleasure and privilege to have you in my squadron.'[5] Praise of this kind from ABC was praise indeed.

In March 1939 Hall visited Godfrey in his old room at the Admiralty. The two men had only met once before, in 1917, when Godfrey had been sent to London on a mission by Wemyss, then C-in-C East Indies and Egypt, on whose staff he was then serving. He had spent some time with the NID.

In his memoirs, Godfrey wrote:

> From then onwards we met frequently.[6] To no one am I more indebted than Reggie Hall … He came to see me on 27 March 1939 and thereafter very unobtrusively offered me full access to his great store of knowledge and judgment on this strange commodity, Intelligence, about which I then knew hardly anything. He realised that I needed contacts and these he produced in large quantities. It was through him that I met Sir Montagu Norman, the Governor of the Bank of England, Olaf Hambro, Chairman of Hambro's Bank and the two Rothschilds, all of whom helped me in a variety of fruitful and unexpected ways, particularly in the recruitment of wartime staff. Above all Hall warned me of some of the political pitfalls that lay in my path in wartime and experience soon convinced me that I had an awkward commodity to sell; that in 1939 the cupboard was bare and the DNI extremely vulnerable.[7]

Hall's warning to Godfrey was prophetic in view of his battles with Churchill, who consistently took an over-optimistic view of U-boat losses, about which the NID was sceptical, and as Godfrey was eventually to be kicked upstairs because of pressure from the Directors of Intelligence of the other services. 'My job had more kicks than half-pence … When in doubt I often asked myself what Hall would have done.'[8]

The exploits of NID and Room 40 in the previous war had made Hall a living legend among the staff of the division. Maclachlan wrote: 'The prestige of Jellicoe's DNI still stood high. In 1939 Admiral Sir Reginald Hall was still about the place, advising and helping.'[9] Some four weeks after his first meeting with Godfrey, Hall wrote to his sister May: 'I have been spending many days and nights with the new DNI, who has asked me to give him some pointers: he is starting on the right lines and gathering together many of my old staff ...'[10] Hall's inspiring presence in the NID while it was securing substantial increases in resources to enable it to function effectively in wartime must have been an immense boost to the morale of all who worked in the Division.

Paying tribute to Hall's veterans, Godfrey noted: 'Of those who worked in Room 40 I was to meet Denniston, de Grey, Frank Birch, Dilly Knox and Travis ... it was they plus Trench, Thring, Brandon, Clayton, Marjorie Napier and Sykes Wright, who carried on the tradition of 1918 which was to bear such ample fruit in 1941.'[11] Jock Clayton, who had been served with Godfrey in the Dardanelles campaign and who had retired as a Rear-Admiral, became Deputy Director of NID in charge of the OIC, where he was highly successful.

Thring, now in his sixties and his skills in no way abated, came out of retirement to take up his old post as head of the submarine tracking section of the OIC, staying on until 1941 when ill-health finally forced him to give up. The writer William Plomer, who was one of Marjorie Napier's colleagues in the Information Section, described her as 'a still youthful veteran of the previous World War' and Hall, a family friend, told May that she was taking up the same work as she had done in his time.

Hall had told Godfrey about Serocold and his contacts in the City, which he had found so useful, and of the many successful missions he had undertaken for the NID. Godfrey accepted his advice to recruit a Personal Assistant with a City background. Hall had introduced him to Montagu Norman, Governor of the Bank of England and Edward Peacock, Senior Partner of Barings, whom he asked to recommend a suitable candidate. Their selection of Ian Fleming proved as astute as it was at first sight, implausible. Fleming, like Serocold an old Etonian, who reputedly had only one regular client, had been bored by stockbroking: a square peg in a round City hole. In contrast Fleming developed a flair for intelligence work. He had a legion of connections inside and outside the City and an ability to speedily and compellingly draft the most complex memoranda. Godfrey and his successor, Edmund Rushbrooke, thought highly of him, entrusting him with substantial responsibilities, just as Hall had with Serocold and Herschell. Hall had initiated the events which had led to Fleming joining the NID, to whose success he made such a valuable contribution. Years later, Godfrey became the model for M, the secret service chief in Fleming's James Bond books.

Godfrey recorded another instance of how Hall's widespread network of contacts proved so useful to him:

I was introduced by Reggie Hall early in 1939 to Lord Tyrell who, after being British Ambassador in Paris, held the post of Permanent Under-Secretary at the Foreign Office for many years. He was old and frail ... but these disabilities in no way impaired the shrewdness of his judgment about European affairs. He encouraged me to go and see him ... and this I did at frequent intervals. In spite of his infirmities he seemed to be remarkably in touch with what was going on and his prognostications were usually correct.

When France was collapsing and A. V. Alexander (First Lord) and Admiral Pound were about make a final effort to get in touch with the French Minister of Marine (Darlan) at Bordeaux, Tyrell ... asked me to come and see him urgently. It was to warn me that Admiral Darlan was likely to be a twister. He had formed this opinion years ago in Paris and knew Darlan, who held the post of Naval Chef de Cabinet. I got back the Admiralty just as Admiral Pound was leaving for France; but he was incredulous. To him it seemed unbelievable that Darlan was anything but an honest straightforward sailor.[12]

Tyrell's assessment of Darlan proved only too correct as he became one of the leading lights of Vichy, implacably opposed to the British and one of Hall's chief 'bêtes noires'.

Bletchley Park

Two recent authors have noted that Hall's influence on intelligence in World War II was particularly significant in the field of SIGINT. In his book on the JIC, Sir Percy Cradock, a former Chairman and Foreign Policy Adviser to Margaret Thatcher, paid him this tribute: 'Adm. Hall ... had laid foundations for modern British cryptography and given intelligence a distinctly better reputation than in the other services.'[13] Alan Judd, the biographer of Mansfield Cumming, wrote: 'Hall was an outstanding DNI ... but his great achievement was his imaginative apprehension of the potential of cryptography.'[14]

In 1938, Sinclair, astutely foreseeing that GC & CS would be vulnerable to bombing if it remained in Central London in wartime, used the secret service funds at his disposal to purchase Bletchley Park, a country house with extensive grounds, approximately fifty miles north-west of London, as the operation's new HQ. He chose well. Bletchley had excellent road and rail communications, sited on the West Coast Main Railway line from London Euston, with branch lines running to both Oxford and Cambridge, permitting easy access to both universities and to their dons who would soon be recruited to join GC & CS's rapidly growing staff. The extensive network of telephone and teleprinter lines, connecting Bletchley with the

NID, the other service intelligence divisions and the Chiefs of Staff, could easily be laid alongside the track on way leaves granted by the railway company.

An adage frequently quoted by leading figures in GCHQ, Bletchley's postwar successor, maintained that 'Room 40 was our grandfather and GC & CS our father.' Hall's traditions were an inspiration to everyone at Bletchley – not least his insistence on security – and Room 40 veterans were its mainstay. Two of these stalwarts, Denniston and Knox, had been chiefly responsible for the acquisition of the ENIGMA machine, which enabled Bletchley to read the German signal traffic, thus continuing Room 40's achievements. Churchill called these decrypts, codenamed ULTRA, his golden eggs. Bletchley was not entirely dependent on ENIGMA. Hall had read diplomatic signals and officials in the Spanish and Portuguese state telecommunications services regularly provided details of coded traffic between German diplomats and the Foreign Office in Berlin to GC & CS. The appointment of Nigel de Grey, who enjoyed considerable prestige for having decoded the Zimmermann telegram, as head of training, ensured the continuance of the procedures which Bletchley had inherited from its predecessor.

As well as those named by Godfrey, W. F. Clarke came to Bletchley as head of its naval section and the staunch figures of Frank Adcock and Walter Bruford, both of them fluent in German, left academia for a return to the field of cryptography for the second time. Relations between Hut 4 at Bletchley, the home of its naval section, and the NID remained close and harmonious throughout the war.

Close cooperation between Bletchley Park and the American cryptography services began as early as the end of 1940. After Pearl Harbor, Captain Eddy Hastings, the NID representative in Washington, negotiated an agreement with his American opposite numbers in which they recognized the importance of adhering to the accepted British methods of security discipline which dated back to Hall and Room 40. Further agreements negotiated by Edgar Travis, by then the effective chief at Bletchley and who like Hall, insisted on the cardinal importance of security, with the US Navy in October 1942 and with the US Army in May 1943, led to the co-ordination of intelligence covering all strategic operations against Germany, notably the Battle of the Atlantic.

While the team at Bletchley admired the technical efficiency of the German cryptologists, they believed with justification that their adversaries were hopelessly inept at intelligence analysis. In what has been called the golden age of allied intelligence against both Germany and Japan in World War II, their mastery of SIGINT ensured that not only the enemy's military dispositions but time and again their strategic objectives were presented to the leaders of the Western powers with almost total clarity.

Bletchley Park – a highly efficient organisation as Room 40 had been in World War I – was once described as '... the greatest single achievement of Britain during 1939–45, perhaps during this century as a whole'.[15] Their success originated from the pioneering work accomplished in Room 40 and NID between 1914 and 1918, inspired by Hall and led by him in the last two years of that war.

The birth of the OSS

However badly British intelligence had become run down in the inter-war years, their American counterparts had fared even more poorly. As Secretary of State in the Hoover Administration, Henry Stimson had abolished the American code breaking operation, reasoning that 'gentlemen don't spy on each other'. At the outset of World War II, the United States had no organisation comparable to the SIS – the FBI's mandate was, and is, restricted to internal affairs. As late as 1940 the Office of Naval Intelligence was in worse shape than the NID had been in 1936–37.

Roosevelt, forward-looking in so many matters, was anxious to recreate an external intelligence service, but in the prevalent political climate of 1940, he had to tread warily. Reaching out across party lines, he selected a personal friend, Colonel William 'Big Bill' Donovan, a Republican, a Catholic, a Southerner and a successful lawyer who had served with distinction in the Army in 1917–18, to act as his 'eyes and ears' on intelligence issues. For several years Donovan had been the Morgan Bank's adviser on intelligence and retaining an interest in strategy and modern weaponry, he had seen the Abyssinian conflict and the Spanish Civil War for himself. His experience of these conflicts had convinced him of the importance of unconventional and psychological warfare. A man of dynamic drive and remarkable initiative, he might be described as an American 'Blinker' Hall.

In July 1940 Roosevelt, suspicious of his increasingly defeatist Ambassador in London, Joe Kennedy, sent Donovan to Britain, knowing that he could rely on his veracity and objectivity. His covert mission was to discover whether Britain was in earnest in continuing to fight the war alone and was thus worth supporting. Roosevelt, anxious to discover what America could do to help, asked him to institute a close co-operation with the Admiralty covering both technology and intelligence, thus restoring the association between Hall, Bell and Admiral Sims that had proved so successful in World War I.

Donovan saw virtually everyone of importance in London from Churchill down and he spent much time with Godfrey with whom he stayed on the night before he returned to Washington. The two men got on well together, forming a strong relationship and Donovan developed a considerable respect for British intelligence. He was deeply impressed by the fighting spirit he found in London and his report to Roosevelt was emphatic: Britain should indeed be supported, effectively counter-acting the negative information which Kennedy was sending to Washington.

From a Naval point of view, the Donovan mission resulted in the deal in which the USN transferred fifty World War I destroyers to the RN in return for America obtaining naval and communication bases in Bermuda and in British Caribbean colonies. Close and effective co-operation on both technical and intelligence issues developed between the two Navies with the formation in March 1941 of the British Admiralty Delegation in Washington. The Delegation included an NID section whose most important function was to keep the Office of Naval Intelligence fully briefed on the most recent reports. Indeed, throughout World War II the US remained highly dependent on British intelligence. One American historian noted: 'Some 85% of our strategic intelligence came from the British.'[16] Hall's reputation, which still stood high in Washington, not least with Roosevelt who remained a fervent admirer, helped to ease the task of the NID's representatives.

Despite this progress Godfrey, backed by his colleagues in the JIC, believed that more needed to be done. A report received on May 4 from the newly-appointed British Naval Attaché, Rear-Admiral Herbert Pott revealed the considerable disarray in the American intelligence community, due mainly to the mutual animosity between the State Department, the FBI and the Army and Navy. He remarked that the ONI was in better shape than its counterparts as its new Director, Captain Alan Kirk, the former Naval Attaché in London and an enthusiastic supporter of closer co-operation between the RN and the USN, had already tightened up its efficiency with some assistance from NID. Relations with the Naval Attaché's staff were excellent, although there was some friction between the ONI and the Operations Divisions, an ominous echo of the situation that had existed inside the Admiralty from 1914 to 1917. Pott noted the detrimental effect of these deficiencies on both Britain and America and the complete and potentially disastrous lack of any joint intelligence function in Washington.

In April 1941 Godfrey, had advocated the 'complete fusion of the British and American intelligence services … with US officers attached to NID sections and vice versa'.[17] After digesting the implications of Pott's report, the Chiefs of Staff sent Godfrey to Washington with a remit 'to set up a combined intelligence organisation on a 100% co-operative basis'. Accompanied by Fleming, he left London for Washington on May 15.

During their journey Godfrey and Fleming discussed how they could best present the concept of a unified American Secret Intelligence Service.

Before leaving London they had prepared a paper describing the sectional organisation of NID which had originated with the reforms Hall had introduced when he had finally taken control of Room 40 in 1917. They decided to use this document to recommend NID as a model intelligence service and to press for the formation of an integrated service that would avoid the current situation in Britain, where four separate agencies reporting to four different political chiefs controlled sabotage and resistance in German-occupied Europe, political conflict, economic warfare and covert HUMINT.

Although Godfrey and Fleming were well-received in Washington, they quickly encountered the inter-departmental animosity about which Pott had warned. Godfrey later wrote: 'We already knew that the relations between the Army and the Navy were bad, but we did not realise how bad until we tried to get them to see eye to eye and collaborate with each other and the State Department about this supremely important matter of intelligence ... after about a fortnight it was clear that we were up against a brick wall.'[18] He sought the advice of William Stephenson, the SIS Chief in North America, and of Sir William Wiseman, who had held a similar position in World War I and who, like Hall, was still available for consultation. Both men supported Godfrey's objective and were in close contact with Donovan.

They were emphatic that only Roosevelt could resolve this quandary and Wiseman succeeded in arranging for Godfrey to be invited to dinner at the White House. After the meal the President took Godfrey into the Oval Office, recalling his visit to London in 1918 when he had met Hall, for whom his admiration was evident. Godfrey recounted that with difficulty, 'I got a word in edgeways and said my piece. More reminiscences – I said it a second time and then a third – one intelligence security boss, not three or four.'[19] Godfrey had been alone with Roosevelt for more than an hour before Mrs Roosevelt came in and told the President that it was his bedtime.

Although Godfrey doubted whether he had got his point across, three weeks later Donovan was appointed as the overall intelligence chief. His new post was initially and euphemistically designated Coordinator of Information, although after Pearl Harbor his organisation was renamed the Office of Strategic Services (OSS); the forerunner of the CIA.

Godfrey later attributed much of his success to Stephenson and Wiseman, both of whom had considerable influence in Washington, and the former had lobbied strongly for Donovan's appointment. Nevertheless, a Rear-Admiral RN had succeeded in spending an hour with the President – an almost unique occurrence. If Roosevelt had not had such a high regard for Hall's achievements, he might not have listened so carefully to, and then accepted, the arguments advanced by his successor.

Godfrey left Fleming in Washington where he used his remarkable talent to draft a series of documents which Donovan used as a basis for setting up the new intelligence organisation along the lines which the two Britons had agreed in advance. As a result the NID exerted a powerful influence on the structure of the OSS. Godfrey's mission had other positive results, setting the scene for the close and effective liaison which grew up between the British and American naval intelligence divisions. The Americans agreed to adopt several British institutions, including the JIC and JIS and, somewhat reluctantly, the OIC. The USN had evidently failed to study the success of the integrated NID/ASWD system in 1917–18 and believed that tracking submarines was entirely a function of Operations. After some early stumbles, including failing to respond to Donitz's moving his Wolfpacks from the Mid-Atlantic after Pearl Harbor to attack the vulnerable traffic off the American Eastern seaboard, which resulted in considerable losses, first-rate co-operation developed between Winn in charge of the Submarine Tracking Room in London and Commander Kenneth Knowles, his opposite number in Washington.

The Cold War era

As captured German leaders freely admitted, in neither war, and to their considerable disadvantage, had they developed an effective system of co-ordinated intelligence as the British had. The outstanding success of British intelligence in World War II owed much to the principles established by Hall in the earlier war.

Hall's influence on British (and indirectly on American) intelligence in World War II had been profound and continued well into the Cold War era. Successive intelligence chiefs operated along the principles which Hall had developed to meet the stress of war and which he had articulated in his unpublished autobiography and in his lecture at Greenwich in 1936.

The onset of the Cold War and the emergence of Soviet Russia after World War II as a major naval power and thus a serious threat to Britain and its NATO allies ensured the survival of the NID, saving it from the decline which it had experienced in the interwar years. Inevitably, intelligence became more closely integrated on an inter-service basis both at a national level and inside NATO.

Mountbatten, the son of a former DNI, had long displayed a keen interest in intelligence. As Supreme Commander in South-East Asia, he had created a joint intelligence staff, combining all three services, headed by Major-General Lamplough, a capable and energetic Royal Marine officer who had served as DDNI under Godfrey. He was a strong believer in an integrated all-service intelligence function, which he introduced during his tenure as Chief of the Defence Staff between 1959 and 1965. His successor as FSL, Sir Charles Lambe, appointed Norman Denning as DNI, the first Paymaster officer to hold the position. In the post-war years he had held several important posts including Director of the Naval Staff College at Greenwich and Director of Manpower in the Admiralty. Denning was also an ardent supporter of an integrated intelligence system and Mountbatten demonstrated considerable confidence in him when in 1964 he appointed him as the first Deputy Chief of the Defence Staff (Intelligence), his chief adviser on all intelligence issues. In the following year the position of DNI was abolished and after 83 years the NID ceased to exist: a victim of changed military requirements and the ever-increasing integration of the three armed forces. The division's achievements in both wars, directed by leaders of the stature of Hall and Godfrey, had well surpassed the call of duty and had made a signal contribution to the victories in both 1918 and 1945.

Epilogue

During the run-up to the invasion of Iraq in 2003, the JIC abandoned one of the basic precepts for handling intelligence, originally developed by Hall and upheld by his successors. As the invasion was controversial, particularly in the Labour Party, the Prime Minister, Tony Blair, decided that his Government should publish a powerful endorsement of its strategy. He entrusted this approach to his Communications Director, Alastair Campbell, a non-elected political appointee. He seems to have had scant knowledge or understanding of the basic principles of intelligence, issuing a further dossier on Iraq to the press without even consulting the intelligence community.

Campbell, it has been claimed, seized upon a report from a single and uncorroborated MI6 source in Baghdad stating that Saddam Hussein had the capacity to deploy chemical and biological weapons within 45 minutes. The Scud missiles in his arsenal had a maximum range of 460 miles, sufficient to hit both Israel and, more importantly from a British public opinion standpoint, the UK sovereign bases in Cyprus. The report was ambiguous and the acknowledged experts on missile systems in the Defence Intelligence Staff regarded it as unreliable, insisting that Iraq would need days to prepare these weapons for action. Blair and Campbell were desperate to vindicate their intention to attack Saddam and Campbell, it was later claimed, demanded that the Government's case should be – a description to be forever associated with the affair – 'sexed up' (though Campbell himself never used the words) by releasing a dossier including the 45 minute report to the press. Despite the analysts' widely-held reservations the Chairman of the JIC, John Scarlett, agreed to its release. His action seems to have had tragic consequences even at home, as one of the Defence analysts, Dr David Kelly, broke confidentiality and leaked his concerns to a BBC reporter. He told her that Downing Street was desperately seeking information which would corroborate the 45 minute report and that he had been put under relentless pressure to confirm the assertion. Dr Kelly's superiors singularly failed to protect him against this coercion. He later committed suicide, thus triggering an investigation which in essence whitewashed the Government.

In both World Wars, the Prime Minister's chief personal advisers on military issues had been serving officers: Maurice Hankey, himself a former Fleet Intelligence Officer, and Pug Ismay. Both men knew the system and thoroughly understood the workings of intelligence and its limitations. In 2002 and 2003 there was no one in Downing Street of the calibre of Hankey or Ismay who had the experience or stature to warn the Prime Minister that such a misuse of intelligence would result in incalculable damage to the reputations of his own government and of the intelligence services.

While in the author's opinion Campbell must bear a considerable degree of responsibility for this fiasco (though this must remain speculation, as there are few hard pieces of evidence about who said what to whom) the ultimate blame must rest with the senior officers of the intelligence services, most notably with Scarlett, a career SIS operative, for their apparent failure to articulate their reservations about the 45 minute report in the dossier. They thus seem to have discarded one of Hall's cardinal precepts: the responsibility of the intelligence services for sifting truth from falsehood and knitting together information to produce a balanced picture. The JIC had failed to maintain its tradition of objectivity, which effectively dated back to Hall. One of its distinguished former Chairmen, Sir Percy Cradock, had set out a guiding principle, which Scarlett and his colleagues had, it seems, abandoned:

> Ideally intelligence and policy should be distinct. ... The analyst needs to be close enough to Ministers to know the questions troubling them and he must not be shy of tackling the major issues. Too close a link and policy begins to play back on estimates, producing the answers the policy-makers would like ... the analysts would become courtiers, whereas their proper function is to report their findings, almost always unpalatable, without fear or favour.[20]

Some observers believed that Scarlett secretly nursed the ambition of becoming Britain's overall Director of Intelligence with control over MI5, SIS, GCHQ and Defence Intelligence, a degree of authority over the intelligence community far greater than Hall had exercised in World War I and comparable to the recent appointment of a National Director of

Intelligence in Washington. In contravention of Cradock's admirably sensible tenet, he and Campbell had become close friends. To promote his career, Scarlett was believed to be ready to go along with the 45 minute ploy despite the analysts' reservations. Although his ambition would not be achieved in the aftermath of this disaster, he was shortly afterwards appointed Director-General of SIS. (As so often in matters of national security and intelligence, we are perforce outside looking in, and therefore speculating rather than asserting.)

Whilst Hall accepted that Government had to decide how to use information to their best possible advantage, he would certainly have been strongly opposed to any attempt to twist intelligence for purely political ends. Although the use of deception to mislead the enemy, of which he had been a master, was a legitimate function of intelligence, the Blair Government's use of the 45 minute claim was unprecedented and clearly open to criticism. One of Hall's most prominent characteristics was total integrity and insistence in providing accurate intelligence based wherever possible on verified information in the NID's possession.

Hall had successfully seen off such formidable adversaries as Northcliffe and Beaverbrook and he would have vigorously defended his turf against Campbell. If any politician had ever suggested to Hall (or Bentinck or Godfrey or many of Scarlett's predecessors in the JIC chair) that he should twist intelligence for political objectives, the resulting explosion would have been heard all over Whitehall. Blair would have had to have taken any threats of resignation from his intelligence chiefs very seriously.

This incident demonstrates extraordinary and disquieting disarray inside the intelligence services in the Blair years, more serious by far than the lack of interface between operations and the NID on the night of Jutland. One wonders whether the lessons of this incident have been learned.

Britain and the Western World now face the enmity of fundamentalist Islam, an adversary arguably more insidious and difficult to combat than Imperial or Nazi Germany or expansionist Japan ever were. Confronted with such dangers, the need for well co-ordinated and effective intelligence services is evident. The men who will lead them will need to possess in full measure the qualities – tirelessness, drive, imagination, integrity, and the capacity for lateral thinking and interpreting the intentions of the enemy – which made William Reginald 'Blinker' Hall one of history's most successful intelligence chiefs.

Notes

[1] Keyes p.135
[2] Information to the author from Mr James Denning
[3] CAC HALL 3/1
[4] TNA ADM 116/6437 Dardanelles Commission Proceedings
[5] Beesly, *Very Special Admiral*, p.95
[6] CAC MLBE 1/2 *The Hall Tradition* p.3
[7] Mc Lachlan *Room 39* pp.17-18
[8] CAC MLBE 1/2 pp. 4-5
[9] Mc Lachlan p.4
[10] CAC HALL 7/1/12 WRH to May Templar April 30 1939
[11] CAC MLBE 1/2 p.5
[12] Mc Lachlan p.53
[13] Cradock *Know Your Enemy* p.14
[14] Judd *The Quest for C* p. 295
[15] George Steiner *Sunday Times* Oct 23 1983 Quoted in Denniston p.66
[16] Mark Reibling 'Intelligence Getting Smart' *National Review* July 19 2002
[17] Beesly pp.180-181
[18] Ibid p. 181
[19] Ibid p.182
[20] Cradock p.296

INDEX

Abney, Sir William 18
Admiralstab 30, 33, 58, 61, 69, 72, 82, 89, 90, 93, 145, 148, 154–6, 187, 188, 213, 220, 232, 233, 249, 274, 277, 280
Adcock, Frank 166, 167, 308
Alfonso XIII, King 46, 139, 267
Anthrax 141, 247, 253, 255, 260
Arbuthnott, Rear-Admiral Sir Robert 67, 148
Archibald, John J. 126, 128
Argentina 178, 187, 247, 253–57, 260, 262
Army and Navy Gazette, the 114
Asquith, H. H. 36, 53, 57, 81, 107, 112–20, 134–38, 225–6, 268
Athens 84, 165
Atlantic Monthly 103, 197
Aud 133–4
Augsburg 30
Ausonia 91
Australia 18, 25, 59, 187
Austria 125, 129, 131, 257, 267–8, 277
Bacon, Sir Reginald 113, 117, 240–1, 265
Balfour, Arthur 50–3, 113, 115, 117, 134, 155–6, 159, 161–2, 184, 195, 201–5, 207, 209, 212, 225–6, 258, 268–9, 284
Baltzer, Kapitanleutnant Hermann 80
Battenberg, Admiral of the Fleet Prince Louis of 45, 57–8
Bayly, Admiral Sir Lewis 28, 37, 133, 221, 229–31
Beatty, Admiral of the Fleet Sir David 7–8, 19–20, 35–6, 64–72, 107, 114, 147–152, 154, 157, 171–2, 174, 225–30, 237–44, 271–74, 278–81, 285, 288
Beaumont, Admiral Sir Lewis 44–5
Beaverbrook, Lord 268–70, 315
Beesly, Patrick 36–7, 39, 65–6, 91, 101–2, 104, 111, 128, 131, 133, 180, 182, 274, 288
Bell, Edward, Secretary to US Embassy 40, 104, 126, 128, 142, 184–5, 192, 196–204, 207, 212, 218–19, 252, 254–6, 259–64, 268, 277, 279, 286, 309
Bell, Sir Hugh 243
Bender, Walther 30–1
Benn, Arthur Shirley 130
Beresford, Admiral Lord Charles 43, 47, 60–1, 72, 244
Berlin 25, 27, 52–3, 56, 61, 63–4, 67, 75, 82, 85–7, 133, 167, 179–80, 182, 187, 190–1, 199, 203–4, 206–8, 212–14, 248–9, 252, 255–62, 268, 275, 277, 279–80, 308
Birch, Frank 163, 166–7, 174, 306
Birrell, Augustine 135
Black Diaries 136–8
Black Tom case 82–3, 257, 296–8
Blackwood, Captain Henry 23–4
Bletchley Park 8, 163, 167, 176, 282, 307–9
Blucher 56, 70–1
Boedicker, Admiral Friedrich 145–6
Boer War 27, 34, 41, 131
Booth, Alfred 92, 97–8
Boy-Ed, Karl 86, 126–9
Brandon, Captain 19, 232, 306
Bremse 236–9
Breslau 57, 77, 79
Bridge, Admiral Sir Cyprian 44–5
Bruford, Walter 166, 170, 308
Brummer 236–8
Buchan, John 42, 77, 83, 269
Bullough, Edward 166
Bushire 83–4
Caillaux, Joseph 261–2
California 200–1
Campbell, Ronald 198, 202, 313–15
Canada 25–6, 129, 187, 276
Canary Islands 72, 248–9
Candidate 96–8, 104
Cape Horn 62–3
Carranza, Venustiano 189–92, 196, 200, 216, 254–5
Carson, Sir Edward 86, 115–16, 226, 228, 235–6
Casement, Sir Roger 87, 104, 130, 132–8
Cavendish-Bentinck, William 50, 288
Cayo Romano 96
Chakravati, Dr 85
Chandar, Ram 85

Chatham 25
Chicago Tribune 211
Chile 59, 178
China 17, 58, 200, 263, 301
Choate, Joseph 210
Churchill, Winston 28–36, 40, 47, 50, 53, 57–8, 60, 65, 69, 72–3, 75, 77–81, 89, 91, 95, 100–5, 107–17, 120, 132, 149, 162, 270, 275, 295–6, 308–9
Clemenceau, Georges 261
Clann Na Gael 86–7
Clarke, Russell 29, 161, 173
Clarke, W. F. 150–2, 162, 168–70, 174, 227, 285, 289, 308
Clemenceau, Georges 261
Cohalan, Judge Daniel 86–7, 133
Coke, Vice-Admiral Sir Charles 93–4, 97–8, 102, 104, 131, 133
Coleman, Flight-Lieutenant J. P. 270
Collins, Michael 137
Connolly, James 134
Copenhagen 132, 179–80
Coronel 58–63, 163
Cradock, Rear-Admiral Sir Christopher 59–61,
Crease, Captain T. E 75, 107, 109, 112–13, 116,
Crippen, Dr. 26
Cromer, Lord 78–80
Cuba 34, 199, 203, 254, 260
Cumberland Bay 64
Cumming, Sir Mansfield 51, 104, 301, 307
Cunningham, Admiral of the Fleet Sir Andrew 42, 242, 305
Custance, Admiral Sir Reginald 44–5
Daily Express 268–9
Daily Mail 41, 119, 222, 226, 294–5
Daily Telegraph 56
Daniels, Josephus 217
Dardanelles 76, 78–9, 81–2, 88, 100, 108–9, 112, 240, 244, 304, 306, 315
Dedeagatch 76–7
de Grey, Nigel 85, 162, 173, 177–8, 180–4, 193, 196, 200, 218, 297, 306, 308
Denmark 41, 280
Denning, Vice-Admiral Sir Norman 163–4, 302, 313
Denniston, Alastair 29–33, 48, 54, 84, 105, 151, 162–3, 169, 175, 281, 283, 289, 301, 306, 308
Derfflinger 71, 147, 154, 157
Dernburg, Dr. Bernhard 86
De Robeck, Admiral of the Fleet Sir John 82
Devonport 60–1, 94, 250, 271
Devoy, John 86–7, 125, 133
Diamond Hill, Battle of 34
Dogger Bank 37, 65, 67–71, 113, 123, 145, 147, 162
Dresden 59, 61–3, 163
Dreyer, Admiral Sir Frederic 67, 242, 244
Duff, Admiral Sir Alexander 100, 221, 226–9, 238, 242–4, 301
Eady, George Griffin 75
Eardley-Wilmot Captain S. W. 44
Earl of Latham 96, 102
Easter Island 59
Edinburgh 161, 165, 213
Edmonds, C. J. 83
Edward VII, King 46, 197
Ehrman, John 40
Ellis, Commodore Heaton 174, 247
Elmhirst, Air Marshal Sir Thomas 80
El Paso Times 211
Emden 27, 37, 58–9, 82, 93–4, 97, 232–3
Erri Berro 142, 247, 249–52
Evan-Thomas, Admiral Sir Hugh 142, 247, 249–52
Ewing, Sir Alfred 28–9, 32, 35–6, 47–8, 50, 66, 84, 104, 161–3, 165, 172–3, 182, 213, 227, 285
British Submarines: E-11 68; E-23 158; E-35 251; E-42 273; E-48 251; J-6 271–3
Falaba 92–3
Fatherland, The 93, 210
Faudel-Phillips, Benjamin 84
Fetterlein, Ernst 175–6
Fisher, Admiral of the Fleet Sir John 18, 28–9, 35, 42, 44,

317

48, 55–7, 60, 65–6, 68–9, 72, 75–8, 89, 91, 104, 107–20, 132, 149, 197, 226, 244
Fisher, Captain W. W. 227
Fitzgerald, Penelope 33, 154, 160, 165–6, 168, 172,
Fitzmaurice, Gerald 55, 75, 78
Fleming, Ian 77, 306, 310–12
Fraser, Lionel 46, 167, 169
Fremantle, Admiral Sir Sydney 244, 274, 278–9
Friedman, William 83, 85, 180–1, 195, 201
Friedrich Der Grosse 150–1
Galibin, Lieutenant 31, 33
Gaunt, Rear-Admiral Sir Guy 52, 54, 94, 125–6, 128, 130, 178–9, 183, 197, 200, 206–7, 210, 212, 222
Geddes, Sir Eric 51, 119, 230, 235–6, 238–41, 243–4, 269, 277, 287
George V, King 46, 136, 139, 232
Lloyd George, David 51, 81, 112–13, 120, 221, 225–6, 228, 234–6, 241, 243, 268–9, 293
Germany: 7–8, 40–1, 52–3, 61, 84, 89–91, 93–6, 100, 103, 104, 126, 128–131, 142, 156, 167, 178, 185, 189, 206, 210, 222, 225, 243, 251, 253, 261, 263–4, 256–7, 279–80, 286, 291, 308, 315; and the naval arms race with Britain 18, 56–7; and undersea cable systems 27–8; and Falklands attack 62–3; alliance with Turkey 75–6, 80; and Spain 139–40; and Zimmermann telegram 180–3, 186, 190, 255; and the sinking of *Lusitania* 189, 211; and Mexico 192, 196, 199, 207, 255, 257; and the build up to the First World War 193–98, 211, 217–18; and Lenin 221; and Austrian bid for peace 268; and failure of intelligence 274; and oil 275; and Black Tom 297–8; and Kingsland 297–8
Gibraltar 25, 55, 141, 248–51
Gila River 200–1
Gilbert, Sir Martin 109, 166
Glanders 247, 253, 260
Gneisenau 58–62
Godfrey, Admiral John 8, 40–1, 81, 142, 242, 244, 288, 304–6, 308–15
Goeben 57, 76–7, 79
Goodenough, Admiral Sir William 67–8
Göppert, Dr. Otto 180, 213
Gough, C. E. 167
Gough-Calthorpe, Admiral of the Fleet Sir Somerset 173, 277
Green, Roger Lancelyn 140
Greene, Sir William Graham 50, 92
Grey, Sir Edward 51, 81
Grieve, Keith 243
Guazo 256
Habenicht, KorvettenCaptain Richard 30–1
Hague Conventions 89, 103
Halifax 206, 214, 253
Hall, Sir Reginald 'Blinker': and Zimmermann telegram 7, 9, 53, 85, 104, 126, 190, 206, 214, 219, 222, 283, 303; attitude to Germans 8, 40, 126; at sea 17–20; as a young man 18; and ill-health 20, 42, 299; and SIGINT 36–7, 47, 64, 195, 307; becomes DNI 39; strained relationship with Admiral Oliver 61, 72, 104, 156–7, 240–2; interrogation techniques 123–4, 127–8, 231–3; and Ireland 130–8; removal of Jellicoe 241–2; and Naval oil supplies 275–7; and anti-Semitism 276; death 299; and legacy 301–16 passim
Hall, Captain W. H. 45
Hall, Ethel (Essie) 18, 20, 251, 294, 298, 300
Hambro, Ebba 168–9, 173,
Hamburg-Amerika 145, 249, 254
Hamburger Fremdenblatt 254
Hamilton, Emma 24,
Hamilton, Admiral Sir Frederick 113–15, 118, 120
Hamilton, Ian 34
Hamilton, Lord George 43
Handelsverkehrbuch (HVB) 15, 30, 32, 63
Hankey, Sir Maurice 52, 54–5, 73, 75–6, 81, 117–18, 238, 243, 314
Hardy, William Cozens 24, 84
Hardinge, Lord 51, 197–8, 201–4, 269, 284
Hardisty, C. W. 166–7
Hari, Mata 124
Harrison, Ernest 167
Harrison, Leland 126, 142, 254–5, 259–64, 277, 279, 286–7

Heaton-Ellis, Commodore Edward 247
Heinrich, Admiral Prince of Prussia 33, 86,
Heligoland 19–20, 60, 68, 117, 171, 273
Heligoland Bight 20, 60, 171, 271
Henderson, Colonel David 29, 41
Herschell, Lord 29, 35, 45–7, 127–8, 136, 139–40, 247–8, 255, 306
Hezlet, Vice-Admiral Sir Arthur 231
Hickling, Vice-Admiral Harold 63
Hipper, Admiral Franz 37, 64, 67–72, 145, 147–8, 151, 271–3, 278–80
Hippisley, Colonel 29
Hirst, Paymaster-Lieutenant Lloyd 61, 163–4, 216, 247
Hitler, Adolf 129, 213
Hohler, Sir Thomas 179, 197
Home Popham signal book 23
Hood, Admiral Sir Arthur 43
Hood, Rear-Admiral Sir Horace 39, 209
Hope, Admiral Sir George 24, 240
Hope, Admiral Herbert 47–9, 151, 153, 162, 168, 172
Hornby, Admiral of the Fleet Sir Geoffrey Phipps 42, 44
House, Colonel E. M. 52, 129, 179, 181, 193, 268
Howell, Major Wilfred 131–3, 139
HMAS *Sydney* 58
HMS *Aboukir* 58
HMS *Australia* 18
HMS *Bluebell* 134
HMS *Britannia* 17
HMS *Canopus* 59–60, 62
HMS *Centurion* 96–8, 104, 156
HMS *Conqueror* 243
HMS *Conquest* 146
HMS *Cornwall* 18–19, 42, 52, 232
HMS *Cornwallis* 18, 131
HMS *Courageous* 239
HMS *Cressy* 58
HMS *Dartmouth* 171
HMS *Defence* 24, 59, 156
HMS *Dreadnought* 11, 57
HMS *Duke of Clarence* 248–50
HMS *Duke of Edinburgh* 94
HMS *Euralyus* 23
HMS *Excellent* 17–18, 42
HMS *Falmouth* 158
HMS *Formidable* 89
HMS *Galatea* 151
HMS *Glasgow* 59–60, 62–3, 163, 247
HMS *Glorious* 239
HMS *Gloucester* 94
HMS *Good Hope* 59–60
HMS *Hogue* 58
HMS *Imperieuse* 17
HMS *Indomitable* 71, 80
HMS *Inflexible* 60, 65
HMS *Invincible* 39, 65, 147, 156
HMS *Iron Duke* 35, 149, 241
HMS *Lance* 32
HMS *Lennox* 32
HMS *Lion* 52, 71, 123, 147
HMS *Loyal* 32
HMS *Magnificent* 18
HMS *Majestic* 82
HMS *Mary Rose* 236
HMS *Monmouth* 59–60
HMS *Natal* 19–20, 172, 243, 293
HMS *Naiad* 24
HMS *Northampton* 17
HMS *Nottingham* 158
HMS *Orion* 67, 94
HMS *Otranto* 59–60
HMS *Princess Royal* 65, 71
HMS *Queen Elizabeth* 112, 149, 275
HMS *Queen Mary* 7, 19–20, 39, 42, 67, 70, 130, 147, 156, 172
HMS *Repulse* 239, 305
HMS *Strongbow* 236
HMS *St. Vincent* 151
HMS *Theseus* 31
HMS *Tiger* 70–2, 147
HMS *Triumph* 82

318

HMS *Undaunted* 32
HMS *Warwick* 266
Houston, David 193
Huerta, General Victoriano 127, 189, 254
HUMINT 52, 311
Hunstanton 29, 273
India 25, 34, 83–6, 197, 235
Inskip, Thomas 167
Ireland 5, 37, 46, 51, 86–7, 92–8, 101–2, 130–8, 145, 203, 226, 230, 262
Irigoyen, Hipolito 253
Irish National Volunteers 86–7
Isaacs, Sir Rufus *see under* Reading, Lord
Jackson, Admiral of the Fleet Sir Henry 25, 48, 108, 118, 158, 162, 225
Jackson, Rear-Admiral Thomas 150–2, 154–5
Jackson, Sir John 75
Jade River 149, 157, 238
Jahnke 257–9
James, Admiral Sir William 'Bubbles' 8–9, 18–20, 40, 120, 172–4, 179, 181, 227–31, 237–8, 273–4, 285–7, 301–304
Japan 28, 183, 190, 196, 199–201, 210, 308, 315
Jellicoe, Admiral of the Fleet Sir John 7, 19, 35–6, 48, 56, 64–6, 70, 72, 89, 108, 114, 119–20, 146–60, 162, 176, 225–9, 235–6, 239–44, 248, 265, 285–9
Joint Intelligence Committee 7, 50, 288, 304
Jones, Sir Henry 85
Jutland, Battle of 20, 35, 37, 39, 68, 72, 101, 145–62, 172, 186, 199, 226–7, 232, 236, 238, 242, 272, 281, 302, 315
J-6 271–3
Kahn, David 32
Kaiser Wilhelm II 65, 76, 90, 145, 165, 186, 188–9, 198, 232, 253–4, 277, 280
Keith, Squadron Leader C. H. 270
Kemal, Mustafa 80
Kendall, Captain Henry 26
Keyes, Admiral of the Fleet Sir Roger 7–9, 19, 39, 68, 82, 156, 160, 237–40, 242–3, 265–6, 301
Kiel 19, 41–2, 56, 232, 279–80
Konigsberg 64, 239
Konig 56, 148, 154
Knox, Alfred Dillwyn 33, 154, 165–9, 175, 182, 289, 306, 308
Krupp armaments 248
Kynaston, David 46–7
Langrishe, Sir Hercules 139
Lansing, Robert 52, 127, 129, 180–2, 185–7, 192, 205–11, 257, 262–3
Laughton, John Knox 42
Laurentic 26
Lee, Ella 168–9
Leeson, Spencer 167, 170, 176
Leipzig 60–2
Lejtenant Burakov 31
Lerwick 37
Leveson, Admiral Sir Arthur 110, 148
Libau 133–4
Lincoln, Abraham 201
Lincoln, Trebitsch 124
Listemann, Dr Helmut 83
Liverpool 26, 39, 91–3, 95–8, 293
Liverpool Post 39
Loughlin, Irwin 202, 204
Lourenco Marques 64
Lowry, Rear-Admiral 20
Ludendorff, General Erich 186, 188–90, 218, 277
Luce, Captain John 59, 62–4, 164
Lusitania 89–105, 110, 127, 133–4, 178–9, 185–7, 189, 198, 211, 226
Luxburg, Count Karl 178, 254, 256–7, 262, 297
Lyautey, General 141
Lytton, Lord 167
Zeppelins: L42 233–4; L48 233–4; L49 233; L50 233
MacCarthy, Desmond 166
Maclay, Sir Joseph 228
Madden, Admiral of the Fleet Sir Charles 35, 242
Madeira, Percy 276,
Maercker, Kapitan Erich 62
Magdeburg 30–5, 174
Malta 25, 55, 173

Manchester Guardian 170
Manisty, Rear-Admiral Sir Henry 163, 229
Marconi, Guglielmo 25–8, 36–7
Marder, Arthur 7, 39–42, 53, 108, 114, 118, 146, 225–6, 236, 238, 241, 243, 282
Marlowe, Thomas 119, 294
Mas Afuera 61, 63
Masaryk, Tomas 125
Mason, A. E. W. 140–2, 258–9
Mauretania 36, 92
Maxse, Ernest 51, 103, 284
May, Admiral of the Fleet Sir William 110
McBride, Colonel 131–2
McKenna, Reginald 107, 109
Meiji Revolution 28
Mersey, Lord 92, 97–100, 103
Mexico 129, 142, 178, 189–192, 199–200, 203–10, 214–5, 219, 223, 254–60
Mexico City 196–7, 199, 216, 219
MI5 15, 50, 123, 168, 314
Moltke 56, 69, 71, 272–4
Molyneux, Edward 167
Montrose 26
Monrovia 27
Montgomery, William 85, 118, 172, 254
Moore, Admiral Sir Archibald Moore 71–2
Morgenthau, Henry 80
Morocco 141, 258
Mountbatten of Burma, Admiral of the Fleet Lord 164, 313
Napier, Marjorie 82, 169, 306
Napier, Vice-Admiral Trevylyan 239
Nauen 27–8, 63, 76, 133–4, 177, 233, 259
Nelson, Lord 23–5, 39, 60, 64, 225, 242, 266, 282
Newport 187, 191
New York Times 125, 128, 209
New Zealand 25
Nicolas II, Tsar 175
Nicolson, Field Marshal Lord 204
Northcliffe, Lord 41, 226, 315
North Sea 19, 27–8, 36–7, 89–90, 124, 145, 148–50, 155–7, 160, 175, 234, 239–41, 273, 278–9
Norton, R. D. 29
Norway 28, 87, 230, 272, 274
Nuremberg 129
Nurnberg 61–2
Odensholm 30
Old Bailey 26, 135
Oldenburg 272–3
Oliver, Admiral of the Fleet Sir Henry 20–1, 28–9, 32, 35, 37, 39, 45, 47–51, 60–1, 65–6, 71–2, 91–7, 101–4, 110, 113, 134, 143, 145, 149–52, 157–60, 162, 171, 225, 227, 236–8, 240–5
Oran 256
Page, Walter Hines 53, 126, 130, 136–7, 185, 193, 196–8, 201–5, 207, 209, 211–12, 216, 218–20, 255–7, 261, 263–4, 268, 296, 298
Pall Mall Gazette 43
Panama Canal 65, 258
Papeete 59
Paris 102, 109, 174, 184, 247, 262, 307
Parsons, Sir Charles 29, 118
Pasha, Bolo 261
Pasha, Djemal 80
Pasha, Enver 75
Pasha, Talaat 75
Pearl Harbor 218, 308, 311–12
Pearse, Patrick 134
Pelly, Captain 71–2
Pendjeh crisis 43
Pernambuco 27
Pershing, General J. J. ('Black Jack') 189–90
Philadelphia 26
Pierce, Lieutenant-Commander 247
Plymouth 25, 130
Poldhu 25–6
Portsmouth 17, 25, 140, 271
Port Stanley 59, 62–3
Portugal 25, 251–2
Posen 68
Pound, Admiral of the Fleet Sir Dudley 164, 305, 307

319

...iana 14, 104–5, 185, 204
...Journal 125, 128
...wn, Vice-Admiral 37, 93, 96, 131
...ctoria Eugenie 139
...Dr. E. C. 166, 267
...John 125, 128
...Prince 139, 248, 253
..., Lord 116
...d, John 86, 136
...son, Captain J. A. T. 30
...d, Admiral Sir Herbert 39, 49, 55, 60, 73, 242–3, 285
...ki Point 26
... Janeiro 61
...velt, Franklin D. 41, 198, 286, 309–11
...sevelt, Theodore 185, 210, 217–8, 223
...t, Elihu 210
...osetta Stone 200
...oskill, Stephen 80–1, 101, 105, 154
Rosyth 69–70, 148–9, 239, 281
Rotter, Paymaster-Commander Charles 32, 36, 48, 162, 181, 184
Rotterdam 51, 103, 124, 284
Rotterdam 126
Round Table Club, the 210
Rufigi, River 64
Russo-Japanese war 56
Saalwachter, Kaptainleutnant 234
Sacramento Bee 211
Safeguard 132
St. Kilda 94
Samuel, Sir Marcus 276
Sandbach, F. E. 167
San Francisco 189
Savory, D. L. 167
Sayonara 130–33, 138
Sayville 27, 125, 177, 180
Sazonov, Sergei 81
Scapa Flow 19, 64, 89, 94
Scarborough Raid 37, 64–8, 148
Scharnhorst 58–62
Schwieger, Kapitanleutnant Walther 90, 93, 96–7, 99, 102
Scotland Yard 26, 51, 87
Serocold, Claud 45–7, 119, 126, 174, 177, 182–3, 200, 255, 287, 299, 306
Seydlitz 73, 145, 147–8, 154, 157
Seymour, Commander Ralph 67–9
Shoecraft, Eugene 204
SIGINT 23–4, 35–7, 45, 47, 52, 55, 64, 66, 104, 157, 174, 195, 231, 271, 304, 308
Simon, Lieutenant F. M. 130–3, 139
Sims, Admiral William 40, 221, 244, 283, 297, 309
Sinclair, Admiral Sir Hugh 290, 301, 305, 307
Sinclair, Sir Archibald 120
Sinn Fein 86, 130, 132, 262–3
Skagerrak 146, 148, 158, 234; *see also* Jutland
Slade, Rear-Admiral Edmund 276–7
Smith, Sir F. E. 116, 133
Sofia 75, 80, 165
Somme, the 185
South Africa 34, 41
Sowrey, Lieutenant Frederick 232
Spain 27–8, 34, 46, 124, 138–142, 247–60, 286
Special Branch 51, 124, 127, 129–30, 134–5
Stafford, David 34, 95, 105
Stileman, Admiral 97–8
Stoddard, Rear-Admiral A. C 59, 62
Straus, Ralph 120, 145
Sturdee, Admiral of the Fleet Sir Doveton 60–3, 172
St Vincent, Lord 42, 60–1, 114, 242
German Destroyers: S-115, S-117, S-118, S-119, 32
Sunderland 148, 157–8, 233
Sussex 185–6, 211
Swedish Roundabout' 64, 178–80, 196, 206, 254, 257, 259–62
Sweden 177, 256–7, 275
Switzerland 128, 263
Szek, Alexander 104–5
Tallinn 30
Teben-Johans, Kapitanleutnant 231
Texas 192, 200–1, 207, 211, 216, 254
Thomson, Sir Basil 51, 87, 130, 134–8

Thomson, Sir J. J. 118, 128
Thoroton, Colonel Charles 142, 247–8, 253
Thring, Fleet Paymaster Ernest 163, 165, 229, 289, 306
Tiarks, Frank 168, 229, 289
Tighnabruaich 85
Times, The 94, 114, 129, 137, 211, 226
Toro 256
Toye, Francis 167, 170
Tralee Bay 134
Transylvania 91
Trench, Captain 19, 232–4, 306
Tuchman, Barbara 27, 125–7, 180, 211,
Tuckerton 27, 177, 180, 258
Turkey 7, 52, 75–6, 81, 85, 104, 129, 257
Tyrwhitt, Admiral of the Fleet Sir Reginald 7, 19, 39, 66, 70, 72, 114, 145–6, 242–3, 283
Usedom, Admiral 76
U-boats: U-19 134; U-20 93–4, 97, 99, 101, 104, 134; U-21 82, 91; U-27 93; U-28 92; U-30 93–4; U-35 253; U-38 129; U-52 158; U-53 158, 187; U-66 158; U-94 234; U-156 251; U-157 251; UC-32 233; UC-61 233
Vergemere 139
Viereck, George Sylvester 210
Villa, Pancho 189, 216
von Bernstorff, Johann Heinrich, Count 86–7, 93, 103, 125, 127, 133, 139, 177–82, 187–8, 191–3, 196–8, 200, 202, 205–8, 211, 213–4, 253–5, 261–2, 275, 297
Von Der Tann 56, 65, 70
von Eckardt, Heinrich 178–9, 181, 190, 192
von Falkenhayn, Erich 186
von Hase, Georg 157
von Hindenburg, Field Marshal Paul 186, 188–90
von Ingenohl, Admiral Friedrich 65, 67, 72, 145
von Kemnitz, Hans Arthur 190
von Levetzow, Kapitan Magnus 69
von Muller, Admiral Georg 76
von Papen, Franz 86, 126–9, 198, 254
von Rintelen, Franz 86, 127–9, 198
von Spee, Vice-Admiral Maximilian Graf 58–65, 128
von Tirpitz, Grossadmiral Alfred 69, 90
von Wangenheim, Hans 80
Voska 125–7
V-26 30–1
Warrender, Vice-Admiral Sir George 37, 66–8
Washington 41, 52–3, 82, 84–6, 93, 125, 129, 133, 139, 142, 177–83, 188, 191–2, 196–202, 204–7, 211–19, 221, 252, 254–6, 258, 261–3, 268, 293, 298–9, 308–12, 314
Wassmuss, Wilhelm 82–3
Waterhouse, Gilbert 166
Weazle 23
Webb, Admiral Sir Richard 91, 99–100, 110
Wemyss, Admiral of the Fleet Sir Rosslyn 107, 119, 173, 236, 238, 240–1, 244, 265, 273, 276, 278, 280, 283, 285–6, 288, 305
Westfalen 158
Whale Island 17
Whitby 65, 67
Whitehall 8, 25, 41, 50, 87, 107, 204, 225, 315
Wilhelmshaven 64–5, 67, 72, 134, 145, 150, 152, 157–8, 230–1, 237, 272–3, 278–80
William Bull 250
Willoughby, Leonard 166, 230
Wilson, Admiral of the Fleet Sir Arthur 35, 108, 117, 149, 155, 162, 179, 181–2
Wilson, Woodrow 52, 126–30, 185–9, 191–8, 203–10, 216–19, 255, 257, 261, 263–4, 268, 279
Wolfram 142, 247–51
Workers Republic, The 134
World's Work 197
Yardley, Herbert 255
Yarmouth 64, 145–6, 148
Young, George 12, 84–5
Ypiranga 254
Zeebrugge 41, 233, 265–7, 277
Zeller, Margaret 124
Zimmerman, Arthur 177, 190, 196, 210, 212, 218, 261
Zimmermann telegram 7, 9 11–12, 27, 53, 83, 85, 126, 130, 162, 173, 177–93, 201, 203, 206, 214, 216, 219, 222, 255–61, 283, 303, 308